Domesticating Empire

Domesticating Empire

ENLIGHTENMENT IN SPANISH AMERICA

Karen Stolley

Vanderbilt University Press

NASHVILLE

© 2013 by Vanderbilt University Press
Nashville, Tennessee 37235
All rights reserved
First printing 2013

This book is printed on acid-free paper.
Manufactured in the United States of America

Library of Congress Cataloging-in-Publication Data on file
LC control number 2012048870
LC classification E143.S76 2013
Dewey class number 980.01—dc23

ISBN 978-0-8265-1938-2 (cloth)
ISBN 978-0-8265-1940-5 (ebook)

To my parents, Jim and Maggie Stolley,

and to my daughters, Kathleen and Elizabeth Littlefield

Contents

Acknowledgments

History shows us that eighteenth-century projects are often left unfinished (Juan José de Eguiara y Eguren's *Bibliotheca Mexicana*, for example), and this one might well have been too, were it not for the many colleagues, friends, and family members whose insightful guidance and unflagging support can never be sufficiently acknowledged here but to whom I am deeply grateful. To all, *un abrazo.*

Domesticating Empire took root over two decades ago as I worked on a chapter on eighteenth-century narrative for the *Cambridge History of Latin American Literature*, edited by Roberto González Echevarría (in whose graduate seminars my interest in the period was sparked) and Enrique Pupo Walker. Everything I have learned about colonial Latin American literature began with Roberto and Enrique, *grandes maestros.*

There are special people and places that made it possible to advance the project at crucial moments. First among these is Ruth Hill, whose unique mix of friendship and erudition kept me going over the long haul. *Ruti, no hay palabras.*

Many years ago, a summer fellowship at the John Carter Brown Library—that jewel of a collection in Providence, Rhode Island, in which so many texts from the early Americas dialogue with one another—provided a foundation for the ideas developed in this book. Rosemary Magee introduced me to the Hambidge Center for Creative Arts and Sciences in Dillard, Georgia, where I was able to return to the project after a long hiatus during the summers of 2006 and 2008. A grant from Emory University's Author Development Program opened a space for writing in my busy life at a critical moment; Amy Benson Brown's wise and empathetic editorial insights have been invaluable in keeping me on track. A yearlong fellowship at Emory's Bill and Carol Fox Center for Humanistic Inquiry made it possible to leave teaching and administrative tasks behind for uninterrupted research and writing in 2008–2009. I am most grateful to Director Martine Brownley, Associate Director Keith Anthony, staff members Colette Barlow and Amy Erbil, and all the FCHI Fellows for their collegial support during that wonderful year.

Emory College of Arts and Sciences generously provided sabbatical leaves and travel funds; I am also grateful for the generous book subvention provided by Emory College and Emory's Laney Graduate School. The Woodruff Library staff—particularly Phil MacLeod and, in the Interlibrary Loan office, Marie

Hansen and Sarah Ward—brought a wealth of eighteenth-century volumes within my reach.

The American Society for Eighteenth-Century Studies (ASECS) and the Ibero-American Society for Eighteenth-Century Studies (IASECS) have been for many years an essential forum for collegial interdisciplinary exchanges, exemplifying the eighteenth-century ideal of enlightened engagement that is *dulce et utile*. Special thanks to my *amigos dieciochistas*.

I am grateful to colleagues and students at University of Virginia, the University of Kentucky, the University of Oregon, Louisiana State University, and the Universidad Nacional de Colombia-Bogotá who heard versions of these chapters and offered valuable comments, as did audiences at various meetings of the Latin American Studies Association, the Modern Language Association, and VACARGA (the Virginia Carolinas Georgia Seminar, now the Tepaske Seminar). As I wrote, I thought often of Antony Higgins and Félix Bolaños— two colonialist friends and colleagues whose untimely passing deprived us of what should have been the fruits of long, productive careers.

Graduate students in my Emory seminars, now valued colleagues, asked thoughtful questions and offered many good bibliographical suggestions: Brittany Anderson-Cain, Amy Austin, Margaret Boyle, Ana María Díaz Burgos, Katherine Ford, Denise Galarza-Sepúlveda, Jeremy Paden, Ryan Prendergast, Eugenia Romero, David Slade, and George Thomas.

On the fifth floor of Callaway, Zinnia Johnston, Dasef Weems, and Amy Linenberger provided unflappable support regarding all things Emory. Zinnia, Lisa Dillman and Dasef helped with the occasional translation of a difficult phrase. Dasef always knew how to solve any problems involving formatting. My dear friends and colleagues in the Department of Spanish and Portuguese—past and present—are too many to name, but you know who you are!

A number of colleagues generously read various parts of the manuscript and offered valuable suggestions: William Acree, Santa Arias, Nick Fabian, Mariselle Meléndez, Jeremy Paden, and Dierdra Reber; Hernán Feldman heroically read the entire manuscript. Peter Bakewell offered a historian's perspective and challenged me to make my argument real, and David Gies graciously extended his exuberant enthusiasm for so many projects to my own work.

In these times of great challenges for academic publishing, I feel extremely fortunate to have found a place at Vanderbilt University Press. Eli Bortz has been the kind of editor every author dreams of—encouraging, reasonable, and patient; Joell Smith-Borne oversaw every detail with impeccable professionalism. Peg Duthie, Wendy Herlich, and Michael Pantozzi provided meticulous copyediting and proofing; Bob Schwarz prepared the index. I am most grateful to the anonymous readers whose detailed and substantive commentaries made this a better book. I regret that my own shortcomings limited my ability to respond fully to every suggestion or correct every error.

To Peggy Barlett, Leslie Harris, Judith Miller, Laurie Patton, and Sharon Strocchia—each an inspiration in her own right and always ready to help with "a few small repairs"—a world of thanks. Bobbi Patterson, my writing hideaway partner, encouraged me to know what I had to do and begin my journey; Maureen O'Toole helped me to hear a new voice.

My family has been unstinting in their support—my brother, Jim Stolley; my sister, Beth Drucker, and her family; the extended Littlefield family, especially my father-in-law, David Littlefield Sr. (a gentleman and a scholar); and Lizzie Hill, who always seemed to know what was needed. My neighborhood friends offered welcome occasions for taking a break—Kim DeGrove and Clyde Partin, Marianne and Larry Gardner, Andrew McIntyre, Jamie Ramsay, Joe and Vicki Riedel, and Lizanne Thomas and David Black. David Littlefield kept the home fires burning, literally and figuratively, for which I am enormously grateful. No one could have been more interested in having this project come to completion than my father, and my deepest regret is that he did not live to see the book's publication.

Domesticating Empire is dedicated to my parents, Jim and Maggie Stolley, and to my daughters, Kathleen and Elizabeth Littlefield. They have kept me grounded in love and laughter throughout the many years it took me to finish the book; their lives have been and will always be the beloved generational bookends for my own.

Introduction

An Insufficient Enlightenment?

Why don't we read eighteenth-century Spanish American literature? This project began more than two decades ago as a meditation on this one central question. More precisely, how do we explain the almost universal omission—at least, until recently—of eighteenth-century texts and authors from the Spanish American canon?[1] It is not only literary historians who give up when faced with the eighteenth-century challenge; in *La expresión americana* (1957), a touchstone essay on Spanish American cultural production, the Cuban writer José Lezama Lima skips a whole century when he jumps from the baroque *señor* to the nineteenth-century romantic as sequential iterations of Spanish American identity.[2] Somehow, the eighteenth century becomes lost in the transition from the sixteenth- and seventeenth-century colonial period to the nineteenth-century post-Independence period. Thus, eighteenth-century Spanish American writing ends up being, to use Concolorcorvo's phrase in *El lazarillo de ciegos caminantes,* a "peje entre dos aguas" (fish between two waters)—infrequently studied and even less frequently read.[3]

In recent years, however, publications and conferences have reflected a growing interest in the Spanish American eighteenth century, with authors and presenters speaking to a crossover audience of scholars doing research on the literature, history, art history, economics, and history of science of eighteenth-century Spanish America.[4] My own work is in constant dialogue with the many valuable insights of these researchers, but most of these scholars do not attempt to make an overarching argument about the period.[5] Their publications focus on either a single author (see, for example, those of Ruth Hill or Margaret R. Ewalt) or a particular aspect of the Hispanic eighteenth century, such as the history of science (Neil Safier), gender and the body (Mariselle Meléndez), visual arts (Magali Carrera), or governance (Gabriel B. Paquette). Moreover, these important studies of the Spanish American eighteenth century represent a groundswell that has not yet permeated the discipline of Spanish American literary and cultural studies more broadly. And to date there has been little attempt within Hispanism to theorize the historic lack of focus on the eighteenth century.[6]

This critical lacuna has implications for the discipline of eighteenth-century studies as well. Scholars of French, English, German, and American literature have constructed an imposing canon and a robust critical tradition in eighteenth-century studies that defines and dominates our understanding of the discipline.[7] Yet even as these scholars of national literatures seek to broaden their view of the eighteenth century by proposing "other" or "peripheral" or "global" enlightenments, they generally overlook the authors and texts of the Hispanic eighteenth century.[8] Striving to diversify an admittedly Eurocentric eighteenth-century canon, scholars have identified texts within the English-language or French-language canon that are taken to be representative of marginalization or difference but do not fully capture a global picture. This partial diversification does not yet map onto the broader Spanish American circumstance. However, if we were to attempt that mapping of difference, we would find resonances and points of convergence.[9]

Why has a period that offers rich possibilities for historians of Spanish America and for scholars of other national literatures attracted so little attention from readers and critics of Spanish American letters?[10] Why has eighteenth-century Spanish America traditionally been regarded as a literary no-man's-land—as not a bridge but rather an abyss between the late colonial baroque and nineteenth-century romanticism and Independence movements? Given that eighteenth-century Spanish American writers engaged in lively exchanges with their counterparts in Europe and Anglo-America, how might we attempt to re-vive that critical conversation in our own work today?

Domesticating Empire proposes to answer these questions by arguing that writing in eighteenth-century Spanish America can be read as a discursive proj-ect of "domesticating empire" that reflects both Enlightenment concerns and the particular preoccupations of imperial Bourbon Spain and its territories in the Americas. This project engages in debates about the importance of cross-cultural contact in the development of human history, the legitimacy of scien-tific evidence, the value of commerce and exchange, the locus of religious au-thority, and the relationship between the eighteenth century and the preceding two centuries of Spanish conquest and colonization by the Hapsburg Empire. The story of the discovery and conquest of the Americas had been writ large, both by those who decried its cruelty and excess and those who celebrated its triumphs and accomplishments. But by the eighteenth century that story was, for the most part, in the past. Gone was the subjugation *a sangre y fuego* (by blood and fire) of territories and their peoples, gone were the urgent questions of survival, gone were the first euphoric rushes of newfound riches, gone was the epistemological shock of the discovery of New World flora and fauna. The eighteenth-century Americas found themselves to be territories whose coloni-zation was a certainty rather than a precarious enterprise. They began a process of consolidation that required a different kind of storytelling, one that I call a "discourse of domestication."

Domestication may be understood in multiple ways. To domesticate is to bring into domestic life, to adapt (an animal or plant) to intimate association with and to the advantage of people in a process directed toward pragmatic or utilitarian ends. More recently, "domestication" has referred to the affairs and activities of a given country or, more particularly, one's own country (as op-posed to a foreign one). All these meanings inform the present study. A "do-mesticating discourse" adapts its subject matter with an eye to utilitarian or social purposes, bringing it "home" for a local audience. That home, by the eighteenth century, had shifted for Spanish American writers away from Spain and toward the New World.[11] While earlier authors in Spanish America addressed themselves largely to a metropolitan peninsular reader in describing their New World experiences, eighteenth-century authors focused on a more local audience, and on a pragmatic approach to an America they increasingly considered their own (regardless of where they had been born). Their writing reflects the degree to which the locus of identity and self-definition had shifted.

Once independence was achieved in the nineteenth century, that eighteenth-century discourse of domestication—the connective tissue between two centuries of conquest and a century of independence—no longer constituted a usable past. Within Spanish American letters, the memory of the eighteenth century was erased discursively in order to move away from domestication to a Creolized place of power similar to that of conquistadors who had gone before. Criollo sovereignty post-Independence had to be established by reaching back, paradoxically, to performatively reject Spain and Spanish conquest.[12] In the process, criollos redefined themselves as independent agents rather than imperial subjects, embracing new forms of mastery. But in doing so, the eighteenth-century criollo apprenticeship that represents the domestic origins of independence had to be erased. An understanding of why this was so further serves to answer the question with which I began this project.

Domestication, of course, also implies taming . . . and there's the rub. The eighteenth-century authors featured in my book take as their point of departure what has been represented in the past (and will again be in the future) as exotic or marvelous and rework it as something that is familiar and, at least potentially, utilitarian. In short, they domesticate it. Ironically, it is precisely this same domesticating project that invalidates eighteenth-century texts for subsequent canonical formulations of Spanish American literary and cultural history. The Spanish American literary and critical canon has been constructed over the past two centuries as a narrative of colonial encounters marked by violence and resistance, heroic confrontations between man and nature in the *novela de la tierra,* yellow butterflies and convoluted genealogies in Marquesan magical realism, wrenching witness in politically engaged *testimonio,* and postmodern fragmentation in the postdictatorial narratives of the Southern Cone. Since Independence, Spanish America has been committed to its own self-created identity as a wild and untamed territory.[13]

In this imagined narrative, the Spanish American eighteenth century has been set aside because it simply doesn't seem to fit. The eighteenth-century's "domesticating discourse" produces works that reflect a very different project of self-identity than the one that would be articulated in the following century. Eighteenth-century writing in Spanish America is much more consonant with the paradigms of the European Enlightenment than has generally been acknowledged, either by scholars of the European Enlightenment or by Latin Americanists, and it therefore resists incorporation into subsequent overarching schemes of Spanish American literary history that come into being in part to contest those paradigms. I propose that the domesticated and domesticating nature of eighteenth-century writing explains its striking absence in the canon.

There's no place at the table for administrators and bureaucrats, military engineers and mining technocrats, reasonable Indians and local saints.

To create a place at that table, *Domesticating Empire* is organized around five key topics that mattered in the sixteenth and seventeenth centuries and that continue to matter in the eighteenth century: conquest, Indians, nature, God, and gold. For each topic, I have selected an eighteenth-century prose narrative text to demonstrate through close reading how the topic is "domesticated," both rhetorically and thematically. I look at conquest in José de Oviedo y Baños's *Historia de la conquista y población de la provincia de Venezuela* (History of the conquest and settlement of the province of Venezuela; 1723); Indians in Juan Ignacio Molina's *Compendio de la historia civil del reyno de Chile* (Compendium of the civil history of the kingdom of Chile; 1795); nature in various writings by Félix de Azara; God in Catalina de Jesús Herrera's *Secretos entre el alma y Dios* (Secrets between the soul and God; 1758–1760); and gold in José Martín Félix de Arrate's *Llave del Nuevo Mundo* (Key to the New World; 1761). In these works we see a commitment to a new version of conquest and colonization involving commerce and conversation rather than war, an interest in engaging nature through scientific observation and measurement, a focus on evolving urban centers of viceregal power, an awareness of the relationship between imperial and local politics (both secular and religious), and a move toward a more complex and interrelated transatlantic economy.

Domestication happens discursively through a number of rhetorical maneuvers that I trace in each text, such as the employment of organizational and descriptive strategies, the choice to include or exclude specific moments in the narratives, and the use of new structuring metaphors. I show how these strategies have the effect of rewriting a given topic, containing rather than expanding or exalting it. Domestication also happens thematically: conquest becomes governance and administration; Indians cease warring and begin to negotiate treaties; nature's specimens are measured and incorporated into new botanical and zoological taxonomies; evangelization is abandoned for local politics; and the lure of gold is reduced to explanations of amalgamation technologies and metropolitan balance sheets. Each of these topics deserves a monograph, but reading them against each other shows the shape of the era and will, I hope, call readers' attention to the potential of resuscitating these forgotten works in order to arrive at a more nuanced assessment of the Hispanic Enlightenment and incorporate that assessment into a fuller understanding of the global eighteenth century.

The following are key concepts that will help orient the reader to the terrain of the no-man's-land I will be mapping.

Geography. The late colonial period witnessed the emergence of new centers of population and prestige, as the balance of power shifted from Lima and Mexico City to the newly created viceroyalties of New Granada (1739) and Río de La Plata (1776), and other viceregal cities like Havana faced growing economic and political challenges. David Livingstone and Charles Withers, coeditors of the collection of essays titled *Geography and Enlightenment,* have reminded us of the plural nature of "geographies of knowledge" in the eighteenth century (vii). Because authors in different parts of viceregal Spanish America necessarily situated themselves differently than their counterparts in Spain and the rest of Europe with respect to scientific, historical, and geographical knowledge, I have chosen to focus on texts produced in the viceregal periphery rather than study the urban centers of Lima and Mexico, which have received the lion's share of critical attention to date.[14] Although the repercussions of Bourbon reforms differ in each of the areas where these featured texts originated (Venezuela, Chile, the Río de la Plata, Ecuador, and Cuba), in all of them an acute awareness of being on the periphery is accompanied by a sense of pride in place and attachment to the local, as well as an appreciation of the reach (and limitations) of imperial power emanating primarily from Madrid and secondarily from Mexico City and Lima (urban centers that often stand in for the rest of viceregal territory). The book begins in Venezuela, moves southward to Chile and the Río de la Plata, and then moves north to Ecuador before returning to Cuba and the Caribbean.

Chronology. Historians of Spanish America have tended to contrast the first half of the eighteenth century, a period of relative stasis as Spain struggled with the challenges of succession, invasion, and civil war, with the second half of the century, when enlightened reform projects gained momentum.[15] These reforms had as their goal "removing the obstacles to the creation of a powerful state capable of generating the wealth and mobilizing the resources that would enable it to hold its own in a ruthlessly competitive international system."[16] As it pursued these goals, the Bourbon Spanish Empire worked to transform Spain and its viceroyalties, centralizing and modernizing the baroque structures of the Hapsburg dynasty. There are compelling historical events that occur during the mid-century period—the Jesuit expulsions of 1767, the British invasion of Cuba in 1762, and the Andean indigenous rebellions of 1780–1781. But the temptation to relate cultural production to economic and political milestones privileges linearity and causality over other kinds of connections.[17]

My approach as a scholar of literature is less chronologically driven. My readings highlight a sea change that marks eighteenth-century cultural production in general, regardless of the decade and irrespective of the particular matter at hand, and I will argue in these pages that we can identify a narrative project of domesticating empire throughout the eighteenth century. I begin with a text published in 1723 (Oviedo y Baños's *Historia de la conquista y población de la provincia de Venezuela*). Molina and Azara wrote multiple works on Chile and the Río de la Plata, respectively, in the closing decades of the eighteenth century and beyond. Herrera penned her spiritual autobiography during 1758–1760, and Arrate wrote the *Llave del Nuevo Mundo* in 1761. However, the rejection of linearity is not a rejection of history. My discussion is, in the case of each particular reading, situated historically and geographically; each writer and his or her work is located within a broader political, social, and economic context.

Chronology complicates this project in another way. The place of eighteenth-century Spanish American narrative in the canon suffers from a fundamental tension that comes from looking both backward and forward at the same time: backward, as eighteenth-century authors confront the anxiety that stems from a sense that the heroic history of America had already been written in the sixteenth and seventeenth centuries, and forward, as later readers look to the eighteenth century primarily to explain the origins of nineteenth-century independence movements or to anchor a foundational history for newly established nations. In these pages my goal is to read each work in the context of its own moment.

Authorial identity. As many scholars have noted, criollo elites are an emerging class in eighteenth-century Spanish America, and any study of the period must take into account the issue of criollo identity.[18] However, it's equally important not to set up rigid oppositions between criollos and their peninsular counterparts. Eighteenth-century authors in Spanish America see themselves at times as belonging to the Hispanic Republic of Letters, at other times as sons and daughters of the Americas, and sometimes as members of a European lettered elite.[19] Their identity is most effectively understood as situational. In fact, we can see how it was continually renegotiated in response to changing political, ideological, and personal circumstances, leading to an eighteenth-century version of what Yolanda Martínez-San Miguel has called an "episteme of ambivalence."[20] Rather than rely on country of origin as an identity marker, my criteria for inclusion are somewhat reminiscent of José de Eguiara y Eguren's in his *Bibliotheca mexicana* (1755), an ambitious and unfinished attempt to bring together all those who had written in or about Mexico.[21] I would suggest that Eguiara's capacious catalog of authors is a more accurate reflection of eighteenth-century realities than narrower categories based on nineteenth-century definitions of national citizenship. Thus, my book deals both with Spanish American authors— criollos, born in America of European parentage (Oviedo y Baños, Molina, Herrera, Arrate)—and with an author born in Spain who spent considerable time in the Americas and whose writing grows out of his American experience (Azara). Rather than construct a binary between Europe and America, between criollos (those of Spanish descent born in the Americas) and *gachupines* (the term used by criollos to refer to Spaniards born in Spain), or between a cosmopolitan, enlightened position and that of the colonized or resistant native, I focus on in-betweenness (the *peje entre dos aguas* to which I referred earlier).[22]

Genre. I have chosen to focus on narrative rather than other genres precisely because narrative speaks, generally, more directly to the complexity of identities and issues I wish to discuss. I will be reading a wide range of texts, all of which might fall under the rubric of "narrative history" (regional history, natural history, spiritual autobiography, urban history).[23] This is not to suggest, however, that some of the same domesticating maneuvers I identify in prose narrative may not also be present in poetry or theater.[24]

Manuscripts and editions. The conventional means by which we categorize literary history—whether by national origin, language, or the dissemination of a given text—falls short of capturing the workings of the Hispanic eighteenth century. Numerous eighteenth-century accounts were published in the nineteenth century, many years after being written, as part of a project to build foundational national literary and historiographical traditions. Other texts are still scattered in archives and libraries throughout the Americas or, like Azara's, were published in unauthorized translations. The Jesuits, exiled in 1767, left Spanish America to relocate in Europe and resumed their writing in Latin or Italian. Much was written about the continent by Spaniards and other European travelers, some of whom stayed for more than a decade and became intimately familiar with the regions they were describing. Today, some eighteenth-century writers, considered minor figures within the larger context of Spanish American letters, are fiercely held up within their own countries as the founding fathers of a national cultural tradition. Most have fallen into oblivion among twentieth-century readers. Furthermore, the relative paucity of easily accessible editions of works by eighteenth-century Spanish American authors is as much a symptom of their exclusion from the canon as it is a possible explanation for this exclusion. The preparation of such editions is essential for the development of Spanish American eighteenth-century studies. Happily, some authors have begun to enjoy wider critical and bibliographical circulation (for example, Pedro de Peralta Barnuevo has received more attention because of work by Jerry Williams and David Slade).

This is in many ways a recuperative project, but it's not a hagiographical one. I do not wish to idealize the eighteenth century or eighteenth-century writing, but I would like to pique the reader's curiosity about forgotten texts and authors and explore the eighteenth-century substrata of the more visible nineteenth-century processes of canon formation in Spanish America. I would like to argue for a less reductionist and teleologically driven view of the Spanish American eighteenth century than has generally been presented—one that foregrounds the period's pragmatic impulses, empirical interests, and its ongoing conversation with both local and metropolitan interlocutors.[25]

The texts I discuss in this book participate in what the late Antony Higgins has called "a contradictory modernity . . . that does not neatly conform to the idealized model of eighteenth-century Western societies," but in which "residual and emergent formations are inextricably bound up with each other."[26] As the authors I'll be discussing navigate between the residue of earlier imperial structures dating from the Hapsburg era and new imperial structures emerging from the Bourbon reforms, they articulate a domestication of empire that involves an ongoing process of critical thinking about the historical moment in which they are writing.[27] Like their enlightened contemporaries in North America and Europe, they operate not only in the past, but decisively place themselves in a concrete and locally defined present.[28]

The authors I study in *Domesticating Empire* are keenly aware of a need to negotiate their various subject positions as Spaniards, as *españoles americanos,* as criollos, and as members of urban communities like Quito or Havana.[29] They participate in a complex network of spheres of authority that are defined by imperial administrative and scientific agendas. They are firmly grounded in local contexts that are simultaneously central and peripheral to Spanish empire, and they are engaged in a domesticating re-articulation of imperial concerns—conquest, Amerindians, nature, religion, and economics.[30] This re-articulation builds bridges between what Higgins has called the "neoclassical, normative discourse" of eighteenth-century Europe and Spain's far-flung peripheries in the Americas, expanding the canon on both sides of the Atlantic ("(Post-)Colonial Sublime," 128).

This book represents a similar kind of bridging project. It positions itself between Spain and Spanish America, between literature and history, between centers and peripheries, between Hispanists and non-Hispanists, and between colonial and eighteenth-century scholars. Since I hope that this book will be of interest to non-Hispanist scholars as well as Hispanists and Latin Americanists, I include bibliographical references that will permit both specialists and a broader scholarly audience to delve more deeply into the topics I discuss. For this reason, I offer summaries of primary and secondary works, and refer in the endnotes and the bibliography to debates in the field, so that the context in which I am rethinking the Hispanic eighteenth century will be clear. I am committed to bringing into our scholarly conversation about the eighteenth century voices, largely silenced, belonging to travelers, missionaries, religious figures, bureaucrats, scientists, and historians who read and communicated widely in a number of languages and who wrote in Spanish. The primary texts I've chosen are challenging, engaging, insightful, and, at times, even humorous. Thus, I have used quotes from the original Spanish as subheadings in each of the chapters in order to give voice to these eighteenth-century authors who have been, for the most part, forgotten or overlooked. I hope that the non–Spanish-speaking reader will view the subheadings in Spanish as an open invitation rather than a closed door.[31]

Whose are the voices I hope will be heard in this book? Readers will meet, for example, Oviedo y Baños—an administrator and historian who proposes new models for settlement and governance in Venezuela to replace the old model of the greedy and ambitious conquistador; Molina—an exiled Jesuit who centers his civil history of Chile on the brave, eloquent, and eminently pragmatic Araucanians; Azara—an Aragonese military engineer who, stranded for two decades in the Río de la Plata, turns his measuring eye away from the contested border with Brazil and toward the region's flora and fauna; Herrera—an Ecuadoran nun who writes a spiritual autobiography marked by a pained awareness of the peripheral status of her city and convent; and Arrate—a favorite son of the elite of Havana, Cuba, who presents his urban history as a claim check for criollo values.

For Spanish America the past has often served as a discursive key to an identity that differentiates Spanish America from its European component. In that discursive process the Spanish American eighteenth century occupies an intermediate zone between making and denying difference, between America and Europe, and between the evocation of the past and an evolving future. It could be argued that the eighteenth century provides an alternative to the oppositional models of center/periphery or coloniality/modernity precisely because of the open-ended, contradictory, and continually negotiated nature of its discursive formulations.[32] This is also why the eighteenth century has resisted reading: it fits neither the sixteenth- and seventeenth- nor the nineteenth-century scheme, neither the discovery model nor the imperial one, neither the colonial nor the postcolonial world. The eighteenth century produced texts that, once the Bourbon Spanish Empire gave way to the newly created Spanish American nations, seemed to have no role to play in the foundational narratives surrounding that transition. In a reading of Spanish American cultural history in which independence came to be understood retrospectively as a consequence of external developments that galvanized criollos—first, the Bourbon reforms and, second, the Napoleonic invasion of Spain—the domesticated eighteenth century drops out of the story.

The eighteenth century thus disappears, much like a stitch that dissolves after a wound has closed. But we cannot continue to look at the long colonial period, spanning the sixteenth to the nineteenth centuries, as if it were undifferentiated. The stitch may have dissolved, but a trace remains to mark an earlier suture that was necessary to close a historical and epistemological gap between conquest and independence. The trace of that suture is only visible, however, if we stop reading the eighteenth century through a retrospective lens or in accordance with nineteenth- and twentieth- (or even twenty-first-) century agendas. What if, as Dennis Moore once suggested in a workshop on "American Enlightenments," we were to read the eighteenth century like a detective novel whose ending we had no way of anticipating?[33] What would it mean to study the eighteenth century and its domesticating project on its own terms?

Eighteenth-century Spanish America, with its increasing racial and economic diversification and the emergence of a criollo discourse of pragmatism and utility, complicates dominant narratives about both the eighteenth-century Enlightenment project and Spanish American cultural identity. As the consensus about the nature of the Enlightenment's heritage has come into question (see Keith Michael Baker and Peter Hanns Reill's *What's Left of Enlightenment?*), a broader and more complex discussion of the eighteenth century becomes possible, one more likely to include Spain and Spanish America as evidence of the Enlightenment's diversity, internal tensions, and discontinuities. At the same time, we see a growing number of challenges to the prevailing view that the eighteenth century in Spain and Spanish America gave rise to a belated, insufficient, or merely uninspired and uninspiring Enlightenment.[34]

This creates new opportunities to understand the Hispanic eighteenth century as something other than the run-up to Independence or a derivative and boring period that merits only an apology. No study to date has attempted to stake out the general terrain of the Spanish American eighteenth century through a close reading of its most salient discursive features, as evidenced in a broad range of narrative works, in order to propose that it can be characterized by an epistemological paradigm shift that reflects a localized and pragmatic internalization of metropolitan discourse—in short, a domestication of empire.[35]

Bringing the Spanish American eighteenth century into conversations about a global Enlightenment enriches those conversations and also helps us to place the eighteenth century on Spanish America's cultural map. As we continue to assess the degree to which "peripheral enlightenments" contributed to a global Enlightenment whose repercussions—for better or worse—still reverberate, eighteenth-century Spanish America has a compelling story to tell.

CHAPTER ONE

Domesticating Conquest

José de Oviedo y Baños's *Historia de la conquista y población de la provincia de Venezuela* (1723)

. . . aquella constelación que corría entonces, de querer
todos los ministros en las Indias aspirar al renombre de
conquistadores.

[. . . the manner of thinking that was then in vogue in
which all administrators in the Indies aspired to the fame of
the conquistadors.]

José de Oviedo y Baños, *Historia de la conquista y
población de la provincia de Venezuela*

I. *"Insepultos los huesos":*
Scattered bones and shards of history

In book 5 of his *Historia de la conquista y población de la provincia de Venezuela*
(1723), José de Oviedo y Baños describes an unsettling moment that serves as
a cautionary tale for would-be conquistadors and for eighteenth-century historians of imperial conquest as well.[1] He traces the route of a Spanish expedition
led by Diego de Losada that set forth to conquer the Caracas Valley in 1567 in
the wake of several failed attempts, including that of Luis de Narváez three years
earlier. Pressing forward despite increasing exhaustion and the threat of Indian
attack, the Spaniards arrive at the scene of Narváez's disastrous defeat and are
sobered to find the whitened bones of their compatriots lying unburied across
the field (218).

In Oviedo y Baños's eighteenth-century retelling, the scattered bones bear
ominous testimony to the perils of sixteenth-century conquest. They also spell
out an unmistakable message about the writing and rewriting of colonial history. Just as sixteenth-century explorers retraced the steps and missteps of earlier expeditions, eighteenth-century historians were inevitably condemned to
follow—and to rewrite—the chronicles of discovery and conquest written during the preceding two centuries. As history moved out of the providentialist
and triumphalist terrain it had occupied during the sixteenth and seventeenth
centuries, it looked to the task of legitimizing conquest on more complicated
and ambiguous grounds, and within a shifting political, economic, cultural, and
ideological context. Narrating the sixteenth-century history of the territory that

is now Venezuela, Oviedo y Baños reveals his own concerns—concerns that are contemporary and local—and implicitly articulates a new project for the eighteenth-century historian.[2] He rejects the epic model of the conquering hero in favor of civil authority and institutionalizing practices of which he provides repeated examples in the *Historia*. He is not writing new history, but I would argue that in this case, putting old wine in new bottles represents a significant act: what we might call "the domestication of conquest."

For Oviedo y Baños and his contemporaries, conquest represents a territory that has been left behind but continues to exert a pull on the eighteenth-century imaginary.[3] Eighteenth-century historiography in Spanish America suffers the fate of belatedness: the eighteenth-century historian knows too well that he has not witnessed the stirring events that must first be described in order to provide a foundational moment before moving on to a discussion of the present. Michel de Certeau has observed that the writing of history can only begin when an "other" time is established as past and separated from the present. This rupture occasions a series of maneuvers that must be accomplished in order to reestablish some kind of continuity with that past. In this process the past is rendered intelligible and suitable to the present. De Certeau observes:

> In the past from which it is distinguished, it [the present time] promotes a selection between what can be understood and what must be forgotten in order to obtain the representation of a present intelligibility. But whatever this new understanding of the past holds to be irrelevant—shards created by the selection of materials, remainders left aside by an explication—comes back, despite everything, on the edges of discourse or in its rifts and crannies: "resistances," "survivals," or delays. . . . They symbolize a return of the repressed, that is, a return of what, at a given moment, has become unthinkable in order for a new identity to become thinkable. (*Writing of History,* 4)

Oviedo y Baños's history reflects the selection process through which the colonial past is rendered intelligible and a new, still-evolving identity becomes thinkable. But the shards created by this process, like the bones of the Narváez expedition, remain visible. The scattered bones are macabre reminders of the greed and violence that, in the eighteenth-century historian's view, had characterized Hapsburg imperial conquest. Even as Oviedo y Baños attempts to advocate for a new Bourbon-era understanding of that past, the bones continue to haunt the historian and his reader until the final pages of the *Historia*.

Oviedo y Baños began writing the *Historia* in 1705 and finished in 1723. The *Historia*, which covers the years from 1492 to 1600 and is divided into six books, is celebrated as one of the founding works of Venezuelan national historiography.[4] Although it's difficult to trace the *Historia*'s immediate dissemination, the Venezuelan historian Guillermo Morón notes that by the early nineteenth century it had become a requisite source for those writing about the origins of Venezuelan history (*Los cronistas,* 132).[5] It achieved this exalted place in the Venezuelan canon despite longstanding questions about the degree to which Oviedo y Baños might have plagiarized from Father Pedro Simón's *Noticias historiales* (Historical notes), written a century earlier—an accusation against which another distinguished Venezuelan historian, Julio Planchart, mounted a vigorous defense ("Oviedo y Baños," 45).[6] More intriguing is the suggestion that Oviedo y Baños based his history, at least in part, on a verse chronicle of the conquest of Caracas written around 1593 by a soldier named Ulloa. Oviedo y Baños, who makes a point of not acknowledging specific sources, never mentions Ulloa, and the poem itself has been lost.[7] However, it's possible that Oviedo y Baños might have come across it during his extensive research in the archives of the Ayuntamiento de Caracas (Town Hall of Caracas) and incorporated specific episodes in his own account of the conquest (*Historia,* xxi). I mention these details—bibliographical curiosities, really—to highlight the important role played by eighteenth-century authors and texts in bridging the colonial era and the period of post-Independence nation building—a role that is often overlooked, given the general amnesia affecting Spanish American literary history with regard to the eighteenth century.

Early critical attention focused less on the *Historia* and more on the author's life, which was read as an example of viceregal interconnectedness. Born in Santa Fe de Bogotá in 1671 and raised in Lima by his widowed mother and her family, Oviedo y Baños traveled to Caracas at the age of fifteen with his brother, Diego. The boys were educated by their uncle Diego de Baños y Sotomayor, who had recently been named bishop of Caracas. Settling definitively in Caracas, Oviedo y Baños made an advantageous marriage and fathered ten children while establishing himself as a local landowner and an engaged participant in Caracas's ecclesiastical affairs and municipal government. He was named regidor in 1703, but served only for a brief time owing to a series of personal and political complications that no doubt inform the following rueful observation: "The art of governance has always been considered by politicians to be very difficult" (*Historia,* 251). Later in life he turned his attention to research and writing.[8] Oviedo y Baños died in 1728.

Despite his many accomplishments, Oviedo y Baños embodies the frustrations of the criollo lettered elite. He spent many years fighting for admittance into the Order of Santiago, only to find his ambitions thwarted, not because of any failing on his part, apparently, but because Caracas had not yet been designated as an approved locale for the conferring of the Order.[9] A protracted lawsuit against the Cathedral of Caracas over his uncle's bequest was finally resolved in his favor, but only after he expended significant amounts of time and money on the case.[10] Oviedo y Baños also fought to affirm the rights of Caracas *alcaldes* (magistrates) to participate with governors in shared administrative decision-making, basing his claims on what he maintained were the clear stipulations of the *Nueva recopilación de leyes de Indias* (New collection of the laws of the Indies; 1680).[11] Oviedo y Baños's numerous personal setbacks crystallize for the reader the confounding of criollo ambition by circumstances rooted in late colonial politics and geography. His critique of the conquistadors may have arisen from a resentful awareness that they had enjoyed access to avenues of professional advancement that were increasingly closed off to him and his contemporaries.[12]

Eighteenth-century criollo disenchantment with the Hapsburg model of conquest informs one of Oviedo y Baños's recurring themes—the enormous difference that exists between conquest and governance (or settlement). The bifurcated title of his work, *Historia de la conquista y población,* points to this tension. Does the conjunction *y* (and) signal simultaneity or a series of separate, sequential events? Should it be read merely as a necessary copulative? Is the story referred to in the title organized chronologically, or geographically, or in response to other unnamed exigencies? The *Historia*'s title recognizes the inevitable priority of conquest, yet the work itself reflects the urgency of the eighteenth-century project of *población*—that is, of population, governance, and settlement.[13] The eighteenth-century historian understands, as earlier historians could not have, that the move from conquest to colonization was not always neatly experienced or chronicled. As Oviedo y Baños presents them, the two projects—*conquista* and *población*—do not constitute sequential events or even binary oppositions, but rather a complex and ongoing negotiation. This explains why Oviedo y Baños frequently uses the phrase *perfeccionar la conquista* (to perfect the conquest) to refer to Spanish endeavors, and why, as we shall see, he devotes a great deal of attention, particularly in later chapters of the work, to matters of colonial administration. His use of the Latinate term *perfeccionar* suggests the necessity of bringing to completion (rather than perfecting) a project initiated by the heroic conquistadors he will be portraying—a project left unfinished precisely because of their folly and error.

In the prologue to the *Historia,* Oviedo y Baños announces his intention: "To bring to light memorable events in Venezuelan history" (11). These include Alonso de Ojeda's discovery of Venezuela in 1499, the early exploration of the region by a number of Spanish and German expeditions, the foundation of cities along the coast and in the interior, the 1561 attack by the tyrannical Lope de Aguirre on the Venezuelan island of Margarita, the long and difficult conquest of the Caracas Valley, the founding of Caracas by Diego de Losada in 1567, and, finally, an account of Francis Drake's sacking of the city of Santiago in 1600. The promised second volume of the *Historia,* which was to have continued the story up to the moment the author was writing, has never been located either in manuscript or print version and has become, in the words of one historian, "a bibliographic myth."[14]

The imperative to revisit issues of conquest that we see in the first part of the history reflects, paradoxically, both a redefinition of Spain's imperial project and an emerging criollo identity that would feed into nascent independence movements toward the turn of the century. "Conquest" represents (recalling once more de Certeau's words) "what must be forgotten in order to obtain the representation of a present intelligibility" (*Writing of History,* 4)—that is, in order to articulate a present defined by an eighteenth-century context. The lack of a historiographical tradition in Venezuela, which Oviedo y Baños notes with some dismay, is another recurring theme in the *Historia.* At the same time, like many eighteenth-century historians, Oviedo y Baños is painfully aware of the belated nature of his task. When in the prologue he refers to "the taxing labor of the historian in our days" (10), the lightly veiled complaint should not be read as a mere *excusatio propter infirmitatem,* but rather as an acknowledgment of the tradition of historic feats and historiographical accomplishment against which his own account will inevitably be measured.[15] Oviedo acknowledges that others—explorers as well as historians—"had the good fortune to arrive first" (73). But he also recognizes the position of the *adelantado* is not necessarily a happy one, as the whitened bones of the disastrous Narváez expedition remind us.[16] Throughout the construction of his history, in the selection of episodes and in his frequent moralizing interventions, Oviedo y Baños repeatedly claims the higher historiographical ground of the eighteenth century, a vantage point from which he can discern the folly and errors of those who went before.

As we have seen, domestication may be understood as taking something that has been represented in the past as untamed or savage and rewriting it as something that is familiar and utilitarian.[17] In this chapter I explore the domestication of conquest as a historiographical maneuver that shifts the focus from a peninsular project of empire building to a more local project of settlement and governance, rewriting an earlier narrative of triumphalism and providentialism. In Oviedo y Baños's *Historia,* both the sixteenth-century legacy of conquest and the figure of the conquistador are domesticated rhetorically within eighteenth-century parameters of local settlement and administrative consolidation. This is accomplished by employing a grammar of balance and civility and by invoking the reformulation of the Hapsburg model of conquest in accordance with Bourbon imperial reinvention. Oviedo y Baños's rhetorical strategy of domestication is articulated on a number of levels: the portrayal of the Spanish conquistadors as vain and greedy men given to excess and lapses of judgment; the representation of power as a shift from the conquistador to the colonial administrator; the portrayal of Aguirre, deformed and practically illiterate, as the disfigured and delegitimized emblem of conquest; and the shift from the search for El Dorado to the founding of Caracas and a host of lesser cities.

Some background is necessary in order to understand the history of colonial Venezuela that Oviedo y Baños is attempting to write. In the eighteenth century, local circumstances in the colonial peripheries became increasingly important as each of these regions developed in relation to the center, whether that center was recognized as Spain or as one of the more established viceregal cities. Thus, the particular nature of the conquest of Venezuela is fundamental to Oviedo y Baños's eighteenth-century reconceptualization of that conquest. It's important to remember that the viceroyalty of New Granada was created twice, with an initial failed attempt in 1718–1719 and then again, with lasting success, in 1739.[18] So Oviedo y Baños was writing his history at a time of transition, when the territory that is now Venezuela and Colombia still formed part of the vast viceroyalty of Peru. Venezuela was a marginalized space in viceregal geography, and Caracas a fledgling backwater outpost far removed from the baroque splendor of Mexico City and Lima. Compared to the legendary stuff of earlier conquests, the Venezuelan colonial experience might be summed up in modest or even negative terms, as in John V. Lombardi's *Venezuela:* "No mighty Amerindian empires, no storehouses of golden objects, and no fabulous cities" (59).[19]

Unlike what happened in Mexico and Peru, where Spanish expeditions were directed against monumental cities and centralized populations, early efforts to conquer Venezuela consisted of fragmented exploratory excursions that spread out inland from the coastal areas, driven by the prospect of indigenous slave raids and the lure of El Dorado. These excursions were often met by resistance from decentralized indigenous groups, and Spanish expeditionary forces struggled to find suitable locations for developing military, economic, and political strongholds.[20] In the early eighteenth century, as Oviedo y Baños was writing, and after more than a century of sporadic and disorganized expeditions that, like Luis de Narváez's, had ended more often than not in disastrous failure, two major military thrusts—one in Coro to the west and another in the region of Cubagua-Margarita-Cumaná to the east—were coming together.[21] As a consequence, pockets of agricultural and commercial prosperity were beginning to emerge that would require for their maintenance and growth a greater degree of administrative stability than had heretofore been provided by Spanish presence.[22]

Venezuelan colonial history was further complicated by the intervention of the Welsers, a small band of Germans who arrived in 1528, having obtained a royal *cédula* (charter) for conquest and colonization in partial payment of the Hapsburg royal debt.[23] They remained for two decades, until the Crown revoked their authorization.[24] This experience of foreign intervention in the conquest of Venezuela—albeit short-lived and anomalous in the larger picture of Spanish conquest of the Americas—looms large in Oviedo y Baños's *Historia*. Perhaps a nascent sense of local, or criollo, identity leads to his rejection of the Welsers as "foreign." It may also be the case that the Welsers' particularly brutal and destructive mode of conquest makes it easier for Oviedo y Baños to reject it. The historian complains that when the Welsers take possession of their claims, their only interest is booty: "Their will and that of the other Germans who followed them was never to attend to the flourishing or conservation of the province, but rather to enjoy it, taking advantage of it for as long as the opportunity lasted" (21). Oviedo y Baños censures here not only Welser greed but also their hedonistic and profligate inattention to the sustainable stewardship of Venezuelan resources. In this he echoes other efforts to differentiate Bourbon imperial ideology, characterized by a kind of civility with roots in Spain's Roman past, from Hapsburg barbarism, which was reminiscent of Spain's Gothic history.[25] Whatever the reasons, condemnation of the Welsers is an integral part of the historian's rhetorical strategy for delegitimizing the larger conquistador project.

Finally, it's important to remember that the territory that is now Venezuela formed part of the Caribbean and thus shared in the benefits and perils of participation in the greater Atlantic world. In the eighteenth century the Caribbean was increasingly an area of conflict between Spain and her European rivals. Contraband trade in cocoa, wheat, and tobacco posed a threat to the development of a diversified economy in the region, and there was great concern about the defense of colonial coastal cities.[26] In his work Oviedo y Baños does not refer explicitly to these issues, but they surely contributed to the historian's sense of urgency regarding the need for stable and responsible government structures.[27]

The War of the Spanish Succession (which began in 1701 and concluded in 1713 with the Treaty of Utrecht) and the resultant switch from Hapsburg to Bourbon rule occasioned a revisionist deployment of the Reconquest of Spain and the Conquest of America as part of a large-scale invention of Bourbon Spanish traditions. As Ruth Hill argues, "At the very heart of it all was a radically different conceptualization of conquest: love, not war, conquered subjects, and peace, not war, permitted the development of the arts and sciences that made a republic powerful and its citizens productive" ("Bourbon Cultural Management," 2).[28] This rationalized and systematized notion of conquest is personified by Benito Jerónimo Feijoo's "peaceful prince" who pursues peace, settlement, and economic development, as opposed to the earlier model of the "prince-conqueror."[29] Arising out of this convergence of geographic and historical circumstances, Oviedo y Baños's *Historia* reflects and reinforces a fundamental shift in eighteenth-century Spanish political culture.

II. "Por asegurarse del peligro . . . dio en manos la desdicha": A grammar of domestication

In the balancing act between conquest and governance that informs the structure and content of Oviedo y Baño's *Historia,* language itself is domesticated. The first-person protagonist so flamboyantly present in the accounts of Hernán Cortés and Bernal Díaz del Castillo disappears behind the cautious and considered mask of the eighteenth-century historian. Oviedo y Baños assumes a bird's-eye perspective that allows him to see many simultaneous events and relate their significance, while always remaining above the fray. Although Oviedo y Baños occasionally abandons a strict chronological presentation in order to include a detail that might otherwise not make its way into the *Historia,* he demonstrates a clear awareness of how he is ordering and presenting his material.[30] Even Oviedo y Baños's syntactic organization is strikingly different from what we see in earlier chroniclers and historians like Cortés and Díaz del Castillo. Their descriptive and narrative accounts of the conquest of Tenochtitlán frequently resort to long, run-on sentences in order to encapsulate a bewildering and chaotic assault of impressions and actions. Eschewing anacolutha as a rhetorical strategy, Oviedo y Baños instead links cause and effect, and consideration and action, in a meticulously constructed layering of dependent clauses.

At the same time, hindsight enables him to make judgments that the protagonists themselves were never in a position to make. This strengthens the authority of the eighteenth-century historian vis-à-vis earlier works that might otherwise make a persuasive claim to primacy. As we will see in his accounts of various conquistadors, Oviedo y Baños is quick to point out the consequences of human error. He pulls no punches in making moralizing pronouncements regarding the history he is narrating. For example, Oviedo y Baños begins chapter 6 of book 2 with this observation: "When ambition overcomes the human heart, there is no understanding that is not blinded, nor reason that is not perturbed" (66). Another statement, regarding the death of Governor Juan Pérez de Tolosa, also carries indisputable moral authority: "In this life there is no happiness or fortune so secure that it is not shadowed by misfortune" (115).[31] These pronouncements reaffirm the role of the historian as a judge of the events he is narrating, and they ultimately reinforce the effectiveness of the eighteenth-century vantage point in perceiving the superiority of an emerging imperial project of governance and settlement.

Perhaps the most striking characteristic of Oviedo y Baños's prose is its thematic and syntactic balance. Here are just a few examples of the carefully equilibrated phrases found in *Historia:*

> they met with death, where they were searching for life (25)
> waiting for death with each step and for shipwreck with each blow (45)
> finding themselves brought down in chains when they believed themselves to be elevated to the throne (124)
> arms could not achieve what was moved by the heart (179)
> by trying to save himself from danger he fell into misfortune (216)

If parallelisms are Oviedo y Baños's preferred rhetorical strategy for communicating through measured language, he also resorts frequently to parenthetical observations that serve to clarify a point or insert a narratorial intervention. The effect is to draw the reader away from sixteenth-century events toward an eighteenth-century awareness of their significance. This awareness is further reinforced by Oviedo y Baños's recurrent use of the imperfect subjunctive mode in his writing to evoke a constant what-if. For example, referring to the conquest of the Omeguas, Oviedo y Baños writes that Juan de Carvajal "would have achieved it had he not been thwarted by events that happened later" (102). Speaking of Pedro Malaver de Silva's quest for El Dorado, Oviedo y Baños writes, "If, chastened by the knowledge of the misfortunes that fate had in store for him, he had opted to retreat, he would have been happy, for he would have avoided suffering the misfortunes to which his destiny led him, and he would not have been given reason to lament the circumstances of his pitiful death" (270). These conditional phrases can be read as the deliberate inscription of historical and narrative contingency—a rhetorical reminder of the eighteenth-century criollo historian's balancing act between past and present, and between conquest and settlement.

The tensions inherent in this balancing act—implicit in Oviedo y Baños's bifurcated title and reflected in his grammar and syntax—permeate the entire history. This is a reflection of the historical circumstances of the eighteenth-century viceregal periphery but also, I will argue, of the historian's domestication of conquest and empire. Nowhere is this domestication more striking than in the portrayal of the sixteenth-century conquistador, where we can read Oviedo y Baños's struggles to connect with and distance himself from the scattered bones of the conquest.

III. "La infeliz descubrimiento y desgraciada conquista": Domesticating the conquistador

It has been observed that the medieval model of *claros varones*—illustrious heroes who exemplify the medieval notion of *fama* (fame)—is invoked and also put to the test as history moves to the Americas.[32] This is certainly true in Oviedo y Baños's *Historia*. In his preface to the English translation of *Historia*, Lombardi challenges traditional views of the Spanish conquest in order to claim a place for the history of Venezuela:

> Where most English-speaking readers leave off studying the conquest of America is precisely where it actually began. It was in the long, tedious, unglamorous, and terribly destructive campaigns of the sixteenth and even into the seventeenth century that America became Spain's territory. Without these efforts, no less heroic than Cortés's or Pizarro's, the Spanish empire in America would never have existed. ("Foreword," ix)

Oviedo y Baños anticipates Lombardi's assessment (while avoiding his troubling triumphalism) when he refers to his subject as the "unhappy discovery and miserable conquest" (*Historia*, 119). While there are illustrious heroes in the conquest of Venezuela, the historian includes their stories as cautionary tales with a clear didactic intent. The campaigns to expand and secure Spanish claims to Venezuelan territory that Oviedo y Baños describes are decidedly unglamorous and destructive, affording numerous opportunities for folly and cowardice as well as bravery.[33] The hindsight provided by the eighteenth-century historian's perspective offers a compelling alternative to the eyewitness perspective trumpeted by earlier chroniclers.

As we shall see, Oviedo y Baños includes in his history many portraits of conquistadors whose whitened bones lie scattered in his path. In his view, they are a complicated cast of characters. At best, they are honest and well-intentioned leaders undone by intrigue or by the hostile and challenging environment. Their successes in battle are often overshadowed by their failures, and their valor and integrity frequently go unappreciated until after their deaths. Oviedo y Baños is more inclined, however, to portray conquistadors as vain, greedy, and foolish men given to excess, hubris, and lapses of judgment.[34] Their failings are not tragic because they cannot claim heroic status, and their downfall inspires little or no compassion in the reader. In many instances, the authority of conquistador figures in Oviedo y Baños's narrative is ultimately trumped by colonial administrators or ecclesiastical authorities who step in as a kind of bureaucratic deus ex machina to resolve their quarrels and restore order. Thus, in the *Historia* the tyrant is tamed, either through the folly of his own actions or by institutional responses to those actions.

In his conquistador portraits Oviedo y Baños problematizes and undermines conquistador authority, even at its most exemplary. By showing time and time again how traditional conquistador behavior leads to negative consequences and thus must either be contained or corrected, Oviedo y Baños uses his history to domesticate the figure of the conquistador, ultimately proving that the pen is mightier than the sword. In what follows, I'll look at the portraits of two conquistadors—Garci González de Silva and Esteban Martín—who merit the historian's admiration. The misguided search by Felipe de Utre (Philipp von Hutten) for the elusive El Dorado receives a more ambiguous portrayal, as does the mestizo Francisco Fajardo, while other conquistadors—Jorge de Spira (Georg von Speyer), Juan de Carvajal, Francisco Martín, and finally Lope de Aguirre—are presented as antiheroes.[35]

One of the most extraordinary heroic portraits in Oviedo y Baños's account is that of Garci González de Silva. He is introduced at the beginning of book 6 as a brave and noble person; equally important, he is presented as a positive counterpoint to his impetuous uncle, Pedro Malaver de Silva (259).[36] Garci González is an *encomendero* who rejects the cruel and abusive tactics of his fellow Spaniards in favor of a kinder, gentler form of conquest consonant with the Bourbon imperial ideals I discussed at the beginning of this chapter.[37] Unlike many of his compatriots, Garci González hopes to subdue the Indians through generosity, "determined to use the experience he'd acquired so that clemency would correct where rigor had erred" (291). Oviedo y Baños offers the reader persuasive evidence of the efficacy of this approach. When the ferocious cacique Parayauta is wounded and captured in an ambush, Garci González—against the advice of all his soldiers—tends to Parayauta's wounds and then sets him free. A grateful Parayauta convenes a meeting of the indigenous leaders of the region and persuades them to lay down their arms and swear obedience to Garci González. Peace is thus achieved in a region where it had previously been elusive (292). Oviedo y Baños later singles out Garci González for having founded several cities without ever unsheathing his sword (313). After so many descriptions of bloody battles and frustrated conquests, Garci González's success is a clear vindication of a different sort of hero.

His exemplary status is consolidated by the description of further exploits.[38] Garci González and his brother-in-law Francisco Infante, traveling in 1566 with two other companions through pacified regions that they held as *encomenderos,* are awakened by a surprise Amerindian attack. In the confusion Garci González cannot find his sword and defends himself using only a blanket for a shield, brandishing first a burning log and then a spur against his attackers (295). This is a far cry from the standard image of the Spanish conquistador, protected by metal armor and superior weaponry. Garci González manages to kill a great number of Indians but is finally brought to his knees by a blow to the shoulder. He ingeniously decides to bluff, shouting to nonexistent companions to join him in his desperate battle. The Amerindians retreat, alarmed by the prospect

of a large number of Spaniards in hiding.[39] Finding his three companions critically injured, Garci González cares for them and binds their wounds—a detail
that reminds the reader that he has previously been portrayed as a healing and
nurturing figure. As the beleaguered Spaniards decide to flee in search of help,
Oviedo y Baños inserts a chapter break, creating a suspenseful pause in the heroic action.

In the next chapter (the final one in book 6), the historian follows Garci
González as he carries the moribund Francisco Infante on his shoulders (the
other nameless companions have died en route). Garci González walks all night
until they finally reach the territory of the Teque tribe, sworn enemies of their
Quiriquire attackers. The Teque cure Garci González and Francisco Infante
with indigenous herbal remedies, "making an honorable effort to favor with
generosity those whom his enemies had mistreated with infamy" (297). With
this phrasing, a sense of balance and justice is restored to the narrative. The
Teque reciprocate Garci González's ministrations in a ritual of healing and recuperation that cancels out their earlier treachery and violence.

Oviedo y Baños adds a narrative coda celebrating the glorious deeds that
secure for Garci González the admiration of his contemporaries (297). The
wrap-up is typical of the *varones ilustres* (literally, "illustrious men") tradition in
which specific feats are invoked to consolidate the hero's richly deserved reputation. In succeeding chapters, however, it becomes clear that Garci González's
moments of greatest authority and glory are behind him, which undercuts this
heroic portrait. He appears briefly at the beginning of book 7, battling the Carib
Indians, but the final mention of him is when Oviedo y Baños recounts his frustrated attempts to found the city of Espíritu Santo.[40] Despite his heroic textual
legacy, Garci González leaves no lasting mark on the Venezuelan landscape.
Since for the historian, lasting settlement is the measure of imperial presence
in the region, Garci González's story becomes further evidence of Oviedo y Baños's project to undermine and domesticate the heroic mode in the *Historia*.

At times Oviedo y Baños advances this project by contrasting one conquistador with another, as in the case of Esteban Martín. Martín is in every way the
chivalrous hero, gallant in word and valiant in action (61). When he is put in
charge of an ill-fated reconnaissance mission organized by the Welser governor
Jorge de Spira, his experience in earlier conquests and his familiarity with local indigenous groups are held up in contrast to Spira's rash and ill-informed
judgment:

> Ascertaining [*tanteando*], with his great experience, the poor disposition of that
> terrain, and the indomitable ferocity of that barbarous nation, he recognized
> the danger to which Spira's ill-considered determination exposed him; never-
> theless, he did not dare refuse to obey him, so that what was in fact an excess of
> prudence would not appear to be a lack of valor: however, [Martín] said to the
> Governor: Your Lordship wishes for me to enter this province to reconnoiter
> it with the very few men you've assigned to me; the Indians (from what I've
> ascertained [*tengo tanteado*]) are many and very skilled in the use of weapons,

the land is arduous and difficult; may God grant that one of us survives to bring news of the disastrous end of the others. (61)

Oviedo y Baños emphasizes the moderate tone of Martín's questioning of the chain of command ("tanteando . . . tanteado"), his reluctance to appear cowardly in the face of danger, and the respectful—even abject—terms in which he frames his response to the governor. The historian chooses to quote Martín directly as the dutiful soldier resolves to leave the matter in God's hands, and he reports Martín's death in battle three days later with regret and admiration.[41] In light of these later developments, the historian's earlier decision to include verbatim Martín's gesture of submission to Spira can be read as an ironic move to subvert Spira's authority. Martín's words foretell the disastrous end of the ill-fated expedition Spira has ordered him to undertake, echoing beyond the grave to condemn yet another instance of conquistador excess. As a final condemnation, Ovideo y Baños notes that even Spira recognizes belatedly his own responsiblity for Martín's tragic end (65).

If Garci González and Martín might be considered *varones ilustres* worthy of inclusion in a heroic tradition, at least initially, Oviedo y Baños's portraits of other conquistador figures are marked by narrative chiaroscuro. Although Francisco Fajardo and Felipe de Utre follow different paths, both represent frustrated heroic potential. Francisco Fajardo stands out in large part because of a compelling mestizo family romance. Fajardo's father is a Spanish nobleman and his mother, Doña Isabel, a Gauiquerí Indian of noble lineage. His mother's enticing descriptions of the beautiful and fertile Maya valley in the Caracas province awaken in Fajardo a thirst for discovery, and he hopes not only to discover but also to settle new lands (*Historia*, 127). Oviedo y Baños presents Fajardo as an exemplary and judicious conqueror, making special note of his fluency in indigenous languages and the cultural affinity afforded by his maternal connections (132); the historian observes that Fajardo's mother was a well-respected *cacica*.[42]

Fajardo is able to take advantage of his bicultural upbringing to legitimize settlement and jurisdiction on both Spanish and indigenous grounds, and he is shown initially to act in measured and constructive ways. For example, when he is invited by the Indians to remain with them as their guest, he is delighted but feels obliged to seek permission from Spanish authorities to accept the invitation. Then, having successfully negotiated his position with the governor, Fajardo puts his men to work building a town—El Panecillo—in order to anchor and strengthen his claim as conquistador. Eventually, though, Fajardo's felicitous model of administrative hybridization goes sour. Suspicions and petty annoyances grow on both sides and finally explode into open combat (130–35). What's more, the local cacique takes the additional step of poisoning the settlement's wells so that the besieged Spaniards will have no source of drinking water. This development augurs poorly for Indian-Spanish relations in general, and is especially disappointing after the peaceful coexistence stemming from Fajardo's hybrid family tree. Finally, even Fajardo's mother dies from the poisoned water. In retaliation Fajardo captures and summarily executes not only the warring cacique, but also a number of indigenous prisoners. The historian judges this to be "an act unworthy of a magnanimous heart . . . and one which stained Fajardo's fame" (135).

As Oviedo y Baños tells the story, an initially promising trajectory is cut short by violence and miscalculation. When Fajardo is sentenced to death by a jealous rival on trumped-up charges and executed several chapters later, he is eulogized as a penniless mestizo (albeit one of noble birth). Here the historian's use of the epithet "pobre mestizo desválido" (poor helpless mestizo) points to Fajardo's low status as the disgraced son of a Spanish nobleman and an Indian *cacica*. The parenthetical phrase has the effect of undercutting Fajardo's noble lineage. And although Fajardo's mestizo identity is key to his early successes, the conclusion of Fajardo's story (both in action and word) points to the erasure of this identity in the history of the conquest and settlement of Venezuela (210).[43]

Felipe de Utre is portrayed as a potentially heroic conquistador who falls under the spell of El Dorado, the legendary city that, according to Oviedo y Baños, was the cause of so many deaths and so much unhappiness. El Dorado is an American variant of the legendary lands of gold that appear in classical myths and their medieval retellings that were brought to the New World (as Irving Leonard has documented in *Books of the Brave*) by the earliest European sailors. The El Dorado legend was given additional credence in Venezuela due to the convergence of several different hypotheses about its exact geographical location that seemed to place it somewhere on the altiplano inhabited by the Chibcha Indians. Indigenous informants reported a Chibcha legend about a Guatavita cacique whose wife drowned herself after having been unjustly accused of infidelity. To make amends for his hasty and cruel suspicions, the repentent cacique would annually dust his body with gold powder and immerse himself in the lake where his wife's spirit resided. This particular legend gave tantalizing form to many others, as "El Dorado" became a phrase that conflated the golden cacique, his submerged treasures, and the existence of hidden cities with vast storehouses of precious metals. Oviedo y Baños offers his own, much more prosaic, explanation, which involves Spanish soldiers in Quito in 1536 who seize on fantastic tales of riches told to them by a manipulative and diabolical Indian (81).[44] The legend of El Dorado is thus reduced in the *Historia* to lies and fictions that lead only to death and suffering for greedy and gullible Europeans like Felipe de Utre.

Utre's fate is presented as a sobering example of how the Welsers squandered material and human resources in their heedless pursuit of El Dorado.[45] Oviedo y Baños recounts that in 1541 Utre gathers a number of men to join him as he strikes out on new conquests, enticing his recruits by naming "El Dorado" as one of the provinces they will conquer (81). Even when Utre becomes a victim of his own glittering rhetoric as he drags his men down a path marked by hubris and hunger, no amount of suffering can dissuade the conquistador from this folly.[46] As Oviedo y Baños traces the route of Utre's ill-fated expedition, he repeatedly contrasts specific geographical indicators with the ephemeral goal of "his false Dorado" (81) or "his fictitious Dorado" (84). In these phrases the combined effect of qualifier—"mentido," "fingido"—and possessive—"su"—is to diminish the lure of El Dorado and undermine Utre's misguided claim to its eventual discovery.

The degree to which Utre's men are misled by their leader is reflected by the miserable state in which they are forced to pass the winter—famished, bedraggled, and covered with rashes and ulcers. They are reduced to eating a repellent mixture concocted by leaving a ball of corn dough at the mouth of an ant hole and then kneading into the dough the ants that emerge in order to supplement the dough's nutritional value (84). As in Alvar Núñez Cabeza de Vaca's *Naufragios*, an initial desire for gold is replaced by a more basic desire for a different kind of yellow treasure—corn.[47] But in these dire straits, even corn is insufficient and must be supplemented by desperate measures. The repeated instances of extreme hunger described in grotesque detail here and elsewhere in the *Historia* reinforce for the reader the advantages of settlement and domesticity over the uncertainties of conquest.

Utre and his men finally return to Nuestra Señora after achieving an important military victory over the Omegua Indians and are received with great jubilation. This provides an opportunity for the historian to recognize and honor collective acts of heroism by Spaniards in a lengthy passage recapitulating a celebrated battle in which thirty-nine Spaniards defeated an Omegua army of fifteen hundred as an example of the "carats [*quilates*] of their bravery and the strength of their fortune" (99). Oviedo y Baños closes the passage by taking credit for having rescued these notable conquerors from oblivion, brandishing his pen as he claims responsibility for converting epic feats into the fame and glory they justly deserve. Although the golden treasure of El Dorado remains beyond the conquistadors' reach, their moral and military strengths become the measure of their worth ("los quilates de su valor"), while Oviedo y Baños's historiographical feat translates the deeds of battle into lasting fame. This necessary maneuver of authorial domestication comes close on the heels of his account of Utre's ill-fated expedition, thus rescuing Utre's reputation from his earlier folly, at least for the time being.

Oviedo y Baños recognizes Utre's accomplishment in having led his men successfully through four years of incredible hardship and misfortune. However, the historian rejects Utre's speculation that the great kingdom of the Omeguas is, in fact, El Dorado: "If we were to ask them what reason they had to say that province was El Dorado, there's no doubt that they would not know how to explain the reason behind their discourse, since this being an imaginary name based on pure chimera, any conquistador who in any other part of America might discover another powerful province could also affirm that it was El Dorado, without there being any more reason for one than for the other" (100). Oviedo y Baños's dismissal of the legend of El Dorado and his impatience with conquistador susceptibility to the El Dorado myth bring to mind Feijoo's discourses on popular superstition. Both men employ arguments against "pure chimera" and in support of the need for evidence that are typical of eighteenth-century philosophical thinking.

Oviedo y Baños is perturbed not only by Felipe de Utre's obsession with El Dorado but also by the way in which he squanders the advantage seized through his conquest of the Omeguas. The victorious leader fails to appreciate the complexities of colonial governance and is caught up in subsequent power struggles with other conquistadors that ultimately lead to his death (102–7). In other words, Utre proves unable to move from conquest to settlement. But rather than dwell on the shortcomings of one of his preferred heroic figures, Oviedo y Baños includes instead a lengthy elegy for Utre that praises his bravery, prudence, and moderation ("no captain of the many who fought in the Indies bloodied his sword less") while also lamenting his misguided pursuit of the riches of El Dorado (105). The tone throughout this passage is one of regret more than anger. The discursive mode is pluperfect subjunctive ("he might have done . . . if they had not anticipated with violence"), pointing to repeated missed opportunities. The vocabulary further reinforces the historian's somber assessment of Utre's legacy: "shadow," "error," "waste," "pitiful" (twice), and "misfortune." Moreover, with Utre's premature death, any chance of capitalizing on his victory over the Omeguas is lost, as the knowledge of that kingdom lies buried with him. Necrological notes like the one written for Utre play an important role in the text, providing the historian with an opportunity to restore a sense of balance and meaning that is missing as the events themselves unfold.[48]

Later attempts to find El Dorado, such as Pedro Malaver de Silva's expedition (narrated in book 6), are equally unsuccessful, and the eighteenth-century historian is in a privileged position to judge the degree to which the exploits of sixteenth-century conquistadors have created a pernicious model. Oviedo y Baños attributes Silva's obsession with the mythical city to his misguided desire to repeat the exploits of Cortés and Pizarro: "The desire to eternalize his fame with the conquest of El Dorado so that his name might equal that of Cortés and Pizarro in the applause tributed him by the world was deeply rooted in his heart" (271). Undeterred even after a first expedition ends in failure, Silva organizes an exploratory voyage along the Venezuelan coast between the mouths of the Marañon and Orinoco Rivers that ends in 1574 with his death (and the death of his two daughters) at the hands of the Caribs.[49] In Oviedo y Baños's account, every reference to El Dorado suggests the foolish conjuring up of unattainable riches. Only the historian himself resists El Dorado's siren song while portraying case after case of conquistadors whose expeditions end in failure precisely because they succumb to the fatal lure of the imaginary city.[50]

Oviedo y Baños's eighteenth-century perspective on the human costs of conquest serves to reduce its significance and undermine its appeal for the reader.[51] If Garci González, Martín, and (to some degree) Utre can be read as exemplary representatives of the conquistador model, most of the anecdotes included in Oviedo y Baños's *Historia* reflect a clear departure from that model.[52] Many of the most egregious examples of greed, ambition, and excess involve the Welsers, who from the 1520s to the 1540s exercised the rights to exploration and conquest granted them by the *cédula* I mentioned earlier.[53] The historian's treatment of the Welsers and their surrogates in the Venezuelan conquest reflects the larger problem the Welsers presented for the Hapsburgs: how to control the intervention of these men—at the same time foreigners and part of the Spanish Austrian Hapsburg Empire—in the imperial project.[54] There is some historical credence to the claim that the Welsers contributed greatly to the ruin and unrest of the region during the sixteenth century; ultimately the involvement of the Welsers ended in failure for both them and the Crown.[55]

Oviedo y Baños strikes a Lascasian chord as he describes the eighteen years Venezuela suffered under Welser rule: "Doing everything with blood and fire, they left nothing that they did not devastate like unleashed beasts: and as their greed drove them to become even richer from enslaving the poor Indians, there were thousands that they took out to sell to the traders who come to Coro, lured by the bait of such an infamous trade, so that most of the province was left completely uninhabited" (108). Welser interests were commercial and short-term, and the eighteenth-century historian finds that the Welsers erred by divorcing what he considers to be the intimately linked processes of conquest and settlement. Over and over again Oviedo y Baños fulminates against Welser short-sightedness and arrogance in viewing Venezuela merely as booty to be plundered rather than as land to be populated and developed, as he does in this long passage where he is discussing the methods of conquest employed by the Welser leader Ambrosio de Alfinger:

> Since his soldiers realized that he had no intention of settling any of what they conquered, and so they could expect nothing from the fruits of their labors, neither *repartimientos* and *encomiendas* for their own interests nor the possession of land for their leisure, and could only make use of what they seized along the way, without being deterred by pity or checked by compassion, like unbridled furies, they cut down and devastated enticing provinces and delightful lands, destroying the benefits that they might have achieved for themselves and their descendants through the possession of their fecundity if, as the most practical and prudent advised them to do, they had settled the lands as they discovered them; but since the Germans, considering themselves to be foreigners, were always aware that their control of the province would not last very long, they paid more attention to short-term gains, by destroying, than to future benefits, by conserving. (23)[56]

Oviedo y Baños attributes the Welsers' willingness to sacrifice long-term stability to short-term interests to the fact that they were foreigners and therefore detached from the Spanish imperial project, with no ongoing commitment to Venezuelan territory and its future development.

The Spaniards, on the other hand, are portrayed as locals who appreciate the need to move from conquest to settlement, eventually overcoming their initial thirst for gold and replacing it with a well-grounded appreciation for the region's agricultural and commercial potential. The Spaniards—or at least some of them—come across as reasonable actors willing to commit to the essential project of domesticating Venezuelan territory. This is, of course, a familiar binary: Gothic barbarity (associated with medieval Spain and with the Hapsburgs) and classical civility (associated with the Bourbons). Oviedo y Baños uses the Welsers to stand in for the vision of conquest exemplified by the Hapsburg Empire, implicitly advocating for the Bourbon model in its place.[57]

Given this larger picture, Oviedo y Baños misses no chance to vent his resentment of the Welsers—Alfinger, Spira, Nicolás de Fedreman, and others—in his narration of their affairs. At one point he makes the familiar providentialist claim that God is on the Spaniards' side in blocking the Germans' conquests until the moment when Don Gonzalo Jiménez de Quesada comes on the scene (46–47). Indeed, it does seem to the reader that the Germans are frustrated at every turn in their ambitions, though it's not always clear whether this is the result of divine Providence, cruel arrogance, or mere incompetence.

In describing Spira's initial forays into the Venezuelan hinterland, Oviedo y Baños makes repeated narratorial interventions to comment on the hapless nature of these expeditions, the inexperience of the German soldiers, the unremitting hardships occasioned by weather, terrain, and Indians, and the frequency with which the best-laid plans go astray. He sums up one expedition in the following terms: "With the dense jungle, the continuous rains, the lack of supplies, and the necessary bother of having to walk with weapons at hand, given the opposition and resistance with which the Indians at every step tried to impede their progress as they were discovering the terrain, the soldiers (most of them recently arrived from Europe) were surprised by that terribly difficult way of waging war, to which they were not accustomed" (37). Welser expectations regarding the standard model of military engagement are undone by the stark realities of the Venezuelan campaign, and Spira's men battle illness and hunger almost to the point of extinction. At one point the desperate soldiers are saved from starvation when they come upon a house where the Indians have hidden over 1,500 *fanegas* (one hundred bushels) of corn—a discovery that Oviedo y Baños describes as "treasure" (43). Once again, food has replaced gold as the object of the soldiers' desire.

At the same time, gold treasure is devalued by the men's dire circumstances. One of Alfinger's subordinates, Iñigo de Bascona, is sent to the city of Coro in an attempt to entice some of its able-bodied men to join the Welser enterprise. Loaded down with the sixty thousand gold pesos he has been given to fund the expedition, Bascona quickly gets terribly lost. Oviedo y Baños observes wryly that Bascona was navigating by the North Star of his unfortunate destiny rather than by a common-sense apprehension of the landmarks around him. Bascona's journey takes him from demonstrated excess to scarcity and want, from fortune to ruin. He is unable to replenish his supplies as they run out, since in the wilderness the gold pesos he carries are of little value. Bascona's men are finally so exhausted that they decide to abandon their precious cargo of gold coins, burying them at the foot of an enormous ceiba tree "in case one of them might have the good fortune of making it out of that labyrinth alive, to come back to look for their hearts, which they were leaving there with the treasure" (26). Bascona's error in having gotten lost is compounded by the folly of this quixotic planting of the useless coins, and the magnitude of the loss is suggested by the conflated abandonment of heart and treasure in the historian's commentary. The sole surviving member of the expedition, Francisco Martín (to whom I will return), is unable ever to find the ceiba tree again. The unavoidable lesson here is that Bascona's inability to read the local terrain leads to his downfall. Having lost his way (as well as his moral compass), he no longer possesses the appropriate symbolic currency to achieve his goals.

With the exception of the rebel Lope de Aguirre (whom I will discuss later in this chapter), the infamous conquistador Juan de Carvajal stands out as one of the cruelest and most tyrannical Spaniards. He arrives in Coro in 1544 to serve as lieutenant general and secretary of the Audiencia until the arrival of the new *fiscal*. Carvajal develops an instant rivalry with the highly respected Diego de Losada and with Felipe de Utre. He schemes ceaselessly to consolidate his political advantage over the two men by hanging anyone associated with either of them (106).[58] News of Carvajal's cruelty finally reaches the ear of the absent *fiscal* and even the king, who quickly sends a new governor to restore order. Carvajal is finally brought to justice and sentenced to death by hanging "from the same ceiba tree that had been the scene of his unjust acts" (110). Oviedo y Baños appreciates, as did the sixteenth-century authorities, the judicious use of violence as spectacle.[59] But he also makes a point of noting that the beautiful and leafy ceiba begins to wither and die once it has been used for Carvajal's execution. In a characteristically balanced and balancing sentence, Oviedo y Baños communicates the moral lesson of the ceiba's fate: its "ruin served to inspire admiration, just as before its beauty had inspired astonishment" (110). It seems that nature herself shrinks from participating in the bloody reprisals occasioned by the conquest—even when they are justified.

IV. "Execrable abominación entre cristianos": Eighteenth-century cannibal scenes

One of the justifications for the cruel excesses of Spanish conquest most frequently employed in sixteenth- and seventeenth-century accounts was the explicit or implicit suggestion that Amerindian populations practiced cannibalism. Cannibalism—understood generally as "the ferocious devouring of human flesh supposedly practiced by some savages"—functions as a marker of otherness in colonial historiography.[60] The cannibal scene posits an absolute opposition between the perpetrator and the victim, an opposition in which the Indian is traditionally the perpetrator and the European either the unhappy victim or the horrified witness. So it is significant that in addition to his portrayals of foolish and arrogant conquistadors, Oviedo y Baños further delegitimizes Spanish conquest by associating it on a number of occasions with instances of cannibalism practiced not by Indians but rather by the Europeans themselves. In Oviedo y Baños's eighteenth-century rewriting of the cannibal scene, the traditional roles are reversed or confused, with Europeans at times practicing cannibalism and Indians functioning as either victims or witnesses.[61] This provides him with an opportunity to drive home an eighteenth-century message about the inherent barbarism of sixteenth- and seventeenth-century imperial conquest.[62] His vision of cannibalism is one in which the practice continues to be barbaric but ceases to be the exclusive province of the Other.

In the *Historia,* references to incidences of indigenous cannibalism seem almost accidental. Oviedo y Baños recounts how a Spaniard named Orejón becomes separated from his companions on a hunting expedition when he pursues a deer over the sabana. Lost and alone, he is eventually attacked and killed by a group of Indians. However, his horse, "having a better sense of direction than its master," manages to find its way back to the Spanish camp, arousing the suspicion and fears of Orejón's companions (39). A search party sent out the following morning comes upon a village (from which the inhabitants promptly flee) where they find Orejón's sword and his partially eaten head, which the Indians had displayed "to celebrate (by eating it) the triumph of their victory" (39).[63] The effect of the parenthetical comment is devastatingly casual; the narrator's offhand explanation of the details of the indigenous celebration in no way suggests any moral reprobation. The Indians are not vilified. Orejón is portrayed as a careless and accident-prone chump whose horse is smarter than he is. The historian's disapproval seems directed primarily at the vengeful Spaniards who lay waste to the surrounding communities as retribution for Orejón's fate, "hanging all the Indians that their anger and diligence could find on that mountain, and leaving the village in ashes" (39).[64] Once again Oviedo y Baños demonstrates his interest in the preservation of settlements across the natural landscape of Venezuela and voices his condemnation of the devastating effects of conquest.

Another cannibalism anecdote that Oviedo y Baños includes in his account of Diego de Losada's expedition sets a place at the table for both Spaniards and Indians. When a group of Spanish soldiers arrive at an abandoned Indian village in search of provisions and plunder, they are delighted to find that the terrified villagers have fled in the midst of preparations for a hearty meal. Appropriating the banquet, the Spaniards tuck in with gusto, only to realize with horror that the stew they're enjoying was made with human flesh: "One of them pulled out of the pot some fingers with fingernails and a bit of skin with an ear hanging from it, and realizing from this that they had eaten human flesh, their revulsion and horror were so great that nauseated and sweating they brought up again what they had just downed with pleasure" (245). Here the indigenous practice of anthropophagy is presented in a matter-of-fact way as culinary custom, framed in an everyday, domestic space. The Spaniards' inadvertent foray into cannibalism serves Oviedo y Baños merely as an occasion for the kind of syntactic balancing act and wordplay of which he is so fond ("they brought up again what they had just downed with pleasure"), rather than for scandalized moralizing or condemnation. In fact, there's a clear sense that the marauding Spaniards have gotten their just desserts.

A much more horrific scene involves a group of Spanish soldiers, part of one of Spira's expeditionary raids, who discover a young Indian child apparently left behind by his terrified mother when she fled. Ravenous, they snatch the child up and cook him (68). The Spaniards are initially driven by greed and hunger as they search the village for booty, but end up sinking into unthinkable depravity, not just eating the child but savoring the broth in which they've boiled him. The historian renames them to reflect their degradation: they are no longer men (*hombres*) but animals (*fieras*), driven by diabolical inhumanity. In taking over an abandoned house and appropriating literally and figuratively its sole remaining inhabitant, the Spaniards assume a new identity.[65] Cannibalism is domesticated: that is, cannibalistic practice is brought home and laid at the Spaniards' doorstep.

A further irony is that the horrified eyewitness to this atrocity is an Indian woman who has converted to Christianity and adopted Spanish customs and language: "Just then a Christianized ladina Indian woman, servant to Francisco Infante, entered the house, and realizing from what she saw and smelled that they were cooking human flesh, without letting herself be spotted, she told her master about the evil of those men" (68). Her transculturation, clearly viewed as a positive metamorphosis by the narrator, stands in stark contrast to the degenerative transformation of Spira's men, and it puts her in the position of being witness, prosecutor, and judge.[66] In these anecdotes the eighteenth-century historian makes effective use of women and children in his history (as Las Casas does in the *Brevísima relación*) in order to emphasize the despicable nature of Spanish abuse; as in Las Casas, the categories of civilization and savagery are reversed.

The most disturbing description of cannibalism is in the story of the Spaniard Francisco Martín. Unlike the Indian woman, Martín is a striking example of negative transculturation. He first appears as one of the men who accompany Bascona on his ill-fated journey to Coro; along with a small group of companions and several Indian guides, Martín becomes separated from the larger body of soldiers. The Spaniards' state of confusion and distress is aggravated by hunger, thirst, and fear until finally they fall upon the surviving Indian porters, kill them, and eat them:

> They committed (in order to save their own lives) such an abominable cruelty that it can never be forgiven, even in light of the extreme danger in which they found themselves, as they began to kill one by one the poor Indians who had remained to serve them, and without overlooking the intestines or any other part of their bodies, they ate them all, with so little heed or fastidiousness that it happened that when they killed the last Indian and were cutting him up, they threw away the genitals (as an obscene and disgusting thing), and a soldier called Francisco Martín (about whom we shall speak later) grabbed them so quickly, and without waiting for them to be seasoned by the flames, ate them raw, saying to his companions: "Would you scorn these at a time like this?" (27)

Although the Spaniards commit a moral sin of ingratitude vis-à-vis those who serve them, this episode might possibly be excused as an unavoidable instance of what is often called "survival cannibalism" had the historian not included several damning details that portray Francisco Martín as going beyond the pale. First, he chooses to eat a particularly taboo body part. Second, he eats it raw, without waiting to cook it. Third, and most shockingly, he puts into words what is normally considered unspeakable depravity: "Would you scorn these at a time like this?" Martín's question to his companions—posed more as a challenge or an uneasy taunt than a true interrogative—remains unanswered. His companions, though they accompany him in this cannibal scene because of their dire circumstances, will go no further.

Francisco Martín's practice of cannibalism makes him a poster child for the barbarism of the Spanish conquistador, as seen through Oviedo y Baños's accounts of the cannibal scene. After polishing off the last of their indigenous companions, the small band of survivors has no recourse but to separate into smaller groups, each to pursue its salvation separately. This disbanding, of course, has the effect of reducing endogamous cannibalism (they can't eat each other if they don't stay together), but it also points to the inherent selfishness that motivates these men. Despite the dastardly measures taken to ensure their own survival, most are never heard from again. From the accounts written about four who do survive beyond this point, however, the reader gains an appreciation of the stark contrast between their continued pursuit of heinous self-interest and the actions of the Indian rescuers who, finding them on the banks of the Chama River, take pity on them and return with canoes laden with corn and root vegetables. The greedy Spaniards fall upon the Indians but, as they are too weak to act fully on their infamous appetites, three Indians manage to escape. A fourth, however, is captured and eaten by the Spaniards, "satisfying their appetite for the time being with the entrails, hands, and feet, which they ate with as much gusto as if they came from a ram: execrable abomination among Christians!" (28). The sin of cannibalism is again compounded by the sin of ingratitude. The Spaniards, who have been stripped of any kind of civilizing or humane aspect and denied any claim to Christian identity by the narrator, flee to the mountains and are lost forever.

Francisco Martín's fate is more complicated. When his companions leave him behind because of a leg wound that has slowed his pace, the implicit lesson of his abandonment as retribution for his earlier gastronomic transgressions is hard to miss. He is eventually rescued by yet another group of Indians who find him floating downstream on a log. Martín manages to insinuate himself into the life of the indigenous community—going naked among them, adopting idolatrous religious practices, learning their language, and, finally, marrying the cacique's daughter and being named captain himself.[67] Martín moves from imitation of indigenous customs to mastery of them in a seamless and rapid sequence until he enjoys, as the historian informs us, "absolute dominion over his vassals" (28). We might speculate that Martín's "crossing over" or transculturation to indigenous culture had been prefigured (or perhaps even prescribed) by his earlier repeated incursions into anthropophagy.[68]

Two chapters later, Oviedo y Baños picks up the trail of this transculturated Francisco Martín, "so converted already into an Indian and comfortable with their rude customs that there was no apparent trace of Spaniard left" (32). Not unlike the whitened bones of the Narváez expedition, Martín's appearance conjures up all that has been repressed. He is what remains of the conquest, an unthinkable reminder of the violence that must be repressed in order to move forward in history. Upon learning that a band of Spaniards is approaching, Martín goes out alone to meet his former comrades, instructing his indigenous companions to remain hidden and poised for ambush. At first the Spaniards do not recognize him, as Martín's transformation into an Indian is apparently complete (32). Only after he has recounted his misfortunes do the Spaniards welcome him, dress him in European clothing, and follow him back to where the other Indians have been hiding. Martín successfully convinces the Indians to make peace with the Spaniards. The Spaniards, after accepting with great relief the Indians' assurances of their peaceful intentions, continue on their way back to Coro, taking Francisco Martín along with them like an Indianized prodigal son.

At this point in the story all is apparently forgiven and forgotten—both the cannibal scene and the subsequent transculturation of its perpetrator. The only discordant note is sounded by Oviedo y Baños. His dour assessment of the overall results of the Spanish expedition, which has left the entire region cruelly devastated, reminds the reader of how infrequently conquest leads to successful settlement and development (33). Oviedo y Baños suggests that one of the reasons for this is that gratuitous and destructive consumption by the Spaniards in the pursuit of conquest involves time and energy as well as more unspeakable costs (of which Francisco Martín's story serves as a reminder).

The futility of the Hapsburg brand of conquest is further underscored by the story's denouement. Not surprisingly, given his propensity for survival and repeated self-invention, Francisco Martín turns up once more in the narrative, to be recast as the confirmed and nostalgic *transculturado*. Homesick for his wife and children and carried away by the "tyrannical violence of desire," he flees from Coro and returns to life among the Indians (34). The Spanish soldiers, however, do not recognize as legitimate his claim to indigenous domesticity; there is no place for this kind of domestic conquest in the Hapsburg Empire. So Martín is brought back to Coro by a squadron of Spanish soldiers, only to escape again at the first opportunity. His inability or unwillingness to embrace a fixed cultural identity—to reconcile his conflicting or serial loyalties to his fellow Spanish soldiers and his Indian family—is finally resolved by transferring him to New Granada, "where he lived with great tranquility in the city of Santa Fe, confessing with repentance the ruin to which his appetite had propelled him" (34). Although this resolution is accompanied (or so the reader is told) by the appropriate gestures of confession and repentance, it is accomplished only by removing the renegade from the physical terrain of the *Historia,* from Venezuela to Bogotá.

In Oviedo y Baños's pages the reader notes a fair amount of ambivalence on the part of the historian regarding the shifting boundaries between civilization and barbarism, and between Spaniard and Indian, as he recounts how Francisco Martín crosses back and forth over those boundaries. The story of Francisco

Martín is profoundly unsettling not because he personifies a definitive rupture with and rejection of Spanish identity (as in the case of Gonzalo Guerrero—probably the most famous, or infamous, of the transculturated conquistadors—whose story is first chronicled by Bernal Díaz del Castillo). Francisco Martín is unsettling because he resists settling on either side of the border. His changes of heart remind the reader of the instability of conquest as it is experienced during its less triumphant phases in the Venezuelan campaign.

V. "Aspirar al renombre de conquistadores": Too many conquistadors

The instability of conquest finds expression in Oviedo y Baños's work in more prosaic terms as well. The overriding message of Oviedo y Baños's account of the conquest in his *Historia* is that by the mid-sixteenth century, Venezuelan territory had become, quite literally, overrun with conquistadors whose competing armies and ambitions regularly collided with one another in a frenzied search for gold and *encomiendas*. The path of every would-be explorer was strewn with the whitened bones to which I referred at the opening of this chapter. In fact, the vision of conquest presented in the *Historia* at times resembles a traffic jam more than an epic event.

At one point Oviedo y Baños tracks two different expeditions—the first under the command of the German Fedreman, and another under the Spaniard Pedro de Limpias—as they advance into territory that had previously been conquered by Gonzalo Jiménez de Quesada, the famed discoverer of the region of Bogotá. Disregarding the indigenous informants who attempt to warn him of other Spaniards in the area, Limpias pushes forward and is dismayed to encounter Captain Lázaro Fonte, who had been exiled by Quesada after quarreling with him. When he is informed of these developments, Quesada (already embroiled in other territorial disputes) becomes alarmed at the possibility of his Spanish enemies joining forces against him (73). But before Quesada can make a move to defend his territory, ecclesiastical authorities intervene to settle the dispute. They effectively buy off Fedreman to the tune of four thousand gold pesos so that he will cede his claim on the territory (it's not clear how Limpias fares in this resolution). Thus, a potentially dangerous and destabilizing situation is resolved without recourse to arms, further validating the importance of colonial administrative authority, whether secular or religious.

Fedreman plays a key role in another episode reflecting the problem of conquistatorial congestion. Having tried unsuccessfully to poach fifty soldiers from a rival contingent in order to swell his depleted ranks, he advances southward through territory governed by the Spanish *adelantado* Pedro Fernández de Lugo. Lugo protests, writing Fedreman an extremely civil letter to request that the German observe the neighborly courtesy of not trespassing on his domain (*Historia,* 59). Fedreman, exercising uncharacteristic discretion (perhaps because he is distracted by the challenge of feeding his men with dwindling provisions), opts to comply with Lugo's request and follows an alternate route. Such courtesy was rare, however, given that the stakes were so high: "In the distribution of *encomiendas* each conquistador hoped for the best, since it seemed to him that his own merits were worthy of the most substantial reward" (251).

In all these anecdotes, we note important elements that signal divergence from the earlier conquest model. First, the enemy is no longer, or at least not always, the indigenous Other, but rather other Europeans competing for territory. Second, disputes are settled most effectively through recourse to colonial authorities in the lettered viceregal city who impose order by means of legal or financial measures (by *via jurídica*).[69] Oviedo y Baños shows himself to be fully aware of the quarrels between *encomenderos* and colonial administrators that were so prevalent during the second phase of the conquest. But he emphasizes by means of his descriptive and prescriptive narrative strategies that, in marked contrast to "the fires that burned in Peru due to Gonzalo Pizarro's disturbances," in Venezuelan territory discord is resolved with the pen (or the purse), not the sword (129).[70]

From his late colonial vantage point, Oviedo y Baños is much less concerned with the search for gold than with the process of naming governors, the procedure for establishing mayoral voting rights, and the ways in which peninsular legislation affects colonial government, particularly in questions of administrative succession.[71] He gives several examples of disorder resulting from contested governmental authority or uncertain succession plans. Cubagua is the scene for one such tussle when both Diego de Losada and Juan de Villegas arrive in 1544 and begin to exercise competing civil and criminal jurisdiction. The problem, as Oviedo y Baños explains, is that

> independent command is such a desired and delicate point, that if the slightest action perturbs it there is no talent that is not falsified nor prudence that is not threatened; being of equal authority and dominion, Villegas and Losada, they could not agree on the governance of that small squadron of soldiers without causing some jealousy between the two, so that beginning with secret resentments, they moved on to open disagreements and finally to openly declared discord. (87)

Oviedo y Baños observes that the enmity between the two continues for years, poisoning relationships between friends and partisans throughout the entire province and impeding the move from conquest to settlement.[72]

The historian's posture regarding the vicissitudes of conquest and the difficult transition from conquest to settlement is evident in his selection of narrative episodes, in the gallery of conquistador portraits he provides, in his balanced and carefully interlocking syntax, in his representation of cannibalism, and in his mapping of conquistador traffic. All these rhetorical strategies come together to undermine conquistador authority, particularly as it is compared to the civil administration beginning to emerge from Bourbon imperial reforms at the time Oviedo y Baños is writing.[73] Oviedo y Baños's condemnatory treatment of the conquistador crystallizes in his portrayal of the rebel Lope de Aguirre where, as we shall see, the heroic portrait becomes grossly disfigured. But this distortion has already been foreshadowed in the *Historia* by his portraits of Hapsburg conquistadors who anticipate Aguirre's excesses and crimes on a minor scale.

VI. *"Así acabó la temeraria tiranía de Lope de Aguirre"*: The tyrant tamed

Lope de Aguirre makes his appearance in the *Historia* within the context of a discussion of administrative authority and governance, and the portrayal of the rebel constitutes the central chapters of the *Historia*. Book 4 opens with an account of various situations that reflect a crisis of leadership in Venezuela, as evidenced by either lack (of exemplary figures or clarity regarding administrative succession) or excess (of greed or ambition), establishing an ominous precedent for the events that will unfold.

Lope de Aguirre has often been seen as embodying the breakdown of the epic model of the conquistador that, fueled by the fantastic discoveries of Tenochtitlán and Peru, had dominated Spanish historiography since the early sixteenth century.[74] The story of Aguirre's rebellion begins when a large expedition organized by Pedro de Ursúa leaves Peru in 1560 to search for El Dorado by traveling downriver along the Marañón (part of the vast Amazonian tributary system). In the face of frequent Indian attacks and widespread illness, doubts about the expedition grow, until finally Ursúa is killed by his disillusioned and mutinous men. These men then declare themselves to be in rebellion against the king, and crown as the prince of Peru, Tierra Firme, and Chile one of their own, Fernando de Guzmán. But the true motivating force behind this bizarre rebellion is a commoner named Lope de Aguirre, whose plan is to travel down the Marañón to the Atlantic and then return to Peru to conquer it in retaliation for what he believes to have been his unfair treatment there by the conquistador elite.[75]

Aguirre is a delinquent in every sense of the word—a violent and destructive criminal who has declared himself outside of the laws of the land. His rebellion is also a belated one; he has arrived on the New World stage too late to make his mark as a conquistador in the way that Cortés and Pizarro have before him, and his reaction is to explode in irrational fury when he realizes he's been left out of the game.[76] Most accounts of the rebellion present Aguirre as a powerful and charismatic madman who terrorizes and fascinates his followers as well as his enemies. Lope de Aguirre's rebellion reflects both the particular rivalries among Peruvian conquistadors and a more general debate about the rights that conquistadors and *encomenderos* might claim before the Crown, a debate that intensified with the passage of the New Laws in 1542. However, as Beatriz Pastor has pointed out, in most accounts "the rebellion is emptied of ideological content and reduced to a paroxysm of meaningless transgression" committed by a single man ("Lope de Aguirre the Wanderer," 88–89). She offers a persuasive reading of Aguirre as the personification of a three-pronged crisis: he embodies "the decadence of existing political structures, the disintegration of the vassal relationship, and the corruption of traditional ideological values" (*Armature of Conquest*, 195).

This is where, I would argue, Oviedo y Baños's eighteenth-century account of the rebellion illustrates another aspect of the evolving ideological context that is often overlooked. In his retelling of Lope de Aguirre's rebellion, Oviedo y Baños presents Aguirre not so much as the breakdown of the Cortesian model but as its terrible and inevitable extension—the result, as he puts it, of the fact that "every administrator in the Indies aspired to the name of conquistador" (*Historia,* 135).[77] The chapters devoted to the rebellion make up most of book 4 and therefore function as the center of the *Historia,* chronologically and structurally. As I will explore in what follows, these chapters present Aguirre as a destabilizing force that is contained and neutralized by the actions of colonial administrators. The retelling of the story results in its domestication, since it is clear from the outset that for the eighteenth-century historian, Aguirre's rebellion has little to do with El Dorado, and everything to do with *el cabildo* (the town council).

Oviedo y Baños begins his account of Aguirre's rebellion *in medias res* to emphasize the sudden irruption of the tyrant into the political and social life of the region: "In the year 1561 all port cities along the coast were called to arms when the tyrant Lope de Aguirre arrived with his armada on the island of Margarita" (154).[78] Unlike most other discussions of the rebellion, Oviedo y Baños's account offers relatively little information about the events leading up to Aguirre's arrival on Margarita. In the extremely abbreviated background he provides regarding the origins of Aguirre's odyssey, Oviedo y Baños refers to the rumors of opulent provinces in Amazon territory and also suggests that Aguirre's splinter expedition may have been viewed by Marqués de Cañete Don Andrés Hurtado de Mendoza as a welcome opportunity to rid himself of a number of corrupt and threatening troublemakers. Oviedo y Baños gives a quick overview of the atrocities Aguirre commited en route to Venezuela in order to consolidate his authority; these are reminiscent of the historian's earlier descriptions of cruelties committed in the name of Spanish conquest.

The focus of the story that Oviedo y Baños wishes to tell about Aguirre is the conflict between Aguirre's Marañones and the inhabitants of the island of Margarita. The treachery and cruelty of the rebellious tyrant are compounded by the initial cowardice and complicity of some of the colonial authorities, who make a disastrous miscalculation in welcoming Aguirre and his men. Aguirre rewards one of the townspeople with a gilded silver cup in recognition of the assistance given to his men as they arrive, and the Marañones' ostentatious generosity conjures up for the locals images of the riches that these emissaries from Peru must be bringing. Even the governor's greed is awakened. Oviedo y Baños includes the detail that the governor goes so far as to hold the stirrup for Aguirre as he mounts his horse—a damning reflection of the degree to which the civil government stoops in facilitating access for the intruders.[79]

This initial euphoria is quickly dispelled by the exchange between Aguirre and the governor (which Oviedo y Baños reproduces verbatim) in which the rebel announces his intention to take them all prisoner: "Gentlemen, we are headed for Peru, where there are typically wars and disturbances; and since you seem to think that we do not go with the intention of serving the King and will likely present an obstacle for our plans, you must put down your arms, since it is clear that otherwise you will not provide the hospitality we desire; and since there is no alternative, you are all taken prisoner" (159). In the historian's reconstruction of Aguirre's speech, the difference between Peru (where wars and disturbances are the norm) and Margarita (where civil authority generally reigns) is presented as an explanation for the subsequent ransacking of property and the destruction of all symbols of governmental authority by the Marañones. In one specific assault, Aguirre orders his men to break down the doors of the building that houses the royal treasury, as he is too impatient to wait for someone to bring the keys. Aguirre is repeatedly described in these pages as an animal and a monster that practices "the barbarous custom of spilling human blood, which fed the heart of that wild beast" (160) and who strides through Margarita "bellowing with rage and foaming at the mouth" (161). These descriptions eerily echo the examples of Spanish barbarism that Oviedo y Baños included earlier in the *Historia,* and they prefigure later atrocities committed by Aguirre and his men that force civil and military authorities to reevaluate their situation and eventually organize a counterattack.

In the context of this struggle between imperial presence and the rebels, it's striking that Aguirre's violent actions are often accompanied by the trappings of legitimate authority. For example, he hangs several soldiers who have tried to escape, putting cards on their corpses that announce being "loyal servants of the King of Castille" as their crime. He also orders the assassination of one of his men, Juan de Turriaga, whom he then buries with elaborate funeral honors (161). Aguirre decrees that official standards be made for himself—black taffeta with red swords—and has them blessed in a public ceremony.[80] All these gestures reflect Aguirre's misappropriation of the legitimate emblems of government and his perversion of Spanish "ceremonies of possession," to use Patricia Seed's term. This improvised, even farcical, misappropriation of authority is markedly at odds with the centralizing, enlightened eighteenth-century formulation of absolutism championed by the historian.

To remind his reader of the importance of orderly succession, Oviedo y Baños includes several anecdotes that point to the tenuous nature of Aguirre's hold on power. When a conversation ensues among Aguirre's men about who might lead them in the event that something were to happen to Aguirre, Martín Pérez speaks up to volunteer. Aguirre, seeing his willingness as a kind of treason, orders Pérez to be attacked and viciously killed. Oviedo y Baños includes not only the description of the assassination, but also its bizarre denouement. While the men are still gathered about the victim, Aguirre passes by and accuses one of them, Antón Llamoso, of being part of Pérez's conspiracy to wrest control of the expedition. In other words, Aguirre redefines the mere discussion of succession as treachery and insubordination. Llamoso, fearful that his protestations of innocence have not convinced Aguirre, resorts to a panicked demonstration of loyalty:

He wished to prove his innocence with deeds, and with a fury directed by some diabolical spirit, he threw himself on Martín Pérez's mauled and bloody cadaver, which had been laid out on the ground to the horror of those present; and saying, "I'll drink the blood of this traitor who tried to commit such evil," he began to suck on the brains through the open wounds in Pérez's head, with the same rage with which a mastiff might feed on a dead cow, and with this inhuman act Aguirre was satisfied with his fidelity, and those present were engrossed in seeing the barbarous mercilessness of that demon. (164)[81]

Acts, not words, constitute political participation. Aguirre's conquest model of authority admits no possibility of orderly succession, as we see in this bizarre and barbaric incident in which governance is replaced by a cannibalistic demonstration of loyalty to an irrational tyrant. This additional anecdote involving cannibalistic acts by Spanish conquistadors reiterates the degree to which the lack of a process for orderly succession troubles the Marañones and haunts the *Historia*.

Oviedo y Baños inserts numerous examples of the many atrocities the tyrant has committed on the island and closes with a summary:

These were the tyrant's operations on that unfortunate island, and if the pen were to express in detail all his excesses, there would not be a heart that could suffer such cruelties, or eyes to weep such sorrow, such were the insults, thefts, and atrocities that the wild beast carried out, so much so that with the island then at the point of its greatest opulence due to pearl fishing, the forty days of his presence there were enough to leave it so destroyed that for many years after, its citizens were unable to complete the repair of its ruins. (171–72)

There are echoes here of Oviedo y Baños's condemnation of the tyrannical Welsers and their indiscriminate destruction of the region to the detriment of the local settlers. But Oviedo y Baños's chronicling of Aguirre's increasingly capricious and desperate acts also makes apparent the rebellion's loss of steam. The historian mockingly describes Aguirre's bedraggled band of rebels as they flee to Borburata, scoffing that "with this they hoped to subjugate the Indies" (174). Rhetorical understatement echoes material reduction, and the effect is a devasting minimization of Aguirre's power to threaten the established order.

Oviedo y Baños organizes his account to dramatize the contrast between Aguirre's tyrannical and ultimately ineffective model of governance and that of Margarita's colonial authorities. The historian reports that as the bloodshed on the island continues, a ship approaches the port of Mompatare. On board is Fray Francisco de Montesinos, provincial of Order of Santo Domingo, who is arriving from the island of Hispaniola as part of an official response to the rebellion. Anticipating that Aguirre might try to commandeer the newly arrived ship for his own purposes and recognizing the futility of any attempts to persuade Aguirre to abandon his rebellious path, the provincial changes course and sets sail for Santo Domingo in order to inform the authorities there rather than pursue fruitless negotiations. Aguirre's hopes of commandeering the ship are thwarted as direct confrontation is replaced by recourse to an administrative chain of command.

Oviedo y Baños further rewrites imperial conquest when he quotes, in its entirety, the rambling letter that Aguirre writes to King Philip II during the final days of his expedition. He justifies its inclusion in the *Historia* as an example of Aguirre's madness and lack of education.[82] Although earlier chronicles had made reference to the various missives penned by Aguirre, Oviedo y Baños's is the first to reproduce the full text of this letter. Tomás Eloy Martínez and Susana Rotker argue that Oviedo y Baños thus goes much further than his sources in giving Aguirre's dissident voice a presence in the text ("Prólogo," xxxii); Ingrid Galster, on the other hand, insists that Oviedo y Baños merely reinforces previous portrayals of the tyrant (particularly that of Simón) while calling attention to his own archival investigations.[83] However, there are small but significant editorial interventions in the version of the letter to Philip II included by Oviedo y Baños that may suggest a different agenda. These changes have to do not with the body of the letter, which the historian preserves intact, but rather with the final paragraphs (in which Aguirre lists the names of his Marañones) and the closing signature ("Lope de Aguirre, the Pilgrim")—both of which Oviedo y Baños omits. What do these editorial changes signify? By including the letter, Oviedo y Baños recognizes Aguirre as both actor and author in the mold of earlier chroniclers like Bernal Díaz del Castillo, driven by the desire to write his story as protagonist and agonist. But he also underscores the transgressive nature of Aguirre's version of that story; by omitting the letter's roster and authorial signature, he denies Aguirre's men and their leader a place in Venezuelan history.

This is a necessary move by the historian, particularly given that the Marañones play a key role in Aguirre's downfall and might therefore challenge colonial authorities in claiming shared responsibility for his ultimate defeat. As the rebels retreat to a small fort, increasing numbers of them abandon their leader and pass over to the royal camp with cries of "Long live the king!" Finally Aguirre is left with only Antón Llamoso (whose loyalty, as we have seen, is absolute) by his side.[84] Aguirre is taken prisoner, but instead of awaiting the imminent arrival of the governor in order to formalize an official surrender, his administrative captors give the Marañones permission to kill Aguirre themselves—an offer they accept with alacrity. This goes against proper procedures, but it also precludes any interrogation of Aguirre by the authorities that might further implicate the Marañones in the many crimes occasioned by the rebellion.

Aguirre's red-and-black banners are presented to the governor, who adds them to his coat of arms, thus reincorporating the errant conquistador into the body politic (198). The ceremony serves to acknowledge the role that colonial authorities have played in Aguirre's capture and death—an important symbolic gesture, given that, as the governor laments, Aguirre has been killed without his official order. As a final punishment, Aguirre's body is drawn and quartered and the parts distributed to various Venezuelan cities as a warning to traitors against the Crown. The malodorous remains are eventually left to scavenging dogs (198). The historian informs the reader in one of his customary necrological codas that Aguirre's defeat and death are greeted with general applause: "Thus ended the audacious tyranny of Lope de Aguirre, whose rebellion began with flamboyance and took hold in all provinces of America; and was undone, as we have seen, more through the industry of cunning than by the power of force, as others celebrated with applause the glory achieved by Venezuela" (198–99). In this valedictory phrase Oviedo y Baños expands the space of the rebellion to include the entire American continent, though the glory of having defeated the rebellion is reserved for Venezuela.

This finale represents an important shift in the way Aguirre's story is told, pointing to the domestication of the figure of the conquistador (and of conquest itself) to which I referred at the beginning of this chapter. Oviedo y Baños eschews the opposition between the exemplary conquistador Pedro de Ursúa and the crazed, criminal Aguirre that anchors earlier accounts, as this opposition only serves to legitimize an idealized model of conquest. Oviedo y Baños chooses instead to organize his own account around Aguirre's incursion into a Venezuelan settlement in order to emphasize that the rebel's dreams of imperial glory have been displaced by a new political reality represented by the colonial authorities who ultimately defeat Aguirre and restore order. Aguirre's downfall is identified with the triumph of civil society over military order and with the displacement of the conquistador by the functionary and the bureaucrat.[85]

What happens in book 4 once Aguirre's rebellion has been contained and defeated by the authorities? In the concluding chapters Oviedo y Baños shifts his focus to a number of peripheral developments. Spanish authorities, having just returned from Margarita, are forced to confront the threat of an indigenous rebellion led by Guaicaipuro and Terepaima. The *Historia* establishes a clear link between Aguirre and this uprising, further tarnishing the historical legacy of the rebel leader. The very real threat of indigenous rebellions in the region leads to widespread resistance to any further attempts to reinitiate the conquest of Caracas, and book 4 ends with the conquest suspended.

The story of Lope de Aguirre functions in the *Historia* as a cautionary tale of conquistador ambition run amok, cast in an eighteenth-century light. Oviedo y Baños inscribes Aguirre as the hyperbolic and dangerous extension of the figure of the sixteenth-century conquistador. But rather than vituperate Aguirre (as Simón had done), Oviedo y Baños provides a domesticating treatment, representing the rebellion in a manner that contains and finally resolves it within the limits of emerging colonial authority.

VII. *"Celebrada esta ciudad": Foundational fictions from El Dorado to Caracas*

Oviedo y Baños's domestication of empire can be plotted cartographically as he maps out the foundation of cities within Venezuelan territory.[86] For the eighteenth-century historian, the foundation of cities functions as an intermediate step in the move from *conquista* to *población,* with settlement replacing discovery and conquest as the originary moment in his history. For example,

Oviedo y Baños lists all the "citizens and settlers" who took part in the founding of the city of Nuestra Señora de la Concepción del Tocuyo, perhaps as a way of distributing protagonism in the foundation of cities and settlements as broadly as possible, and perhaps also to emphasize exemplary acts in the larger context of Francisco de Carvajal's tyrannical reign (106). The historian's gesture, which contrasts markedly with his omission of the roster of Aguirre's Marañones, reflects a shift from old blood to new blood, from a traditional aristocracy to a service aristocracy. Newly founded cities serve as visible evidence of Spanish presence in Indian territories. They are placemarkers in the turf wars among rival conquistadors, and trade centers for emerging exports like cotton, cacao, and hides.[87] Oviedo y Baños cites approvingly the opinion of Governor Juan de Villegas that, rather than contemplate yet another armed attack on the Amerindians, it was preferable to found cities "in whose neighborhood the luster and permanence of the land is secured" (120).[88]

However, like conquest, the founding of cities (the focus of book 3) is a vexed endeavor.[89] The *Historia* is replete with examples of cities that, once founded and settled, were eventually abandoned, only to be reestablished a second, third, or even fourth time. These problematic foundings—urban fits and starts—mirror the beginnings of the viceroyalty of New Granada (which coincides exactly with the period when Oviedo y Baños is writing). These foundational initiatives are described as every bit as arduous as military campaigns. One particularly striking example of a tenuously held urban space is the city of Trujillo/Miravel, whose double name reflects a rivalry between two conquistadors, Francisco Ruiz and Juan Maldonado. When Ruiz establishes a city on the site of an abandoned town (formerly named Trujillo), he changes the name to Miravel to indicate its new administration (137). But when Maldonado arrives to challenge Ruiz's rights to the town and succeeds in having those rights revoked, he promptly renames the settlement Trujillo. The naming rivalry becomes moot, however, when the town must be relocated because of the damp and inhospitable environment. Unfortunately, new sites—"humid and infested with mosquitoes, ants, tigers, and other creatures"—prove equally unsuitable for settlement (138). Oviedo y Baños laments that the "portable city" suffers a "thousand decampments," but he is actually quite amusing as he describes the city's misfortunes, occasioned in part by the hostile environment but also by its inhabitants' persistent inability to agree on anything (138). There is a happy ending when the city, definitively named Trujillo, moves to its present location. But this eighteenth-century version of Columbus's Adamic imperative to rename as a sign of possession—in which towns are named, renamed, and renamed again—signals the contested nature of discovery and conquest in Venezuela.

The jewel in the crown, from the perspective of the eighteenth-century historian, is Caracas. Indeed, according to many critics, the chapters in book 5 dealing with Losada's hard-fought conquest of Caracas are the most original section of the *Historia*.[90] Following closely on book 4 (and the account of Aguirre's rebellion which, as I have argued, can be seen as constituting the transgressive center of the *Historia*), the chapters on Caracas succeed in displacing the disgraced conquistador and offer an alternative center of gravity for the text.

The *Historia* consolidates its move from conquest to settlement, as the founding of what will be the city of Caracas is presented as the crowning achievement of a new kind of conquistador.

Caracas also displaces El Dorado. In marked contrast with the quixotic efforts to locate El Dorado, the campaign to conquer the Caracas Valley in the wake of earlier defeats is ultimately successful. Diego de Losada, who was named in 1665 as general of this new expedition, is introduced in the narrative with a description of his experience, prudence, and noble spirit—qualities that compare favorably with what the reader has seen not only with Aguirre and his Marañones but also with the Welsers' desperate search for El Dorado.[91] The historian informs the reader that Losada spent an entire year making preparations for the march into the Caracas Valley. Oviedo y Baños then calls a halt in his narrative to include a long list of the names of Losada's men, many of them seasoned captains with a wealth of experience in earlier campaigns who have been unjustly overlooked by history (215).[92] Here Oviedo y Baños returns to his theme of Venezuela's forgotten heroes. The chapters that follow include numerous incidents that demonstrate Losada's wisdom and bravery. Particular emphasis is placed on his reticence in resorting to violence: "He never unsheathed his sword, except in the most desperate situations" (224).

It's clear, however, that Losada is no coward. In the first challenge to his advance, Losada is met by ten thousand Indians who have joined forces to resist him. Oviedo y Baños recounts in elegant and balanced prose how Losada makes ready for battle: "Losada, in whose magnanimous heart fear never found a welcome, disregarding the wariness of his men, demonstrated his resolve to open a path with his sword through enemy squadrons, preferring to risk his life in the arms of temerity in the name of daring, rather than fixing his security in retreat with an appearance of cowardice" (220). It's worth remembering that this section opens with the description of the scattered bones of the Narváez expedition, an indication of the historian's preoccupation with heroic models, past and present.

In Oviedo y Baños's discussions of Losada's negotiations with the Caracas Indians regarding prisoner exchange and peace treaties (which alternate with vivid descriptions of pitched battles), one glimpses an eighteenth-century awareness of the complex nature of Indian-Spanish relations. David Weber notes, "Although the destructive effects of raiding and warfare often gave Spaniards and Indians incentives to take the first steps toward peace, peaceful relations endured only when leaders on both sides believed that peace served their economic interests" (*Bárbaros*, 200). Oviedo y Baños presents Losada's valor as the result of a judicious calculus, a careful weighing of the costs and benefits of his decision to engage the enemy, rather than as a headlong rush to bloodshed: "He knew how costly war would be" (*Historia*, 223).

Losada's decision to found a city in the San Francisco Valley, which he names Santiago de León de Caracas, is presented as another element of his prudent strategy of pacification (231). Ever the conscientious historian, Oviedo y Baños is clearly distressed at not knowing the exact day on which the city was founded.[93] But the lack of precise historical data frees him in a sense to move from sixteenth-century history to the present moment in order to describe the city as it exists at the time of his writing. As Oviedo y Baños moves from conquest to settlement, he changes the verb tenses he is employing, shifting from preterit to present perfect and then to the present tense. As he turns from the past to the present, he also turns discursively away from the heroic mode and epic narrative toward domesticating description.

The vibrant city of Caracas, described by Oviedo y Baños in all its early eighteenth-century splendor, takes hold of the reader's imagination and claims a place in the *Historia,* unseating the illusory and disappointing El Dorado.[94] Located in a beautiful and fertile valley, Caracas enjoys a moderate climate, and its spacious patios, gardens, and orchards harbor a wealth of plants and flowers. The city's population includes "an innumerable multitude of blacks and mulattos," as well as over a thousand Spaniards, but the historian is primarily concerned with the criollo inhabitants, who are attractive, courteous, and well spoken:

> Its criollos are of quick and sharp minds, courteous, affable, and polite; they speak the Castilian language perfectly, without those bad habits that mar it in other port cities in the Indies; and because of the benevolent climate they are of sound body and gallant disposition, without any defect, or ugly deformity, being generally of dashing spirits and good-hearted, and so inclined toward diplomacy and education that even blacks (being criollos) are scornful of those who cannot read and write. (232)

There is a specific mention made of the gracious hospitality shown to foreign visitors to the city (perhaps a reflection of the author's own experience in moving to Caracas from Bogotá), and Oviedo y Baños boasts that any visitor who spends two months in Caracas will never again choose to leave.

Caracas's many convents, hospitals, *colegios* (schools), and seminaries are described with careful attention to architectural details as evidence of criollo accomplishment and merit.[95] Ecclesiastical finances and administration receive particular attention, and there are several references to the patronage and influence of the historian's uncle, Bishop Don Diego de Baños y Sotomayor. Oviedo y Baños displays a typically eighteenth-century interest in agriculture and trade; by virtue of his marriage to a wealthy widow, he owned a cacao plantation as well as cattle-grazing lands, and was a member of the criollo landholding class.[96] After a long enumeration of the many fruits and vegetables that are cultivated in the Caracas Valley, he concludes:

> Adding to the aforementioned excellent qualities is the frequency of its business dealings, the continued commerce with New Spain, the Canary and Windward Islands and elsewhere, in which considerable amounts of cacao, tobacco, hides, brazilwood, and other commodities are traded; these are parts that make up a whole for which the city is to be celebrated as one of the best among those that make up the extended Empire of America. (238)

Oviedo y Baños describes Caracas as a city that exemplifies the benefits of the move from conquest to settlement, one that is enjoying the fruits of civilized and civic endeavors. His criollo pride, which engages in the defense of American flora and fauna made in response to European charges of degeneracy, is evident in these pages.[97] If in earlier chapters of the *Historia* corn replaces gold as the object of conquistador desire, here a more sweeping agricultural panorama replaces conquest as the engine of empire in a continuous process of transvaluation that is typical of the eighteenth century.

Although Oviedo y Baños continues to address "matters of the past," his narrative focus in these final chapters of the *Historia* is continually drawn toward the moment in which he is writing.[98] When explaining the prolonged nature of the efforts to pacify the indigenous population in the Caracas Valley as the result of the diversity of neighboring tribes, he anticipates their eventual pacification through continued communication and exchange: "Trade and communication served to domesticate them" (274). This is a typically eighteenth-century observation regarding the domesticating force of commerce and conversation, and it reflects the degree to which the eighteenth century regarded commerce as conquest by other means. As we shall see in the following chapter, Molina makes a similar argument about the Araucanians.

Oviedo y Baños represents Losada's strategy as consonant with his own prioritization of settlement over conquest. Thus, the sixteenth-century conquistador Losada and the eighteenth-century historian Oviedo y Baños seem to share a commitment to the rationalization, institutionalization, and systematization of conquest through administrative procedures. For example, several chapters in book 5 explain how Losada decides to submit traitorous Indians to a formal legal process in order to establish blame by *via jurídica* instead of relying merely on circumstantial evidence.[99] It is, in fact, archival documents from these proceedings that provide the historian with the information he uses to write his account.

Oviedo y Baños's principal concern is the eruption in 1586 of administrative quarrels in Caracas that wreak havoc with the newly established colonial order. These quarrels will threaten Venezuela for years to come, well past the limits of the history he is narrating. Oviedo y Baños opens chapter 8 of book 7 with a lengthy diatribe:

> We come to the year of '86 [1586] when all the military expeditions necessary for the total conquest and pacification of the province had been concluded, when its neighbors should have enjoyed in repose the desired fruits of peace, which at the expense of great shedding of blood had been achieved through the indefatigable constancy of their will. They [the citizens of the province] began to experience as a reward for their labors outrages and abuses, offspring of the violence produced by an impassioned lack of reason, the spitefulness of a baseless issue giving rise to disagreement and discord, which lasted for many years afterward, to the general perturbation of the Republic. (318)[100]

This governmental calamity is followed by a natural one (a plague of worms that decimates crops), and then by an attack on Santiago by the celebrated and feared corsair Sir Francis Drake that occurs in 1595 while the governor has been called away to another part of the province. The afflicted city organizes itself admirably, surrounding and besieging Drake and his pirates until they finally give up and sail away, though not without first burning and pillaging many of the houses in the town. Taken together, these events are an unsettling note on which to end the *Historia,* particularly since the account of Drake's attack is reminiscent of Aguirre's invasion of Margarita. Nevertheless, this final chapter addresses a number of important issues for eighteenth-century Venezuela that would have been very much on Oviedo y Baños's mind as he wrote.

As we have seen, the foundation of cities plays a key role in Oviedo y Baños's domestication of conquest, replacing discovery as the originary moment in his history. Cities represent a requisite phase in the move from *conquista* to *población* and are important placeholders for empire in Venezuelan territory.[101] Thus, the historian discounts the many failed attempts to locate and conquer El Dorado, rejecting the pursuit of its legendary but illusory riches. He focuses instead on the establishment of Caracas as an example of successful settlement and the emergence of a diversified economy based on agriculture and trade. The trajectory of the *Historia* moves away from military history to civil—in every sense of the word—history.[102] Unlike El Dorado, which proved ever out of reach for the many conquistadors who tried to find it, Caracas was already home to a large and growing criollo population at the time Oviedo y Baños was writing. Despite the fact that the historian begins by stating his intention to chronicle the memorable events of the conquest of Venezuela, these concluding chapters leave the reader with the distinct impression that the greatest chapter of Venezuela's history is yet to be written. That, of course, would have been the focus of the missing second part of Oviedo y Baños's work.

VIII. *"Para materia del segundo tomo":*
The missing link

Having taken his *Historia* up to 1600, Oviedo y Baños closes the first volume with these words: "We conclude this first part, leaving, with God's favor, as material for the second volume the events and happenings of all the following century" (327).[103] But the promised second volume of the *Historia* (to which the author refers on numerous occasions in the text), purportedly an account of the seventeenth century, has never been found in either published or manuscript form. We are left only with the *Tesoro de noticias,* a working notebook containing details culled by Oviedo y Baños from viceregal archives and not published until 1967.[104] The author describes the *Tesoro* as a general index of the records of the town council of Caracas. It is peppered with complaints about missing documents, references to ongoing lawsuits, and many mundane details of landholdings, titles, and appointments. However, none of the material has been given narrative shape; as the title *tesoro* (treasure) suggests, it has come down to us in unelaborated form as the raw material of colonial historiography.[105]

The question of the missing second volume has long vexed Venezuelan historians. Was it ever written? Was it published? If so, what happened to it and why? A number of distinguished Venezuelan historians have proposed answers to these questions that offer a fascinating glimpse into the obsessive speculation provoked by this textual lacuna. They also shed light on the negotiation of a historiographical foundational fiction in which Oviedo y Baños plays a key, albeit contested, role.[106] Among the possible explanations are that the manuscript was confiscated by Spanish authorities, or that those implicated in its pages managed to buy up all the copies of a published version.[107] In *Leyendas históricas,* Arístides Rojas speculates that a second part did exist at one point in manuscript form, though he maintains that it was never published and was eventually burned because of the inflammatory material it would have contained regarding some of the founding families of Venezuela (223). In Rojas's view, any history of seventeenth-century Venezuela would have to focus on the development of a new mestizo and criollo aristocracy. This new urban history would necessarily make reference to the *mantuanistas* (from the *mantos,* or blanket-like capes, worn by daughters of indigenous caciques) and to the tensions that emerged between this new aristocracy and the direct descendants of the Spanish conquistadors (233–34). It would also have to include an account of the licentious and abusive Bishop Mauro de Tovar (to whose family Oviedo y Baños was related by marriage), the public flogging of a venerable dowager, and a host of other scandals that took place during these years, similar to the ones that enliven Juan Rodríguez Freyle's *El carnero* (1636).[108] Because of this background, Rojas proposes, although without providing any real proof, that a member of the Tovar family stole the manuscript from the *ayuntamiento* and consigned it to the flames.[109]

In any continuation of his history into the seventeenth century, Oviedo y Baños would have also had to deal with the aftermath of Lope de Aguirre's incursion into Venezuelan territory, a crime whose punishment is narrated in the *Historia* with exemplary finality. However, Oviedo y Baños does not—cannot—explain that Aguirre's Marañones for the most part went unpunished and insinuated themselves into colonial Venezuelan life by marrying into the best Caracas families. This legacy of the rebellion—itself a kind of insidious domestication—cannot be documented by the historian, since to do so would be to acknowledge the failure of colonial authority to definitively contain the rebellion. Such an admission does not lend itself to the kind of history Oviedo y Baños was prepared to write.

Morón, who has done exhaustive research on Oviedo y Baños's personal library, suggests that the more recent events that would have been the subject of the second part of the *Historia* would have been beyond the historian's scope and talents, which he argues leaned more toward describing "warlike actions" than discussing the organization of civil society (*Los cronistas,* 121). I would counter, however, that Oviedo y Baños's predilection for civil society informs every aspect of his account of the early, more conflictive period of Venezuelan history. The historian's concern for issues of economic and urban development and civic literacy is implicit in his treatment of the conquest. I would agree, therefore, with Tomás Eloy Martínez and Susana Rotker's suggestion that the absence of the second part—regardless of whether it was hidden, destroyed, or never completed—should be read as both the sign of a criollo epistemological conflict and as a rupture with earlier examples of colonial historiography ("Prólogo," xxix).

The missing second part of the *Historia* also points to eighteenth-century criollos' anxiety about the discontinuity between earlier colonial history and their own present moment. This anxiety, never completely resolved, may help to explain the absence of the eighteenth century in the move from coloniality to modernity. The eighteenth century is a missing link in that move; like the copulative "y" in the title of Oviedo y Baños's *Historia de la conquista y población de la provincia de Venezuela,* it refers to a relationship that has never really been defined.[110]

The preoccupation with primacy—who came first?—that marks colonial historiography from the moment someone on Columbus's ship cries "Lumbre tierra" (Land ho) shifts in the eighteenth century to concerns about who (and what) comes next.[111] This is why Oviedo y Baños presents the reader over and over again with situations of administrative chaos occasioned by a lack of clarity about the process of succession. These episodes often serve to open or conclude a particular chapter or book, pointing to their significance in the structure of Oviedo y Baños's history as well as in the structuring of viceregal administration.[112] At the time Oviedo y Baños was writing, it was increasingly unclear on what basis administrative appointments would be assigned or maintained, and criollos responded warily to Bourbon reforms that threatened to sideline them. For this reason, perhaps, anxieties over the question of governmental succession permeate the *Historia.*[113]

The eighteenth century was a period of enormous consolidation and progress, one in which a criollo man of letters would have aspired to play a role.[114] So at this juncture it may be useful to compare briefly Oviedo y Baños's trajectory (and even the catastrophic failure of Aguirre's ambitions) with the life of José Baquíjano, whose story has been studied by Mark Burkholder in *Politics of a Colonial Career.* Burkholder portrays Baquíjano as a colonial pretender, an obscure office seeker who was rescued for posterity precisely because of the unremarkable nature of his life. Burkholder's aim is to examine how the environment of ambition shifts in the eighteenth century through the examination of Baquíjano's negotiations with power, focusing on a civic—rather than epic—definition of that environment. As Burkholder argues, "Far more than the famous conquistadors (conquerors) the urban bureaucrats represented Spain's domination of the Indies; their presence was imprinted indelibly on the colonial landscape" ("Bureaucrats, 79"). Oviedo y Baños (like Baquíjano) is a *letrado* (a member of the lettered elite), and he too aspires to negotiate successfully the administrative hierarchies of his adopted patria.

The eighteenth-century criollo's reformulation of a political identity based not on arms but rather on administration can be read on every page of the

Historia de la conquista y población de la provincia de Venezuela.[115] In his condemnations of nefarious and misguided conquistadors as well as his tributes to noble but misguided ones, in his remapping of the routes of discovery and conquest so that they lead not to El Dorado but to Caracas, in his capture and containment of the tyrant Lope de Aguirre at the very heart of his narrative, and in his measured and balanced language itself, Oviedo y Baños domesticates the representation of conquest in order to put it to work in service of an emerging Bourbon imperial project.

CHAPTER TWO

Domesticating Indians

Juan Ignacio Molina's *Compendio de la historia civil del reyno de Chile* (1795)

Los Araucanos son en sus comarcas los enemigos más
comunes, más intrépidos,
y más irreconciliables de la España.

[The Araucanians are in these regions the most common,
most intrepid, and most intransigent enemies of Spain.]

> Guillaume-Thomas-François Raynal, *Historia de las dos Indias*

I. *"La nación chilena": Molina and his "bárbaros"*

Oviedo y Baños's *Historia de la conquista y población de la provincia de Vene-zuela*, the focus of the preceding chapter, deals with one particular place on the map of Spain's eighteenth-century viceroyal periphery. Chile represents an even more distant and contested point on that map. Initial Spanish efforts to conquer Chile in the sixteenth century were an expansion of Francisco Pizarro's Andean expedition, and the Peruvian conquest was both an inspiration and a cautionary tale for Spaniards endeavoring to expand their conquest southward. The Araucanians who inhabited that region were one of the few groups that had managed to remain outside of Inca imperial control, and their spirited resistance to conquest was the stuff of legend.[1] When Spaniards first encountered the Araucanians in 1546, the European invaders were handily defeated. But Pedro de Valdivia arrived from Peru four years later, leading a Spanish advance to the BíoBío River and founding the fortified city of Concepción.[2] With these victories the Spaniards appeared to have been successful in bringing the Araucanians under control and began employing them as forced labor in Spanish gold mines. However, in 1553 the Araucanians reinitiated armed resistance that would continue sporadically until 1882.[3]

Because of its strategic location on the periphery of the empire and because of the ongoing conflict with a local indigenous population that proved difficult to subdue in any definitive way, Chile commanded a great deal of imperial interest during both the Hapsburg and Bourbon periods.[4] It became home to a number of Jesuit and Franciscan missions that complemented (and sometimes competed with) military efforts to secure the Spanish frontier. In the eighteenth century the BíoBío River still served as it had since the sixteenth century to mark the border between Araucanian territory and that of the Spaniards.[5] But in Chile, perhaps more than any other place in the Spanish Empire, the discursive boundary between savagery and domestication was not clearly drawn. Eighteenth-century Araucanians inhabited a complex middle ground, as the Jesuit writer Juan Ignacio Molina demonstrates in his *Compendio de la historia civil del reyno de Chile*, a history of Chile from 1546 to 1787.[6] Interspersed with a chronologically organized account of Spanish efforts to conquer Chile are numerous chapters devoted to Araucanian customs, religion, and governance.

In the *Compendio de la historia civil*, Molina in effect claims new territory for the Araucanians by domesticating them.[7] That is, he rewrites their savagery by recasting military feats as virtuous and pragmatic acts of civic engagment and diplomatic oratory. As Hapsburg imperial strategies for dealing with Indians were being re-envisioned through a Bourbon imperial lens, Molina retouches earlier portrayals of the Araucanians produced in the sixteenth and seventeenth centuries, reimagining his subject in response to the ideological imperatives of his own moment.[8] Through a reading of how the indigenous inhabitants of Chile were represented to eighteenth-century criollo and European readers in the *Compendio de la historia civil*, we can trace Molina's project: to introduce to his readers a new kind of Indian protagonist, characterized not by brute savagery but rather by reason, political pragmatism, and rhetorical eloquence.[9] This reading affords us an opportunity to broaden the scope of Enlightenment-era thinking on racial and cultural difference and to consider Molina's Araucanians as an example of how New World Indians operated in a particular natural, social, and political context.[10]

The eighteenth century saw a significant demographic shift as the Amerindian population began to recover after having been decimated during the preceding two centuries. This resurgence in population coincided with the transition from the Hapsburg to the Bourbon dynasty, and a corresponding shift in imperial administrative practices. Responding to enlightened critiques of bloodthirsty Spanish conquistadors and to their own economic and political interests, Bourbon officials created new structures for consolidating and exercising authority in the Spanish borderlands in hopes of "replacing war with commerce, colonists and diplomacy."[11]

In his splendid book *Bárbaros: Spaniards and Their Savages in the Age of Enlightenment*, David Weber distinguishes between *indios no sometidos*—those who had managed to resist the Spaniards and were still unconquered as the eighteenth century began—and *indios domésticos*—domesticated Indians who had been conquered and incorporated economically, politically, and culturally into the Spanish colonial system (281n45). The distinction is a useful one, as it reminds us of the importance of thinking of the category of Indian in the plural, and as politically (as well as ethnically) defined. Weber explores a wide range of local factors that influenced the implementation of Bourbon Indian policies in Spain's American empire: a given region's strategic importance, the material resources available for exploitation, the particular interests of local Spanish administrators and elites, and the degree to which the indigenous population had mastered acculturation. He reminds us that Bourbon officials responded to local conditions in the dynamic and contested contact zone of the eighteenth-century Spanish frontier with a mix of accommodation and military strategies (offensive and defensive) in an ongoing dialogue with their colonial subjects, including conquered and unconquered Amerindians (9). During the eighteenth-century, as Weber observes, "on a day-to-day basis . . . neither absolute peace nor unqualified war characterized relations between independent Indians and Spaniards, even during times of peace and times of war" (83).

Echoing this view, recent scholarship on the history of Chile has challenged the prevailing myth that armed conflict between the Araucanians and the Spaniards was constant and unmitigated. Rather, war alternated with intermittent periods of peaceful coexistence and developing commercial ties.[12] At the same time, however, resistance—real and rhetorical—is key to the collective identity of the Araucanians, who considered themselves (and were considered by others) the most ferociously independent of indigenous peoples. Among the *indios no sometidos,* Weber proposes that "perhaps no Native Americans developed the military capability of maintaining independence from Spaniards more rapidly or effectively than the Araucanian-speaking peoples of south-central Chile."[13] He notes that eighteenth-century Araucanians referred disparagingly to neighboring tribes who had been conquered and Hispanicized as *zapatudos* because they wore shoes (*zapatos*), or *reyunos* because they served the king (*rey*). In these instances language clearly communicates resistance to domination and rejection of the acculturation represented by European clothing and labor structures. But the derogatory terms *zapatudos* and *reyunos* also implicitly acknowledge acculturation as a gradual but inevitable encroachment on indigenous life. Weber's distinction between *indios no sometidos* and *indios domésticos* does the same, highlighting an ongoing conquest as well as a process of acculturation and domestication.[14]

Molina sees the Araucanians as neither *indios no sometidos* nor *indios domésticos,* and he uses the *Compendio de la historia civil del reyno de Chile* to map out the middle ground they inhabit. As the author moves forward in Chilean history from sixteenth-century battles to eighteenth-century treaty negotiations, he inscribes Araucanian Indians into local and imperial history and politics in a move of rhetorical domestication that takes place well before the Araucanians are finally subjugated in the nineteenth century. Thus, Molina's eighteenth-century intervention in the domestication of the Araucanian Indians plays an important—albeit often overlooked—role in bridging the colonial epic with subsequent national foundational fictions.[15]

II. *"Para beneficio común de mis compatriotas": Molina's life and works*

Juan Ignacio Molina was born in 1740 to a well-established criollo family at the hacienda of Huaraculén, near what is now the Chilean city of Villa Alegre.[16]

He displayed an early interest in the study of natural history, an enthusiasm he shared with his father and which continued throughout his long life.[17] Molina began his studies at Jesuit *colegios* in Talca and later studied in Concepción, where he was accepted into the Jesuit novitiate in 1755. In 1767 Molina's Jesuit training was interrupted when Charles III issued a royal decree expelling the Jesuits from all Spanish territories. With a small band of fellow Jesuits, Molina left his homeland in late October of that year, sailing from Callao (Lima's port city) to Italy, stopping in Pisa, Florence and, finally, Imola, where he lived until resettling in Bologna in 1774.[18] Facing exile, Molina had unsuccessfully attempted to smuggle aboard the ship his research notes on Chilean flora and fauna; he was forced to leave behind not only those notes but his entire library and all other scholarly materials as well.[19] Once established in Bologna, however, Molina was able to recover many of these materials and return to the projects interrupted by the expulsion. In later years he took on a number of important teaching and scholarly roles, corresponded widely, and wrote extensively.[20] At one point after 1814, Molina considered returning to Chile in order to deal with matters related to his inheritance, but despite the pull of nostalgia, he ultimately decided against the trip, given his age and the uncertainties occasioned by the ongoing wars of independence. Molina died in Bologna in 1829, having confessed shortly before his death that after so many years he felt more Bolognese than Chilean.[21]

Molina's oeuvre, like that of many of the exiled Jesuits, consists of works that were written, rewritten, translated, and reedited in Europe and, often at a much later date, in the Americas.[22] Molina produced several volumes on the natural and civil history of Chile, writing first in Italian and revising his thinking in subsequent publications and translations.[23] The *Saggio sulla storia naturale del Chili del signor Abate Giovanni Ignazio Molina* (1782) and *Saggio sulla storia civile del Chili del signor Abate Giovanni Ignazio Molina* (1787) were both published in Bologna (an even earlier work, *Compendio della storia geográfica naturale, e civile del regno del Chile,* was published anonymously in 1776 but is generally attributed to Molina).[24] The Spanish translation of the first part of Molina's history, the *Compendio de la historia geográfica, natural y civil del reyno de Chile* (Compendium of the geographic, natural, and civil history of the kingdom of Chile), appeared in Madrid in 1788. The 1795 Spanish translation of the second part, Molina's *Saggio sulla storia civile,* was titled *Compendio de la historia civil del reyno de Chile* and published in Madrid with various notes added by the translator, Nicolás de la Cruz y Bahamonde.

In composing these works, Molina relied heavily on source materials, most notably accounts written by European travelers and the *Historia militar, civil y sagrada* (Military, civil and sacred history; complete Spanish edition published 1870) by Miguel de Olivares, a fellow Jesuit also living in exile in Italy.[25] As he labored over the continuation of his history of Chile, Molina endeavored in vain to acquire the second part of Olivares's *Historia militar,* as he hoped it would provide him with valuable material regarding events in Chile from 1655 (where Olivares's first volume, already in his possession, left off) to the present moment. Molina's brief preface to the *Compendio de la historia civil del reyno de Chile* begins, in fact, with a discussion of his frustrated efforts to obtain this second volume. Molina finally gave up, resorting to other, less exhaustive sources in order to complete his civil history, including the oral testimony of his fellow exiled Jesuits regarding the salient events of late seventeenth- and eighteenth-century Chile. Molina hastens to affirm his impartiality regarding those events, noting that he will avoid at all costs any reflection that might compromise an otherwise objective narrative. Molina also includes in the preface a description of the various maps he had hoped to include in the volume and an account of his difficulties in obtaining them. Finally, he explains that at the conclusion of the history, he has added sections on Chilean language and a catalog of authors who have written about Chile.

Some scholars have criticized Molina's style as bland; others note that his scientific observations often miss the mark. Molina himself lamented the limitations imposed by his lack of access to source materials. Like those of many of his contemporaries, Molina's writings on the geographical, natural, and civil history of Chile are not widely read these days, although they were hotly debated during the eighteenth century.[26] They provide valuable insight into the preoccupations of eighteenth-century Chilean criollos and were enormously influential for the evolution of Chilean historiography during the nineteenth century.[27] Molina's *Compendio de la historia civil del reyno de Chile,* questions of historical accuracy and style notwithstanding, offers a revealing perspective on how Indians were domesticated by one writer during the period of the Bourbon Spanish Empire. As I will explore in this chapter, Molina puts Araucanians on the map, both literally and figuratively.

III. "Las insuficiencias de las razones de Paw": Molina and the dispute of the New World

Molina conceived of his natural and civil histories as two parts of the same work (he announced in the preface to the *Saggio sulla storia naturale* the imminent appearance of the *Saggio sulla storia civile*). However, they were published in Italy (and later, in a Spanish edition) as separate volumes.[28] As the title of the first volume indicates, Molina's intention was to begin by offering a natural history of Chile. He organizes the work into four parts, using Linnaean classification throughout to provide a description of Chile's geography and climate, minerals (particularly precious metals and mining techniques), and flora and fauna (with an emphasis on llamas, vicuñas, and guanacos); he concludes with a discussion of the autochtonous inhabitants of the region.[29] As did other exiled Jesuits writing in Bologna, Molina compares Chile's temperate climate with that of Italy. The fact that the Araucanians inhabit a temperate zone, isolated by the Andean cordillera, provides a foundation for comparing Araucanians to the classical civilizations of Greece and Rome. In the chapters of the natural history devoted to indigenous peoples, Molina singles out three groups (the Araucanians, the

Cunchos, and the Huillichies), but it is the Araucanians who will dominate the discussion and in a sense subsume all other indigenous groups in Molina's account of Chile's history.

Molina writes in the tradition of the sixteenth-century Spanish Jesuit historian José de Acosta, whose *Historia natural y moral de las Indias* (1590) provided a model for subsequent investigations of New World flora and fauna, geography, and customs.[30] Acosta represents a particular moment in intellectual and imperial history in which Spanish historiography about the Americas was informed by theological principles, on the one hand, and intra-European rivalries fueled by the Reformation and Counter-Reformation on the other. Molina, writing almost two centuries later, combined "natural" and "moral" description, locating both within his own historical framework. In doing so, he picks up on Acosta's understanding of "moral" history as having to do with *mores,* or customs.[31] Araucanian customs, as Molina will attempt to show in the *Compendio de la historia civil,* are important for the kind of comparative ethnography that both Acosta and eighteenth-century enlightened philosophes were pursuing. They provide the foundation for Molina's argument that Araucanians have the capacity to be incorporated into a universal cosmopolitan republic, as I will explore later in this chapter. The shift from natural and moral history to civil history in Molina's own authorial trajectory reflects a deeper shift in his thinking: while earlier European historians and chroniclers had included Amerindians as part of natural and moral history, Molina ascribes to them a significant agency in Chile's still unfolding civil history.[32]

Molina came somewhat belatedly to what Antonello Gerbi has called "the dispute of the New World" on the supposed inferiority of New World species.[33] He published his first work (the anonymous 1776 *Compendio della storia*) without any apparent familiarity with the charges and countercharges being lobbed by scholars in Europe and the Americas regarding American flora and fauna. However, several years later he begins the preface to his *Compendio de la historia geográfica* with this sweeping declaration:

> Europe at this time turns all its attention to America, desirous of knowing with erudite curiosity about the diversity of its climates, the shape of its mountains, the nature of its fossils, the form of its vegetation and animals, the languages of its inhabitants; in sum, all that might engage its attention in those various regions, among which, according to the testimony of the authors who write about that part of our globe, the Kingdom of Chile is one of the most worthy of consideration. (iii)

As is clearly reflected in these prefatory remarks, Molina has joined the debate, taking pen in hand to refute Cornelius de Pauw.[34]

Molina faults de Pauw's lack of firsthand experience with America, a strategy employed by many criollo authors in contesting European critiques, but he also criticizes de Pauw's careless reading of works written by those who have traveled and studied in the New World.[35] He challenges de Pauw's description of the American climate as humid and debilitating, his characterization of American species as generally degenerate, and his portrayal of Amerindians as cowards.[36] Molina, emphasizing the particularity of Chile's indigenous inhabitants, objects to de Pauw's tendency to rely on isolated data points to characterize the vast diversity of the continent's indigenous groups. Guillaume-Thomas-François Raynal resonates more positively with Molina, and in the natural history Molina includes a number of quotes from Raynal's *Historia de las dos Indias* (*A History of the Two Indies;* 1780) praising Chile's climate and inhabitants.[37]

As a missionary order, the Jesuits had long cultivated an interest in indigenous peoples across the globe. And while their insistence on a universalizing view of human development can be faulted for erasing differences among cultures, it is also the case that Jesuits viewed many of those whom they were attempting to convert as members of a civil republic, albeit one very different from their own. Anthony Pagden has argued that Jesuit historians—Francisco Javier Clavigero foremost among them—were instrumental in providing an overarching account of "a continuous, instructive, and politically legitimating past" linking criollos and Amerindians.[38] They accomplished this by reappropriating pre-Hispanic Amerindian civilization as a New World classical antiquity and claiming it as their own cultural patrimony, obviating any reference to Spanish conquest.[39] Given the differences between Chile, Mexico, and Peru, Molina's project involving the Araucanians will require a different approach.

Molina's lifelong interest in the provenance of peoples is reflected in all his writings. His thinking about Amerindian culture mirrors that of other eighteenth-century conjectural historians and economic theorists such as Adam Ferguson (1723–1816), William Robertson (1721–1793), and Adam Smith (1723–1790).[40] He shared their views about the development of peoples and nations and explained the difference between savage and citizen as corresponding to the stages of human development: hunters, shepherds, farmers, and finally tradesmen, "the stage at which the truly civil man is formed" (*Compendio de la historia civil,* 12).[41] Molina develops these arguments about stadial history throughout the *Compendio de la historia civil* to explain that, because of its semi-savage stage of development, Araucanian culture combines admirable customs with inevitable vices (55). He argues that this combination characterizes the development of Araucanian society so far ("hasta ahora"), a view that holds forth the promise of continued development in the future as a result of the expansion of commercial exchanges with surrounding regions and other peoples. Commerce, the foundation of the fourth and final stage in the development of civil society, plays a key role in eighteenth-century discussions of how best to integrate conquered peoples, and it becomes an important element in treaty negotiations between Araucanians and Bourbon Spanish administrators. So Molina's insistence on viewing society through the lens of stadial history gives him considerable latitude to paint a new portrait of the Araucanians.

On the whole, therefore, Molina's account of Chile's indigenous population has a recuperative thrust; he describes the Araucanians' current level of cultural accomplishment in detail in order to provide a basis for the expectation of future progress. Molina notes that "the nature, the customs, and the harmonious language of [Chile's] ancient inhabitants lie as unknown as the marvelous efforts with which they have endeavored to defend their freedom with the many battles they have fought since the beginning of the conquest until our days" (*Compendio de la historia geográfica,* v). Here he expands the criteria for which the Araucanians are to be admired—not only their love of liberty and military prowess but also their customs and harmonious language.[42] He speculates that increasing familiarity with European customs will result in the development of a people worthy of universal admiration. In the *Compendio de la historia civil,* he elaborates on this view, foregrounding those qualities shared by Araucanians and Europeans in order to domesticate the former. Withers names these qualities as "the power of rational choice, language, the importance of individual and societal self-preservation and of personal and social well-being."[43]

Molina sets the stage for this project of domestication in his prefatory comments to the first part of his history, the *Compendio de la historia geográfica.* First, he registers a lament regarding the historiographical oblivion into which Chile has fallen—a frequent topic in eighteenth-century writing, as we have seen with Oviedo y Baños. Given the fact that Araucanian-Spanish hostilities were ongoing even as Molina was writing, it's somewhat of a stretch for him to insist that those battles have been forgotten. In fact, Molina goes on to observe in a note that continued wars, along with the region's commercial dependency on Spain, have resulted in stagnant population growth and limited the degree to which the inhabitants have been able to take full advantage of the country's rich resources (37n1). But Molina's sense that Chile is a forgotten chapter in Spain's imperial history is undeniable, and his efforts to rewrite that history in order to include Chile and the Araucanians are part of a larger project. Second, the historian emphasizes Araucanian prowess in battle, echoing earlier characterizations of their ferocity in which Araucanian aggression is explained as an admirable effort to defend freedom rather than as an expression of hostility against the Spaniards. In doing so Molina shifts the focus in subtle but significant ways. His emphasis on the perfection of civil society, both in general philosophical terms and in the particular case of the Araucanians, leads him to view military valor not as an end in itself, but rather as a stepping-stone to other, more developed forms of civic virtue.[44] Finally, and most significantly, customs, language, and military valor are collapsed together in Molina's characterization.[45] This convergence goes beyond earlier idealizations of the freedom-loving Araucanian warrior. Molina's domestication of the Araucanian warrior reflects an evolving role for Indians in a new, post-conquest Bourbon Spanish Empire—a role that puts to the test eighteenth-century cosmopolitan thinking.

IV. *"Los más desconocidos salvajes":* *Araucanians and the cosmpolitan imaginary*

There was an explosion of interest during the eighteenth century in the global cross-cultural contact zone as the circulation and exchange of people, commodities, texts, and ideas increased exponentially. The Americas were both laboratory and stage where the Enlightenment worked out its theories about human development, difference, history, and civilization; they represent a space where those theories were challenged by complex and contested realities on the ground. Buffon, de Pauw, Raynal, Robertson, and others posed questions about the degeneracy of New World species and proffered critiques of Spanish conquest; Spaniards and criollos (or *españoles americanos*) were quick to respond. In this charged context, Molina's portrayal of the Araucanians is meant to substantiate his claim for their incorporation into a universal cosmopolitan republic.

Cosmopolitanism, a term that in the eighteenth century might be understood to sum up "the relationship between the European Enlightenment and the rest of the world," is generally acknowledged to be one of the central values of the Enlightenment.[46] In *The Cosmopolitan Ideal in Enlightenment Thought,* Thomas Schlereth argues that the eighteenth-century cosmopolitan ideal is usually "allied with humanism, pacificism, and a developing (*although ambivalent*) conception of universal human equality" (xii–xiii; emphasis mine). For Karen O'Brien, eighteenth-century cosmopolitan history represents "an intellectual investment in the idea of a common *European* civilization" (*Narratives,* 2; emphasis mine). Yet these deliberately neutral formulations belie the conflictive backdrop and legacy of cosmopolitanism. Challenges to enlightened thinking about an increasingly harmonizing and inclusive trajectory of cosmopolitan history come from within the Enlightenment itself.[47] In the *Esprit des Lois* (Spirit of laws; 1748), for example, Montesquieu discusses the inevitability of different systems of government arising from differences in climate, geography, and history. Johann Gottfried Herder, in a more pointed critique, charges that in positing an undifferentiated and universal human nature, his contemporaries have "taken words for works, Enlightenment for happiness, greater sophistication for virtue, and in this way invented the fiction of the general amelioration of the world."[48]

The progressive, cosmopolitan view of stadial history runs the risk (1) of denying non-European cultures the very agency that is another central tenet of the Enlightenment, (2) of seeing these cultures merely as prior stages of cultural evolution, and (3) of erasing the cultural specificity that would make them visible to a European reader.[49] Postmodern critiques of the Enlightenment have offered a reevaluation of cosmopolitanism, linking the eighteenth-century embrace of the exotic to the practice of colonialism or to the "denial of coevalness," to use Johannes Fabian's term.[50] On the other hand, Dena Goodman points out that although postmodern critics use the Enlightenment as a "synecdoche for universalism," one can also argue that "difference" was equally an Enlightenment concept ("Difference," 129).

It is undeniable that the Enlightenment's classifying gaze, when turned on issues of race and difference, exhibits a curious blindness with regard to Spanish America. In the introduction to his anthology of Enlightenment writings on race, Emmanuel Chukwude Eze proposes that the classical (that is, Aristotelian) distinction between "cultured" and "barbaric" based on reason is reformulated in the Enlightenment as a distinction between "civilized" and "savage" or "primitive" (*Race,* 4). His anthology includes many authors whose names would have been familiar to Molina: Buffon's writings on the "savages of South America" discuss the role of climate as a factor in skin color (18–20, 27), while David Hume rejects the influence of geography and climate on man's "temper or genius" (31). Some writers included in the anthology point to the Peruvian and Mexican empires as examples that challenge the supposition that all other men are inferior to whites, but most Enlightenment schemes that use climate and heat to explain both skin color and cultural development do not address the South American Indians (particularly those of the temperate Southern Cone, like the Araucanians, who would challenge those schemes).[51]

We must remember that eighteenth-century debates about cosmopolitanism took place not only in the salons and libraries of European philosophes, but also in imperial Europe's peripheral territories. Molina's history reflects the challenge of the spatial and temporal positing of the categories of civilization and savagery—or of domestication and barbarism—in Enlightenment thought. Like his contemporaries, Molina struggles with issues of difference and universalism, but finally concludes that all peoples are fundamentally analogous.[52] Many of the arguments that will be key to this conclusion are already outlined in his earlier work on natural history, and Molina returns to these issues—a preoccupation with source materials, mapping, language, and war as it relates to governance—in the preface to the *Compendio de la historia civil.*

Molina begins the *Compendio de la historia civil* with a haunting and evocative speculation about a lost past: "The origin of the first inhabitants of Chile, like that of other Americans, is enveloped in dense darkness" (1). Molina goes on to enumerate all that Chile is missing that might shed light on these lost origins. Chile can claim no archaeological or architectural monuments. Nor is there evidence of writing or any other semblance of a scriptural tradition. Molina's opening confession points to the lack that lies at the heart of his history of Chile, a lack that is not shared by "other Americans" and that he must attempt to fill with his *Compendio.*

Who are the "other Americans" with whom the first inhabitants of Chilean territory are compared . . . and not necessarily favorably? For Molina both the Aztecs and Incas loom large. As a diligent scholar and voracious reader, Molina was familiar with the different Amerindian writing systems that had been studied and praised by other historians and scholars, such as the *khipus* (knots) of the ancient Incas chronicled by the Inca Garcilaso in his *Comentarios reales de los Incas* (Royal commentaries of the Incas; 1609), the "Disertaciones" on the archaeological ruins of the ancient Mexicans included by Francisco Javier Clavigero in his *Storia antica del Messico* (1780–1781; published in Spanish as *Historia antigua de México* [Ancient history of Mexico]), and the *piedrecillas* (small stones) described by Juan de Velasco in his *Historia del reino de Quito* (History of the kingdom of Quito; 1795)—in short, with other indigenous traditions that had left behind some trace, which was essential for European readers to acknowledge their historical and historiographical legitimacy.

Because of their geographical proximity, however, the Incas are the standard against which Molina's Araucanians must be measured. Accounts of Inca civilization captured the imagination of readers from the sixteenth century onward, with their descriptions of the monumental terraces and pyramids of the Andes, of the Incas' elaborate social and political hierarchies, and of the rich traditions preserved orally and through Inca *khipus*. During the eighteenth century such accounts still represented a model that historians of other Amerindian cultures felt compelled to either echo or contest. One might even argue that Garcilaso's *Comentarios reales,* which was translated and circulated widely in the eighteenth century, haunts Molina's portrayal of the Araucanians. Apart from Buffon, who is briefly mentioned in the first chapter, Garcilaso is the first author cited explicitly by Molina. In chapter 2 of the *Compendio de la historia civil,* Molina refers to "the historian Garcilaso" in describing early Araucanian resistance to attempted encroachments by Peruvian forces (11). This is one of the few times the *Comentarios reales* are explicitly mentioned; however, there are repeated references to various aspects of Inca civilization, particularly the "quippos" (*khipus*) used to preserve historical memory in the Andean region. Molina acknowledges with considerable regret that this "admirable art was absolutely unknown to the Chileans" (26).

Garcilaso, Clavigero, and Velasco all create a kind of textual museum in which pre-Hispanic culture is displayed.[53] But Chile could lay claim to none of the source materials that figure so prominently in their accounts—neither archaeological ruins nor evidence of writing systems such as Inca *khipus* or *piedrecillas*. Araucanian civilization is evidenced not by the kind of antiquarian artifacts that are showcased by Clavigero, Velasco, and other eighteenth-century Jesuit writers, but rather, Molina argues, by their participation in a process of civic engagement. Thus, he begins his account of Araucanian Chile in an apologetic mode, trying to claim for "his" savages both exceptionality and universalism. Molina must demonstrate that the Araucanians, while ferocious and brave "*bárbaros,*" cannot be summarily dismissed as a people "sin rey, sin ley, sin fé" (without king, without law, without faith). His aim in describing the Araucanians is to inscribe them within the history of Chile, within Spain's imperial history, and within a broad, cosmopolitan human history. He will also invoke them to refute European charges of American inferiority and degeneracy (these are, of course, aims he shares with many of his fellow Jesuit exiles, whose writings are also marked by the same nostalgic patriotism). In order to do so, he must explain Araucanian motives for their continuous warring against the Spaniards, reconfiguring their ferocity not as bloodthirstiness or a desire for vengeance, but rather as the result of their love of liberty and as a quality consonant with other forms of civic and civil engagement.

Molina therefore displaces Araucanian ferocity (traditionally center stage) by including in his history other, non-military aspects of Araucanian life that he claims have been overlooked by historians. He does this by shifting the focus to Araucanian language—"the harmonious structure and richness of the language of this nation" (*Compendio de la historia civil,* 5). He describes in great detail not only the protocols of Araucanian warfare but also their *parlamentos* (parleys)— the war councils in which the Araucanians debated among themselves issues of self-governance, military strategy, and ethics, with eloquence and with great philosophical and political sophistication. Molina's focus on Araucanian *parlamentos* responds to the eighteenth-century preoccupation with the rationality of language and with Amerindian linguistic variants, as I will explore later in this chapter. What's more, he shows how in the eighteenth century (a period obviously beyond the reach of earlier historians of Chile) these endogamous *parlamentos* have evolved into complex treaty deliberations with the Spaniards that put into practice cosmopolitan ideas. Molina writes a civil history of Chile organized around—but not limited to—the prolonged Araucanian wars, and he continues his account up to the present day. His representation of the Araucanians is effected not through recourse to a distant Amerindian antiquity but rather by implicating Amerindians in an ongoing negotiated present. This ultimately leads to the portrayal of a domesticated Indian that reflects not only its openly acknowledged roots in the sixteenth century but also—and most significantly—an emerging enlightened cosmopolitanism.

V. "El fiero pueblo no domado": Exemplary Indians

Molina's account of the fierce and freedom-loving Araucanian Indians is informed not only by historical sources such as Olivares's chronicle but also by literary treatments idealizing Araucanian bravery.[54] First and foremost among these is Alonso de Ercilla's *La Araucana*.[55] In this sixteenth-century epic poem devoted to Spanish efforts to subdue the Araucanians, the poet creates a collective indigenous hero who epitomizes the classical virtues of love of freedom and military prowess. As has been frequently noted, Ercilla rewrites the European epic tradition in order to narrate his experiences in Chile, inserting himself as combatant/narrator and invoking the Araucanian people as a collective hero.[56] His poem became a classic and, one might argue, a Chilean foundational fiction. David Brading has observed that "few countries in Spanish America were so dominated by one primordial text as was Chile by *La Araucana*" (*First America*, 449).

Molina is not exempt. Just as the whitened bones of previous Spanish explorers mark the path Oviedo y Baños must follow in telling the story of the conquest and settlement of Venezuela, *La Araucana* marks the trajectory of Molina's *Compendio de la historia civil*. Although the eighteenth-century historian of Chile skips over the bucolic, classical, and fantastic digressions that are such an important part of Ercilla's epic, he draws on *La Araucana* for his representation of warriors like Galbarino and Caupolicán, for his descriptions of Araucanian war tactics, and for his narrative of the early phase of Araucanian-Spanish hostilities. Molina includes extended quotes from *La Araucana* in footnotes, a rhetorical strategy that underscores the poem's historical authority.[57] And, as I will discuss later in this chapter, Molina even includes in his own work a map of Chile that had originally been published in the 1776 Madrid edition of *La Araucana*.[58]

Molina shares Ercilla's dilemma: how to represent a ferocious adversary who is at the same time a sympathetic hero with whom the reader is meant to identify? How does one establish some degree of rhetorical control over a subject defined in terms of resistance to any form of subjugation? Numerous readers have observed that the Janus-like portrait of the Araucanians in Ercilla's epic—as noble heroes as well as ignoble barbarians—corresponds to the myth of indomitable Araucanians characterized by their ferocity in battle and love of freedom (themes that will be echoed by Molina).[59] For both the sixteenth-century poet and the eighteenth-century historian, the Araucanians' motives for warfare, which in a different context might be construed as savage behavior, are not linked to base motives such as bloodthirstiness or vengeance, but rather to an idealized love of independence. War for the Araucanians is not emptied of its ideological significance. Nor are the Araucanians reduced to tragic figures by their defeat at the hands of European imperialism.[60] Their heroic resistance is precisely what defines them and their role in Chilean history.[61]

What is each author's role in the construction of Chilean history? For the poem's narrator-combatant, *La Araucana* ends not with a bang but a whimper. Ercilla returned to Spain in 1561 without having secured any glorious and definitive conquests. He and a small band of companions close out their imperial offensive with a meandering and ill-advised expedition to the archipelago of Chiloe—a slog reminiscent of some of the disastrous forays recounted by Oviedo y Baños in his *Historia de la conquista y población de la provincia de Venezuela*. Shortly before this expedition begins, toward the close of the poem and just as his own participation in the conquest of Chile is about to end, Ercilla recounts how he carved his name on a tree trunk, adding the date and time: "Here came, where no other had come / Don Alonso de Ercilla" (canto 36, stanza 29, lines 1–2; pages 385–86). The carving marks in time and space the extent of Ercilla's involvement in the Chilean enterprise. This signatory flourish reflects what Margarita Zamora has called "the cathartic function of the text" ("Epic Poetry," 233)—that is, Ercilla's compulsion to record his own protagonism in an extended and fraught imperial effort. It might also be read as an anticipatory epitaph, recorded at a time of no less certainty than the bloodiest moments on the battlefield. In any event, with this gesture Ercilla writes the conquest (and his role in it) on his own terms.

Molina, in turn, repeats the gesture, literally inscribing Ercilla's signature within his text: "The famous poet Ercilla who was part of the delegation, wanting to have the glory of having pushed southward further than any other European, went to the aforementioned gulf and on the far shore left written in verse in the bark of the trees his name, and the date of his discovery, which was January 31 of this year [1558]" (*Compendio de la historia civil*, 189). I read Molina's inscription of Ercilla's signature as an attempt by the eighteenth-century historian to co-opt the sixteenth-century poet's authority and appropriate his place as chronicler of Araucanian Chile. Like his contemporaries, Molina is mindful of an existing historiographical tradition to which he must respond, expanding on it and incorporating it even as he moves beyond it in terms of his chronological framework. So his account of the signature attests to an authorial sleight of hand, as Molina uses Ercilla's Araucanians as models and rewrites them in accordance with his own eighteenth-century context.

Given the moment at which he is writing, Molina as a historian is presented with a unique set of challenges and opportunities in terms of his representation of the Araucanians. Molina may have shared in a general sense that the bar for civil histories of the New World was being raised as a result of disputes between the Council of the Indies and the Royal Academy of History. There was pressure for the academy to support only new research and writing projects, as previous histories were judged to be unscientific and of limited value. Jorge Cañizares-Esguerra quotes Manuel Pablo Salcedo of the Council of the Indies regarding these histories, which "enjoy praising heroes . . . but are silent on the origins of wars; the causes and outcomes of victories; the impact of economic systems, laws, and mores that are introduced" (in *How to Write,* 164). Molina's two-part project clearly aspired to do more. He focuses on the Araucanians to make possible a renegotiated Indian identity that makes sense in a new imperial context. Molina comes to terms with the exemplary Indians who populate the pages of Ercilla's epic and Garcilaso's commentaries by turning his history away from war and conquest to diplomacy and governance. Alphabetic writing (clearly a preoccupation for sixteenth- and seventeenth-century historians but one which, as we have seen, finds no purchase in Araucanian civilization) is replaced by oratory. In Molina's civil history, a different kind of negotiation plays out both among the Araucanians and in their dealings with Spaniards through *parlamentos* and treaties.

This negotiation is reflected in the *Compendio de la historia civil* and becomes especially apparent as Molina diverges from his principal sources, Ercilla and Olivares. It does not go unnoticed by the reader when, after the death of the Araucanian leader Caupolicán (in 1561, the point at which *La Araucana's* account of Spanish-Indian hostilities leaves off), Molina must continue his story without further reference to Ercilla (*Compendio de la historia civil,* book 3, chap. 7). This leaves a period of almost one hundred years (1561 to 1656) for which Olivares's *Historia militar* functions as Molina's principal source. These chapters correspond to a time during which military leadership frequently changes on both sides, Spanish forts are constructed in an effort to secure the frontier, and the Dutch threaten Spanish control of the coastal regions. The heroic phase of the Spanish-Araucanian conflict cedes its place to a new and increasingly complex reality.

Much mention has been made of Molina's dependence on Olivares's first volume and the frustration that ensued when he was unable to secure a copy of the second volume. Molina notes the precise moment when "with great sorrow on our part" he can no longer rely on Olivares (*Compendio de la historia civil,* 290). Olivares's history stops in 1656; Molina's account continues until 1773, and concludes with a brief final chapter titled "Current state of Chile." This section develops at a fairly expeditious pace, condensing the account of multiple battles and negotiations between Spaniards and Araucanians as if Molina no longer felt entirely authorized to tell the story. Yet by filling in the gaps left by his predecessors, Molina is able to inscribe Araucanian accomplishments in the development of civil society in Chile. By continuing the story of the Araucanians beyond the moment when Ercilla and Olivares stopped writing, Molina paints a new portrait of a domesticated, eighteenth-century Indian.

VI. *"Contra el método común de los Geógrafos": Araucanians on the imperial map*

But first Molina must situate the Araucanians for his European readers, many of whom had only the vaguest notion of Spain's viceregal periphery.[62] Molina's interest in cartography is apparent in the frequent references that he makes to maps and mapping, and in the prominent role that maps play in the various editions of his works.[63] The same is true of many of his Jesuit contemporaries, whose keen sense of place (it might be argued) comes from an equally keen sense of their own displacement following Charles III's 1767 expulsion edict. Fascination with geography was widespread at the time, however. Withers has observed that "people in the eighteenth century understood their world to be changing as a fact of geography, and as the result of processes of geographical inquiry—in the shape and dimension of continents, for example, in the types of human cultures making up mankind, in the reasons plants, animals, and humans were located as they were" (*Placing the Enlightenment,* 5).

These changes had imperial implications, of course, and a great deal of scholarly work has recently been devoted to the ways in which mapping and surveying (along with other forms of scientific appropriation) were employed in the service of European political and economic expansionism in the eighteenth century.[64] As J. B. Harley has argued, "maps were used to legitimize the reality of conquest and empire."[65] Lines on an imperial map may be drawn to confirm the reach of imperial power or to suggest its inevitable expansion. At other times, as is the case with Molina's maps, the lines reflect a fundamental instability; in the relationship between Molina's employment of maps and the story he is trying to tell about Araucanian Chile, a discursive tension emerges between cartography and narrative.[66] This tension points to the many ways in which the Chilean territory was a contested space whose contours and boundaries continually shifted as Araucanians and Spaniards met, fought, traded, and parleyed.

As Molina notes at the beginning of the *Compendio de la historia geográfica,* at the time he is writing, Chile is divided into two parts: "the country inhabited by the Spaniards, and that which is still possessed by Indians" (9).[67] Molina's incorporation of maps in the 1795 Spanish version of the *Compendio de la historia civil* follows earlier efforts to provide cartographic complements to his accounts of Chile's history, both in the anonymous 1776 *Compendio della storia* and the 1788 *Compendio de la historia geográfica.*[68] The first includes a map in which the mythological figures that traditionally served to decorate a map's borders have been replaced by the stylized figure of an Araucanian Indian.[69] The second re-

produces the same partial map of Chile that appeared in the 1776 English translation of Ercilla's *La Araucana,* albeit with a different title. While in the Ercilla
volume the map describes "the land where famous events between Spaniards
and Araucanians took place," Molina titles the same document "Map by Poncho
Chileno of the country that the Araucanians inhabit in Chile."[70] In this presentation of the map, there is no mention of the Spanish-Araucanian wars or, in
fact, any recognition of the past; the Araucanians inhabit the Chilean territory
in the present. Molina's choice of language is perhaps merely a grammatical reflection of a textual present, or perhaps it is in recognition of the Araucanians'
ongoing presence in eighteenth-century Chile. Santa Arias reminds us of the
role played by cartography in legitimizing imperial design; it is all the more interesting, therefore, to note Molina's subtle acknowledgment of the Araucanians
not as mere ornament (as was the case with the *Compendio della storia* map),
but as real players in an imperial project.

Replacing the maps that had been confiscated or left behind in Chile along
with other documents and source materials proved difficult, and Molina on
various occasions must settle for something that imperfectly approximates the
geographical information he wants to convey.[71] When he enumerates in his
preface to the *Compendio de la historia civil* the sources he has used to compose
the work, Molina makes the following confession: "I had also hoped to draw a
new general map of Chile, but I have not been able to obtain any documents
other than a beautiful printed map of that region inhabited by the Araucanians, whose author has chosen to hide behind the name of 'Poncho Chileno.' As
this can be of great utility for the matter of my History, I have expanded it and
added it to this Compendium" (vii). Practicality and utility seem to inform his
decision to include a map of Araucanian territory, even as he directs readers
interested in a more complete and accurate cartographic representation to the
anonymous *Compendio della storia*. Molina's Araucanian map has been distorted to conform to the exigencies of the editorial process, as Arias has studied in great detail ("Geografía, imperio," 340–42). Molina explains that he has
turned the map sideways—"contrary to the method common to Geographers,
with the East in the upper part; this has been done because, since the Kingdom
of Chile is too long from North to South and too narrow from East to West, a
normal map would be very inconvenient for those wishing to view it" (xviii). If
necessity is the mother of invention, here Molina is obliged to invent Chilean
cartography, first by manipulating its most striking geographical features (that
is, its long narrow extension), and second by inscribing the Araucanians in its
center. In the process indigenous territory space ends up substituting itself for
the Spanish territory the author initially intended to portray.[72]

Molina's difficulty in successfully reproducing and disseminating a Chilean
map as he originally intended reveals how challenging it will be for him to definitively control Araucanian knowledge and territory in his history of Chile. The
editorial placements and displacements of maps in his history serve to remind
us that, in the eighteenth-century, Chile occupies a contested space on Spain's
imperial map. Matthew Edney notes that maps have always functioned as instruments of governance, "as devices by which governments of all sorts have

sought to extend their authority and transform land into territory" ("Irony," 11). This transformation is itself a kind of foundational domestication, in which a "European discourse of landscape deterritorializes indigenous peoples, separating them off from territories they may once have dominated."[73] But in Molina's history, Spain's ability to execute the transformation of Araucanian land into imperial territory in a sustainable and mappable way is constantly being renegotiated, and the Araucanians continue to inhabit their lands and resist the extension of Spanish empire. Rather than affirming empire, therefore, Molina's maps point to the limits of Spain's imperial project.

The maps also serve to remind the reader of the author's lived experiences in Chile and suggest that Molina's account of the Araucanians carries the force of observation, even when he is dealing with historical events that he has not witnessed himself. The claim to authority by the eyewitness is a constant refrain in colonial historiography, and it has not lost its significance for the authors I study here. In Molina's case the claim has an added twist: it reminds the reader that the author maps his history of Chile from a distance, as a Jesuit in exile, and in some ways as a victim of empire himself.

If imperial history, as it has been argued, involves assigning "meaning retrospectively and from without, rejecting context, locality, and specificity," then Molina cannot be said to be writing imperial history.[74] Rather than map Chilean history so that the "preexisting places and alternative conceptions of space that preceded the colonialist enterprise vanish from view," Molina allows the exact opposite to occur.[75] Molina's maps point to an ongoing negotiation in which the rhetoric and ceremonies of possession (to use Seed's term again) are real, rather than performative.[76] At the same time, his narrative project—to domesticate the Araucanian Indians in order to inscribe them within eighteenth-century historiographical discourse, by shaping and reorganizing that representation to fit the ideological imperatives of the moment—is barely under control.

The Araucanians threaten to overrun the textual landscape just as they dominated Chilean territory, forcing the remapping not only of earlier European cartography but of Molina's narrative project as well. One example will suffice to explain what I mean by this. Recounting the Spanish struggle in 1554 to recapture the city of Concepción from the Araucanians, Molina permits the description of Araucanian *parlamentos* and military strategies to dominate his account, while overlooking the reaction of the terrified citizens of Concepción and the ineffectual response of colonial administrators to indigenous attacks—both issues that are foregrounded in other accounts.[77] The editor of the 1795 edition adds these details later in a footnote, reenacting Molina's earlier move in displacing Spaniards and criollos to the margins (*Compendio de la historia civil*, 153). Molina's text is marked time and time again by such displacements, suggesting the degree to which the Araucanians eclipse their criollo and Spanish adversaries in the battle for Chile, at least in the short term. Molina charts Araucanian territory not only through the specific maps he includes in his works, but by placing Araucanians in a broader eighteenth-century context—in a frontier zone that is both real and figurative and that challenges received notions of the absolute and fixed difference between its civilized and barbarian inhabitants.[78]

VII. *"La perfección del estado civil"*: *Domesticating savages*

One of the most important shifts represented by Enlightenment historiography is the move away from military, political, and diplomatic history toward something more eclectic that combines all these with natural and cultural history. In keeping with this shift, Molina's *Compendio de la historia civil,* while a chronologically organized account of the Araucanian wars, is also an account of Araucanian culture. Several chapters in book 1 are devoted to a description of the Araucanians' political, military, social, religious, philosophical, and artistic development, as is all of book 2. Molina links warlike resistance to culture in the opening chapters of the *Compendio de la historia geográfica* and continues this rhetorical strategy throughout the *Compendio de la historia civil,* emphasizing at every opportunity the rational nature of Araucanian warfare as a foundation for governance.

As we have seen, Molina's views on the stadial evolution of civil society inform his observation that Araucanian culture at the time of the arrival of the Spaniards had reached the third stage, that of agriculture. Molina offers specific examples in support of his argument that Araucanians demonstrate a level of cultural development beyond that of hunters or shepherds. He describes the use of flour and yeast among the Araucanians, noting that the turn from raw grain to cooked bread reflects the advances of civil society. He compares the storage of alcohol in clay jars to Greek and Roman practice, taking what had often been a topic for recrimination by Europeans—indigenous customs related to alcohol and drinking—and affirming the practice as a "refinement of domestic economy" (*Compendio de la historia civil,* 18). Agriculture leads to the establishment of fixed communities and the right to private property among the Araucanians. They can lay claim to a small but vibrant poetic tradition; they use clay to create ceramic vessels for daily and ceremonial use; and they are skilled metallurgists who work with gold, silver, iron, copper, and tin (20–22). Molina is quick to observe that although one might have expected the inhabitants of Chile to have made even greater progress toward "the perfection of civil society," "the passage from barbarism to civil life is not as easy as might be believed at first glance," as can be seen even in the history of civilized nations like those of Europe (25). Having introduced the issue of cultural development in a comparative context and as a universal challenge, Molina plants himself squarely in the camp of those who, like Robertson and Ferguson, view human history as a progression through a series of stages. Thus, his Araucanians are presented as being involved in perfecting civil society in a process that continues to the present day. This absolves them (and the historian) from having to present concrete evidence of the kind of cultural accomplishments that other historians of ancient Amerindians have been able to incorporate in their accounts. Molina proffers a conjectural opinion about the future: "If plausible customs and innocent European knowledge were to be introduced among them, they would quickly form a people worthy of universal esteem" (55).

Just as war has interrupted the development of civilization in Araucanian territory, Molina interrupts his meditation on the evolution of civil society in order to narrate the historical events surrounding Pedro de Valdivia's return to Chile and the ensuing battles between Indians and Spaniards. Molina will argue in the following chapters that these events not only provide the Araucanians with an opportunity to demonstrate their valor in battle, but also to receive and profit from the external cultural influences that are inevitable when two peoples come into contact. Character and customs are as relevant in these encounters as strength and bravery are in times of war. Thus, the historian concludes book 1 by announcing a necessary digression to discuss "the character and customs of this warlike people" (51). Book 2 is organized as an ethnographical project, with extended descriptions of the condition, character, dress, homes, and customs of the Araucanians. Molina weaves together in his opening chapter various threads: the recent history of Chile, defined by conflicts between Spaniards and Araucanians; an overview of Araucanian cultural practices; and, finally, the author's views on human cultural development as both universal and cosmopolitan. He closes by emphasizing that the story of the Araucanians provides the background for "*our* history" (emphasis mine). The historian's rhetorical gesture of appropriating the history he is about to tell, an inclusive and open-ended narrative that will take the historian and his readers up to the present day, opens the door for a convergence of Araucanian and Spanish history and the positing of a collaborative, rather than adversarial, story.

By Molina's time, praising the Araucanians' love of liberty had become a familiar gesture. Book 2 begins with "This people, constantly devoted to independence, relishes being called Aucá; that is, independent, or free," and compares Araucanian Chile to Holland, claiming that the Spaniards named the region "Araucanian Flanders, or that of the indomitable state" (52). Warlike resistance, aestheticized in Ercilla's epic idealizations, is presented in Molina's history as essentially rational. Molina argues that the level of Araucanian cultural development can best be observed in their conduct of war, and he repeatedly conflates war and governance in his account of the Araucanians: "The military government of the Araucanians is not only reasonable and more systematic than civil government, but it seems in some ways to go beyond the intelligence of an uncultured nation" (67). War practices are presented as rationalized protocol, as when Molina describes how the Araucanian leader (or *toqui*) claims for himself a stone ax as a sign of his authority and dignity (68), or when war councils send messages to one another by means of small arrows linked by a blood-red thread.[79] Araucanian provisioning strategies are likened to those of the ancient Romans (73). Molina argues that, far from lacking a visible political structure, the Araucanians have a very tightly constructed hierarchy that can be sustained even when their *toqui* dies or is killed in battle through the election of another *toqui*.

Molina's comments also reflect the reality that over time, familiarity with a common Spanish enemy encouraged intertribal unity in the region.[80] He points to collective actions on the part of warring Araucanians that signal a higher degree of civil development than that evidenced by other Amerindians, as when neighboring groups inform the Araucanians of possibly threatening activity on the part of the Spaniards. This collaboration represents a marked departure from the typical behavior that Molina has described earlier, in which indigenous groups fail to come together in their own self-defense. Araucanians also learned to appreciate the strategic value of a cavalry through their encounters with the Spaniards.[81] In addition to becoming expert horse breeders, they augmented their stock by rustling horses being sent to Spanish forces along the frontier; by the early seventeenth century, they had become daring and experienced horsemen. What emerges from these examples is a picture of Araucanian engagement in a process of scientific observation and experimentation that will eventually lead to their mastery of European knowledge. Araucanians are portrayed as agents in their own process of domestication as they put to pragmatic use a range of European practices and commodities.

Molina includes an anecdote that reveals the degree to which Araucanians have abandoned the barbaric practices employed in earlier times. When a new *toqui*, Putapichion, is named in 1630, he hopes to energize his warriors for battle by reinstating the *pruloncon,* a long-forgotten tradition of sacrificing a captive with an ax blow to the head (Molina explains this ritual earlier in the *Compendio de la historia civil,* though he claims it has not been practiced more than once or twice in the past two hundred years, since the Araucanians, inclined to clemency, prefer to participate in prisoner exchanges instead). Molina judges this cruel act to be unworthy of an otherwise praiseworthy leader, and he expresses his objections in terms that are reminiscent of Las Casas and reflective of eighteenth-century thinking on universal human rights. Perhaps because he is describing a practice the Araucanians have for the most part abandoned in their progressive evolution toward civil society, Molina includes horrific details of this savage ritual—the ripping of beating hearts from the chests of victims, the drinking of the victims' blood from flutes made from their bones, general drunkenness, and the placing of a cow head on the shoulders of the unfortunate captive (79–80). He quotes Francisco Núñez de Pineda y Bascuñán, an eyewitness who reported that many of those present protested the inhuman spectacle.[82] Molina concludes the passage by comparing this ritual to those practiced by the Goths, a reference that distances both the Araucanians and Bourbon Spain from their less civilized ancestors.[83] Molina's account confirms Araucanian participation in a cosmopolitan humanity that had clearly progressed beyond the savage stage. It must be recognized, however, that notwithstanding the negative response they provoke, Putapichion's barbaric actions might also be understood as an example of the reinvention of tradition that characterizes nation-states in their early stages of formation.

Molina's descriptions of Araucanian involvement in commerce (the fourth stage of human development) similarly reflect the degree to which he views them as engaging in a process of perfecting civil society. Molina's deeply felt convictions regarding the importance of commerce and trade informs much of what he has to say about Araucanian culture and echoes enlightened thinking. Molina observes that the Araucanians are the most commercial of all the savages living in Spanish territories. Though they have not yet introduced the use of coins, he points with pride to their well-developed trading practices, through which they participate in a wide range of commodity exchanges among themselves and with the Spaniards (involving horses, tools, wine, and ponchos). As Weber notes, "Vast trading networks developed in frontier zones where the economies of Spaniards and independent Indians articulated with one another. In such places, the stabilization of economic relations promoted peace, borders became diffuse, and trade became the norm" (*Bárbaros,* 83). Military negotiations from the mid-seventeenth century onward increasingly encompass commercial concerns as well. Reporting on the successful conclusion of an exchange of prisoners in 1640, Molina pronounces with satisfaction, "Commerce, inseparable from the good harmony of peoples, was established between the two nations, and the lands abandoned because of continuous enemy raids became populated again, and reanimated with regular products the industry of their tranquil owners" (*Compendio de la historia civil,* 287). Molina's choice of words is revealing. He speaks of how commerce between two nations leads to the repopulation of war-ravaged territories and increases the tranquility of those who inhabit them.[84]

In using the term "nation" to refer to Araucanians, Molina enters into contemporary debates that were redefining the meaning of the word.[85] The Enlightenment understood "nation" to refer to "a coherent tradition of beliefs and customs, often identified with a *printed* heritage."[86] This emphasis on print culture—a familiar topic in histories of the New World—led many eighteenth-century philosophers to debate whether barbarous communities could even be called "nations." Straddling these two definitions, Molina's Aragonese contemporary Félix de Azara (the subject of the following chapter) defines "nation" in these words: "I will call nation any congregation of Indians who share the same spirit, forms and customs, with their own language as different from others known there as is Spanish from German."[87] Given his frequent laments that Araucanians had not yet had the opportunity to develop a lettered civilization, Molina is cognizant of how precarious his positioning of the Araucanian nation may seem to the reader. At the same time, his account of Araucanian life is clearly constructed so as to leave no doubt that it cannot be relegated to the savage space constructed by many historians for Amerindians. Thus, Molina repeatedly uses terminology that suggests Araucanian unity and political maturity.

Nowhere is Molina's domestication of the Araucanians more intentional than in his discussion of how they employ language both to conduct and avoid war. Prudent and reasoned language tempers warlike instincts. Book 3 includes a description of Caupolicán's exhortation to his warriors that draws on Ercilla's depiction of the same moment and emphasizes the Araucanian leader's oratorical skill: "No less a politician than a warrior . . . he contained their ardor with prudent reason" (*Compendio de la historia civil,* 141). But it also encompasses strategic operations. In Araucanian culture all important decisions having to do with war—whether or not to go to battle, how booty is to be distributed, what to do with prisoners—are thoroughly examined and decided by means of deliberative meetings or *congresos* (congresses). This is the rationalized protocol for governance that distinguishes the bellicose Araucanians from their more savage counterparts. During these meetings the participants (all male warriors, regardless of age) deliver speeches, "which the Spanish call *Parlamento,* and the Araucanians *Huincacoyag*" (80). Molina describes these *parlamentos* as a sort of linguistic rehearsal of the act of war itself: "They make in the Chilean language an extensive harangue [*arenga*] on the motives that led to war, and on the most opportune ways to conserve good harmony between the two peoples" (81). Molina's move here from "war" to "harmony" is significant, as it signals a change in emphasis from warfare to governance and diplomacy that is central to his domestication of the Araucanians.

VIII. *"Dueños del decir": From war to diplomacy*

Molina demonstrates a particular interest in Araucanian language in all his writings, emphasizing the richness and eloquence of Araucanian speech in the natural and the civil history even as he laments the lack of a written tradition. Molina's *Compendio de la historia civil* opens with an acknowledgment that in the absence of any monuments or writing systems, all knowledge of Araucanian history prior to the arrival of the Spaniards has been buried by the passage of time. Yet Molina insists, repeating an earlier speculation, that past Araucanian grandeur is still somehow present in the rich and harmonious structures of Araucanian language. Araucanian language, Molina suggests, represents the residue of a moment of former glory, the remnant of an illustrious and enlightened people.

Since the perfection of language, he argues, follows naturally from the perfection of civilization, it therefore holds that a savage nation is incapable of speaking a cultured, expressive, and abundant language: "Perfection of language consistently follows that of civilization; it is not possible to understand how a nation that has always been savage, that has never been polished neither by wise laws, nor by commerce, nor by the arts, might speak a cultured, expressive and abundant language" (5). What's striking here is Molina's shift from the declarative to the subjunctive mode and from the exposition of a fundamental philosophical principle to speculation. The list of negatives—"neither by wise laws, nor by commerce, nor by the arts"—is quickly counterbalanced with an affirmation of Araucanian language.

Molina concludes the preface to the *Compendio de la historia civil* by returning to the topic of language, noting that research on the languages of savage nations is of great interest to eighteenth-century philosophers. He will elaborate on this in an extended discussion of Araucanian language, vocabulary, and syntax in subsequent chapters, and in the appendix that he promises will give "an idea of Chilean speech, which for its structure and harmony deserves to be known" (viii; the appendix begins on 332). While noting that there are diverse indigenous languages spoken in the southern Andean region, Molina explains that Araucanian, because it is the most elegant, gives its name to the general population (332). Araucanian compares favorably with other "barbarous" languages in terms of its constituent parts—verb tenses, prepositions, adverbs, interjections, and conjunctions—as well as its orderly nature and its possible classical roots (4–8). Molina emphasizes the Araucanians' concern for linguistic purity, marveling at their refusal to incorporate any foreign words into their lexicon (101). He includes a wonderful anecdote about how the Araucanians would interrupt Spanish missionaries to correct their feeble attempts to use indigenous language, preferring instead to rely on Spanish translation: "They would rather suffer the inconvenience of listening to a tedious interpreter than degrade their native language" (102).[88] This ironic inversion of European concerns about safeguarding the purity of their language against the inevitable incorporation of indigenous words echoes other ways in which Araucanians resisted acculturation.

When Molina moves beyond the grammatical structure of Araucanian language to its larger cultural role, he is equally encomiastic. He points to the Araucanians' employment of sophisticated rhetoric as proof of their cultural superiority.[89] Rhetoric is especially esteemed "because this knowledge, as in ancient Rome, leads to honors and to the management of business" (100). Molina praises the allegorical and figurative nature of Araucanian rhetorical oratory and suggests that its structure corresponds to classical rhetorical norms. After a description of their locutionary style, their poetic traditions, and their songs, Molina reports that Araucanians honor their poets by calling them "dueños del decir"; that is, "masters of speech" (104).[90]

For reasons that become apparent in later chapters devoted to more recent Chilean history, Molina is particularly impressed by Araucanian oratory. He stresses the importance of the performative aspects of any communicative situation: "One must listen to an Araucanian oration to form some idea of its energetic and abundant expression" (350). In other words, Molina appreciates language as performance and values speech as oratory, and he insists that only someone intimately familiar with Araucanian language can understand its energy and abundant expressivity. He is not alone in privileging performative speech. The eighteenth century saw an increasing focus on rhetoric and oratory as philosophers and politicians sought to find a universal language capable of expressing all human thoughts and feelings, regardless of cultural differences.[91] Oratory, intially identified with evangelization and preaching in the early Americas, gradually assumed a secular dimension and began to challenge the primacy of alphabetic writing as constitutive of authority in the public sphere. Conversation, oratory's private companion, similarly privileged a civil and deliberative exchange. Without forcing a comparison between Anglo- and Spanish America (or, for that matter, between Jefferson and Molina), it bears keeping in mind that the transatlantic and hemispheric resonances of eighteenth-century oratorical conventions and aspirations extend to Molina's Chilean history.[92]

Molina's thoughts on indigenous language are in many ways similar to those of his fellow Jesuit Lorenzo Hervás y Panduro (1735–1810).[93] In fact, as the Jesuit historian Charles Ronan explains, Molina gave Hervás valuable information about Araucanian language that the Spanish philologist included in his *Catálogo de las lenguas de las naciones conocidas* (Catalog of the languages of the known nations; Madrid, 1800-1805).[94] Beyond these efforts to systematize and classify all languages, we can point to broader philosophical discussions about language in the eighteenth century that have implications for Molina's representation of the Araucanians. As Cañizares-Esguerra has observed, "In the eighteenth century, European scholars collected and studied Mesoamerican codices and Inca quipus to demonstrate the evolution of mental facilities in conjectural and philosophical histories of progress" (*How to Write,* 7).[95] Amerindian sources composed in non-alphabetic script were increasingly called into question as untrustworthy and biased. The move to discredit Amerindian sources might actually have made it easier for Molina to write his history of the Araucanians, as it undermined the importance of the very scriptural systems— *khipus,* codices—that the Araucanians lacked. According to Cañizares-Esguerra, conjectural historians viewed writing as something that evolved gradually and thus tended to focus on speech when considering primitive societies.[96] Molina's insistence on the richness and sophistication of Araucanian language must be understood in this broader context, in which an abundant and richly expressive vocabulary pointed to the sophistication of Araucanian thought.

There is, of course, an extensive bibliography related to Andean notational systems such as the Inca *khipus* and, to a lesser degree, the *piedrecillas* described by Velasco in his *Historia del reino de Quito,* both discussed earlier in this chapter. Gary Urton and Galen Brokaw, among others, have studied the signifying potential of the knotted threads that captured the imagination of eighteenth-century travelers, philosophers, and writers (Françoise de Graffigny's *Lettres d'une Péruvienne* is a noteworthy example of this enthusiasm). The Inca Garcilaso's discussion of the sources—oral and written, Andean and European—for his *Comentarios reales* reflects his efforts to justify a strong Inca historical tradition in the absence of alphabetic writing. However, what Molina is trying to do is quite different from the Garcilasan project, or even from that of his fellow Jesuit Velasco. Both Garcilaso and Velasco point to nonscriptural recording systems used by Amerindians to register and transmit the past. Molina focuses on Araucanian use of spoken language to effect governance not only in the past, but also in a continually evolving present. Lacking the archaeological artifacts that could be used by Mexican and Peruvian historians to cement their idealized recreation of Amerindian antiquity, Molina chooses to domesticate his Indians by monumentalizing Araucanian language and speech. In the process he civilizes Araucanian warfare and domesticates Aruacanian ferocity, inscribing Araucanians in emerging conjectural and philosophical histories of human progress.

In addition to the aforementioned appendix on Chilean language, Molina also adds an "Index of some Chilean verbs" (*Compendio de la historia civil,* 361–76) and a "Catalog of writers on Chilean matters" (377–82).[97] The decision to include such appendices is not unusual in Spanish American eighteenth-century historiography (think of the dissertations that Clavigero added to his *Historia antigua de México*). However, in this particular case the idea is not to actually espouse the study or much less the adoption of indigenous language, but rather to invoke the idea of it in order to link Araucanians with a criollo, cosmopolitan reader and with other Amerindian groups more commonly associated with monumental civilization. In light of this goal, it's worth noting that the appendices are preceded in the Spanish edition by two tables or graphs: one listing the names, locations, and makeup of various militia units; the other listing all Fransciscan missions operating in 1792—both added by Nicolás de la Cruz y Bahamonde when he translated the *Saggio sulla storia civile* into Spanish for publication in 1795. In these editorial supplements, military men and missionaries vie for the authority to represent imperial Spain. But in the body of the text, Molina seems to be making a move away from these more hierarchical or oppositional aspects of colonial administration in order to focus on *parlamentos*—a form of linguistic engagement that has the potential, at least, to function in a more horizontal and collaborative manner.

IX. *"Una arenga bien entendida"*: *Parlamentos in action*

Parlamentos are moments in which military force and language meet. Taking place within the larger context of bloody and unrelenting conflict, they represent pauses in the conflict during which the Araucanians debate among themselves, quite eloquently, issues of self-governance and military strategy.[98] The long descriptions of the Araucanian *parlamentos* that appear both in Ercilla's epic and in Molina's history represent a textual space where the positive and negative elements of the Araucanian warrior are brought together, or rather where the positive qualities of eloquence and rationality are meant to cancel out the negative ones of savagery and ferocity.

The *bon sauvage* in reasoned dialogue with a European interlocutor is a familiar Enlightenment narrative device employed to challenge conventional wisdom about the superiority of European customs.[99] But these dialogues are, by their very nature, exceptional exchanges involving exceptional individuals—staged, fictionalized encounters with a philosophical or ethnographic focus. Molina, however, puts Araucanians first in dialogue with each other, and then with their Spanish and criollo counterparts. His focus is historical rather than philosophical; the *parlamentos* he describes always occur in a specific place and at a specific moment. When Molina first mentions *parlamentos* in book 2, rather than explain the practice in general terms, he moves from the ethnographic to the historical, eschewing the chronological organization of his history to speak instead of a particular *parlamento* that took place in 1723 to resolve a recent outbreak of hostilities between the two nations. In his account Molina oscillates between narrating an ahistorical present and a very concrete historical instance. Subsequent chapters demonstrate that many of the particular features of the 1723 encounter can also be used to describe *parlamentos* more generally.

The 1723 *parlamento,* Molina explains, took place on an open plain—a sort of no-man's-land between the BíoBío and Duqueco rivers that served as territorial boundaries for Spanish and Amerindians. Both groups sent large delegations, headed by "Ulmenes" (for the Araucanians) and by an unnamed "Spanish President." In a ceremony symbolizing future friendship, the *bastones* (staffs) of the Spanish and Araucanian leaders were bound together, after which an Araucanian orator presented a cinnamon branch and delivered "in Chilean language a very well understood declamation." This was followed by a similar speech by the Spanish representative. Both remarks were duly translated so that all might understand the exposition of the causes of the war and conditions for maintaining the peace. Treaty provisions were hammered out and ratified, and the process was sealed by the sacrificial roasting of Chilean *camellos* (llamas or alpacas, presumably), the exchange of gifts, and a communal meal (*Compendio de la historia civil*, 81).[100]

The Araucanians' ability to negotiate effectively with the Spaniards represents a marked departure from earlier instances of failed or vexed intercultural communication that are frequently recorded in the chronicles of the Spanish conquest, beginning with Columbus and the infamous *requerimiento* (literally, "requirement"), the legal document read aloud in Spanish to Amerindians that laid out the reasons for submission to the Spaniards and the consequences of refusing to do so. Tzvetan Todorov's insistence in *The Conquest of America* that the Spaniards were masters of rhetorical improvisation has been met with justified resistance on the part of many scholars of colonial Spanish America, but the larger point—that Amerindians often engaged the Europeans at a notable rhetorical and legal disadvantage—certainly holds. Even so, eighteenth-century Amerindians, particularly those in strategic frontier zones, were often able to leverage their interests with Spanish and criollo administrators as they shifted their focus from conquest to defensive war, and to commercial and demographic expansion.[101] Molina's emphasis on Araucanian success in diplomacy at different moments in Chilean history is part of this larger picture, and his choice to introduce the practice of *parlamentos* by means of a recent example is not insignificant.

Molina's description of a 1557 meeting between Spaniards and the Araucanian representative Millalaulco (included later in the *Compendio de la historia civil*) can then be understood in this broader context. When he identifies the Araucanian envoy sent by Caupolicán to negotiate an agreement with the newly arrived governor of Chile, Don Garcia Hurtado de Mendoza, Molina uses the honorific *embajador* (ambassador) to convey the importance of Millalaulco's status and mission (*Compendio de la historia civil*, 171). Millalaulco speaks first, "expressing in a few words the desire of his people to collaborate in order to establish an honorable peace" (172). Both sides emphasize their willingness to negotiate not because they fear the enemy's power, but rather because they are motivated by a humanitarian desire for peace. Both sides also use the meeting as an opportunity to assess the enemy's strength and to display their own military might. Both sides are talking peace while preparing for war, which they clearly consider to be inevitable. The chapters that conclude book 3 chart the fortunes and misfortunes of Spaniards and Araucanians, closely referencing the concluding cantos of Ercilla's *La Araucana*.[102] These chapters, as well as the opening chapters of book 4, are marked by a sense of resigned weariness on the part of the narrator. He knows, as the protagonists themselves could not, that the periods of apparent calm would not be sustainable, and that none of the Spaniards who arrive from the metropolis to subdue and govern these peripheral territories had any real understanding of the people they hoped to conquer. So it becomes even more important that the reader understands *parlamentos* by having been introduced to a successful eighteenth-century example.

With the advantage of hindsight, Molina is aware that winning one battle against the Araucanians will not mean definitive victory for the Spaniards: "These repeated victories, for which the Spaniards congratulated themselves so much, were the prelude to the most lamentable disasters that were ever suffered in that kingdom," he notes, referring to Spanish victories in Mariengu and Tucapel in the late sixteenth century (246–47). His account at the beginning of book 4 of the opening years of the seventeenth century gives the reader some idea of how much war has been transformed from its earlier epic phase. More and more, rival European powers played a role in the conflict, as when the Dutch sacking of the island of Chiloe in 1600 wiped out the Spanish garrison there (256).[103] Defensive fortifications became increasingly important along the frontier, replacing earlier Spanish settlements that had been abandoned. Hunger beset the inhabitants of the few remaining Spanish cities, and intermarriage between Spaniards and Indians led to growing numbers of mestizos, whose allegiances were often unclear.[104] Molina sums up the situation: "And so were destroyed, in the space of a little more than three years, all the settlements that Valdivia and his successors had established and maintained through so many wars in the vast country that lies between BíoBío and the Archipelago of Chiloe, none of which have been rebuilt" (257–58).

In this discouraging context, only a negotiated peace held out any possibility of lasting success. Molina would have understood that in the seventeenth century, as in his own time, "to attempt to conquer all of the independent peoples throughout the edges of the empire would have tested Spanish resources beyond their limits."[105] So treaty negotiations become a strategic response on the part of both Spaniards and Araucanians. Molina's account of the negotiations leading up to the 1641 Treaty of Quillín occupies much of book 4 and anticipates later events that the historian will sketch out in his final chapter on the present state of Chile. The negotiations, pursued over several decades in the face of numerous setbacks, are presented as a pragmatic and deliberative approach to realizing imperial goals.

The process began in the early seventeenth century when a Jesuit missionary named Luis Valdivia traveled to Spain to persuade King Philip III that converting the Araucanians was impossible in an environment of continued war. Valdivia urged the king to find some way to forge a lasting peace with the Indians. He returned to Chile in 1612 with a royal letter addressed to the "Araucanian Congress" in which the king expressed his desire for peace and the establishment of Christianity in the region. (Molina, *Compendio de la historia civil,* 263).[106] Valdivia and the Spanish governor initiated discussions with Araucanian representatives regarding key items: the establishment of the BíoBío River as the frontier between Araucanians and Spaniards; an agreement for the mutual return of deserters; and a guarantee that missionaries would be permitted to preach Catholicism in the contested territories. Unfortunately, the peace negotiations unraveled when the Spanish-born wife of the Araucanian leader

Ancanamon fled to the Spanish encampment with her children and entourage, in effect seeking asylum with the governor and converting to Catholicism. Molina reports the outcome with remarkable understatement: "One cannot easily imagine the indignation that he [Ancanamon] felt, not so much because of the flight of the women but at the courteous welcome that the Spaniards gave them. Once he heard about that, he abandoned all thought of peace and requested that the governor return the women" (266).[107]

Tensions were exacerbated when, in a separate incident, three missionaries who had accepted an invitation extended by another Araucanian leader, Utaflame, to enter his territory were killed by a rival leader who greatly resented both the Spaniards and Utaflame. The result of all this, as Molina reports, was that war broke out again with even greater fury. Molina emphasizes the repercussions in terms of the loss of life and property and of the failure to secure a lasting peace, but the ensuing years of intermittent warring eventually left Araucanian and Spanish leaders once again disposed to negotiate (285).[108] A summit to negotiate a peace treaty took place in Quillín in January 1641.[109] The Treaty of Quillín, ratified by both sides, recognized the Araucanians as members of an independent nation with sovereignty over its territories:

> The Treaty of Quillín, with its implicit recognition of the independence of the crown's Araucanian "vassals," represented an exception to the Habsburg policy of requiring Indians to surrender, settle in reducciones, become Catholics, and pay tribute. This treaty was also exceptional because it was written rather than oral, ratified in Spain, and the only treaty with Indians to appear in a twelve-volume published compendium of treaties that Spain signed with other nations through the mid-1700s. (D. Weber, *Bárbaros,* 208)[110]

Molina's description of the Quillín peace summit repeats many of the same details he had reported in his account of the 1723 *parlamento:* well-articulated speeches by Araucanians and Spaniards, the sacrifice of twenty-eight *camellos,* and the presentation of a cinnamon branch as a symbol of peace (*Compendio de la historia civil,* 286–87). The ratification of the treaty was celebrated with more speeches and a banquet.

Molina had already explained that *parlamentos* were repeated and treaties renewed whenever a new viceregal administrator arrived from Spain, "because to proceed in any other manner would mean that the Araucanians would feel looked down upon, and for no other reason they would resume hostilities" (83).[111] What might be reduced to irrational behavior on the part of the Araucanians can also be seen as savvy realpolitik on their part—a reflection of their awareness that new political bonds must constantly be forged with Spanish viceregal administrators, who continually rotated in and out of their positions. Moreover, each *parlamento* occasioned a wide range of new commercial transactions, further consolidating political relationships through mutual trade.[112] The Treaty of Quillín included provisions stipulating that the Araucanians were to allow no foreigners to disembark on their shores, nor were they to offer aid or provisions to any foreigners.[113] These provisions reflected the growing awareness of both groups of signatories that Spanish-Araucanian hostilities were playing out in a larger context of inter-European imperial rivalries. Clearly, the treaty was designed not only to secure peace with the Araucanians, but also to enlist them as allies of the Hapsburg Empire. The Quillín accord eventually—perhaps inevitably—broke down, a development Molina attributes to those on both sides who for various reasons were invested in the continuation of hostilities.[114] But the importance of the treaty, historically and symbolically, cannot be overstated.

It is at this precise moment that the first volume of Olivares's history leaves off, and Molina must rely on contemporary sources, both written and oral, as he writes the closing chapters of his *Compendio de la historia civil.* There are important new developments involving the Araucanians during the eighteenth century that signal both a consolidation of earlier practices and a new emerging paradigm for Spanish-Indian relations in Chile. Molina's earlier representation of *parlamentos* as a protocol for rational diplomacy and governance anticipates his privileging of the role a new, domesticated Araucanian will play in subsequent *parlamentos* as Chile moves forward into the Bourbon imperial age.

Two events dominate Molina's account of Spanish-Araucanian relations in his penultimate chapter, which deals with the years 1722 to 1787: a new outbreak of war in 1766, and a *parlamento* held in 1773.[115] Both serve as concrete examples of Weber's argument that, Bourbon policies notwithstanding, events on the ground were frequently determined by the proclivities of individual players. As these came and went, the implementation of policies led sometimes to war and sometimes to peace. Thus, any attempt to read viceregal history from an exclusively metropolitan perspective, overlooking peripheral regions and peripheral actors, will inevitably result in a distorted picture. Those attempting to assess Enlightenment views of difference risk overgeneralization if they do not take into consideration the ways in which Spaniards and Amerindians met and dealt with each other in frontier contact zones like the Araucanian region.[116]

The first instance that Molina discusses involves a newly appointed and overly ambitious governor, Don Antonio Guill Gonzaga, who in 1766 decided to enlist the Araucanians in the building of Spanish cities. Wiser and more experienced colleagues tried to dissuade the governor from this project. The Araucanians, alerted by their spies to this potentially dangerous assault on their liberty and the privileges they had so assiduously negotiated, followed his plans with great interest and formulated their own plans in response.[117] Molina lays out the Araucanian strategy. First, they went along with the governor, making false promises in order to accumulate the tools and instruments used in the construction process. Only those directly implicated in the work order declared war; all others observed neutrality in order to be in a credible position to mediate in the conflict. It was agreed that in the event mediation proved futile, all would join in a general war, but not without first permitting all missionaries serving in the battle zone to leave.[118] In advance of the potential conflict, a *toquí* was elected to oversee provisioning and other preparations. Araucanians then engaged in a work slowdown that prevented any progress in the construction of cities and forts even as they continued to amass a great quantity of tools, oxen, and supplies. Finally, in a cunning inversion of the Biblical imperative to convert swords to plowshares, the Araucanian laborers used their shovels and hoes to attack and kill their Spanish supervisors (299). The governor then enlisted the Pehuenches as allies against the Araucanians; the strategy backfired, however, resulting only in a lasting enmity between Pehuenches and Spaniards. Disheartened by the failure of his enterprise, the zealous governor died soon after, but the conflict continued. By 1773, Molina calculates, it had cost the royal treasury one million seven hundred thousand pesos.[119]

Mindful of the potentially devastating consequences that continued conflict would mean for the region, both sides agreed to hold a convention in 1773. A fifty-year hiatus had transpired since the 1723 *parlamento,* and the imperial landscape had changed. Spanish imperial energies were stretched thin, and the Araucanians had become increasingly integrated into formal and informal commercial and social networks in the region.[120] The Araucanians requested that the congress be held in Santiago rather than on or near the battlefield; Molina adds that "the Araucanian plenipotentiary made another proposition that seemed even more extraordinary than the first . . . that his compatriots be permitted to have a stable Ministry in the very city of Santiago" (301). The request was extraordinary because it signaled Araucanian willingness to move off the battlefield and into the imperial city, establishing a diplomatic presence in the urban space. It reflected a strategic acceptance by the Araucanians of acculturation as manifested in civility and diplomacy. This was a request that could have been made by and granted only to an eighteenth-century domesticated Indian. Colonial administrators, after much debate, were persuaded of the utility of the proposition, "since in this way they could more easily respond immediately to any reciprocal differences" (302).[121]

Through the collapsing together of warfare and *parlamentos,* the Araucanians are civilized in Molina's recounting of sixteenth- and seventeenth-century events. This means, in turn, that the eighteenth-century Araucanians whose story he tells in the closing chapters of the *Compendio de la historia civil* can be represented as engaging in new and potentially productive interactions with Spanish and criollo administrators.[122] But as they enter into these engagements, Araucanians leave the territory they have dominated for centuries and enter a new metropolitan, imperial space where their claims to sovereignty will face new and different challenges. Imperial policies toward indigenous peoples were firmly grounded in a belief in their inevitable acculturation, driven by commerce and communication; these policies had the effect, over time, of diminishing the Araucanian agency we see at work in eighteenth-century *parlamentos.*

Even as Molina reports the Spaniards' enlightened acceptance of the Araucanian proposal to establish themselves within Spanish metropolitan boundaries, he expresses some ambivalence: "However, the two propositions, keeping in mind the way of life of those nations, can give rise to many interpretations" (302). Molina does not elaborate on what he means by the oblique reference to Araucanian customs and way of living, preferring to leave the matter open to multiple interpretations by his readers. Instead, he adds the detail that the Araucanian delegation was housed in the Colegio de San Pablo, which had been previously occupied by the Jesuits until their exile in 1767. The effect is to shift the focus away from questions about Araucanian suitability for sustained cosmopolitan engagement and remind the reader instead of past injustices suffered by Molina and his fellow Jesuits at the hands of Bourbon imperial authority. Even so, Molina reaffirms his support for good governance with a brief mention of the prudent and beneficent administration of the current governor of Chile as he moves to his final chapter, "Present state of Chile."

X. *"Estado presente de Chile": Imagined empires*

Endings are a dilemma for Molina, as they are for Oviedo y Baños. In his treatise on Chile, the eighteenth-century historian faithfully rehearses what's come before the moment at which he is writing (this, in fact, constitutes the bulk of the *Compendio de la historia civil*). At the same time, he is emphatic in arguing for the utility of his work in the present. Faced with the challenge of anticipating what might come next, however, his narrative reveals some uncertainty. For this reason, perhaps, Molina's final chapter strikes the reader as abbreviated or rushed—a hodgepodge of information and argument.

Molina begins by recapitulating the history he has just finished recounting, emphasizing once again the military successes of the brave Araucanians over the course of the previous three centuries. As he draws a verbal map of the territory currently occupied by the Spaniards, the reader cannot help but be struck by how much that territory has been reduced—an ironic observation, given Spanish attempts to confine Amerindians to *reducciones*. Molina explains the political, military, and religious organization of the territory at present. He describes the layout of a typical Spanish urban settlement, lamenting the fact that too few have been built along Chile's largest rivers. He is pleased to report that the population of "Spanish Chile" has been rebounding of late, and he offers a characterization of Chilean criollos who, like their counterparts elsewhere, are talented and morally upright. Lamentably, the state of education and the arts in Chile lags behind that of other viceregal regions, though Molina notes with pride that progress is being made in this regard. Araucanian customs, comparable in many ways to those of the Argentine gauchos, still prevail in rural regions. Blacks, mestizos, and *mulatos* are subject to slavery, but Molina insists that this generally means domestic labor; the plantations where "this unhappy class of people" labors in other parts of America and which, according to the historian, suffocate all sentiments of humanity have not yet been established in Chile (324). Molina includes a description of the region's commercial and agricultural potential, which is inhibited in his view by the lack of copper coinage (the only coins circulating in Chile at the time are minted from gold and silver). All these observations reflect a keen sense of Bourbon imperial priorities in fomenting domestic and transatlantic growth.[123]

This chapter is followed by a series of appendices: "Idea of the Chilean language," "Index of some Chilean verbs," and "Catalog of writers on Chilean matters" (all discussed earlier in this chapter). What role do these appendices play in the overall history? They are strikingly similar to the appendices in other eighteenth-century works (such as Clavigero's *Historia antigua de México* and Eguiara y Eguren's *Bibliotheca mexicana*) that represent attempts to put Bourbon Spain's eighteenth-century periphery on the map, politically and culturally. They also reflect Molina's interest in promoting his lost Chilean homeland and reveal the challenges of differentiating it from Araucanian territory.[124] Along with the preface, the indices and catalogs serve as a paratextual frame for the landscape of Araucanian Chile that Molina has mapped in his history and for his portrait of a domesticated Araucanian.

As we saw in the previous chapter, eighteenth-century historians were uneasy with earlier Hapsburg models of conquest.[125] New models of conquest required a new kind of exemplary Indian. Thus, Molina paints a portrait of an eighteenth-century Araucanian who is defined not only by ferocity in battle but also by a demonstrated capacity for reasoned, deliberative thought. *Parlamentos* are the evidence of this capacity.[126] Language is still the standard by which the development of Amerindian civilization is assessed, but in Molina's *Compendio de la historia civil,* spoken speech and oratory replace writing as its measure. While written histories of the Americas inevitably involved a somewhat defensive posture vis-à-vis the European historiographical tradition, the *parlamentos* that Molina describes are horizontal negotiations positing as their point of departure two equally engaged and empowered participants.[127] They take place in a particular time and place, and respond to a particular set of imperial circumstances and contingencies.

Eighteenth-century Chile is especially interesting in this context because of its character as a perpetual frontier zone whose contested lands continue to be spaces of transition and negotiation.[128] This creates a dilemma that the historian—looking both backward and forward—must resolve. Molina's dilemma, as we have seen, is that the intractable Araucanian conflict is a double-edged sword. On the one hand, it makes difficult, if not impossible, the evolution of the foundations of a Chilean nation. Historically, the continuing struggle to pacify the Araucanians created an extraordinary situation that disrupted normal population and settlement patterns in Chilean territory and led to the almost complete absence of historical sources—two factors that are key to the national development. As Molina notes, despite Chile's natural advantages and resources, the population growth that one might expect in the region has not occurred, primarily because of "the continuous war that has been waged since the beginning of the conquest to our present days between Araucanians and Spaniards, with few intervals of peace, swallowing up innumerable people on both sides" (*Compendio de la historia civil,* 37). It's ironic that the criollos in Chile, like the Araucanians, find themselves without the most visible signs of culture: population, urban architecture, and written historical records. But, on the other hand, the Spanish-Araucanian wars provide a compelling myth around which to organize Chilean identity and articulate an incipient national identity.

How do Molina's Araucanians end up functioning in Chilean history? Is Molina's Araucanian history (as opposed to Ercilla's, for example) a "usable past"?[129] Benedict Anderson observes that in the biography of nations, violent deaths "must be remembered/forgotten as 'our own'" (*Imagined Communities,* 206). But who is understood by that first person plural? Because of Chile's status as a frontier territory under constant attack, eighteenth-century historians there did not have the option of denying the existence of the contact zone.[130] In other eighteenth-century accounts of indigenous culture, Spaniards (or criollos) and Indians never come into contact; they are always at some remove from one another, separated by space, time, or the mythologizing process itself. Indians exist not as a political reality but as a forgotten exhibit in a national museum. My reading of Molina's portrayal of the Araucanians points to "the contradiction that lay at the heart of Enlightenment thinking on other peoples, of their being viewed simultaneously as exotic and familiar, exemplary and exploitable."[131] Molina's portrait of the Araucanians clearly reflects this contradiction. But I would argue that it also points beyond cosmopolitanism abstractions by providing us with a historically and geographically specific example of the eighteenth century's engagement with the concept of difference, played out on the ground, in conflict, commerce, and *parlamentos.*

The transformation of indigenous presence into an absence by means of an idealized abstraction becomes a constant in the context of nineteenth-century nationalist rhetoric in the Americas, North and South. When Eric Wertheimer uses José Martí's celebrated essay "Our America" to initiate a discussion of the role Amerindian figures of the conquest and colonial period play in shaping later foundational fictions in the United States, he also underscores "the problems of creating possessive pronouns like 'we' and 'our' when making narratives of history and nationality" (*Imagined Empires,* 1). Eighteenth-century cosmopolitanisms often imply an expansive and idealized sense of "we." The enthusiasm with which eighteenth- and nineteenth-century North American writers embraced Inca and Aztec figures in order to articulate an incipient national identity (and which Wertheimer traces masterfully in the writings of Philip Freneau, Joel Barlow, William H. Prescott, Herman Melville, and Walt Whitman) parallels the enthusiasm with which late colonial criollos—among them exiled Jesuits like Clavigero in the *Historia antigua de México* and Velasco in the *Historia del reino de Quito*—turned to those same cultures in order to claim a glorious pre-Hispanic cultural heritage differentiated from the Spaniards with whom they were increasingly coming into conflict. But if, as Wertheimer suggests, "for the cosmopolitan poet abroad, New World history was a kind of symbolic museum" (4), replete with exemplary artifacts such as Aztec calendar wheels or mummified Incas, we must also keep in mind that the museum harbored more problematic exhibits, like those devoted to Molina's warring Araucanians.

The Jesuit expulsions of 1767 led to a reinvention of America by exiled Jesuits that was driven in large part by nostalgia—by the memory of a place and space that had been lost to them.[132] The Jesuits' contradictory self-positioning (as authorized by and distanced from their experience of American reality) and their geographical (though by no means intellectual or cultural) isolation lead them into a double bind. They are faced with the difficult task of writing or rewriting colonial history in the absence of the documents and other sources that had informed their historiographical labors in the past. They must rely on the secondary accounts available to them in Europe (as does Molina, for example, with his fellow exile Olivares's *Historia militar*). They write in Italian or Latin and later translate their works in order to reach a broader audience. Their histories reflect the prejudices of their age. Even Ronan, Molina's most enthusiastic biographer, points to areas where modern research has confirmed the hyperbolic shortcomings of Molina's view of the Araucanians' degree of civilization, the sophistication of their language, and the portrayal of unmitigated enmity between them and the criollo population (*Juan Ignacio Molina*, 261–63).

There is a tension in Molina's historiographical project: the Araucanians are at the same time the source of Chile's epic history and the force that constantly threatens to prevent it from being written. Molina must contend with a double and at times conflicting imperative: to relegate the Araucanians to the space of history (that is, to the past) while inscribing them in Chile's present and future. Despite the divided heroic image of the Araucanians—and, in fact, of Amerindians in general in the eighteenth century—as barbarians and noble savages, Araucanians in Molina's history are neither marginalized nor romanticized nor consigned to a distant and petrified past.[133] The author moves inexorably in his history toward the present day and to scenes of enlightened and rational deliberations about political and commercial matters by Araucanians and viceroyal administrators, highlighting Araucanian agency in a highly localized and pragmatic eighteenth-century imperial context.[134] In subsequent formulations of a Chilean national narrative, however, Araucanian agency is erased: the constitution of 1822 extended Chile's borders to the Strait of Magellan and denied indigenous peoples, including the Araucanians, autonomous status.[135] Perhaps this is why Molina is most remembered and celebrated as a naturalist rather than a historian.

At the end of the day, all the actors on this Chilean stage are repatriated and domesticated in one way or another—Molina as well as the Araucanians—as nineteenth-century nation building invokes the pre-Hispanic and colonial periods.[136] This attempt, driven by an appropriating kind of nostalgia, brings expanded and much-debated opportunities for displaying Amerindians: "In 1900, the Santiago newspaper, *El Porvenir,* got wind of a plan that 'certain entrepreneurs of spectacles' were preparing to take a group of Araucanians to the Grand Exposition in Paris. 'What national interest does it serve,' the newspaper wondered, 'to cart around, in order to exhibit in Paris as a sample of Chile, a handful of Indians who are almost savage, brutalized, degraded, and repugnant in appearance?'"[137] The newspaper's query makes clear that by the beginning of the twentieth century, Araucanians are positioned outside of modernity and national self-image. Relegated to the metropolitan margins, they are denied their power to speak and can only signify through their physical appearance. Refuting this marginalization is the project of current-day Mapuches; the continuing role that the Mapuches play in contemporary Chilean political life reminds us of the significance of Molina's delicate balancing act.[138]

Molina closes the *Compendio de la historia civil* with the following challenge to his readers: "Let us be impartial and confess that all nations, be they American, European, or Asiatic, have been similarly in the savage stage, from which none has had the privilege of exempting itself" (359). These words represent a succinct formulation of his view of the universality of stadial history and of his efforts to bring together Araucanians, Spaniards, and criollos in Chilean territory on Bourbon Spain's imperial map. Thus, Molina's eighteenth-century domestication of his Araucanian subject might well be seen as an anticipation of Pogo's ironic pronouncement: "We have met the enemy and he is us."

CHAPTER THREE

Domesticating Nature

Félix de Azara's *Viajes por la América meridional* and Other Writings

Es desgracia de la Historia Natural, que todos quieran votar
en ella, y que a todos se haya de contestar.

[It is the misfortune of Natural History that all want to have
their say, and all must be answered.]

Félix de Azara, *Apuntamientos para la historia natural
de los quadrúpedos del Paragüay y Río de la Plata*

I. *"Los objetos que me presentaba la Naturaleza": Azara as accidental naturalist*

In 1781 the Spanish Crown dispatched the Aragonese military engineer Félix de Azara to the Río de la Plata as part of a commission charged with resolving an ongoing border dispute with the Portuguese in that region.[1] Azara would spend two decades in South America, during which time he compiled a wealth of detailed cartographic, ethnographic, geographic, zoological, and botanical observations. Although he had no formal training in natural history, his writings reflect a sustained corrective impulse with regard to earlier Spanish chroniclers, including Alvar Núñez Cabeza de Vaca, and philosophical natural historians, most notably George-Louis Leclerc, Count Buffon. Azara's voluminous treatises, which were published both in the original Spanish and in translation throughout Europe, proved highly influential in enlightened debates about nature in the New World.[2] For example, Charles Darwin refers repeatedly to "the high authority of Azara" in *The Origin of Species* and *The Voyage of the Beagle*, quoting at length Azara's meticulous observations of the fauna of the Southern Cone and echoing his interest in the domestication of feral animals (*Voyage of the Beagle*, 71).

Azara and his various interlocutors took part in a transatlantic exchange on the philosophy and practice of natural history that both reinforced and rewrote imperial thinking about the New World, particularly with regard to the relationship between metropolitan centers and peripheral borderlands that provided the urgent background for the work of Azara's commission. Spanish-born, but having lived for many years in America, Azara is an example of the phenomenon that Ralph Bauer has called "circum-Atlantic triangulations" ("Atlantic Triangulations," 7–8). Azara engages in exchanges that are cultural and textual as well as material, commercial, and political, linking Spain, the rest of Europe, and the Americas. He is at the same time an imperial agent, a scientist, and a propagandist, and he blurs the frequently overstated distinction between Spaniard and criollo.[3] The challenges he experiences in negotiating the difference between natural and political boundaries are repeated and reflected in the epistemological challenge of incorporating the nature of the New World into traditional natural history and emerging national polities.[4] In Azara's work the contested ground of the Río de la Plata region becomes fertile territory for an emergent narrative that attempts to articulate enlightened science in a local borderlands context.

Azara's experiences in the region of the Río de la Plata reflect a gradual move from imperial conquest and expansionist border disputes to more domestic concerns. Azara negotiated—literally and figuratively—between Europe and the Americas, between Spain and Portugal, and between what would become Brazil and the Spanish American republics of Argentina, Paraguay, and Uruguay. Most importantly, he negotiated between different ways of observing, knowing, and representing nature. A careful reading of Azara's writings—not only his treatises on natural history but also his extensive official correspondence and memoranda—tells us a great deal about the articulation of a particular kind of eighteenth-century criollo epistemology, grounded not so much in national origin or received tradition as in lived experience and local expertise.

Azara was born in Barbuñales, Aragón, in 1742.[5] His parents hoped that he would follow in the footsteps of his older brother, Nicolás, who had already begun what would be a spectacularly successful diplomatic career.[6] But after studying history, law, and philosophy at the University of Huesca, Félix de Azara began training as a soldier and military engineer, first at the Regimiento de Infantería in Galicia, and then at the Academia Militar in Barcelona. In 1767 he was named infantry lieutenant and engineer in charge of boundary delineations and participated in the reconstruction of the main plaza in Mallorca.[7] After he was badly wounded in 1775 during Spain's Algerian campaign, a long and arduous recuperation slowed the pace of his professional advancement.[8] Two years later, however, having been promoted to captain, Azara returned to active duty. He oversaw engineering projects in Gerona and Guipuzcoa and was named to the newly founded Real Sociedad Económica Aragonesa de Amigos del País (Royal Aragonese Economic Society of Friends of the Nation). Azara was the model eighteenth-century man of arms and letters, and his carefully plotted career trajectory in the Spanish military made him an ideal candidate to survey one of the most highly contested frontier areas of Bourbon Spain's imperial territories in the Americas.[9]

On October 1, 1777, Spain and Portugal agreed to the signing of a new border treaty, the Preliminary Treaty of San Ildefonso. This treaty was to serve as a starting point for efforts by Azara and his commission to rationalize the border between Spanish and Portuguese territories in the Americas that had been drawn originally—and infamously—by the Treaty of Tordesillas in 1494. Dis-

putes soon erupted on both sides about whether the Treaty of San Ildefonso
was binding or transitory, and despite their initial acceptance of the terms of
the treaty, the viceroys of Brazil and Río de la Plata resisted complying with the
demarcation contingencies.[10] The tense situation of conquest and settlement in
the South American borderlands led to continuing conflicts between Spaniards
and Portuguese, both of whom wanted a clear commercial route to Potosí and
control of the Río de la Plata. Spain's interest lay not so much in conquering
new territories as competing with rival European powers to ensure prosperity
for her citizens. This change was, as Pagden has observed, a shift that characterized not only the transition from Hapsburg to Bourbon rule in Spain but also
the European eighteenth century more generally (*Lords,* 73).[11] Thus, the ensuing
wrangling amounted to a tamer, bureaucratized version of earlier conflicts.

Azara, who was among a number of Spanish officers named to complete the
demarcation, traveled from San Sebastian to Lisbon and then on to Rio de Janeiro in 1781. After meeting with the Portuguese viceroy Luis de Vasconcelo y
Souza, the Spanish delegation continued its travels, first to Montevideo, where
they met with Juan José de Vértiz y Salcedo, viceroy of the Río de la Plata, and
then to Buenos Aires, where they met with the governor of Río Grande de São
Pedro.[12] Azara would later note in his diary that the instructions they received
from the governor were vague and incomplete.[13] Azara spent his first thirteen
years in the Americas traveling throughout what is now Paraguay. He visited
a number of Guarani Indian and missionary settlements and traveled to the
Iberá Lagoon as well as the cities of Candelaria and Corrientes before returning to Asunción in 1788. Subsequently, he traveled throughout the region of
the Yaguarey and Corrientes Rivers to establish borders and inspect Portuguese
forts in the province of Chiquitos. He was later charged with the reconnaissance
of the southern frontier marked by the Paraná and Paraguay Rivers, and sent to
survey the territory inhabited by the Chaco Indians and map the territories of
Córdoba, Salta, and Mendoza.[14]

Azara's official responsibilities included making periodic official visits to
Spanish settlements (traveling throughout the region by horse and canoe), surveying the territory, producing maps, and negotiating a new treaty with the Portuguese. However, Azara and his colleagues were repeatedly thwarted in their
mission by faulty instructions, breakdowns in communications, and delays occasioned by the Portuguese, who proved notoriously averse to showing up for
the scheduled negotiations. As deliberations with the Portuguese dragged on,
Azara came to see mapping, collecting, and measuring the natural environment
as both a pleasant diversion and a productive way of occupying his time. These
activities not only provided a welcome distraction from the vagaries and frustrations of his administrative reponsibilities, but also led to increasing familiarity with the territory. As Azara felt more and more at home in his surroundings,
his growing mastery of the region contributed in significant ways to his role as
representative of the Spanish Bourbon Empire, even as he was blocked from
carrying out the specific duties associated with the demarcation delegation.

As all-out war with the Portuguese threatened in 1801, Azara, who was in the recently founded settlement of San Gabriel de Batoví, received an official communication from the royal palace in Aranjuez recalling him to Spain and instructing him, before leaving, to surrender "to a Person of complete confidence all Papers and other materials relative to the establishment of the border with Brazil for which he had been commissioned years earlier; and also to give such Person custody of all materials respective to the three Kingdoms—Mineral, Vegetable, and Animal—which he had collected with his indefatigable curiosity."[15] The fact that the instructions gave equal weight to safeguarding both Azara's labors with regard to the border negotiations and his explorations and experiments in natural history is eloquent testimony to the high regard that his work in both areas enjoyed in metropolitan circles in Spain and beyond.

Upon his return to Spain, Azara traveled to Paris for a long-awaited reunion with his brother, Nicolás, then serving as Spanish ambassador to France. He spent two years there doing research at the Muséum National d'Histoire Naturelle and consulting with other natural historians living in France.[16] These connections would later prove extremely useful for the publication and dissemination of Azara's writings. The visit ended with Nicolás's death in 1804, at which time Azara returned to Spain. In 1805 he was named to the Junta de Fortificaciones y Defensa de Ambas Indias, a military unit responsible for the construction of defensive fortifications for the Spanish Empire. Three years later, in 1808, Azara retired to private life in Barbuñales but was almost immediately called out of retirement following the Napoleonic invasion of Spain. After the war, Azara remained active, maintaining a lively correspondence with numerous friends and colleagues and writing several reports for the Real Sociedad Económica de Amigos del País, until his death in 1821.

Azara was an accidental naturalist—a career officer who found himself in the wilds of South America with a few cases of scientific instruments and a great deal of time on his hands. In this regard he is perhaps typical of his age: "In some senses the eighteenth century rather witnesses the 'amateurization' of science; natural history is the creation par excellence of amateurs, and there is nothing incongruous about the conjunction of amateur with high-quality science."[17] Azara, keenly aware of his lack of formal training, explained his transformation from military man to scientist merely as the inevitable result of frequent delays, which led to a desire to put his time to some good use, using his professional cartographic skills and his natural curiosity.

Azara complained constantly about the isolation and loneliness to which he was condemned, plaintively describing himself as "a soldier who had never looked carefully at an animal until now. I have neither books nor the means to acquire information and instruction. I am an original naturalist, who doesn't even know the right vocabulary, and many of my notes are taken without a chair, table, or bench."[18] In the letter of May 16, 1802, in which he dedicated *Apuntamientos para la historia natural de los quadrúpedos del Paraguay y Río de la Plata* to his brother, Nicolás, Azara compares, not without some bitterness, the different paths their lives have taken—Nicolás having held important government positions in Spain and abroad, while he has been forgotten even by his friends: "I have spent the best twenty years of my life in the far-off corner of the Earth, forgotten even by my Friends, without books or rational discourse, and traveling continually through deserts and immense, fearsome forests, communicating only with the birds and the wild beasts" (*Apuntamientos . . . quadrúpedos,* n.p.).[19]

Azara's complaints about his isolation notwithstanding, he wrote constantly.[20] In fact, the furious pace of his composition seems to have developed in inverse relation to the progress of his commission. Azara's many works include *Apuntamientos para la historia natural de los quadrúpedos del Paraguay y Río de la Plata* (Notes for the natural history of the quadrupeds of Paraguay and Río de la Plata; hereafter *Apuntamientos . . . quadrúpedos*) and *Apuntamientos para la historia natural de los páxaros del Paraguay y del Río de la Plata* (Notes for the natural history of the birds of Paraguay and Río de la Plata; hereafter *Apuntamientos . . . páxaros*), both geographical and zoological studies following up on and critiquing Buffon's research.[21] Their publication history is complicated. Azara sent *Apuntamientos . . . quadrúpedos* as a work in progress to a French colleague who published it without consulting with him, a source of considerable distress for Azara.[22] Azara's *Descripción e historia del Paraguay y del Río de la Plata* (Description and history of Paraguay and Río de la Plata) was published posthumously by Azara's nephew in 1847, but is better known as the *Viajes por la América meridional* (Travels through South America).[23] The first part of this work is devoted to the geography, flora, and fauna of the region, while the second examines its indigenous inhabitants, including their conquest by the Spaniards and subsequent pacification and government, before concluding with an abbreviated chapter on the discovery and conquest of the Río de la Plata and Paraguay. Other diverse writings by Azara were collected and published in Buenos Aires in 1943 under the title *Memoria sobre el estado rural del Río de la Plata y otros informes* (Memorial on the rural state of Río de la Plata and other communications).[24]

Although Azara (like José Ignacio Molina, the Jesuit who wrote on the natural and civil history of Chile) was frequently frustrated by his lack of control over the different translations and editions of his work, his writings enjoyed better dissemination in Europe than those of many of his Hispanic contemporaries, such as the Spanish naturalist José Celestino Mutis.[25] Azara seems to have published on his own, with his own money, and without any kind of official Spanish support. He enjoyed the friendship and collaboration of the well-known French naturalist C. A. Walckenaer, who was responsible for the 1808 annotated French edition of *Viajes,* the *Voyages dans l'Amérique méridionale.* The close relationship between the two Azara brothers also had positive repercussions, since the siblings complemented each other professionally and their connections served both science and empire. Nicolás's prominence in the Spanish Bourbon court and in enlightened circles in Paris helped to extend Félix's reach as a natural historian and to expand what Antonio Lafuente and Nuria Valverde would call his "technoscope," the "network of signs, symbols, patronage, and conventions of representation . . . that depends on empire and at the same time underpins it" ("Linnaean Botany," 134). The number of editions and translations of Azara's writings that appeared during the eighteenth and nineteenth centuries attests to a lively transatlantic exchange on scientific matters in which Spain and Spanish America participated fully.

The reader notes throughout Azara's work an increasing level of comfort and mastery with regard to the objects of study.[26] The author begins to make frequent use of the possessive when referring to his observations of flora and fauna, writing of "my quadrupeds" and "my birds" (*Viajes,* 1:300–301). The grammatical marker of possession signals a process of domestication that occurred as Azara mastered his environment through productive observation and study, a process I will explore later in this chapter. His frequent meditations on species development and dissemination strike a proto-Darwinian note. Likewise, his musings on the spontaneous cultivation of certain crops reflect both his critical view of the region's inhabitants and his interest in pragmatic uses of the knowledge he is acquiring. These are also issues to which I will return.

Azara was an engaged and interested participant in debates about nature in the New World, as demonstrated by the appendix in the *Viajes* on the birds of Paraguay and the Río de la Plata. In this appendix, which will be more fully developed in his *Apuntamientos . . . páxaros,* Azara draws on his own observations to refute Buffon's contention that Old World birds are not to be found in the New World.[27] Surrounded by the raw material of natural history and balancing between lack and excess, Azara charts a new kind of discovery and conquest. At times, the author confesses, he is not sure whether what he is describing is new or has already been discovered and reported by others. In his isolation he can only "make reconnaissance, which even if it is never of any use, will entertain me in my leisure," as he confesses in a letter to the viceroy (*Memoria,* xxvi).

At the same time that he was recording his observations of his natural surroundings, Azara was engaged in a voluminous and charged correspondence with peninsular and viceregal authorities that has been collected in the volume *Memoria sobre el estado rural de Río de la Plata y otros informes.* This correspondence includes a number of political and economic documents that become an archive of the border disputes and complement Azara's reflections on natural history. Which is the "true history" of Azara's expedition—the observations of the accidental naturalist, or the political and economic arguments, alternately angry and despairing, of the soldier turned bureaucrat? Each must be read against and through the other; both are domesticating discourses that spring from Azara's firsthand familiarity with his subject.

Like the other authors discussed in this book, Félix de Azara has been all but forgotten in the larger story of Spanish American literary and cultural history. One biographer, Enrique Alvarez López, laments, "Among the most glorious figures of Spanish science, Félix de Azara is, if not one of those completely forgotten then one of those insufficiently known, this lack of recognition being even more surprising given that his life can serve as a magnificent example of the virtues of our people, and his character and patriotism combined make him deserving of the admiration and devotion of all Spaniards" (*Félix de Azara,* 7).[28] Alvarez López's impassioned claims for Azara's place in Spanish posterity may, in fact, suggest a clue regarding his relative obscurity. Although Azara is Spanish (more specifically, Aragonese), he spent the most productive years of his adult life in the Río de la Plata region, and his publications all deal with the flora and fauna of the Southern Cone. Thus, Guillermo Furlong included Azara in his 1948 volume on Argentine naturalists of the Spanish colonial period, apparently by virtue of his interest in "*our* flora and fauna" (*Naturalistas argentinos,* 360; emphasis mine). Azara has also been claimed by Uruguayan historians and literary critics, as reflected by Gustavo Verdesio's inclusion of Azara in the Uruguayan canon.[29] Yet because he was born in Spain, Azara's name is omitted from other important works such as David A. Brading's exhaustively researched and comprehensive *The First America.* Azara might therefore be described as a "new Creole," to use Ralph Bauer's term—a European by birth who spends long periods in the Americas, sometimes remaining there and sometimes returning to Europe (*Cultural Geography,* 240). Azara challenges conventional notions of the antagonism between criollos and peninsulars. He is Spanish-born, but his writings represent an example of a hybrid epistemological project that depends equally on New World and Old World underpinnings.[30] His simultaneous roles as administrative representative for the Bourbon Spanish Empire and enlightened naturalist of the Río de la Plata resist the opposing nationalist loyalties that emerge in the nineteenth century and that become inscribed in canonical historical and literary accounts on both sides of the Atlantic. His project resists as well, I think, the facile charge of imperialist appropriation of American reality. Azara's name in Spanish—*azar* (meaning "chance" or "coincidence")—suggests the fortuitous and risky nature of his enterprise; he is conquered by nature even as he attempts to conquer it.

Azara represents a hybrid criollo subject who is epistemologically rather than racially or ethnically defined. That is, he is typical of the criollo subject who emerges from a particular combination of circumstances that may include country of origin, education and professional training, transatlantic travel, empirical observation, and familiarity with a wide range of enlightened thought produced both in Europe and in the Americas. Through his lived experiences and his writings, Azara represents the attempt of eighteenth-century writers in Spanish America to create their own discourse of authority in the process of shifting away from Spanish conquest and consolidation to settlement. He also represents the development of an emerging (though complex and continually renegotiated) sense of criollo identity in which scientists, bureacrats, and border disputes come to the fore against a backdrop of imperial domestication.[31]

Azara's double mission as Spanish engineer and amateur naturalist of the Río de la Plata must be set against the background of the rewriting of natural history in eighteenth-century Europe and the Americas and, more particularly, in the Hispanic world. Before turning to a discussion of Azara's explorations of the flora and fauna of the Río de la Plata, and the role that collecting and measuring play in his evolution as a natural historian, it is necessary to examine the ways in which the Americas became a much-debated proving ground for enlightened scientific theories generated in Europe.

II. *"Sin que hasta ahora se haya sabido caracterizar a sus diversas especies": Categorical imperatives*

From their discovery, the American continents presented a challenge for European natural historians: how to absorb, manage, and organize so much new information? As historians proceeded to address this challenge, the relationship between received knowledge and experienced knowledge would be inverted and renegotiated. If initially European writers struggled to reconcile what they found in and heard about the New World with what they had read about natural history, as time went on, local discoveries would lead to the comparison and integration of new empirical data.[32] In her book *New Science, New World*, Denise Albanese considers the way that discourse ultimately becomes the "contested ground" of natural history: "The conditions of intelligibility for a scientific ideology in the process of emergence are . . . discursive, foregrounding the issue of textuality, both because 'nature' is an ideological construct that exists in language, and because the figures who inaugurate scientific modernism must be considered as propagandists—agents, whether intentional or not, of a new discursive formation" (57). Those who, like Azara, write about the New World must negotiate contested ground on various fronts—discursive, political, and epistemological—and this is reflected in their writings.

Beginning in the sixteenth century, as the New World became a source of material resources (both mineral and natural), it served as a locus for an increasingly institutionalized collaboration between explorers, administrative officials, and entrepreneurs. Antonio Barrera-Osorio studies the often-overlooked importance of the Spanish American Empire to the early scientific revolution, and the foundational role the sixteenth-century Atlantic world played in the development of modern epistemological practices. As he points out, "from the point of view of the Spanish rulers and people engaged in the American enterprise, the accumulation of empirical evidence constituted a sensible basis for political and economic decisions and for dealing with the increased flow of things and information circulating in the Atlantic world" (*Experiencing Nature*, 6). Barrera-Osorio observes that in the texts of Gonzalo Fernández de Oviedo y Valdés and José de Acosta, "one can trace the role that empirical observation played in the disruption of the hegemonic authority of the classical texts of medieval humanism" (1–2). Both Oviedo y Valdés in his *Sumario de la natural historia de las Indias* (Summary of the natural history of the Indies; 1526) and Acosta in his *Historia natural y moral de las Indias* (1590) renegotiated the relationship between personal experience and collective knowledge, Oviedo y Valdés in the context of a rewriting of Plinian notions of diversity, Acosta by viewing New World nature as a means of studying the workings of God.[33]

Barrera-Osorio goes on to suggest that the institutionalization of these practices—what he calls "the early scientific revolution"—anticipates the seventeenth-century scientific revolution that would follow (*Experiencing Nature*, 2). Seventeenth-century science is perhaps best exemplified by Francis Bacon, who makes natural history central to his new philosophy. As Bacon argued, "It would, indeed, be disgraceful to mankind, if, after such tracts of the material world have been laid open which were unknown in former times—so many seas traversed—so many countries explored—so many stars discovered—philosophy, or the intelligible world, should be circumscribed by the same boundaries as before."[34] Bacon viewed the world, whose limits had been expanded as a result of fifteenth- and sixteenth-century voyages of discovery, as a fitting object for empirical observation and scientific study, and he urged his contemporaries to embrace a new scientific method for learning.

By the eighteenth century, the new discursive model was full fledged. Travel, and scientific expeditions more specifically, became a literal and philosophical point of departure, and written accounts of those journeys generated an enthusiastic readership. Benito Jerónimo Feijoo, the Benedictine essayist who is considered one of the leading thinkers of the Spanish eighteenth century, affirms the benefits of the publication of so many travel narratives: "There is no Region so remote that it is not frequented by many Europeans for reasons of commerce or missions. So one is no longer free to lie as before, because one finds someone at hand to set straight the lies of another, and considering the risks of being caught in a lie, each one tries to preserve his good reputation."[35] While the sixteenth-century traveler attempted to reconcile the natural world of the Americas with received epistemological models, the eighteenth-century traveler measured, classified, and deployed nature in the service of clearly defined pragmatic or utilitarian goals.[36] This transition is evident in the evolution of the impulse to possess or collect nature: Renaissance cabinets of curiosity, which were characterized by a glorious and chaotic promiscuity, gave way to museums of natural history, which were meticulously normatized, systematized, and controlled. For eighteenth-century "scientific Americans," curiosity no longer functioned as an end in itself but rather as a means to material and social progress through the expansion of scientific knowledge.[37]

The eighteenth century saw not only a veritable explosion of interest in scientific knowledge, but also a corresponding expansion—both in Europe's metropolitan centers as well as its far-flung peripheries—of the various activities and institutions dedicated to producing, ordering, and disseminating that knowledge. Ultimately, during this time of exploration, the propagandists for this new discursive formation of natural history established what in essence became a new "categorical imperative" in the form of the primacy of classificatory systems inspired by, though not limited to, Linnaean taxonomy.[38] This categorical imperative of natural history informed both the work done by naturalists in the field and the uses to which the epistemological and material fruits of their labors were addressed—all grounded, as Mary Louise Pratt reminds us, "within the totalizing, classificatory project that distinguishes this period" (*Imperial Eyes*, 28).[39] In fact, two methods of apprehending nature in all its emerging diversity—observing and ordering—had been in evidence and in dialogue with each other from the earliest attempts by Spanish chroniclers to describe the New World. Natural history writing in the Americas, as we have seen, had always involved a tension between the authority of received tradition and local conditions that challenged that authority.[40]

After the obscurantism and Tridentine dogma of the seventeenth century, the reform of eighteenth-century scientific activity in Spain was spearheaded by a relatively small intellectual elite whose faith in rational thinking and empiricism was matched by a commitment to utilitarian goals and reformist practices. During the reign of Charles III their investigations in the full range of the sciences and natural history—medicine, agriculture, botany, zoology, geography, chemistry, and mining—flourished with royal support.[41] Charles III's 1776 order regarding the establishment of the "Gabinete de Historia Natural" decisively articulates the convergence of royal and individual interests, and of new theoretical and practical approaches to the study of natural history:

> The King has established in Madrid a Cabinet of Natural History to bring together not only all animals, plants, minerals, rare stones, and everything that Nature produces in His Majesty's vast dominions but also all that might be acquired from foreign dominions. In order to complete and enrich the series and collections of the Royal Museum in each of these classes, the subjects in charge of the provinces and towns of the Spanish Kingdom should take care now and in the future to collect and send to the Cabinet of Natural History the curious specimens that they find within the districts under their control. (qtd. in Pérez Murillo, Casas Rivas, and Dueñas Olmo, "El interés," 60)[42]

Charles III also established Madrid's Royal Botanical Garden. He attempted, albeit unsuccessfully, to found a Spanish academy of science, and he sponsored a number of scientific expeditions that involved the participation of Spaniards and criollos, as well as European scientists from France, Germany, and other countries in a vast network of thinkers and practitioners.[43]

The collaborative nature of the many scientific expeditions launched during the eighteenth century—such as those led by Alejandro Malaspina, José Celestino Mutis, Alexander von Humboldt, and others—must be understood in a larger context of European rivalries and jockeying for strategic information about potential imperial interests in the Americas. Although the Treaty of Utrecht officially brought the War of the Spanish Succession to an end in 1713, Spanish territories in the Americas continued to be regarded as contested territories. They were seen as sites of potential political and commercial expansion as well as opportunities for more disinterested scientific exploration.[44] The Charles Marie de La Condamine expedition is a well-known case in point. Two Spaniards, Jorge Juan and Antonio de Ulloa, participated in that expedition. Depending on one's perspective, either they had been invited to collaborate with the Frenchman or they had been dispatched by the king to monitor the trip and defend Spanish interests.[45] International expeditions like La Condamine's often ended up being a "marriage of science and imperialism"; the "imperial eyes" of enlightened scientists imposed a European order on American nature through map-making, specimen gathering, and the naming of new species.[46]

Several important eighteenth-century developments help to explain what Pratt has called Europe's emerging "planetary consciousness": the growing importance of natural history and a turn to continental (as opposed to maritime or coastal) exploration.[47] Azara is a good example of these developments. His demarcation commission clearly represents the Bourbon Crown's shift away from an earlier focus on circumnavigation and the mapping of coastlines, both of which had been replaced in the eighteenth century by attempts to explore the vast interior American territories in a kind of second conquest.[48] Another important development was the growth of patriotic science, which was increasingly espoused and proclaimed by enlightened criollos and Spaniards on many occasions and in a range of contexts.[49] These articulations, grounded in local knowledge and hands-on experience, mediate between what is American and what is European. Thus, the figure of the "new Creole" scientist becomes a focal point for leveraging acquired knowledge to serve both local autonomy and imperial goals.[50]

III. "No he ceñido mis trabajos a la geografía": On the nature trail

An accidental naturalist without training or colleagues, Azara represents a departure from the model of the scientist-explorer affiliated with one of the internationally or nationally organized scientific expeditions that have received so much scholarly attention. Nor does he belong to the cohort of Jesuits who documented American flora and fauna before and in the wake of their 1767 expulsion.[51] Azara's perspective is somewhat similar to that of the seventeenth-century male European subjects who helped to launch scientific modernization—Albanese's "agents . . . of a new discursive formation." (*New Science, New World*, 57). Azara is a propagandist, both for Spanish imperial interests and for the natural world that surrounds him, but in an eighteenth-century context. A close and careful reading of his work—in this case, *Viajes por la América meridional, Apuntamientos . . . quadrúpedos,* and *Apuntamientos . . . páxaros*—offers us glimpses of how he implements a discursive proccess of domestication on contested ground, and it is to those texts that I turn now.

Once Azara is launched on his South American expedition, he devotes himself wholeheartedly to the activities of traveling—observing, mapping, measuring, collecting specimens of the natural world around him, and recording everything in copious notes and detailed journals. He produces a narrative of travel and observation, of measurement and cataloging that occurs in a parallel universe to that of his diplomatic correspondence and official meetings.[52] Azara's writings, like much of the flora and fauna he will study, have little in common with classical models of natural history. They rarely, if ever, reflect the Horatian attitude of quiet retreat and contentment that characterizes the vade mecum genre so popular among eighteenth-century Anglo-American farmers and gardeners. Nor does Azara find recourse in the Horatian simile "Ut pictura poesis," an idea that informed eighteenth-century appreciation of landscape gardens.[53] Azara's view is decidedly more prosaic, his intentions markedly strategic and pragmatic. Azara was not writing from a locus of aestheticized nostalgia; rather, he sent dispatches from the trenches.[54]

Azara's jottings retain the markers of time and place that situate his observations and experiences in a concrete location. For example, he notes, "In terms of the turtles, I should not omit that I caught two fishing one day in the Santa María River, near 30, 15' degrees of latitude" (*Viajes,* 1:123). He emphasizes that he is not interested in writing an autobiographical narrative or a novelistic account: "I have always tried to avoid the novelistic style; that is, to concern myself more with words than with things" (1:78). Even so, he very decidedly positions himself as the protagonist of his scientific adventures. Azara begins the *Viajes* with a lengthy introduction, explaining the circumstances that brought him to the wilds of South America. Promising not to dwell on the many dangers and costs associated with his travels so as not to discourage readers who might be interested in following in his footsteps, he offers instead a self-portrait of a curious and actively engaged observer (frequently using phrases such as "I have seen" or "I have found"). This engagement is the foundation of his scientific authority and a source of obvious pride, as when he describes his knowledge of a particular kind of crab that lives in the floodwaters near the port of Montevideo: "I have eaten these crabs, and I have found them to have the same color, the same size, and the same taste as European ones, and I believe that I am the only one to have eaten them, because nobody here pays any attention to them" (1:121).

Crabs may be familiar to a European reader, but other examples of flora and fauna present a picture of daunting variety:

> Finding myself in an immense country, which seemed unknown to me, ignorant almost always of what was happening in Europe, deprived of books and pleasant, instructive conversations, I could only attend to those objects with which Nature presented me. . . . Moreover, I could not avoid thinking that an isolated man like myself, overcome by fatigue, busy with geography and other indispensable concerns, would find it impossible to describe adequately such a great and varied number of objects. (1:70)

Azara's musings reflect his efforts to do justice to the impossible task of adequately describing the objects nature has put in his path. The textual and material collections resulting from his years in the Río de la Plata region reflect not only a changed mental and physical landscape but also a shift from earlier modes of bringing together and organizing objects.[55]

Wonder as a response to natural phenomena is replaced by the imperative of organized curiosity, as can be seen in the description of the Asunción River that Azara includes in the second chapter of his *Viajes.* Azara explains that having observed with astonishment the abundant water flow, he measured the width and depth of the river at a number of different points. He observed the velocity of the river currents by watching the speed with which a cotton boll floated downstream. By calculating how many cubic units of water passed downstream every hour, he was able to conclude that the Asunción River was twice the size of the Ebro (1:105).[56] The Aragonese engineer was thus able to channel his powers of observation and experimentation in such a way as to render the South American river measurable and comparable for his readers.

Other natural phenomena prove more challenging. Faced with the awe-inspiring spectacle of the Salto del Canendiyú, a breathtaking waterfall that spills into the Paraná River, Azara begins with a familiar trope as he suggests that only poetry can adequately describe the spectacle: "It is an awesome cascade and worthy of description by the poets" (1:107). Then, after making an attempt to reduce the force of its waters to measurements in cubic *toesas* (as he had done with the Asunción River) and its height to "Parisian feet," Azara slips into a description that is a hybrid of wonder and science:

> The dew or vapors that form at the moment when the water crashes against
> the inner rock walls and some rock outcroppings that are found in the path
> of the waterfall can be perceived at a distance of many leagues, in the form of
> columns, and nearby with the rays of the Sun they form different rainbows
> of bright colors and in which one perceives some movement of trepidation.
> Moreover, these vapors form an eternal rain all around the area. The sound can
> be heard from six leagues away, and the nearby rocks, which are so pointed that
> they tear one's shoes, seem to tremble. (1:108)[57]

To reach the waterfall, visitors must travel thirty leagues through the surrounding desert and then build a canoe from one of the large trees that grow on the riverbanks. Azara's account of the geographical distance the European visitor must traverse in order to reach the desired locale and of the laborious process of using local materials to construct the necessary means of transportation to reach the waterfall highlights the strangeness and grandeur of the cascading spectacles of America. There is, Azara insists, no possible comparison between Canendiyú (and other similar New World waterfalls that he has also seen firsthand) and European waterfalls. American incommensurability is absolute: "If one wishes to look for points of comparison, it is in America where one must find them, because in this part of the world the mountains, the valleys, the rivers, the waterfalls, in a word, everything is of such great proportions that objects of the same nature that could be found in Europe wouldn't seem to be more than miniatures or small copies of these" (*Viajes,* 1:110–11). To bring home his point, Azara makes reference to a number of American waterfalls, including the Salto de Tequendama in Colombia, Iguazú Falls, and Niagara Falls, many of which would later be celebrated by romantic poets.[58]

But the overall effect of Azara's trip to the waterfall is ultimately neither that of awe and wonder nor of imperial mastery. The "potentially destabilizing category of the sublime" cannot in Azara's experience be fully harnessed, but it can be domesticated through a careful process of observation, measurement, and dialogue with other scientific references.[59] We see this when he turns his gaze from the turbulent waters themselves to the rocks that for centuries have channeled the torrential force of those waters. Azara recognizes the importance for natural history of studying the particular characteristics of these rocks, but he confesses, "Unfortunately, I have no knowledge of rocks" (1:113). Although he is unable to conduct experiments with the rock formations (as he did with the river currents), the regret he expresses at not having sufficient knowledge to do so reflects a turning away from the awe-inspiring spectacle toward a more measured perspective. For Azara the domestication of nature is a work in progress.

Nature is a source of both infinite exoticism and potential utility. This is evident when Azara proposes to "speak at length of some trees that are notable for their utility or their strangeness" (1:135). Azara sees no conflict between these two characteristics, which are ultimately brought together by the pragmatism of the eighteenth-century gaze. His engagement with nature is consistently experiential rather than theoretical. Like many travelers to the Southern Cone then and now, Azara adopts the custom of drinking maté, whose utility, he insists, can only be appreciated by those who have tried it and know it well (1:142). But though he becomes an enthusiastic maté drinker, he prefers to observe as others sample the medicinal properties of local plants, explaining that since he is rarely ill, he has little interest in them (1:148). For instance, during a walk in the Paraguayan jungle with the governor's wife and daughter, Azara introduces the ladies to the much-vaunted effects of the "piñón purgante" (purgative pinenut). He explains that those who indulge in the sweet fruit fall victim to its purgative properties and are immediately wracked by violent vomiting. The governor's family is no exception. The reader can only imagine the diplomatic repercussions of Azara's hands-on lesson in natural history.

At times Azara clearly rejects the *Wunderkammer* tradition that, as many have argued, is both about the wonders of display and the power of possession.[60] Azara exults instead in the opportunity to study flora and fauna alive and in situ. He pities those who can see animals only as specimens in a much diminished state, like prisoners in some kind of display, "exhausted, plucked and dirty in cages or chained," or "in the cabinets where, in spite of all care, the injuries of time have much altered their colors, changing black to brown, etc.: no pelt, nor the best prepared skeleton, gives an exact idea of their form and measurements" (*Apuntamientos . . . quadrúpedos*, i–ii). As one of the fortunate few who has had the chance to observe firsthand the animals of the Río de la Plata region, Azara goes to great lengths to provide meticulously detailed descriptions of these animals for his reader. Azara's descriptions are the foundation of his sustained engagement with and contestation of the works of Buffon.

Key to this engagement are his concerted efforts to gather animal specimens to send to Spain. Although the transportability of animal specimens was more problematic than that of plants, Azara seems to have concentrated mostly on fauna rather than flora.[61] Azara frequently acknowledges the essential collaboration of colleagues and acquaintances who provide him with specimens, either as gifts or objects for purchase (he notes proudly that he has sent between six and seven hundred specimens back to Spain).[62] Don Pedro Blas Noseda—"my friend

Noseda," as Azara calls him—offers advice and often assists him in acquiring specimens (*Apuntamientos . . . quadrúpedos,* 323).[63] In the *Apuntamientos . . . quadrúpedos,* Azara refers to the *lanoso,* or sloth, with the following disclaimer:

> I haven't seen any except for this male, which D. García Francia presented me with in Paraguay, assuring me, as have others, that the female has a pouch similar to that of a Micuré [opossum], where it keeps its young. They gave it to me dead, and I think that is why it didn't smell bad. I made a description of it when I was not so informed as I am now, and putting it in *aguardiente* [a kind of brandy made from local ingredients], I dispatched it to the Royal Cabinet in Madrid." (221)

Azara also writes in the prologue to his *Apuntamientos . . . páxaros* that he initially tried stuffing his animal specimens in order to send them to Madrid until moths wreaked havoc with his careful efforts (ix). When the hot, humid climate foiled Azara's taxidermic efforts, *aguardiente* became Azara's preferred method for preserving his specimens, and he is pleased to report that smaller specimens preserved in this manner arrived in good condition. Azara's ingenuity in turning to local ingredients to meet the challenges of enlightened scientific inquiry is an example of how he adapted to his surroundings and made them his own.

In these and other notes we see not only Azara's commitment to continually revising and updating his conclusions about the flora and fauna of the Río de la Plata, but also his awareness of the relationship between natural history and empire in eighteenth-century Spain. Paula De Vos, who has studied various collections of specimens destined for the Royal Botanical Garden, the Royal Pharmacy, and the Museum of Natural History in Madrid, stresses that these collections reflect a long tradition of information gathering in the service of Spanish imperial interests.[64] The cases sent to Madrid were often filled with objects sent not by formal scientific expeditions but rather by individual imperial administrators, as in the case of Azara.[65] Azara's method for taking possession of nature is less an imperial appropriation of the kind evident in later writings than a reflection of his curious and interested immersion in his surroundings. When Azara refers to "my birds" or "my quadrupeds," the possessive marks his own domestication as much as that of his specimens.

Even though some individual experiments fail, Azara's project of domestication generally meets with success. Ironically, this success may help to explain the conflict that Azara encountered with the governor of Paraguay, Joaquín Alós. This incident is mentioned by many of Azara's biographers as an unfortunate complication in an otherwise illustrious career, and it seems that administrative and scientific rivalry may have had something to do with the governor's sudden change of heart regarding his Aragonese colleague. Alós at one point had proposed to Azara that they collaborate on a natural history of the province of Paraguay. The Crown granted permission for this joint enterprise on May 26, 1788, with a warning that the scientific work should not affect Azara's primary responsibilities with the border commission. But the project never went forward. Azara wrote a letter to Alós on July 13, 1788, to explain that he had not yet sent his field notes to his collaborator for lack of an assistant to copy them. As a goodwill gesture, he sent instead a box with eighty-four birds preserved in *aguardiente,* assuring Alós that he would continue to share specimens and data with him. This collaboration seems not to have been mutual, however, and the only tangible contribution that Azara mentions as having come from Alós was a bat that had been caught in the governor's house. Asín recounts that later, when the *cabildo* of Asunción honored Azara with the title "Most Distinguished Citizen of the City of Asunción," Alós became quite irritated and secretly ordered that Azara's map and description of the city be withdrawn from the municipal archive, where it had been deposited. When these orders became public, Alós tried to defend himself by accusing Azara of treasonous complicity with the Portuguese. The resulting scandal went all the way up to the viceroy and may have negatively affected Azara's career prospects for a time, until his name was eventually cleared.[66] In the final analysis Azara's reputation rests on his observations of the animals of the Río de la Plata and the numerous experiments in which the gaze of the empirical observer and the tools of the meticulous engineer come together.

IV. "He evitado siempre el juzgar por aproximación": Azara measures the world

As an engineer, Azara was familiar with a wide range of scientific instruments and brought many of them with him to the Río de la Plata region. He sometimes complains that he lacks the precise instrument needed to carry out a given task; for example, he notes that his thermometer cannot measure extreme temperatures of hot or cold (83).[67] Nevertheless, he boasts, "In my travels I have always avoided judgment by approximation" (*Viajes,* 1:65). Azara's efforts to apprehend his natural surroundings in the Río de la Plata are concrete, objective, and measurable.

Unlike what happened on many scientific expeditions to Spanish America, no illustrator accompanied Azara on his travels nor, as he confesses with chagrin, is he himself an artist.[68] Azara's voluminous writings were not initially supported by drawings or other graphic representations of the kind that proved so important in disseminating and popularizing New World flora and fauna.[69] As a result, he communicated those elements commonly represented through drawing or painting—form, color, similarity or difference, wonder—using other descriptive tools. Furthermore, he often framed those representations within a broader descriptive context, in the same way that an artist might surround a drawing of an eagle or a toucan with foliage or water.[70] At one point, Azara requested and received copies of the *planches enluminées,* or plates, that had been issued to illustrate Buffon's encyclopedia, but he complained that the illustrations were of such poor quality that they were almost useless (*Apuntamientos . . . quadrúpedos,* 190). As a result, the engineer Azara resorts to painting by numbers.

Azara's ability to take accurate and repeated measurements became a filter through which he experienced the flora and fauna all around him and by means of which those experiences were authorized.[71] Numbers mediate between his lived experience and the understanding of his metropolitan readers. As an indication of the importance of correctly evaluating those numbers, Azara begins the *Apuntamientos . . . quadrúpedos* with a note to the reader regarding his measurements: "The measures used are inches from the foot of the King of Paris" (xi). The clarification reminds us that at the time he is writing, scientists had not yet arrived at a point of standardization (although clear gains were being made in this regard), and that in order to be comprehensible and utilitarian, the New World still had to be measured in terms of the Old World.[72]

Mindful of this imperative, Azara provides meticulously precise measurements of all aspects of his animal specimens—height, length, circumference, length of the tail or ears, and so forth. This precision stands in marked contrast to the shifting fortunes of his diplomatic efforts, and it imbues his writings with a kind of quantitative aesthetic. Azara's description of an adult male *capibára* (or *capigüara*) will suffice to give a sense of his enthusiasm for measurement:

> Length 45 1/2 inches: no tail. Height front and back 19, but the talons retract. Circumference there, 32, and here, 36. The head is 8 1/4 long until the base of the ear, where it has a height of 6, because it is longer than it is wide. The edge of the ear in the anterior part consists of two straight edges, forming a fold that the rest of the ear doesn't have; its width is 1 1/2; and since it is very thick on top, the back edge has three soft waves, with little hair on the inside and none on the outside. Black whiskers, divergent, and 2 2/3. (*Apuntamientos . . . quadrúpedos,* 1:10)

In this account, minimal narrative elements combine with a profusion of numerical detail to sketch a portrait of the adult *capibára.*

The widespread use in the eighteenth century of the new Linnaean taxonomic system led to a particular descriptive rhetoric, in large part because Linnaeus's taxonomy was often meant to accompany the observation of actual specimens.[73] Pamela Regis argues that one of the advantages of the Linnaean system was its simplicity and portability: "The New World of exotic mystery, of distance-shrouded indistinctness, gives way to a sharp-edged, delineated, concrete description systematically and rationally related to the Old World" (*Describing Early America,* 14). Linnean taxonomy is characterized by its absence of verbs and is thus static and descriptive rather than active narrative (21). Azara's numerous anecdotes regarding his interactions with "his" animals serve therefore to activate Linnean discourse and to open a discursive space in which those wild animals are domesticated. In his description of the *capibará* and elsewhere in his notes, Azara provides a dizzying profusion of detail, calibrated to within a Parisian inch. Azara's precise descriptions were initially intended to accompany the specimens he gathered to send to Madrid. They became even more crucial when circumstances such as mold, humidity, or physical deterioration destroyed the specimens and rendered those shipments useless for the purpose of scientific study. In those cases, the measurements stand in for the specimens themselves.[74] In Azara's descriptions, the frequent numerical references interrupt the narrative flow that describes the scientist's experience. However, the fragmented discourse that results reminds the reader of the scientific activity in which the writer was engaged and on which the narrative depended.

Moreover, the precision of his measurements enables Azara to persuasively counter or correct a number of earlier writers, including José de Acosta and the Inca Garcilaso, in addition to his principal scientific interlocutor, Buffon.[75] Buffon, whose "infinite elegance" Azara acknowledges, is an important point of departure for the Spaniard (*Apuntamientos . . . quadrúpedos,* vii). But Azara went far beyond his precursor in describing American flora and fauna.[76] He directly engages Buffon in the prologue to *Apuntamientos . . . quadrúpedos:* having read the 1775 Spanish translation of Buffon's *Histoire naturelle, genérale et particuliere,* he finds it full of "vulgar, false, or mistaken information" and initially rejects the odious and difficult task of attempting to rectify its many errors—particularly given the fact that he does not have access to the authors cited by Buffon (v). Upon further reflection, however, Azara is persuaded by the importance of such a task.[77] Although he disagrees with Buffon's conclusions about many animals—panthers, wild boar, and wild horses among them—he also blames the travelers and naturalists on whom Buffon has relied for his information (vii).[78] It's worth noting that as Azara rewrites his European precursors, he appropriates and domesticates them just as he has done with his American animal specimens, as when he refers on numerous occasions to Buffon as "my Author."[79] Azara's possessive rhetorical gesture and his masterful obsession with precise measurement are evidence of the extension of the Spanish Bourbon Empire as it radiates out from the Iberian peninsula to its Southern Cone periphery and back again to Europe. At the same time, the homemade, improvisational nature of many of Azara's interactions with his new Río de la Plata world—for example, his fraught efforts to adequately preserve his specimens for shipment—reminds us that empire's reach sometimes exceeds its grasp. Azara's writings on natural history sound a cautionary note for the reader, warning that when a scientific text or specimen traverses the Atlantic, neither is likely to survive the crossing intact.[80]

Azara's use of the possessive also extends to the maps he produced of his various travels throughout the region: "The principal objective of my travels, as long as they were frequent, was to produce an exact map of those regions, because that was my profession and I had the necessary instruments" (*Viajes,* 1:63).[81] He refers on numerous occasions to "my map."[82] As we have seen, the charge of the demarcation mission was to negotiate the consolidation or—better yet—expansion of Spain's territories along the southern borders of Brazil (1:60).[83] Azara's interest in imposing order on the lands of the Río de la Plata stemmed in large part from his mission to survey those lands in order to draw a boundary that would convert terra incognita into imperial territory.[84]

Azara's cartographic practices took place on the ground and were determinedly referential and experiential; in other words, he was mapping places that he knew from experience.[85] He explains in detail his method for determining geographical positions using a compass. When the compass proved inadequate, he would send riders off on horseback and calculate the time needed for them to cross long distances in as straight a line as possible. He could then compare the times and trajectories. When surveying streams and rivers, he used a similar technique. Azara was interested in establishing as many control points as possible in order to minimize error; triangulation—which resolved the messiness of earlier geographical observations—served him well. As Matthew Edney argues, the new emphasis on cartographic representation through triangulation led to a shift in the eighteenth century away from narrative accounts and memoirs as validations of geographic data, since certainty was now assured by observational methodologies rather than by the experience of the geographer.[86] But rather than use triangulation merely as a mapping tool, Azara positioned himself as a fixed point of reference. This enabled him to triangulate between metropolitan and peripheral points of view and ways of knowing.[87]

We might characterize Azara's cartographic practices as a kind of reconnaissance, particularly given his training as a military engineer: "Reconnaissance—the purposeful movement through and examination of the world—was practiced by merchants, missionaries, civil and military officials, scientists, surveyors, and even tourists who all observed, examined, and documented the constituent features of the landscapes through which they passed."[88] Far from presenting his reconnaissance as unproblematic, however, Azara notes time and time again the resistance posed by the territory to the purpose of his mission. He is cognizant of the fact that maps function to flesh out his written commentary, much in the same way that his specimens flesh out his numerical measurements. But he is equally cognizant of the fact that neither map nor specimen can be fully understood and appreciated in the absence of his own mediating and domesticating discourse.[89]

IV. "Todo río es caudaloso": Border patrol

Azara's scientific mediations are complicated by the larger context in which he operates—namely, that of the border disputes with the Portuguese—and his triangulations are as much personal and political as they are cartographic. Pamela Regis explains in *Describing Early America* that travel accounts written by natural historians bring together two fundamental processes, collecting and observing, and two discursive modes, narrative and descriptive. The narrative mode locates a traveling subject as he or she passes along a chronological and spatial itinerary; the descriptive mode is used to define and fix the objects encountered along that itinerary. Azara employs both processes and both modes, as we have seen. But epistolarity represents yet another discursive strategy for Azara. Azara depends on letter-writing as a student of natural history, since his scientific interlocutors, both implicit and explicit, are to be found *ultramar*. He also turns to letter-writing as he attempts to carry out his administrative responsibilities. Thus, the "back and forth" of Azara's correspondence unfolds in a discursive space that is neither the timelessness of Linnaean taxonomy nor the quotidian, clock- and calendar-driven world of the traveler.[90] The contractual documents that were expected to result from Azara's commission failed to materialize, but they were substituted for by a constant chain of epistolary complaints, explanations, and suggestions contained in Azara's memoranda and missives—a paper trail that leads writer and recipient unerringly toward their shared imperial objectives.

Azara assumed responsibility for representing Spanish interests in the border negotiations at a crucial moment for the Spanish Crown, and his border commission had to negotiate among a variety of competing claims and interests. Spanish inattention had opened a space for Portuguese expansionism and colonization, effected largely by means of *bandeirantes,* informally organized expeditions that moved into the dense interior in search of gold and slaves.[91] At stake as well was control of the mouth of the Río de la Plata and the increasingly important trade—both licit and illicit—that flourished there. The Portuguese were understandably reluctant to enter into negotiations that almost certainly promised to limit their claim to territory they had already appropriated. Local Spanish officials and landowners (all of whom had a vested interest in permitting illegal contraband to continue circulating) apparently also colluded to stop—or at least slow—the progress of the commission.

The practice of imperial mapping is predicated on a sense of "one's own community as the natural center of the world, and by implication superior to the communities arrayed around that center."[92] But what was happening in the Río de la Plata region in the eighteenth century was complicated by realities on the ground involving a very long history of competing imperial powers. In a sense, Azara's "Portuguese problem" had its origins in earlier attempts to trace boundaries between Spanish and Portuguese territories in the Americas—namely, the series of bulls issued by Pope Alexander in 1493 and the 1494 Treaty of Tordesillas. Those attempts—at the same time solomonic, quixotic, and presumptuous—created the circumstances that eventually led to the territorial wrangling in which Azara was a committed if frustrated protagonist. Thus, the border negotiations that Azara was charged with bringing to successful resolution came with considerable historical baggage. Neil Safier, discussing the imperial cartography of the Amazon region, notes that Alexander von Humboldt complained about the Spanish and Portuguese rivalries being "vain territorial disputes" that had contributed to "the imperfection of the geographical knowledge which we have hitherto obtained respecting the tributary rivers of the Amazon" ("Confines," 134).[93] These disputes are as much a part of the background scenario for Azara's writings as are the trees and the riverbanks.

The result is that, in addition to his notes on natural history, Azara's writings include a large corpus of documents, letters, and memoranda related to his administrative responsibilities with the border commission.[94] These documents bear anguished witness to the delays experienced by the commission and incorporate the conclusions Azara drew from his experiences. Two sets of documents discussed here will provide an example: "Official and unpublished correspondence on the border demarcation between Paraguay and Brazil" (a series of letters dating from February 28, 1784, to March 17, 1795) and "Memorial on the border treaty of South America celebrated between Spain and Portugal in the year 1777 and on the disputes that have occurred in its execution" (written in 1805, several years after the author returned to Europe). These texts put in context two different versions of the demarcation mission. "Official and unpublished correspondence" is a one-sided, blow-by-blow account of the interminable wrangling that accompanied the demarcation mission; "Memorial on the border treaty" is a more organized account, shaped by Azara's retrospective view of the mission's ultimate failure.

"Official and unpublished correspondence" consists of forty-one letters Azara wrote to Don Pedro Melo de Portugal and to Don Joaquín de Alós (both of whom served as governor of Paraguay), to Viceroy Marqués de Loreto, and later to Loreto's successor, Nicolás de Arredondo. The letters, collected and published in *Memoria sobre el estado rural del Río de la Plata y otros informes,* offer a fascinating glimpse of Azara's travels and activities as head of the demarcation commission. They also provide the reader with evidence of Azara's increasing familiarity with the Río de la Plata region and with the development of his convictions regarding its potential for settlement and growth. Azara writes to Viceroy Loreto on August 12, 1784, informing the viceroy of his decision to supplement the narrowly defined mission of negotiations with the Portuguese with a broader reconnaissance of the territory in question (*Memoria,* 93). Here and elsewhere Azara minimizes the seriousness of his scientific observations, perhaps in part because of his awareness that he is at best an accidental naturalist. But the reader also suspects that the military engineer views scientific observation as an opportunity to survey the scene—to conduct a "reconnaissance" that might eventually prove useful in his treaty deliberations with the Portuguese. In other words, if Azara's administrative responsibilities provide an occasion for scientific activity, the reverse is also true: his scientific activities provide a pretext for furthering his administrative duties in support of the Bourbon Spanish Empire.

Azara assiduously pored over the existing agreements regarding the region and the maps that had been drawn up to substantiate them, recapitulating his understanding in a long letter that he writes to Viceroy Loreto on April 12, 1784. In that letter Azara underscores the region's economic potential, which he insists had been misrepresented in earlier reports: "It seems that the last demarcation delegation believed that these lands were hot, humid, unhealthy, prone to flooding, and useless for raising cattle; but the continued efforts by the Jesuits to establish themselves there, and the many towns and *reducciones* that have been founded and abandoned there, not because of the poor quality of the land but rather due to violence and fear of the Paulistas, lead us to form better ideas" (*Memoria,* 81–82). On June 11, 1784, he updates Viceroy Loreto: "I have nothing to add to my earlier missives, except that I wish to find myself in the territory to see things up close, because without this it is impossible to resolve with certainty many questions" (89). Days later, having heard nothing from the Portuguese, he proceeds with the reconnaissance.

His correspondence captures the many hardships and frustrations of this journey. The Portuguese prove elusive, although local caciques inform Azara that they are aware of the existence of a nearby Portuguese fort because they can hear gunshots when they go to the river to fish (83). Distances are hard to measure, and the names commonly used in the region do not always correspond to those stipulated in existing agreements. Moreover, European nomenclature often proves inadequate to deal with American nature.[95] For example, at one point Azara proposes to resolve a cartographic uncertainty by using a river to draw a new boundary line: "I will settle for looking for a river . . . that might serve as a boundary for these dominions without leaving neutral territory between them" (90). But Azara quickly learns the limitations of relying on a natural tool to articulate and realize political goals, when he attempts to bring a newly appointed viceregal administrator up to date on the work of his commission. In a lengthy letter that he writes on January 13, 1785, to Commissary General José Varela y Ulloa, Azara explains that the official instructions he had received referred somewhat ambiguously to the Igurey River as "the first large river" above the great falls on the Paraná River. Azara objects to this, stating that "I do not consider this to be well-founded reasoning, since it seems that the phrase 'large river' is very general, and in a rigorous sense it means nothing, since every river is by definition large" (99).[96] The exchange reflects the difficulties of mapping imperial intentions onto the natural landscape.

The logistics of moving his men from one location to another also take a toll, and the complications of climate, distance, and hostile indigenous tribes are compounded by the most basic questions about the task of the commission. Azara appeals to the viceroy for much-needed guidance regarding what he and his men are expected to accomplish, and how they are expected to proceed (98–99).

By the time Loreto is replaced by a new viceroy, Azara's communications have taken on a more substantive and less reactive tone. Having successfully familiarized himself with the region, Azara writes with authority and as an informed local to Viceroy Arredondo. Increasingly concerned with the territorial usurpations made by the Portuguese and with the commercial and military implications of Spanish concessions to these usurpations, his letters become more and more insistent: "I feel obliged to inform Your Excellency of some reflections prompted by my knowledge of these lands" (100). In a subsequent letter, written on February 13, 1791, Azara's sense of urgency is expressed in even stronger terms: "The zealous consideration for royal interests commands me to communicate to Your Excellency some reflections that agitate my spirit greatly in recent days" (104).

Although Azara's letters are often marked by a tone of officious mastery or righteous indignation, on July 30, 1791, he permits himself a rare moment of despondency:

> I do not know what ideas the Portuguese might have had to have delayed so many years in the life of one man in telling us that they would be coming; and after what they have done, I am afraid that the current century will pass without their showing up here. I leave aside how sensitive it is that I have spent the best part of my life and the most useful years of my existence uselessly; other-

wise I will have to request my retirement from this veteran project, as men are
not eternal. (120)

The emphasis on utility that permeates Azara's correspondence is typical
of Azara as an enlightened administrator, and this threat of resignation merely
rhetorical. Azara quickly recovers his equilibrium. The next letter he writes to
Viceroy Arredondo, on January 19, 1793, is a less agitated, clearly reasoned
summary of the results of almost a decade of labor by his demarcation commission, affording him the opportunity to bring that work to epistolary conclusion
even though the treaty negotiations had been inconclusive.[97]

"Memorial on the border treaty" is also a summary of those labors, but written retrospectively. Like Cabeza de Vaca in the *Naufragios,* Azara in both his
correspondence and "Memorial on the border treaty" carefully shapes his presentation of what was, by all accounts, a disastrous failure. Azara's overriding
strategy throughout the document is to lay blame squarely at the feet of the Portuguese delegation. The "Memorial on the border treaty" is an anti-Portuguese
diatribe predicated on the author's conviction that "there is nothing more evident than the falseness of anything alleged by the Portuguese" (*Memoria,* 53).
Azara holds the Portuguese fully responsible for the breakdown in the border
negotiations. Looking beyond that breakdown, Azara challenges the reader—
namely, his superiors in the Bourbon imperial court—to envision a bold and
promising future for Spain's viceregal Río de la Plata territories.

Tellingly, Azara begins his account in the preterite tense—"Spain
proposed"—a grammatical choice that in Spanish (*se propuso*) anticipates failure even as the author enumerates the goals of the treaty deliberations: "Spain
proposed in this treaty the elimination of contraband and all discord and disagreements between the two powers, which have not ceased since America was
discovered" (*Memoria,* 29). The reference to contraband as the primary factor
in the disagreements separating the two parties is revealing, as it signals the degree to which economic interests were driving both the Spanish and the Portuguese. Azara is writing from hard-earned experience as he explains the mis-
conceptions that contributed from the very beginning to limit any chance for
success that his mission might have had. But he also cautions that distance is
subjective and measured very differently in America than in Europe. Acknowledging that those who had never been in the Americas might find this truth
difficult to accept, Azara echoes a long line of Spanish chroniclers who claimed
authority by virtue of firsthand experience.

Azara recounts the various disputes that arose regarding the details of the
proposed treaty, rewriting geographical cartography as political cartography.
As we have seen, he had voiced many of these concerns in the letters written
over the years to his superiors. Azara emphasizes that the preliminary treaty
documents confused everything by employing inadequate and imprecise terminology. For example, in suggesting where the border might be drawn, they
referred to places on a map marked by rivers and streams (*ríos* and *arroyos*).
Azara explains (complains, really) that these terms cannot be clearly differenti-

ated from one another, especially in the Americas, where they do not signify in the same way they do in Europe (32). Moreover, seasonal variations in rainfall lead to topographical changes that further alter the mapped landscape. In some ways Azara's project resembles William Byrd's efforts in his *History of the Dividing Line betwixt Virginia and North Carolina*. Both Azara and Byrd were engaged in state enterprises of mapping and delineation, with the intention of fixing boundaries that would be both political and cultural. Yet, for each man, the local reality acted to thwart his mission.[98] Byrd was attempting to draw a dividing line along a sandbank, while Azara attempted to establish a border by following a riverbank. In both cases, as the ground literally shifted beneath the feet of the enlightened administrators, imperial mapping gave way to American nature.

"Memorial on the border treaty" chronicles Azara's increasing frustration not only with the recalcitrant Portuguese, but also with Spanish authorities, whom he often views as either naive or lazy. Spanish lack of attention in the region has resulted in the surrender of pine forests, cattle grazing lands, mines, and rivers for commercial transport to the Portuguese, with dire consequences for Spanish hegemony in the Americas. Azara concludes his memorandum by invoking three hundred years of history: "It is thus evident that the Portuguese persist in the same system as always. One knows this by observing their conduct since the discovery of America" (*Memoria*, 73). Spain's current situation is critically precarious, demanding urgent attention. However, the remedies that Azara puts forth, here and elsewhere in his administrative writings, are economic and civic rather than military. If, as it has been argued, "bureaucracy and militarization are the central instruments of empire," then it's worth remembering that Azara is wielding a compass or a draftsman's pen rather than a blunderbuss.[99]

VI. *"Todo lo que sea neutral es pura pérdida para nosotros": Writing back to empire*

Azara's extensive and charged bureaucratic correspondence is related to a number of other documents that do not directly address the border disputes, but rather look beyond them to issues of colonization and settlement.[100] Like the texts we've just been examining, these reports reflect Azara's keen awareness of the Río de la Plata region as a strategic peripheral zone in the eighteenth-century Spanish Empire as well as his deep conviction regarding the need to strengthen Spanish presence in that area.[101] They provide a discursive counterpart to Azara's naturalist writings on the flora and fauna of the region, and at times go even further than the reports on the border commission in making specific recommendations. Azara's missives constitute a series of entreaties that verge on the imperative. They reiterate his unwavering conviction that observation and study can and must lead to a conclusive outcome, and that reconnaissance—defined (as we have seen) by Edney as "the purposeful movement through and examination of the world" ("Reconsidering Enlightenment Geography," 176)—can and must lead to a more strategic engagement by Bourbon Spain in its southernmost territories in the Americas.

As David Weber has noted in *The Spanish Frontier in North America,* the frontier is both a space of interaction between cultures and peoples and a set of political boundaries that mark the limits and aspirations of imperial expansion.[102] Azara notes on repeated occasions that the neutral territory established by the preliminary border treaties with the intention of separating Spanish and Portuguese holdings in the Río de la Plata region had become, in fact, a refuge for "criminals, thieves and contrabandists" (*Memoria,* 29). Moreover, the Portuguese had seized the opportunity to populate those neutral territories with their own settlers, leading Azara to conclude, "All that is neutral is pure loss for us, and a source of difficulties, disputes, complaints, and disorders for us in the demarcation practice that will never end" (30).[103]

One aspect of the proposed negotiations involved the need for a no-man's-land (a "band of neutral territory," as Azara describes it)—a sort of buffer zone between Spain and Portugal's imperial holdings (29). Spanish claims on the Río de la Plata borderlands were challenged both by their Portuguese rivals and by various indigenous groups, most notably the Chaco.[104] Of course, the very notion of a no-man's-land reflects the degree to which the Europeans did not recognize or even see the indigenous inhabitants of the territories they so confidently and arrogantly had claimed.[105] Azara rejects vehemently the position held by some Spanish administrators—among them Joaquín Alós, governor of Paraguay, and Joaquín del Pino, governor of Montevideo—that it was to Spain's advantage to maintain open or empty territories, and he advocates the founding and location of settlements and forts, the development of ranching and agriculture, and the fomentation of commerce and trade. Moreover, he is profoundly interested in how the indigenous inhabitants of the Río de la Plata might be eventually integrated into the Bourbon imperial project.[106]

In "Memoria sobre el estado rural del Río de la Plata" (1801), Azara opens with a brief explanation of what propelled him to write: he has traveled throughout the region, he has produced a map of the territory, and he has read all the published and manuscript histories of the Río de la Plata environs. His authority is grounded in both practical experience and his study of existing sources. Azara tells the reader that he is finalizing a more polished version of his report that he hopes to publish soon, but that in the meantime he wishes to offer a preliminary account of facts and reflections pertaining to the region.

Azara's description of rural life reflects enlightened thinking about what makes a people productive and happy. The inhabitants of the Río de la Plata are peasants and small farmers involved in some limited agriculture, but mostly *pastoreo*—livestock breeding and herding (*Memoria,* 3–5).[107] Azara argues that "organized work is a virtue that makes men happy," and he advocates the building of parishes and schools that will serve to foster community and civic engagement. He proposes the development of agriculture appropriate to the terrain; he also calls for the regularization of the cattle industry and the establishment of more formalized structures of government and economic administration (5–7).

Azara worries that prolonged delays in the border negotiations will afford the Portuguese an opportunity to fortify their settlements at Coimbra and Albuquerque in defiance of the treaty provisions (133). Fearing that the diplomatic impasse might then develop into a real military threat, Azara carries on an extensive correspondence with Viceroy Arredondo about this issue, in which he strongly suggests the Spanish take similar steps to build forts as a countermeasure.[108] In Azara's opinion, Spain must not only fortify the borders but also populate the contested border regions. By saturating the territory with settlers, Spain will prevent the Portuguese from moving in—an eighteenth-century version of the maxim *gobernar es poblar;* that is, "to govern is to populate" (16).[109] Azara suggests the following:

> Having concluded that which refers to military service and the security of the frontier, I will deal with the method of populating the frontier zone. The Portuguese and other foreigners, when they want to expand and populate their borders, foment and assist those who offer themselves for this end, and moreover they distribute land to them, because they know that the right to property that they give them not only leads to building but is also a chain that fixes men in place forever. (174–75)[110]

Like many of his contemporaries, Azara embraces the possibilities of commerce. He worries that Spanish commercial opportunities both in the countryside and in urban areas will suffer if the Portuguese are allowed to take advantage of the border negotiations to expand their territory (169). Azara even includes a list of very specific suggestions regarding the utility of permitting some forms of contraband in the region, as he is convinced that contraband is both inevitable and potentially beneficial for the Spaniards.[111] Azara also compares the potential of the cattle industry to a mining-based economy, concluding that all the mines in the Americas do not provide half the benefits of a robust cattle-based economy. Countering the view that cattle herding might prolong barbarism, Azara argues that it will, on the contrary, foment industry and commerce (22–23).[112] Many of Azara's ideas will find enthusiastic advocates in nineteenth-century debates on civilization and barbarism in Argentina and Uruguay. In fact, Domingo Sarmiento was an avid reader of Azara and frequently quoted him.

Azara's various proposals—preferred status for married settlers and family men, the equitable distribution of property, start-up resources for towns and settlements, regulations prohibiting new settlers (*vecinos*) from abandoning their houses, funds to support parish priests—are all efforts to respond to the American reality that Azara experienced. They reflect eighteenth-century Bourbon *proyectismo,* which always involved a negotiation of philosophical ideals and pragmatic goals.[113] In effect abandoning the goals of his mission to draw official boundaries, Azara proposes instead to build settlements that will mark the Spanish imperial frontier in more concrete ways. Azara was instrumental in relocating a number of families that had been brought from Spain in 1778 to settle in Montevideo, Maldonado, and Colonia del Sacramento. When these settlements proved unsuccessful and the continuing cost of maintaining the families became a burden for viceregal authorities, Azara proposed to move the families to the Brazilian border region, near the Ibicuy River (which had caused him so many headaches as a surveyor). He established the town of San Gabriel de Batoví for this purpose and was, in fact, visiting there when he was called back to Spain.[114]

At every turn Azara opts for the pragmatic and domestic over the imperial and the ideological. As he argues fervently for a successful resolution to the simmering border dispute or—failing that—for an ambitious program of colonization and settlement, Azara invokes the Spanish tradition of conquest: "If to some it might seem risky . . . it will be because they do not remember that we are Spaniards, that Garay founded the forts at San Salvador and Santi Espiritu, and Oyolas the one at Asumpción, at great distances from Spain . . . and surrounded by a greater number of savages, more warlike and vigorous than the ones around here" (181). We must remember, however, that conquest is employed here merely rhetorically, as part of a historical legacy rather than a lived present. Ultimately Azara proposes a new kind of empire, consonant with Bourbon (not Hapsburg) ideals, which will be achieved through a pragmatic, domesticating presence in the region.

VII. "The accurate Azara": Darwin's debt

I conclude this chapter with a meditation on Félix de Azara's legacy. One of the few critics who studies Azara in depth calls him "the Humboldt of America."[115] I have always found the comparison somewhat jarring: What does it mean to be the American Humboldt? What is implied by that analogy? Why does it prove so difficult for Azara and other eighteenth-century writers of the Hispanic world to stand alone, on their own terms?[116] In this concluding section I will explore the idea of Azara as a predecessor of two giants of natural history whose work was defined by their own long sojourns in the Southern Cone and who subsequently served to define (and eclipse) their precursors: Alexander von Humboldt and Charles Darwin.

Darwin and Humboldt are to eighteenth-century natural history as Independence is to eighteenth-century historiography—that is, the lens through which everything that comes before is viewed and the scale against which all measurements are taken. But Azara's legacy is sui generis. Much like the flora and fauna he spent his life observing and analyzing, he is a homegrown and hybrid variant of the enlightened naturalist, a specimen that can only be considered in relation to itself. I have commented earlier on the ways in which Azara resists nationalist and nationalizing categories. One might also propose that he resists taxonomy and measurement, and in this way represents the Hispanic eighteenth century more "accurately" than has been previously acknowledged.[117]

Humboldt does not mention Azara in his voluminous writings; the Prussian explorer and the Aragonese engineer covered different territories. But their paths as geographers run in parallel, even if they do not intersect.[118] Pratt argues for a connection between Humboldt and early explorers: "Though deeply rooted in eighteenth-century constructions of Nature and Man, Humboldt's seeing-man is also a self-conscious double of the first European inventors of America, Columbus, Vespucci, Raleigh, and the others. They, too, wrote America as a primal world of nature, an unclaimed and timeless space occupied by plants and creatures (some of them human), but not organized by societies and economies; a world whose only history was the one about to begin" (*Imperial Eyes,* 126).

But this vision of America as a primal space, hearkening as it does back to sixteenth-century explorers, overlooks the world that followed—an eighteenth-century world dedicated to the project of organizing itself socially, politically, and economically.[119] What's more, it was this very world that made significant material and epistemological contributions to Humboldt's expedition: "Despite the emphasis on primal nature, in all their explorations, Humboldt and Bonpland never once stepped beyond the boundaries of the Spanish colonial infrastructure—they couldn't, for they relied entirely on the networks of villages, missions, outposts, haciendas, roadways, and colonial labor systems to sustain themselves and their project, for food, shelter, and the labor pool to guide them and transport their immense equipage."[120] The economic, political, and missionary networks that sustained the Humboldtian expedition appear intermittently in its written accounts, but many of the Spanish and Spanish American enlightened scientists who served as Humboldt and Bonpland's hosts, guides, and interlocutors disappear.[121] Enlightened scientists of the Hispanic world—criollo and new Creole natural historians—are almost completely overshadowed by their metropolitan contemporaries.

We know of Humboldt's importance in the formation of Charles Darwin's earliest impressions of South America, but Darwin's many references to "the accurate Azara" have been largely overlooked.[122] The first mention of Azara comes in *The Voyage of the Beagle,* where Darwin refers to him as "Don Felix Azara" and repeats his description of having seen a wasp "dragging a dead spider through tall grass" (50). Darwin later continues his discussion of the "gregarious spider," using the same possessive pronoun whose use we have noted in Azara—"perhaps even the same species with mine" (52). Darwin also refers to Azara on several occasions when he is discussing Carrancha carrion birds: "To these observations I may add, on the high authority of Azara, that the Carrancha feeds on worms" (71).[123] In these comments, Darwin's own observations are corroborated or complemented by Azara's earlier ones, and his respect for the Spaniard's experience is patent.

Curiously, both Azara and Darwin were deeply intrigued by the process of domesticating feral animals.[124] We've seen the care Azara took with the animals he kept as specimens, and the various experiments he devised to track their eating habits, reproduction, and behavior in captivity. Darwin repeats many of Azara's observations in *Variation of Animals and Plants under Domestication.*[125] Darwin uses the considerable evidence he gleans from Azara's writings on the quadrupeds of Paraguay to conclude that the gauchos' notorious lack of interest in selective breeding may account for the uniformity of cattle and horses throughout the Argentine pampas. Darwin adds, "With respect to animals, Azara has remarked with much surprise that, whilst the feral horses on the Pampas are always of one of three colours, and the cattle always of a uniform colour, yet these animals, when bred on the unenclosed estancias, though kept in a state which can hardly be called domesticated, and apparently exposed to almost identically the same conditions as when they are feral, nevertheless display a great diversity of colour" (2:246).[126]

Darwin's writings reflected an ongoing and substantive engagement with Azara's observations and experiments, and he quotes the eighteenth-century natural historian with obvious admiration. This influence notwithstanding, the lively debates about Darwin in late nineteenth-century Argentina make little or no mention of Azara. Those debates were sparked by Sarmiento's repeatedly expressed belief that Darwin's thinking on evolution had been inspired by fossils the British naturalist had seen in the Argentine pampas.[127] But Azara's role as intermediary and resource for Darwin's thoughtful processing of his Southern Cone experience, while acknowledged by Darwin himself, is, for the most part, erased by others.

Because he is both scientist and imperial administrator, Azara's writings—taken in their entirety and in dialogue with each other—offer us the opportunity to better understand the Hispanic eighteenth-century project in the Americas as a hybrid of curiosity and interest.[128] The juxtaposition of natural history and imperial administration informs and directs all of Azara's activities in the Río de la Plata in ways that fall outside the traditional vision of the disinterested scientist. Again, as Azara emphasizes in his correspondence with the Bourbon Crown, when it comes to imperial borders and borderlands, "all that is neutral is pure loss for us" (*Memoria*, 30).

Azara is invoking here a civic community—an "us"—that encompasses Spaniards, criollos, new Creoles, and an as-yet-to-be-developed Amerindian population. Azara's survey of the contested borderlands of the Río de la Plata finally relinquishes any definitive claim to what Santiago Castro-Gómez calls the "hybris del punto cero"; that is, the neutral and perfectly objective vantage point of the enlightened criollo (*La hybris,* 11–19). Azara's rejection of neutrality may be used as a point of departure to explore the position of the imperial administrator who is informed by scientific observation but who does not at any point claim to be a disinterested observer. Rather, in all his practices of reconnaissance, observation, measuring, mapping, collecting, and communicating, Azara is motivated by a desire to support and foment an imperial project.[129]

Michel Foucault's work on the relationship between scientific knowledge and the construction and exercise of power has informed to some degree the rejection of the Enlightenment's legacy, understood narrowly to mean positivist science and imperialist universalism. Yet enlightened scientific and geographic processes also challenged the same overarching and monolithic universalism they served, as can be seen in Azara's insistence on local knowledge and his contestation of Buffonian taxonomies. Azara's ongoing efforts to implement the biopolitics implicit in the mission of the demarcation delegation and institute from afar a policy of colonial control over the Spanish-Portuguese border are thwarted time and time again.[130] Thus, rejecting neutrality on practical terms and recognizing the limits of the measuring gaze of the natural historian, Azara argues instead for a Spanish imperial presence that would emerge in the contested borderlands as a human landscape of houses and churches, schools and stores. In other words, Azara argues for the domestication of empire in a New World natural setting.

CHAPTER FOUR

Domesticating God

Catalina de Jesús Herrera's
Secretos entre el alma y Dios (1758–1760)

Llamásteme, Señor, según me han dicho, a la
Contemplación. Me habis [*sic*] puesto ahora en la vía activa.

[You called me, Lord, according to what they have told me,
to contemplation. Now you have placed me on the active
path.]

Catalina de Jesús Herrera, *Secretos entre el alma y Dios*

I. *"Qué hago yo con este alboroto?": Edification and agency*

Cloistered behind convent walls in mid-eighteenth-century Quito, a Dominican
nun labored over the time-honored exercise of writing a spiritual autobiography,
an account of her struggles to overcome sin and vanquish doubt on the path
to salvation. As she wrote, Catalina de Jesús Herrera's solitude was often interrupted by events occurring beyond those walls. The nun would later recall how,
when a powerful storm threatened Quito with tremendous winds and rain, the
city's terrified inhabitants poured out into the streets, driven by rumors of an
imminent disaster:

> All the Churches opened their doors, as with one voice everyone cried out that
> the city would be lost to the torrential downpour that was coming to inundate
> it. The sound of the wind was already so great that all were terrified, and the
> fearful anticipation made it worse, so that, caught by surprise and begging for
> mercy, they abandoned their homes and fled to the Churches to await their
> death. (*Secretos*, 261)

Churches, monasteries, and convents offered shelter to those seeking refuge
from the pounding storm. Herrera was not immune to the tumultuous climate
of fear, and her recollections bring home to the reader a vivid sense of the panic
shared by religious and secular *quiteños* at a time of great danger:

> And I became even more frightened, seeing that the nuns in the Choir had no
> idea what to do with the holy images. But after careful consideration, I won-

dered: What avenue of water is this that is so slow to arrive? And even more so as I heard waves of people entering the Church, and that some said that they had come from the Plaza escaping from the water, such was the apprehension created by their fear, and I finally thought: What will I do with this tumult to die or live? (261)

Herrera's response to this catastrophe—and others large and small, natural and man-made, which she incorporated into her autobiography—bolsters her narrative authority and demonstrates her special relationship with God. But more importantly, the storm provokes a consideration of the possibilities of her own agency: "What will I do?"

Herrera's spiritual autobiography, recorded in a long-forgotten bundle of notebooks and titled *Secretos entre el alma y Dios,* represents her attempt to answer this question. Herrera wrote not only to chart a private journey of spiritual awakening, but also to register her encounters with the larger world as she attempted to build a life for herself inside the convent. *Secretos* may be situated within the Hispanic tradition of convent narratives but it must be read paying attention to her particular historical moment and place. By constructing a local—that is, conventual, urban, regional—foundation for her struggles, Herrera domesticates the "tumult" (*alboroto*) of life in eighteenth-century Quito. Writing in a viceregal city in the heart of the Andes at the midpoint of the eighteenth century, she engages a metropolitan tradition of female religiosity, proposing her convent (and herself) as home base. Her relationship with God is expressed through a narrative that focuses on daily preoccupations and *quiteño* concerns such as convent politics, urban unrest, and natural disasters. Herrera reimagines and domesticates the earlier Hapsburg imperial project of spiritual conquest in markedly local terms that reflect criollo preoccupations on the periphery of the Bourbon Empire during the late colonial period. In spite of the fact that history has traditionally relegated cloistered nuns to a marginal position, Kathryn Burns argues persuasively that they protagonized the reproduction of prestigious and powerful social relations in the colonial period (*Colonial Habits,* 2–3). Thus, what links the diverse memories within *Secretos* is Herrera's effort to establish and defend a convent home within a spiritual and political world that is firmly grounded in eighteenth-century Quito.

Catalina de Jesús Herrera Campusano was born in Guayaquil in 1717. The legitimate daughter of Captain Juan Delfín Herrera-Campusano y de la Bárcena and María Navarro-Navarrete y Castro, she was a member of a distinguished family in colonial Guayaquil. Herrera's strong religious vocation became apparent at an early age, and as a young girl she was assigned to the spiritual tutelage of a Dominican confessor, Carlos García de Bustamante.[1] Because there was as yet no convent in the city of her birth, Herrera, at the age of twenty-three, made the arduous journey from Guayaquil to Quito to pursue her religious vocation.[2] Andrés Paredes de Polanco y Armendaris, bishop of Quito from 1734 to 1745, took a particular interest in Herrera and gave her permission to visit various convents so that she might choose the one most to her liking.[3] She chose the Dominican Convent of Santa Catalina de Siena and was able to secure the required convent dowry thanks to the generosity of an anonymous gentleman from Guayaquil (*Secretos,* 54, 64).[4] She took her vows on April 23, 1741. Over the next half-century, Herrera performed various roles within the convent: *escucha* (that is, listener and companion for nuns in the *locutorio,* or convent parlor), mistress of novices, and prioress.[5] She died in 1795.[6]

Herrera began writing *Secretos entre el alma y Dios* on February 8, 1758, by order of her confessor at the time, Friar Tomás Rosario Corrales, and left off writing on August 29, 1760. The title of her lengthy manuscript makes reference to the privileged nature of Herrera's authorial project, which, as God himself has dictated, will be a selective confession meant for his eyes alone.[7] Perhaps because of a heightened awareness of the vulnerability of her writings (a topic to which I shall return), Herrera includes in her text a number of explicit references that locate her writing process in time (this explains how we know that she began writing in 1758). Herrera also wrote poetry, although few of these compositions remain (most are included in *Secretos*). The autobiography concludes abruptly, and no subsequent writings have ever been found. Either Herrera never wrote again, or her writings were not preserved.

The notebooks containing *Secretos,* like many other vitae written by cloistered nuns in Spain and Spanish America, lay almost completely forgotten until the beginning of the twentieth century. In 1906, Father Juan María Riera discovered Herrera's notebooks in a storehouse of the Convent of Santa Catalina and undertook the laborious task of copying them, first by hand and later with the aid of a typewriter. Father Riera's work remained in manuscript form until 1950, when it was published in Quito under the title *Autobiografía de la Venerable Madre Sor Catalina de Jesús Herrera.*[8] Father Alfonso A. Jerves provided editorial guidance for the 1950 publication, writing an introduction and adding chapter divisions, each with its own summary. In 1984, Hernán Rodríguez Casteló brought further attention to Herrera's writings by including a brief fragment in his edited volume, *Letras de la Audiencia de Quito* (Letters from the Audiencia of Quito). In the prologue to that collection, Rodríguez Casteló offers a panoramic vision of eighteenth-century hagiography in Quito, as well as a brief analysis of each of the selected works. His observations about *Secretos*'s lexicon, narrative construction, and stylistic turns represent the most rigorous critical treatment that Catalina de Jesús Herrrera's work has received to date.[9]

The selections from *Secretos entre el alma y Dios,* when compared with the other fragments of spiritual autobiography included in Rodríguez Casteló's *Letras de la Audiencia de Quito,* present a strikingly unconventional picture.[10] Rodríguez Casteló observes that *Secretos* is not really an ordered autobiography but rather a loose collection of memories. Moreover, those memories at times fall short of the exemplary narrative one might expect from a spiritual autobiography. As he copied Herrera's manuscript in 1906, Father Riera lamented that "certain not very edifying things will be found in some passages of this work; nevertheless, one should look on them as shadows that make the portrait of God's servant shine with even greater brilliance: in such things the reader can glimpse the difficulties—neither insignificant nor few in number—that crossed Sister Catalina's path in monastic life; difficulties that, far from weakening her solid virtue, forged it even stronger."[11] Father Jerves echoes this judgment in 1950: "Not all that the venerable author, moved by her unshakable spiritual rectitude and burning love of truth, consigned to her autobiographical account is normal and edifying" ("Introducción," 10–11).

These comments made by Father Riera and Father Jerves about edifying spiritual autobiography merit further consideration. Edification suggests a correspondence between individual female exemplarity and monastic tradition, and between a textual project and an architectural or institutional one. Behind the veiled reprobations of Herrera's editors is a sense that her work does not quite live up to expectations. But Herrera's authorial project is edifying, although not necessarily in the conventional sense of the word. As Herrera builds a case for herself as God's privileged interlocutor, she moves from contemplation to action in order to construct a female monastic tradition for herself and for the Convent of Santa Catalina where she resides.

Despite the fact that the notebooks that constitute *Secretos* have remained cloistered until recently, the figure of Sor Catalina created in those pages circulated—and continues to circulate—in a wide political, spiritual, and institutional network.[12] The identification of Catalina de Jesús Herrera with viceregal Quito extends to the subsequent production of a nationalist hagiography with roots in the eighteenth century. So *Secretos* is a text that mediates between the two master narratives of religion and nation that Jean Franco identifies in *Plotting Women*.[13] In the spiritual economy of Quito, the vita that Herrera initially drafted for domestic consumption is inscribed in the national consciousness, not in the manner in which the author would have intended, but through a curious melding of texts and remains, and of textual persona and historical persona, that I explore in this chapter.

Written from the viceregal periphery, toward the end of the colonial period, *Secretos* can be read as a Teresian *Libro de las fundaciones* (Book of foundations)—*après la lettre*—that is every bit as focused on institutional monumentality as on individual spiritual exemplarity.[14] The history of Catalina de Jesús Herrera reflects a preoccupation with constructing both a female genealogy and also the domestic conventual space from which that genealogy is written. The geographic *traslatio* initiated when Herrera left her father's home in Guayaquil to enter the convent in Quito can be read not only as a spiritual quest but also as the first step of a journey toward an imagined community of religious women in eighteenth-century Quito. In *Secretos,* Herrera employs women's spiritual autobiography as a foundation on which she builds an edifying narrative of her own place in her religious community, the place of her convent in Quito's spiritual economy, and Quito's place vis-à-vis other viceregal cities in Spain's empire.

II. *"Me parece tuve más luz para conocerlo todo": Faith-based Enlightenment*

In order to appreciate how Herrera's parochial world figures in Spain's imperial sphere, we need to consider the larger forces affecting the complex and continually renegotiated relationship between church and state in Bourbon Spain and its viceregal territories.

The traditional insistence on a secularized Enlightenment—one of a number of factors that have limited our appreciation of the global eighteenth century—ignores the ways that enlightened thinking played out in Catholic countries such as Italy and Spain, and in the far-flung Spanish Empire. In his introduction to *Magistrates of the Sacred*, an exploration of priests and parishioners in eighteenth-century Mexico, William B. Taylor opens with a description of a mid-nineteenth-century British academic's impatient, even appalled reaction to the exuberant baroque ornamentation that interrupted his line of sight whenever he visited a colonial church in Mexico (1).[15] Taylor uses this anecdote to suggest how colonial religious art and architecture interfered with the recovery of a pristine indigenous past; I read it as emblematic of the challenges faced by scholars of eighteenth-century Spanish America. As we attempt to reconcile the widely accepted—at least, until fairly recently—notion of a secular Enlightenment and our own work involving the Enlightenment's peripheral manifestations, many of which emerged in historical and cultural contexts that were profoundly influenced by Catholicism, all too often the question of religion literally gets in the way.

The picture appears much more nuanced if we look beyond a small group of antireligious philosophes in France and England. The eighteenth century was, in fact, not only a time of concerted efforts to challenge religious beliefs and organizations but also a period in which religious beliefs and practices shifted to accommodate enlightened thinking. As Dorinda Outram has argued, "The Enlightenment produced a wide variety of responses to organised religion, ranging all the way from violent Voltairean hostility to religion, through to attempts to bolster orthodox belief by demonstrating its rationality and accordance with natural law" (*Enlightenment*, 113).[16]

In Spain there was certainly some ambivalence regarding the Catholic Church's economic and political agenda. Charges made by enlightened reformers of corruption and extravagance within the church spurred internal efforts to respond to those charges.[17] We might think of these responses as domestic attempts to put one's house in order by strengthening inner spirituality (similar to what happened during the Counter-Reformation in Spain). Suspicions regarding the long reach of papal authority and an interest in appropriating lucrative revenue streams led to attempts to increase centralized control over ecclesiastical institutions. Jansenists, regalists, and enlightened reformers were natural, albeit uneasy, allies who came together through their distrust of the Jesuits.[18] The 1767 expulsion of the Jesuits from Spain and its overseas territories is an important touchstone—or flashpoint—for discussions of religion in the global eighteenth century, although it falls outside the scope of this study.[19]

It is important to remember, though, that for the most part reform did not mean rejection of the church: during the eighteenth century, Spaniards and Spanish Americans remained loyal to the Catholic faith.[20] Margaret Ewalt argues that Bourbon Spain participated in "an eclectic Catholic Enlightenment that unites sentiment and reason, allows for emotion within scientific inquiry, and values wonder in accumulating, enumerating and disseminating knowledge" (*Peripheral Wonders,* 2). There is persuasive evidence that the Hispanic eighteenth century was characterized not by antireligionism, but rather by spiritual and pastoral renovation in a larger context of secularization. Coupled with a crisis of institutional ecclesiastical authority, this provided fertile ground for the invention of localized and domesticated discourses of religious authority, of which Herrera's *Secretos* is an example.

Another example is the emergence of local saints in the Americas whose popularity contributed to a flowering of post-Tridentine late baroque Catholicism among both the elite and larger populace; the effects of that flowering would later shock and dismay that nineteenth-century British traveler in Mexico.[21] The emphasis on the "social presence" of the church, with its attendant sacralization of objects and places, dovetails in Spanish America with criollo concerns about their place in the Bourbon Spanish Empire.[22] These concerns find expression in New World Mariology, whose most noteworthy exemplar is the Virgen de Guadalupe (Virgin of Guadalupe). Eighteenth-century criollos in New Spain invoked and reworked earlier accounts of the Virgen's miraculous apparition to the Indian Juan Diego in 1531 at Tepeyac, on the outskirts of Mexico City, using New World Mariology as a means of furthering their claims to exceptionalism and legitimacy.[23] But there are many other examples of local saints who gave an eighteenth-century cast to the traditional linking of providentialism and Spanish imperial history, including Rosa of Lima.[24]

The eighteenth century also witnessed a redefinition and reorganization of the Spanish imperial project of evangelization. During the sixteenth and seventeenth centuries, Spanish missionaries were committed to the goal of spreading Christianity to the indigenous population by means of the *requerimiento,* mass conversions, and the establishment of missions, churches, and schools. Initial optimism regarding the lasting results of these evangelical efforts gave way in many cases to pessimism, leading to campaigns for the extermination of idolatrous practices in New Spain and the Andes. The eighteenth century saw yet another shift, as "Indians became less the epitome of weakness, laziness, and sin, and more the objects of improvement, if not perfectability, capable of full 'conversion' in the new Hispanic order."[25] Despite this new optimism, missionaries were often isolated, geographically and linguistically, from imperial reach, while the day-to-day obligations of administering the agricultural enterprises on which mission life increasingly depended proved to be a distraction from their evangelical focus.[26] Indigenous rebellions occasionally erupted, revealing the limits of missionaries' control over their flock and threatening viceregal authority. Reform efforts aimed at subordinating the Catholic Church to Bourbon bureaucracy contributed to a blurring of boundaries between Spanish and Indian spaces in both urban and rural areas, sharpening criollo anxieties about their identity during a period of institutional instability and racial miscegenation.[27]

While nuns were not directly engaged with imperial religious expansionism or the missionary project, convents had always functioned as a locus of agency for women in colonial Spanish America, and spiritual autobiographies often became narratives of that agency within a broader political, social and economic context.[28] Concerns about the challenges of evangelization, political tensions within and between religious orders, debates about common monastic life (*la vida común*), and events taking place outside the convent walls—earthquakes, epidemics, and indigenous rebellions—make their way into the pages of Herrera's notebooks.

III. *"Tú también has de escrebir": Rewriting the vida in eighteenth-century Quito*

The command to write comes to Herrera directly from God, as she explains in her diary: "You know well how much repugnance I have felt since they first ordered me to write. And when I started reading some things that your servants had written, you said to me, 'You must also write'" (*Secretos,* 17). Herrera implicitly acknowledges her familiarity with the spiritual writings of other exemplary religious women and also alludes to earlier attempts (presumably by her father confessor) to induce her to produce the kind of confessional autobiography that was often a requisite part of a nun's spiritual formation. Indeed, the opening chapters of the *Autobiografía* reflect Herrera's ongoing negotiation of the demands of obedience, holy ignorance, confession, and humility. In the pages that follow, she continues this juggling act as she incorporates details of her upbringing before becoming a nun and of the struggle to realize her vocation once she has entered the convent.[29]

The conventions of female spiritual autobiography mirror those of confession, Inquisitorial practice, and hagiography.[30] Teresa of Avila's *Libro de la vida* (Book of life; 1565) circulated widely in Spain and Spanish America and served as a model for nuns seeking to chart an acceptable path toward God while balancing their own experiences of the divine against orthodox expectations of female piety. The father confessors who frequently ordered nuns to write about their spiritual journeys looked for "evidence of heroic retreat from the world, penitential practices, obedience to the church, and personal knowledge of God that had not been learned from books."[31] Given the tensions that often arose from these competing demands, women's spiritual autobiographies have been characterized as "conflicted self-portraits," fraught with anxiety about female subjectivity and at the same time "infused with creativity, self-affirmation, and subversion."[32] The nuns who penned these autobiographies often resorted to the *vos me fecit* (you made me) *topos* to remind both God and their readers that they were chosen for all the trials, tribulations, and triumphs that they were experiencing; such assertions alternate with gestures of exaggerated humility and self-doubt. In their accounts, visions of the devil compete with visions of God, confessors are either arbitrarily unjust or paternalistically supportive, and danger and temptations lurk everywhere. Mystical experiences, strategically exercised, had the potential to provide women with a privileged position within their own communities, but also ran the risk of angering church officials who sought to control and contain female spirituality. By the post-Tridentine eighteenth century, the Catholic Church viewed many mystic practices as a dangerous manifestation of "baroque excesses."[33] Nevertheless, the mystic model of extreme religiosity still prevailed in female spiritual autobiography at the time Herrera was writing, and *Secretos* reflects the conventions of the hagiographic confessional mode inherited from seventeenth-century models such as Teresa of Avila. Herrera follows a well-trodden path in describing her upbringing, her mystic visions, her negotiation of the vow of obedience to her father confessor, and her focus on the privileged nature of her conversations with God.

At first glance, Herrera's religiosity and her rewriting of the *vida* seem relatively tame, particularly when compared with other instances of extreme mystic practices and popular sainthood. An exemplary childhood was the starting point for most spiritual autobiographies, as it was for hagiographical narratives, and Herrera's *Secretos* is no exception. But Herrera's presentation of her parents and their respective influence on her religious vocation suggests the interest in constructing an exemplary female lineage that informs the entire work. Early in *Secretos,* Herrera recounts an extraordinary conversation that as a very young girl she initiated with her mother immediately following the birth of a baby brother. Herrera, having witnessed the long labor and childbirth with astonishment, contemplates her exhausted mother:

> Seeing that a child was born from my mother surprised me and I became pensive, thinking that in the same way she would have produced me and all my siblings. But my mother, where had she come from? Without a doubt it would have been from another woman. And that one, from another woman; and so on for all us living creatures. But the first woman from whom we began to be born, from whom would she have been born? Here my discourse became stuck and I felt extremely overcome with doubt. I went over my discourse again and again from the beginning and, arriving at the first woman, I became increasingly perplexed and fatigued, until I could bear it no longer. (21)

Herrera traces a long line of mothers and children back to the very first woman to discover how those generations began. The young girl's articulation of the classic question "Where do babies come from?" takes a decidedly theological turn as Herrera quizzes her mother. In her responses, Herrera's mother shows herself to be "a great and capable person," explaining to the curious child that God had created the first man and woman, and also the heavens, the angels, and all things. She further explains the concept of the Holy Trinity, the idea of good and evil, and the manner in which God became man in the person of Jesus Christ. Her mother's answers awaken in Herrera an even greater curiosity and lead to an even more provocative query: "Lord, where did You come from?" (21). Since Herrera addresses this question directly to the Lord, it is not her mother but God himself who answers, letting her know that the exchange can go no further. For Herrera, as for the reader of the autobiography, the divine answer, which effectively closes off further discussion, seems much less satisfying than the wide-ranging mother-daughter conversation she has just recounted.

All the details of this incident—the exhausted mother who, despite having just given birth, is presented as a source of theological revelation, and the curious young girl who watches, questions, and listens—serve to establish implicitly but forcefully in the opening pages of the autobiography a model of female authority regarding spiritual questions. Moreover, the very same biological condition that in other contexts has sufficed to disqualify women for theological and intellectual discourse is here precisely that which opens a space for the transmission of theological wisdom from mother to daughter, from woman to woman.

It is not unusual to invoke maternal images in religious writing, of course. Carolyn Walker Bynum points out that despite what the misogynist tradition of the late medieval period might suggest, the idea of Christ's maternity frequently served as a metaphor for his compassionate and redemptive role in the Catholic Church. In Bynum's view this association permits a tropological movement "from images of lactation or giving birth directly to theological matters, such as the Eucharist and redemption" ("And Woman His Humanity," 265).[34] In Herrera's text, however, maternity does not operate metaphorically, but rather concretely. It is not associated with Christ, but rather with Herrera's own mother, who plays an intellectual and theological role as an instructor at the same time that she fulfills her biological role by giving birth.[35] By placing this moment of double "enlightenment" in the opening chapters of her spiritual autobiography and within the walls of her childhood home, Herrera both acknowledges and rewrites the conventions of the genre.[36] The matrilineal tradition in Herrera's text takes as its point of departure not only the *vidas* of other exemplary religious women recognized by the church, but also the life of Herrera's own mother as it unfolds within the domestic sphere.

This incident is even more striking when we compare it with the portrait that Herrera has painted of her father in the previous chapter. The nun describes how on three separate occasions her father threatened her in a paroxysm of anger: first because as a newborn she cried continuously, later because her childish games annoyed him, and finally when he splits her head open accidentally with a mug he has thrown at a servant. In each instance, a female figure miraculously appears to save the child—her mother (in the first two instances) and, in the last case, a maidservant who hurries Herrera off to the safety of her mother's side. That her father's violence does not end in tragedy is due not to his self-control or any reflection or rehabilitation on his part, but rather to maternal intervention. Herrera closes the account of her father with a laconic description of his death:

> Later, God and loving Lord, who does not wish for the death of a sinner, you tamed my father's character with so many trials, giving him a happy death after a long illness which he tolerated with great patience and awareness of his mortality, leaving me at the age of eleven years, for by that point he had already given me all the counsel necessary for my whole life. (20)

Herrera narrates the supposed repentance and deathbed conversion of her father in an exaggeratedly pious and respectful tone. Given all that she has already shared with the reader, this tidy denouement, far from contradicting the implicit condemnation of the father that we've read in previous pages, only serves to reinforce it ironically.

It's worth noting that in later biographical accounts of Herrera, all of them marked by a whiff of hagiography, this paternal portrait is often retouched so that it conforms to the image of an exemplary father whose model would be, obviously, the father of Teresa of Avila.[37] In his introduction to the 1954 edition of *Secretos,* for example, Father Jerves offers the following commentary: "She was orphaned at the age of eleven when her father died but, as she says in her *Autobiografía,* having already given her and reiterated all manner of good counsel for the correct governance of her whole life" (5).[38] The transformation of "all the counsel necessary"—Herrera's slyly ambiguous phrase—into the more categorical "good counsel" reflects an editorial process aimed at rehabilitating both father and daughter.[39] Herrera's strategy is to shift emphasis away from paternal authority and emphasize instead female wisdom and maternal authority.

Her father's outbursts of rage are not the only disruption Herrera experiences on the home front. Herrera later makes a spine-chilling disclosure about her principal motive for seeking the cloister: "Here I say many times, my God, that since my brother took his wife's life, that I wished to put a lock on my Monastery so that none of my relatives' voices might reach me by any means, because that event was what made me understand how far I needed to be from all flesh and blood [*carne y sangre*]" (*Secretos,* 67).[40] Herrera mentions here almost parenthetically the fact that her brother has commited uxoricide, a heinous act that affirms her decision to remove herself from the world and retreat behind the locked gates of the convent. Herrera's use of the words *carne* and *sangre* evokes the tragic and brutal consequences of this honor play—familiar in every sense—and reminds the reader of the paternal violence that the nun has already described.[41]

In her notebooks Herrera sketches a society full of dangers for young women—a society that does not protect them adequately from moral ruin and that incites them to evil while condemning their failings.[42] Herrera recounts that as her religious vocation intensified, she tried to excuse herself from the social visits that often put a young girl at risk of unwanted or questionable encounters (*Secretos,* 34). But if life outside convent walls meant danger and uncertainty, young women were also exposed to danger, temptation, and strife inside the convent. Some of these dangers arose because the relaxing of monastic customs gave rise to a state of affairs in which the parlor of a cloistered convent functioned as a relatively open space to which many visitors, both secular and religious, enjoyed access.[43] Over the course of two long years, Herrera was forced to reject the unwanted amorous advances of an imprudent priest: "He was so daring, that in front of those who accompanied him in my company he dared to try to caress me with his hands, pretending not to notice my negative gestures, giving his caresses a positive air. And wherever one of his hands touched me, I was left with intolerable pain" (109).

Spiritual autobiographies were often organized around the struggle against sin and the daily temptations of laxity. Indeed, no spiritual journey could take exemplarity as its uncontested point of departure; instead, a course had to be charted away from sin toward ever-greater rectitude and religious fervor. Veiled allusions to temptation and confessions of peccadilloes were generally sufficient to suggest a positive trajectory and proved much less risky for the writer than fully fleshed-out accounts of serious transgressions. Thus, in *Secretos* one finds many allusions to sins committed but not confessed in detail and unexplained conflicts that are invariably resolved with God's help. It should be recognized, however, that even when Herrera writes according to the rhetorical norms of the genre of spiritual autobiography, she rarely sets herself up as overly virtuous. In fact, the anecdotes she includes are characterized by a marked lack of exemplarity. Herrera describes her spiritual commitment as initially lukewarm, noting that she frequently gave in to the temptation to pass the time by telling jokes and laughing with the other novices (140) or to skip prayers: "I remained awake in bed, wishing that something hurt so that I might stay in bed without scruple" (148).

There are moments when Herrera explicitly rejects the path of spiritual perfection through illness and bodily mortification.[44] Her resistance to conventional expectations of religious fervor is most strikingly illustrated by the episode of the *cilicio* (hairshirt), which she has been instructed to wear at all times. To the great consternation of Herrera, as well as her mother and sisters, the effects of this mortification soon become evident: Herrera's waist and back become swollen and sore, and she can no longer eat nor sleep (60). But in contrast with the long-suffering or even joyful resignation to pain evidenced by other, more ecstatic nuns, Herrera merely observes, "I was left badly with my scruples, and with the *cilicio* even worse, because I began to think, Lord, that spiritual life was very trying" (60).[45] She decides to remove the *cilicio* in order not to worry certain family members who have come to visit her. Once the visit is over, she looks for the *cilicio* but cannot find it. Its mysterious disappearance, which frees her from a bothersome torment, is never fully explained. Herrera only ventures that she later found the tattered *cilicio* in a crevasse on the mountain, without ever being able to find out who had left it there. This suggests some kind of divine intervention, which is further corroborated by her relatives, who, when confronted by Herrera, disclaim any involvement in the disappearance of the *cilicio* (60). Herrera concludes her story by insinuating that God himself excuses her weakness and redeems her from an exercise of devotion that has become an unwelcome calvary for her. The anecdote's lack of clear resolution opens up a narrative space in which God and Herrera become accomplices in order to subvert not only the expectations of the monastic regime, but also the norms of spiritual autobiography. It is as if the nun were using her own failings as a pretext to affirm a privileged relationship with God.

Like many other nuns who wrote spiritual autobiography, Herrera records frequent periods of psychic and physical disturbances. She confesses that she experiences many strange visions, some of them highly erotic. At one point she is visited in her cell by a vision of a former member of the convent, a deceased nun who tells her that she suffers still in purgatory because "I loved you" (130).[46] When Herrera presses the apparition for a more detailed explanation of her suffering and punishment, the nun disappears and then reappears, naked and sweaty. Book 3 opens with a vision in which God appears to Herrera as a lamb who licks her breasts (192–93). The devil appears to Herrera in various forms: as a black dog (17), a vile beast (267), and a raging bull (387).[47] But other visions unfold in an atmosphere of quiet domesticity. Book 2 ends with a recurring vision of God as a sweetly willful little child: "You appeared to me as a beautiful Child, seated on my lap, playing with your little shoe. . . . You took the shoe off your little foot, and you threw your little sandal at me" (179). Each time that Herrera tries to put one shoe on, the baby Jesus removes the other. Eventually the game leads her to exclaim with affectionate exasperation, "Don't be naughty, Child!" (179). Here the repeated use of the diminutive—"sentadito," "calzadito," "piesecito," and "sandalita"—accentuates the familial and domestic nature of Herrera's relationship with the Divine.

Perhaps in order to further emphasize that privileged relationship, Herrera's visions often portray the punishment of those who have opposed her or threatened her vocation.[48] This is the case with the wayward priest mentioned earlier, whom Herrera later envisions as a drowning man flailing away in an immense sea, his hands blackened as a mark of the indiscretions he committed against Herrera while he was alive (109). At another point she recalls how at the age of about four she happened to enter unnoticed a room where a group of girls were enticing another young girl to commit some unexplained sin. Though Herrera never offers details, she does record the fact that many years later, after having taken her vows, she has a vision of those same girls, long dead and suffering eternal damnation (152). These visions of divine punishment meted out to others are balanced by many instances of divine mercy regarding Herrera's own spiritual weaknesses. Thus, we see that in the *Secretos*, mystical experience is effectively incorporated by Herrera so as to consolidate her own spiritual position; the visions, even though they occur outside the realm of the rational, serve to order, anticipate, and reinforce her narrative authority.

As is the case with many other spiritual autobiographies written by women, Herrera's text reflects a constant negotiation between the formulaic conventions of the *vida,* on one hand, and the autobiographical impulse on the other, and between writing as obedience and writing as the construction of an authorial "I." Herrera attempts to impose narrative control over the series of religious figures who served as her father confessors even though they were often not her equals in terms of spiritual commitment. When Herrera speaks of these men, she generally does not refer to them by name, preferring to invoke a generic figure of masculine authority.[49] Only Tomás Corrales, who orders her to write the *vida* and is recognized as an important person in her spiritual development, is named as a protagonist in the narrative. When Herrera meets him for the first time (without knowing that years later he would become her confessor), she senses an immediate connection (*Secretos*, 53). The astute young girl recognizes her future spiritual director, thus claiming agency in what was traditionally a highly hierarchical relationship.

Herrera never misses an opportunity to praise Corrales's spiritual guidance, but there are several narrative twists that undermine the confessor's authority with respect to the young nun under his charge. The most daring of Herrera's editorial maneuverings is effected through a vision in which she is permitted to observe the friar's most intimate thoughts: "Since that Father became my Confessor, it was granted to me that I should know all that passed in his interior. And so, much harm in which he might have involuntarily lost himself was prevented. And I said to myself: That with my declaring to him his own inner thoughts, he seemed much improved in many things" (99). There is another revealing incident when God asks Herrera to shield Corrales from a diabolical danger, telling her to warn her confessor that Satan has prepared a trap for him at five o'clock that afternoon (266). Herrera's intervention to defend her confessor from Satan's plotting has a Mariological cast. Like the Virgin Mary, Herrera is a protective maternal figure who intervenes on behalf of those who are needy, sinful, or in danger. By including these episodes, Herrera proposes an inversion of the traditional relationship between nun and confessor, appropriating her spiritual director's function when she becomes his visionary guide and protector, a role that counterbalances Corrales's influence on her manuscript.

Herrera employs other strategies to minimize her dependence on her father confessor. One of the most frequent is the direct invocation of God and her repeated affirmations of a relationship with the Divine that requires no mediation by ecclesiastical hierarchy.[50] When Herrera interprets a shocking vision in which she sees the choir of her convent full of manure, God confirms and rewards her hermeneutical authority, sharing with her his disappointment over the abuses and frivolity of the clergy: "Ah, daughter! you would say to me, at times compassionate and at others annoyed: *They give full rein to their appetites and passions. And they have no scruples*" (266). The conversations between God and Herrera—the secrets to which the title refers—establish a tone of intimacy and complicity between the two that reminds the reader of the exchange between young Herrera and her mother.[51] In these pages the triangulated relationship between Herrera, her father confessor, and God is replaced by a direct colloquy between Herrera and God, her true interlocutor.[52]

When she experiences mystical visions, Herrera insists on her capacity to interpret and record them, thus shifting the focus from the contemplation of a somatic visionary experience to an active intellectual process. Translating her visions into writing is an exegetical exercise that allows for their meaning to be fully understood. Herrera explains how she deciphered a vision that initially seemed incomprehensible: "And as I did not understand, I had required myself just to write it down as it is here, leaving the question of intelligence to Him that is a Theologian . . . who made me a scholar [*bachillera*]?" (198). The jocose and self-deprecating comment masks a serious intent. Writing is presented as a requisite first step for understanding, even though the nun's discourse of humility dictates that she cannot openly claim the theological intelligence necessary to interpret the vision. Herrera explains that any insight she might have regarding the vision is not hers, but rather belongs to God. She announces, "I will say that which is not mine, but rather Yours," and she concludes this passage with the requisite *excusatio*, "For I am a poor idiot" (198, 199).

Formulaic humility notwithstanding, what stands out in the multiple entries devoted to this vision is the repetition of the verb *entender* (to understand) in first person. The passive *se me da a entender* (I am given to understand) is replaced by the active *entendí* (I understood) and *entiendo* (I understand)—verb forms that appear seven times on a single page. The grammatical shift undermines Herrera's protestations of humility and underscores the nun's active intelligence in understanding and interpreting her mystical experiences. Thus, the writing process itself becomes an essential stage of Herrera's hermeneutical journey.[53] As the nun explains upon awakening from a trance, "I didn't know what to say except to say that I didn't know. Not even to the Confessor could I ever say it, because I did not find words to express it, until they ordered me to write. Then it became clear to me how I was to write it" (119).[54]

IV. *"Prepara el tinterillo": Writing home*

Herrera acknowledges the existence of an extensive tradition of religious writing and, like so many women authors before her, she vigorously affirms God's defense of women's writing in general, and her own writing in particular. Writing—how, when, and about what—is a constant theme in Herrera's notebooks. There are repeated references in *Secretos* to another version of Herrera's autobiography, begun a decade earlier and subsequently burned by the nun by order of her confessor (15). Acts of obedience represented by the destruction of one's writings are a frequent topic in convent narratives. In Herrera's case these references serve to create a phantom text that is evoked at times with shame and at other times with nostalgia and even defiant pride. Herrera writes a letter to her confessor that is included in an appendix to the *Autobiografía* in which she states that when he told her to burn her writings, "I felt that God's mercy had been reduced to ashes" (*Secretos*, xiv).

When Herrera later begins to write again, it is with a markedly resentful tone toward her confessor's command that she incinerate her text. God responds directly to her "loving complaint" by explaining that the burned pages represented the sins she recounted in them, and that henceforth she is to write "without specifying her wickedness" (16).[55] Thus, a pact of complicity between Herrera and God is sealed, and her narrative authority rises like a phoenix from the ashes of her earlier obedience. The nun is given divine license to perform the editorial functions previously assumed by her confessor, and her earlier sense of neglect and doubt is replaced by clarity and confidence. She anticipates the fulfillment, eleven years later, of God's promise to her: "You will write again"—a promise that will sustain her throughout many difficult moments and that will eventually find manifestation in *Secretos* (16).

When Herrera explains toward the close of book 4 of *Secretos* how she began to write again in 1758, the providential revelation is enacted through a dialogue with God in which he instructs her, saying, "Prepare the little inkwell" (333). When she protests, God repeats his command twice more, until Herrera finally cedes to divine insistence: "Well, all right, Lord. . . . Then I will prepare the little inkwell. And now don't rush me" (333). The use of the diminutive for "inkwell"—"tinterito" in one instance, and on another occasion, "tinterillo"—

once again underscores the intimate relationship Herrera enjoys with God, as does Herrera's request that God not push her to fulfill his command. Unlike what we often see in the mystic experiences recorded by other nuns, this is an intimacy expressed through the quotidian. Herrera's dialogue with God takes the form of a familiar and loving tug of war—a discourse of reminders and nudges.

Herrera eventually fills more than thirty notebooks with her confessional prose, despite her protestations and notwithstanding occasional difficulties. For example, the third chapter of book 5 picks up after a nine-month hiatus, during which Herrera did not take up her pen a single time. She is confused about what she has recorded and where: "I don't know if I've already written all this, or if I'm writing it twice. That's why I'm merely making notes, because I've lost track of whether I have written this in one of the Notebooks that are with Your Mercy" (387). The notebooks, as she suggests here, often end up in the hands of her confessor. But during the periods when she does not have access to them, she continues to write at times on bits and pieces of paper or on blank pages in the convent prayer books. This serves to preserve those miscellaneous writings when others threaten to destroy or confiscate them.

Toward the end of book 5, Herrera describes how a beautiful angel has appeared before her with an arrow and a silver scythe to announce Herrera's proximate death. Instead of ceding to the angel in a show of holy obedience, Herrera interrupts her angelic visitor to propose an alternative timetable more in accordance with her own authorial agenda:

> Wait for me a bit. For I have to take care of, particularly, three things. One is that I have in my possession some Papers from among the ones that I was ordered to write in Obedience about the Benefits of God. And it wouldn't be right that, were you to carry me away now in silence, that they might fall into the hands of others. In these Papers I still have to write about another Benefit, and this one that is happening to me now with you. I'll write that and I will turn the Papers over to my Confessor and Prelate. (446)

In this wonderfully familiar exchange, Herrera asks the angel for more time. In addition to finishing her writing, she must also return some jewels she has borrowed and take care of a number of outstanding debts. The angel assures her, "I'll arrange that and other little things" (446). Here the use of the diminutive again underscores the quotidian nature of the exchange, as does the mundane specificity of Herrera's to-do list.

The fusing of this and other moments of mystical visions and the later moments in which those visions are recorded in writing reinforces Herrera's autonomy precisely in her most vulnerable hour and underlines the relationship between the nun's spiritual project and her scriptural one. The reader, by now accustomed to Herrera's persuasive abilities, is not surprised to learn that the angel cedes to Herrera's implacable authority, merely urging her to hurry. Having succesfully bargained for this heavenly extension, Herrera later confesses that because she has been feeling tired and lazy, she has not kept her end of the bargain: "I did not pick up the pen to do any of the things that I promised the Angel" (447).

But this confession of inactivity is an exception, as Herrera shows herself repeatedly in the *Secretos* to be a woman of resolve and initiative. Responding to the pedagogical imperative that she has assigned herself in the text, Herrera uses the biblical story of the two sisters, Martha and Mary, to explain in down-to-earth terms how in her own case the passive suspension of self that characterizes the mystic experience is complemented and fullfilled by action:

> Settle this Doubt for me, my Loving Master: If Mary hadn't had her sister Martha, what would she have done? Would she have left you without food when You were in their House, because she was seated at your Divine Feet? . . . And it seems to me that this is your response, according to the light that you, Lord, give me. That I understand that just as in that House, where within it you attended to Mary and Martha, I understand that House is the Soul, where at times one feels your Divine Majesty within. And you concede to it at the same time the active life and the contemplative life. That is what is meant by Martha and Mary being together and living within the same House. (435)

Herrera reminds God and the reader that Martha and Mary live together in the same house. The two sisters complement each other in serving God, as Martha's attention to the details of everyday life makes possible the mystic and contemplative life of her sister, Mary. The obvious and unapologetic valorization of the active life that stands out in Herrera's reading of the story of Martha and Mary extends to her characterization of the Virgin Mary, who is able to encompass both action and contemplation in one being. Herrera comments to her divine interlocutor, "As I understand it, if I am not mistaken, only your sainted Mother was always and habitually, at the same time, active and contemplative" (435). The domestic sphere of the convent provides a space where Herrera, like the Virgin Mary, brings together contemplation and action as she seeks to legitimize her spiritual community not only through her writing but also through her hands-on pragmatic initiatives.[56]

V. *"Toda mi inclinación era irme a Santa Rosa de Lima": Local saints and model nuns*

Herrera never loses sight of the local geography through which her spiritual path takes her. Awakening from her visions, Herrera often experiences a heightened awareness of her own location: "I became aware of *the land where I was, the Convent,* and that I was a nun" (120; emphasis mine). When Herrera laments the fact that Christ was born, lived, and died so far from America, God shares with her a secret that answers her concerns and vindicates her Andean homeland. God explains that he spent the forty days that passed after his resurrection and before his ascension on a kind of global listening tour: "I walked all these lands with my divine footsteps, so that no one might complain to me as you do now" (262). Although God's response might be read as a gentle rejoinder to Herrera's recriminations, it also affirms a divine boots-on-the-ground familiarity with the Americas that the nun uses to shore up her own authority.[57]

Noting that female religious writing has generally been regarded as somewhat removed from patriotic discourse (much as the nuns themselves were separated by convent walls from the surrounding community), Mariselle Meléndez contests the commonly held notion that women's spiritual autobiography and monastic chronicles "were not articulations of a local sense of national identity or deeply rooted in patriotic sentiments" (*Deviant and Useful Citizens,* 91). We can see both a deeply felt sense of local identity and an interest in promoting local prestige in Herrera's writing. As she casts about for spiritual models, Herrera, who has recourse to a host of canonical exemplary figures, invokes her own Holy Trinity: Teresa of Avila, Catherine of Siena (of fundamental importance for the Dominicans) and Rosa of Lima.[58] Herrera writes at length in *Secretos* about these venerable nuns, viewing them as local heroines who have brought renown and blessings to their convents.

Because of her chronological and geographic proximity to Quito, Rosa of Lima is the model saint to whom Herrera feels most attracted.[59] Herrera frequently speaks of her desire to travel to Lima to enter Rosa's convent, and after an earthquake destroys the Convent of Santa Catalina, leaving the nuns homeless and exposing them to inclement weather and the threat of violence, she announces her intention to depart immediately for Lima (*Secretos,* 295). But because of a series of complications (among them the role she agrees to play in rebuilding her Dominican convent), the trip never takes place. Herrera must—as in other moments—find a narrative resolution for her frustrated desires. Herrera achieves this by describing a beautiful vision of Rosa of Lima, who appears before her, embraces her, and speaks with her at length about various religious topics. Herrera exclaims, "For God's Sake, even the Saint graciously held forth upon seeing me suffer without a Confessor, and she came to me, teasing and offering herself as my Confessor!" (352). This conversation is reminiscent of the scene discussed earlier in which a young Herrera discusses theology with her mother. Here we see that Rosa offers herself as a "mother confessor" for the nun, whose own masculine confessor is not available. After this intimate exchange, Herrera feels emboldened to critique the various portraits of Rosa that can be found throughout the convent. She offers a verbal portrait that replaces the official hagiographic paintings in the same way that her visionary conversations with the sainted woman replace the absent father confessor:

> After this I have walked around looking at the images there are in the Convent, and only in one do I find that certain air that she has about her mouth. The glorious saint's mouth was somewhat large, but not too much, and her lips, when she spoke, curved up a bit with much grace. . . . Her face, somewhat full, but sharp-nosed, and pink and white, like the glorious white that one sees and that I cannot put into words: it seems to me that the pink and white colors are transparent and very delicate, according to the one breast I glimpsed. She was

small, and not fat. And what pleased me most is that she arrived from Glory with her Limeñan ways and speech. (352)[60]

Herrera employs a familiar tone throughout the description and includes details that suggest intimacy. These characteristics aside, what is most striking about the portrait that Herrera paints of Rosa is her insistence on the aspects of the saint's speech and demeanor that suggest a connection to Lima. Physically, the vision corresponds in every way to a traditional celestial apparition; however, the saint's American—even Andean—origins are revealed in the verbal and gestural language that she uses.[61] Herrera's search for and celebration of local spiritual authority mirrors broader reform movements within eighteenth-century Hispanic Catholicism.[62]

The campaign that Herrera undertakes to locate monastic exemplarity in her own sphere reaches its culmination with another vision that appears to her above the main altar of the convent. Herrera mistakenly believes the vision to be Catherine of Siena. She rushes out of the chapel, calling out, "Thanks be to God, there is a Saint with this name in God's Church!" (*Secretos,* 428). The vision lingers, and Herrera approaches the image to venerate it, falling to her knees to kiss and embrace its feet (429). But then God interrupts her adoration to clarify that the "Catarina" who has appeared above the altar is not Catherine of Siena but Herrera herself: "*Yes, Daughter. You are that one whom I have in my Church*" (429).[63] With this divine revelation Herrera's earlier gestures of devotion (kneeling, kissing the vision's feet) take on an unexpected element of auto-exaltation. *Imitatio* has become a perfect mimetic gesture by means of which Herrera appropriates the hagiographic tradition in order to assign to herself a central position within it—above the altar, no less.

I turn now to perhaps the most audacious moment recorded in *Secretos,* an incident that exemplifies both Herrera's sense of initiative and her desire to establish Quito's Convent of Santa Catalina as home and home base for a localized spiritual authority: the exhumation of Sor Juana de la Cruz. In order to understand what motivates this incident, we must remember that Herrera had moved from Guayaquil to Quito in order to enter the Dominican convent of Santa Catalina after long and complicated debates with herself about where she should take her vows.[64] The issue of which convent to choose comes up again and again in *Secretos* as a carefully considered decision in which others frequently attempt to influence Herrera (71). Herrera explains that her initial decision to enter a Dominican convent was owing to a combination of chance and divine intervention. Having promised God that she would go to church and follow the vocational advice of the first priest to emerge from the confessional, she sees a Dominican friar who has just arrived from out of town. The friar provides her with counsel on the pros and cons of various convents, but it is her confessor who finally announces, "God wants you for Catarina, as I know and well understand from his Divine Majesty" (74).

This background explains in part Herrera's oft-expressed anguish and frustration regarding the prestige of her convent. She recognized that there were many other convents in the Americas that enjoyed older and more distinguished traditions and that played a larger role in viceregal circles than the convent in which she has pledged.[65] As we have just seen, Herrera's admiration for Rosa of Lima is one way in which this awareness manifests itself in her writings. More generally, Herrera laments the fact that her convent cannot claim as part of its history an illustrious founding figure:

> *For God's Sake! How unfortunate my convent is, that it was founded so many years ago and one hears nothing about any nun having flourished here!* This thought made me feel indifferent: *Why wouldn't I go to Lima to some Monastery where so many flourished* (as if others' virtues could serve for my own perfection)? *Here* (I thought) *there is not a single nun of whom to say: I will follow this example. Since not even the Founding Mothers have anything memorable about them.* (162)[66]

Herrera's confession of disappointment is followed by a vision of a beautiful nun whom she describes in detail (narrative once again providing an answer to her dilemma). Asking her fellow sisters later who the nun might have been, Herrera is told that it must be Juana de la Cruz, an exemplary nun who had previously lived in Herrera's cell. Realizing that when the few remaining nuns who had known her pass away, Sor Juana de la Cruz will be forgotten, Herrera organizes a daring expedition to locate and excavate the nun's final resting place within the convent walls. By unearthing this exemplary religious figure, Herrera hopes not only to rescue her memory but also to legitimize the history of the convent to which she and Sor Juana both belong.[67]

The description of the expedition overflows the boundaries of the spiritual autobiography genre and approaches the picaresque, reminding the reader of Herrera's earlier championing of Martha's active agency.[68] The nuns who join Herrera must disrobe in order not to dirty their habits during the excavation. Herrera recounts that they do not know where to look for the nun's burial place; what's more, they are pursued by demons that attempt to disorient them and dissuade them from their objective. Miraculously, a statue of Christ that stands nearby opens its eyes, gesturing to indicate to Herrera where she will find Sor Juana's remains (163–65). But when she and her companions follow the statue's directions, they find only an empty burial place.[69] The crestfallen nuns return to their cells. Renewing their efforts the following night, Herrera and her band of intrepid followers are once again frustrated. On the third day, Herrera successfully secures official permission for the search from the prelate, luckily an elderly and forgetful nun. That very night, digging in the same place as before, the nuns come upon a coffin covered with a multitude of tiny crosses and hear, coming from inside it, the sound of jangling bones. A voice confirms their discovery: "This is it" (165).[70]

Removing the cover of the casket, the nuns find that the remains are encased in a mysterious crystalline covering, and the skull gives off an unearthly fragrance. Comparing the disposition of the remains with convent documents detailing Sor Juana's funerary rites, they find that the written record confirms their discovery. For example, the skeleton lies in a particular position—"one shinbone extended, and the other, withdrawn upwards" (165). These details correspond to stories told by the older nuns of Sor Juana's burial, at which time an Indian sacristan was terrified when, as he attempted to rearrange one of Sor Juana's legs in the casket, the leg moved itself up and out of his grasp. Herrera notes that there is a shoe missing—a detail that is also confirmed by existing documents. Apparently a member of the clergy, a devotee of the sainted nun, had carried one shoe off with him at the time of Sor Juana's burial with the obvious intention of using it as a relic (165).[71] While Herrera's account incorporates miraculous elements that receive no explanation, other more mundane details like these are corroborated by the same convent documents that Herrera hopes her expedition will supplement as she takes action to rewrite convent history.

We can read the incident of the exhumation of Sor Juana as an internal pilgrimage—the only type of pilgrimage permitted to these cloistered nuns.[72] The six participants, led by Herrera, share a keen awareness of the marginality of their own convent and claim solidarity in having committed to a mission whose purpose is to glorify the institution where they themselves feel somewhat alienated. In an epilogue to this episode, Herrera informs the reader that "the older nuns took it badly, saying that we had taken away from those who knew her the chance of removing her themselves. That we were busybodies who wanted to steal the bones from the dead. So what should the living expect from us?" (166). The complaints of the older nuns notwithstanding, Herrera affirms and is affirmed by the search for a feminine geneaology for her convent, and her account chronicles a trajectory that moves from transgression to exemplarity and edification.[73] Just as Sor Juana Inés de la Cruz does in the "Respuesta a Sor Filotea" through the enumeration of "la gran turba de las que merecieron nombres" (the great throng of those [women] who deserved renown), Herrera articulates a strategy for the vindication of her own narrative authority at the same time that she consolidates the spiritual and institutional authority of the religious order and convent she has chosen.[74]

Some of her contemporaries penned histories of their convents as part of a personal and institutional public relations campaign. Meléndez explains the goals of these chronicles: "First, to present the history of the institution and, second, to relate the story of its exceptional founders and members. In addition, the chronicles also called attention to activities performed by nuns within and outside the monastery walls" (*Deviant and Useful Citizens*, 91).[75] Herrera does not present her narrative as monasterial history, perhaps because she struggles with a sense that her convent cannot yet claim the kind of institutional exemplarity that would warrant such a chronicle, although she clearly hopes that the parallels she draws between herself and models like Rosa of Lima and Catherine of Siena, as well as the excavation of Sor Juana's remains, will help to address that issue. However, *Secretos* clearly reflects what Meléndez calls "religious patriotism—a type of discourse that claimed a love of one's country on the basis of religious principle" (*Deviant and Useful Citizens*, 85). Herrera structures her personal story and her search for origins in a way that clearly aspires to connect with a discourse of local institutional prestige produced for domestic consumption.

VI. *"Una Casa que a toda prisa se iba arruinando": All convent politics are local*

As we have seen, convents (and the nuns who dwelled therein) played an important role in bridging the sacred and the material in what Burns has called the colonial "spiritual economy."[76] They also reflected the hierarchies of race and social class that informed colonial urban centers. Monasteries, convents, and cities functioned on the basis of a mutual dependency that one can glimpse in the system of monastic patronage, the contributions made by monastic orders to public charity, the pomp and ceremony of viceregal life, and the constant political intrigues in which nuns were both victims and instigators.[77] These conflicts inevitably found their way into the spiritual autobiographies written by nuns. *Secretos* is no exception, and Herrera's preoccupation with the spiritual authority of her convent (and her own authority as a leader in the convent) must be understood within a broader context of convent politics and ecclesiastical reform playing out in eighteenth-century Quito.

In the late seventeenth century, the Convent of Santa Catalina had suffered a governance crisis that still resonated in Herrera's day. Growing numbers of nuns (each accompanied by servants and companions) had mandated a move in 1615 from the convent's original location to larger quarters, but the move did little to calm rising tensions. Increasingly, the convent was divided by debates about jurisdiction between older nuns, who wished to continue under Dominican supervision, and younger nuns, who advocated for a kind of self-governance, albeit within the strictures of ecclesiastical rules.[78] Among the abuses that the young reformists hoped to address were instances of Dominican chaplains wandering freely about the convent, refusing to permit even dying nuns to confess with anyone except a Dominican friar, and demanding that the nuns perform menial tasks for the friars.[79]

In 1678, with the upcoming election of a new prioress, these tensions came to a head. A number of younger nuns were determined not to vote for the candidate designated by the Dominican provincial Jerónimo Cevallos. Cevallos, described by his contemporaries as a stubborn and inflexible man, took the extraordinary step of whipping several of the rebellious nuns, who then appealed to the bishop for protection and redress.[80] The merits of both sides of the conflict were hotly contested among secular and ecclesiastical authorities, as well as by the families and friends of the nuns, many of whom were members of Quito's elite.[81] When the Audiencia ruled in favor of the Dominicans, the conflict worsened. Dominican friars ignored official orders to stay away from the convent in order not to exacerbate tensions. The rebellious nuns resisted their attempts to enter the cloister, crying out "We will not obey!," and a veritable melée ensued.[82]

The scene was made even more chaotic by the rainy weather, which made it seem as if the heavens themselves were weighing in on the scandal. This was by all accounts a generational dispute: "The old nuns, seated on the ground with their legs crossed and veils covering their faces, remained silent, contemplating with cold indifference the suffering of their sisters."[83] The Audiencia, reconsidering its earlier decision, ordered the convent to be put under protection of the bishop. After repeated petitions and appeals by all sides, the matter was eventually taken up by the Council of the Indies and then Rome, where it was finally determined in 1690 that the convent would remain under Dominican control.[84]

Similar instances of convent politics (often generationally inflected, as we have seen) were still very much a concern in the eighteenth century and found their way into Herrera's account.[85] Herrera frequently wrestled with the implications of her own votes in matters of convent governance and complained that she was the victim of convent intrigues. In frustration she addresses God directly, exclaiming, "Oh, what pain it causes to see these disorders in the Houses of your Brides! Is it possible, Lord, that I must die with this pain of not being able to see my Monastery in best Observance! or not to see myself, if that is not possible, where Religion is observed?" (*Secretos,* 110). In matters of convent politics, as in almost all other matters, Herrera finds her position ultimately and definitively vindicated by God. Part 3 of *Secretos* concludes with a wide-ranging conversation between God and Herrera that further reinforces their mutual understanding with regard to ecclesiastical authority. Herrera recalls, "From here on you began to give me to understand how irritated you were with humankind. And you said to me, 'The cause of all the perdition in the world are priests and religious men and women. The ecclesiastical State is the cause of the perdition of the secular State'" (271). God even goes so far as to suggest that he's about to throw all clergy out of his house, using the domestic space as a metaphor for ecclesiastical governance. These conversations clearly reflect ongoing debates about Bourbon reformist efforts to limit ecclesiastical influence in the viceroyalties and point to a convergence of the interests of local authorities and nuns in opposing a tradition of male monastic authority. Herrera's leadership role in these debates is affirmed not only by her privileged dialogue with God but in more mundane terms when, toward the end of part 4 of the *Secretos,* the other nuns inform her that she has been proposed as a candidate for prioress (398). After much prayer and despite many misgivings, Herrera accepts the nomination. Her political ascendency is miraculously confirmed when a small basket containing alms for the needy becomes always mysteriously full of coins—material witness to Herrera's preferred status on the convent ballot (402–3). The convergence of a putative miracle and Herrera's explanation of her role in the governance of her convent home brings home the degree to which her narrative is informed by matters of politics and property.[86]

Herrera's tenure as prioress is not without difficulties. She must calm her fractious community with loving words, exhorting them to come together as one: "Oh my Sisters! Let us love one another. For because we are born of different wombs, have we not already renounced those wombs and by our will have we not become daughters of one Mother, Religion?" (*Secretos,* 439). The genea-logical terms in which Herrera frames this exhortation recall once again her search for female origins and remind the reader of the young Catalina's bed-side conversation with her mother. Other crises have to do with the push for reform of *la vida común,* directed at impious customs, indolence, and corrupt administration, which were widespread at the time.[87] Herrera must deal with an anonymous letter that has been sent to the dean of Quito, criticizing the strict rules the nuns of the Convent of Santa Catalina must follow, including the re-quirement of nocturnal choral prayer. Herrera responds to the letter by inviting any nuns who wish to transfer to a more lax convent to do so with her bless-ing. The nuns, however, come together in a show of support for their prioress, renouncing the anonymous critique in a signed letter they all write to the dean (440–41). While Herrera's efforts at domestication—that is, to impose order and discipline on her own convent must be understood in a broader context of eighteenth-century reform efforts, they are ultimately concrete evidence of her success in wielding authority within convent walls.

But the tenuous balance between order and disorder in the Convent of Santa Catalina is structural as well as administrative. Even in its early years, the con-vent suffered from shaky foundations. A deposition made in 1600 includes the following assessment of the physical condition of the monastery: "The church is very old and exposed because of quakes, and because the convent is so poor and the building so old, last year part of the convent buildings fell into the street, and since there is no way to raise it, it has not been rebuilt and it has not yet been raised."[88] Despite the move in 1615 to larger and better-maintained quar-ters, the nuns were still faced with considerable challenges a century and a half later in terms of the upkeep of the convent. When a powerful earthquake oc-curred on April 26, 1755, the convent was irreparably damaged by the powerful tremors. The peaceful, reflective life that Herrera had hoped to find in the con-vent crumbled as well.

Earthquakes and other natural disasters were frequent in the Andean re-gion, creating aftershocks that not only were felt concretely, but that also rippled through the social, economic, political, and religious order.[89] As Burns notes, "The story of volcanoes, earthquakes, and migrating nuns at the turn of the seventeenth century also raises to view more figurative varieties of instability, exposing the anxieties of identity in an emerging colonial aristocracy" (*Colo-nial Habits,* 94). The same conditions were prevalent a century and a half later throughout the Andean region, and were exacerbated by the emerging fractures of the late colonial period. After each earthquake, civil and ecclesiastical au-thorities were faced with the considerable challenge of rebuilding—both in a physical and a moral sense—as Charles Walker has shown in *Shaky Colonialism.*

Life in eighteenth-century Quito was shaken by repeated eruptions of the Cotopaxi volcano, which had first erupted in the colonial period in 1534. After more than a century of lying dormant, it did so again several times in 1742, and again in 1744, 1755, and 1768.[90] One observer described the 1768 eruption: "It not only caused violent earthquakes but it added to the general consternation and terror with frightful thunder, with dense clouds of ash that darkened the light of the sun, with lightning and balls of fire that flew up into the air, and with extended subterranean rumblings that could be heard at great distances."[91] After the 1755 earthquake, which caused similar havoc, the nuns of Santa Catalina were obliged to evacuate their convent. Dispersed by this forced exodus, they were exposed to the world outside the convent walls: "Only in the Convent were we regarded as your Brides," Herrera writes, lamenting how outside of it, the nuns received "the contempt of all as if we were the most miserable persons, suffering disdain and hardship" (*Secretos,* 292).[92] Herrera faces a double domestic crisis, because the earthquake has destroyed both her convent and the familial home (leaving Herrera's mother also homeless).[93] Furthermore, the prelate warns Herrera that there is little possibility of rebuilding because of financial and logistical constraints (295). Herrera repeatedly announces her intention to depart immediately for Lima, where she hopes to enter the convent of her model and inspiration Rosa of Lima: "My only inclination was to head off to Santa Rosa of Lima" (295).[94] Herrera's confessor authorizes her to go, but she vacillates, and the desired trip to Lima never materializes. Instead, fleeing the uncertain rubble of Quito, Herrera makes her way to the neighboring town of Pomasqui. She eventually finds lodging with a pious, elderly black woman who shares her modest hut and meager rations with Herrera and another nun until conditions are such that Herrera can return to Quito to undertake the arduous work of rebuilding her convent.[95]

Herrera describes this homecoming as a time of disappointment and disillusionment (307). The return to her ruined convent is traumatic, particularly since it coincides with a period when she has no confessor. Herrera begins to sweat blood and has frequent and devastatingly distressing visions, until she is finally assigned a new confessor, Tomás del Santísimo Rosario y Corrales (318).[96] Herrera's prophetic spells continue to include visions of her ruined monastery, but the bricks and mortar reconstruction of the convent gradually advances, accompanied by the development of a new and deeply satisfying confessorial relationship.[97]

Herrera's complaints about the disorder of monastic life and her account of the 1755 earthquake open a textual space where she can once again exercise authority. Herrera's *excusatio* regarding her ordering capabilities—"I, Lord, am a poor ignorant woman, for I do not know where and how to write things in order, but can only do what I can with Your help!" (100)—belies the degree of narrative control that she exercises throughout the autobiography. What serves to impose order in Herrera's life is not, as one might expect, the cloister (those convent walls are easily breached), but her narrative, in which material and spiritual edification come together as the nun organizes and resolves her trials and tribulations.[98] During most of the autobiography, Herrera is able to use moments of crisis to demonstrate her unshakable faith and confident mastery of the situation, even offering herself to God at one point as a sacrifice to save the city of Quito: "I offered, if it would be of any use, to carry the torments of this life by myself, in order that You might forgive those who dwell in this city"

(260).[99] While this offer acknowledges the possibility of divine providence as a factor in natural disasters, Herrera's gestures at other moments in *Secretos* generally reflect an exemplary (and typically eighteenth-century) pragmatism.

VII. *"Todo en alboroto y guerras": Criollo fear and trembling*

Herrera's convent could eventually be rebuilt, but there were cracks in the imperial façade of the Audiencia of Quito that were not so easily repaired. Herrera's private writings attest to these cracks. The seventeenth century was a period of economic and demographic growth for the region during which Quito became an important urban center for the surrounding hinterland and home to a diverse economy based on mining, textiles, and commerce. In the eighteenth century, however, the city experienced a number of economic and administrative crises in addition to the natural disasters discussed earlier.[100] Droughts and flooding alternated in destructive cycles, negatively affecting agriculture, commerce, and construction.[101] Economic uncertainties were further aggravated by Bourbon reformist efforts to impose new taxes on agriculture and the success of European contraband in penetrating Andean textile markets. Social and economic tensions came to a head in 1765 with uprisings in Quito's popular neighborhoods, known as the *rebelión de los barrios*.[102] These uprisings, which anticipated the 1780 rebellion of Túpac Amaru in Peru, involved a widespread plebian mobilization that represented a significant challenge to viceregal authority and Quito's urban elite.[103] Voicing a general view among criollos that mestizos embodied a particular potential as troublemakers, the Jesuit historian Juan de Velasco in his *Historia del reino de Quito* blamed the *rebelión de los barrios* on a mestizo plot.[104]

Hierarchies founded on race and ethnicity historically had provided the foundation for social order and ethnic *convivencia* in the Audiencia of Quito but, as Velasco's accusation demonstrates, this foundation was shifting.[105] With the accelerating pace of miscegenation in the eighteenth century, the city became home to growing numbers of mestizos, mulattoes, and *zambos* (individuals of mixed African and Amerindian ancestry) who occupied a complicated legal and economic territory.[106] Hispanic notions of urban design, informed by a concern for order and symmetry and exemplified in the Americas by the grid and the plaza (the central location of the seats of ecclesiastical and civic authority) were challenged by late colonial developments.[107] Despite official pressures to maintain ethnic and racial segregation, in Quito the "integration of indigenous and Spanish populations exceeded that of some other major cities in Spanish America."[108] Racial categories responded to economic and legal negotiations, thus permitting some degree of social mobility but also exacerbating criollo fears about societal instability.[109] In her own references to her adopted home, Herrera oscillates between the tradition of *encomia* or *laudes* (praise) and an opposing portrait of the city as dangerous and disorderly. Herrera's criollo anxieties about the precarious situation of eighteenth-century Quito are both unsurprising and revealing.[110] And although specific events to which historians refer in discussing this situation took place after Herrera had completed writing *Secretos* (most notably, the *rebelión de los barrios*), her narrative in many ways anticipates those events.[111]

The most extreme reflection of the anxieties produced by the political and social fissures underlying life in eighteenth-century Quito can be found in Herrera's private letters, a number of which were discovered bound with the manuscript of the *Secretos*. These letters (which are not dated) are addressed to Herrera's father confessor, who at the time she was writing him was traveling outside of Quito. Herrera repeatedly expresses a sense of being abandoned and adrift during his absence, and in each letter she asks her confessor, whom she affectionately calls "Taita mío, Padre de mi alma" (my Taita, Father of my soul), when he plans to return. She also recounts a number of visions that she has experienced, describing them for her confessor with the vivid details that the reader of the *Secretos* has come to expect. But these visions refer not to the divine or the diabolic but to more worldly manifestations, and instead of permitting a masterly demonstration of theological exegesis they open a door to anxieties that remain unresolved in Herrera's epistolary narrative.

The penultimate letter begins with an expression of concern regarding the repeated bouts of illness from which Herrera's confessor has been suffering.[112] But Herrera quickly moves from these mundane preoccupations to more unsettling matters. She describes for her father confessor a Dantesque vision of the end of Quito, which she fears may be a foreshadowing of actual events. Herrera explains that the previous night she had spent the evening praying not only for the good health of her confessor, but also for the health of all the inhabitants of Quito. As dawn approached, she either fell asleep or fainted (it's not clear which—as is often the case during her visions) and had a nightmarish vision that she describes in chilling detail (and which I quote here in its entirety):

> I saw Quito overrun by so many heathen Indians, and so ferocious, that it still causes me horror to write of it. All armed with bows and arrows and other instruments. And these, united with all the Christianized Indians of Quito, made a terrible destruction. They spoke a language that no one understood, not even the other Indians from around here. Then I saw that, united with these, came a sea of black men and women, heathens and heretics, whom I knew to be the offspring of those who had fled Christianity and lived united with those Indians. These ones came together with the blacks of Quito. And each was worse than the other, as if the heathens had come from Guinea. And they made worse destruction than the Indians, because the first thing these Ethiopians began to do was overrun the churches and grab as many books as they found, and scatter them. They took from me a book about the lives of the saints that I was going to hide. And I tried to save and hide a book by the patriarch Saint Joseph. They took from me the papers I was holding, because I was beginning to write a notebook. This church of ours was worse than a stable, only fit to house blacks. It was so filthy, and I saw that the blacks were living off those they had begun to kill. They spoke among themselves in their Guinean language. And the black women of Quito served as their interpreters. I asked one of these interpreters

what would happen to us nuns and to the priests and friars, and she said that
we nuns would be their servants, and that the priests and friars would be killed.
(xv)[113]

Herrera's deepest fears and most shocking prejudices regarding miscegenation,
the threat of rebellion, the babelic confusion of languages, and idolatry emerge
from this eschatological landscape.

Clearly the greatest danger to order is posed by the coming together of Indians and blacks. The alliance between a marginalized urban population of mixed
blood (*castas*) and the indigenous inhabitants of the surrounding mountains in
a spectacle of mob violence is reminiscent of the circumstances leading up to the
rebelión de los barrios.[114] Herrera repeatedly uses the word *unirse* (to unite, or to
come together) to describe what is happening; this verb, in addition to suggesting the convergence of an unruly crowd, also evokes the threat of racial mixing.[115] As Herrera contemplates with terror "the sea of black men and women,"
her language recalls the terrifying winds and waves of earlier meteorlogical
catastrophes. Herrera realizes that these menacing hordes are the offspring of
those who had violated the religious, geographic, and racial boundaries of the
viceregal city: they are "who I knew to be the offspring of those who had fled
Christianity and lived united with those Indians" (xv).[116] These offspring are the
embodiment of criollo concerns about the efficacy of indigenous evangelization
and skepticism about the dependability of recent converts to Christianity.

Herrera reflects in her autobiography on the difficult circumstances of those
who serve in isolated missions throughout the Audiencia of Quito, circumstances that challenge the imperial project of evangelization (338).[117] Andean
geography made travel throughout the region exceedingly difficult: the surrounding mountains closed in on the city, where deep ravines separated urban
neighborhoods and served to heighten divisions between them.[118] This spatial
and psychic geography informs another vision in which Herrera and a small
group of nuns attempt to cross a narrow and rickety bridge to reach a remote
mission. The bridge, according to Herrera's description, is muddy, slippery, and
marked by broken spots, underscoring the dangers and difficulties that confront
missionaries sent to the hinterlands to minister to a resistant or even hostile
Andean indigenous population. It's striking that in this vision Herrera and the
other nuns have left the safety of their cloistered convent to venture into dangerous and uncertain terrain, transgressing the gendered boundaries of monastic
life. The description of their slow and difficult progress reminds the reader of
the pilgrimage to unearth the remains of Sor Juana. In this case, however, there
is no triumphant conclusion to the pilgrimage. Rather, here and in Herrera's letter to her father confessor, Quito is overpowered by indigenous heathens and
heretics who have renounced the Christian faith they had previously accepted.

Echoing terminology employed by Benedictine Benito Jerónimo Feijoo in
his essay "Color etiópico" (included in the *Teatro crítico*), the Dominican nun
refers to blacks as "Ethiopians" or "Guineans."[119] Although this is standard terminology for the time, Herrera's choice of words underscores an additional level
of otherness having to do not with race or ethnicity but rather with domicile.[120]

The marauding blacks are not from Quito; that is, they are not locals but rather outsiders. Unlike the domesticated "blacks of Quito" who also figure in Herrera's autobiography, like the pious elderly woman who offers Herrera shelter after the earthquake or her young servant in the convent, "the sea of black men and women" who flood Quito in Herrera's epistolary nightmare are implicated in the emergence of new generations that are profoundly unsettling for the elite political and social order to which Herrera belongs.[121]

Herrera makes a clear distinction in her writing between "the Indians from around here" and "those Indians" as well, resorting repeatedly to demonstrative adjectives—"these" and "those"—in an effort to differentiate between the two groups.[122] The result, however, is not clarity but rather a bewildering and threatening proliferation of plebian bodies. In eighteenth-century *casta* paintings, the pictorial taxonomies that portray racial mixing in a domesticated and familiar setting can be read as an attempt to contain miscegenation by framing and labeling it.[123] What Herrera glimpses in her vision resists any effort at taxonomic control, threatening both the boundaries of the viceregal city and her carefully controlled narrative efforts. The degree to which Herrera's world is turned upside-down is revealed by one of the black women interpreters who assures her that the nuns will be serving them in the future; she translates for Herrera not only words in an unknown language but also the ramifications of unimaginable social change.[124]

In Herrera's vision Quito is overrun by barbarians who speak a language that no one can understand, not even the urbanized Indians of Quito. She has already expressed concern about the difficulties of the church's evangelical mission in a context in which the indigenous population does not understand Spanish. In one vision included in the *Secretos,* Herrera finds herself in "a town of idolatrous Indians where there was no language except for theirs that I still do not understand, nor can any interpreter, so that they spoke to me and I did not understand them nor they me, and in great straits I found myself where it might end in them killing me" (302).[125] This scene is an inversion of the ceremony of Hapsburg conquest in which the *requerimiento* is read in Spanish to a group of uncomprehending Amerindians, and it indicates how far removed the periphery of the Bourbon Spanish Empire feels itself to be from that paradigmatic moment. Just as the indigenous infidels speak an incomprehensible language, so do the blacks, whose "Guinean language" requires interpretation.

Herrera also refers specifically to the destruction of books written by the church fathers—books she tried unsuccessfully to protect—and to the theft of the barely begun notebook that the rebellious hordes tear from her hands. These acts are commensurate with all the other instances of atrocity she witnessed in her vision and represent an assault on the eighteenth-century lettered city. *Secretos* contains numerous references to the precariousness of the written text, Herrera's own writings as well as those of others.[126] In one of her earliest visions of the devil, he spills ink over a number of papers on her desk. The nun explains:

> The first thing I wrote I had inside a desk that had a crack in the middle of the top; this beast knocked an inkwell over it and all the ink ran inside. And

You, my God, who knows to take care of your things, saved them, so that not a single drop of ink fell on the papers that were inside, and the ink I don't know how ended up wetting some old Bulls and letters that were there. (17)

Here, Herrera's writings are miraculously spared. But in the vision Herrera describes in her letter, there is no miracle. The result of the political turmoil that threatens Quito is the destruction of history itself, represented by the sacking of church libraries and by the theft of Herrera's own pages. The authorial mastery evinced in *Secretos* at other moments of crisis cannot be sustained in Herrera's private epistolary correspondence in the face of this fearful onslaught.

Herrera's letter concludes: "Quito was left in darkness. The whites did not appear: some hidden and unable to escape from where they were hiding, and others dead. And we were all awaiting death. Here is where I lost my fear of the plague, because we would have been better off dead than seeing all this disaster" (xv). The enlightened viceregal city has been enveloped in darkness—a darkness that for the writer is both atmospheric and racial. Herrera moves from historical reporting in the third person—"los blancos"—to a more inclusive first-person plural in which she herself is implicated—"nosotros." She concludes with a deeply felt individual confession ("I lost my fear of the plague") that returns to—and, in a sense, moves beyond—the epidemiological preoccupation that marked the letter's opening.

In Herrera's eschatological nightmare we recognize the most unsettling preoccupations and deep-seated prejudices of the Andean criollo: racial mixing, linguistic confusion, idolatrous practices, indigenous uprisings, and the general dismantling of the enlightened lettered city.[127] By describing how the threat of epidemic becomes a rampant pathology that extends over the entire *quiteño* landscape, Herrera reveals the precarious situation of her criollo contemporaries who, in this vision, are rendered incapable of defending themselves against the collapse of viceregal order. Part of Herrera's anxiety stems from the fact that it's not clear what kind of institutional or imperial authority might be called upon to defend Quito from the threats she envisions. As Bourbon reforms change the structures of viceregal administration and demographic shifts change the face of Quito, there are profound implications for the delicate balance of secular and ecclesiastical claims to property and authority in the eighteenth-century lettered city. If at other moments Herrera uses her narrative to construct a textual and institutional barricade against the instability of her epoch, in this epistolary parenthesis Herrera's constructive and ordering will relinquishes control as she witnesses Bourbon hierarchies overtaken by events and overwhelmed in a nightmarish scenario of crisis and chaos.[128]

VIII. *"Acta de apertura del cofre": A relic of one's own*

Herrera could not have anticipated the ways in which her vita would circulate in an Ecuadoran spiritual economy beyond these moments of crisis. Nor could she have known how it would contribute to the construction of foundational national and urban narratives beyond the breakdown of empire. As we have seen, Herrera suddenly broke off the composition of her manuscript, with no formal conclusion or closure. For that reason Herrera's story lacks the narrative element of a "good death" that is characteristic of hagiographic accounts.[129] Faced with this dilemma of *habeas corpus,* scholars and historians have gone to great lengths to include in their accounts and editions of Herrera's writings all extant *actas* (records), testimonies, and other documents that might compensate for the absence of a rehabilitating conclusion to her not always edifying life. The 1954 edition of *Secretos entre el alma y Dios,* for example, includes photos of the convent and of the images mentioned by Herrera in her text, as well as a portrait of the author painted after her death. In his biography of Herrera, José María Vargas also includes a number of photographs and reminds his reader that these portraits and images can still be seen by visiting the Convent of Santa Catalina.[130] These details create a kind of mise en abyme for the reader in which the material and textual traces of Herrera's life work to reinforce each other.

No aspect of this mise en abyme is more vertiginous than a series of documents related to Herrera's remains. Vargas explains that the catalyst for his biographical-hagiographical study of Herrera was the founding of a Dominican convent in Guayaquil, her birthplace. Both in Europe and the Americas it was common practice to sacralize a new church or convent with the formal establishment of a reliquary, so the founders of the convent, which was to be named "Santa Catalina" in her honor, wrote on the occasion of its inauguration in 1977 to ask that Herrera's remains be exhumed and to request a number of relics from those remains to honor the new convent.[131] The Dominican authorities agreed to this request.

The "Acta de apertura del cofre que contiene los restos de Sor Catalina de Jesús María Herrera" (Act of the opening of the coffin containing the remains of Sor Catalina) is the final document included in the appendix to Vargas's biography (*Sor Catalina,* 114–17). The *acta* states that "following a brief deliberation, the ecclesiastical authorities present, priests, nuns, and the medical expert agreed to separate out the following remains of Sor Catalina de Jesús to be sent to the city of Guayaquil: right temple, sacrum, shoulderblade, and two vertebral fragments" (117). Dispersion and fragmentation paradoxically create opportunities for new, local invocations of spiritual authority.[132] The transferral of the remains also represents a kind of homecoming for Herrera, a triumphal return to the city of her birth.

We see here reproduced the very same circumstances of the exhumation of Sor Juana that Herrera had organized two centuries before to consolidate the prestige of her convent in Quito, except that now the expedition is an official one, and it is the consecrated remains of Herrera that will serve to represent and disseminate feminine religious exemplarity. The connections between these two exhumations are reinforced by the fact that both the 1954 edition of *Secretos* and Vargas's biography reproduce the *acta* documenting the discovery of Sor Juana's remains that was bound with the original manuscript of *Secretos.*[133] The identification or—more accurately—the confusion of Sor Juana and Sor Catalina as model nuns is definitively inscribed in Ecuadoran historiography with

the 1987 publication of the *Diccionario biográfico del Ecuador*. The essay dedicated to Catalina de Jesús Herrera Campusano in that volume states that her remains were discovered in 1845, fifty years after her burial. The find is described
thus:

> They found the bones of the right leg withdrawn upward, because soon after
> she died they wanted to bury another person at her feet and the Indian who
> opened the grave put his hand in to touch her and as he went to grab her foot,
> she moved it away from the Indian's hand. And he began to shout, and a nun
> came to certify what had happened and found the foot withdrawn as has been
> described. (Pérez Pimentel, *Diccionario biográfico del Ecuador,* 2:102)

The source of this quote is not identified in the brief biographical note, but
anyone familiar with *Secretos* will realize immediately that it has been included
in the *Diccionario* by mistake. The cited description comes, in fact, from the
1745 *acta* testifying to the discovery of the remains of Sor Juana de la Cruz by
Herrera and her band of semi-naked and muddy coreligionists, the details of
which Herrera narrates in her *Autobiografía* (*Secretos,* 165). The confusion is instructive, however, as it reflects the degree to which the story of the nuns functions as both an archive and a lipsanotheca where documents and bones are
mixed up together in an undiscriminated but inspired fashion—all in order to
testify to the prestige of the convent, the Dominican order, and the nation.[134]
The repeated unearthing of these remains, and their textual repercussions as
they circulate in Quito's spiritual economy, serve to buttress the edification of
personal and institutional genealogies that lie at the heart of Herrera's *Secretos*
and that become a touchstone for the transition between premodern and modern notions of empire.

CHAPTER FIVE

Domesticating Gold

José Martín Félix de Arrate's
Llave del Nuevo Mundo (1761)

Compónese dicho escudo de tres castillos de plata sobre
campo azul, alusivos a las tres fortalezas que guardan la
boca del puerto, y una llave de oro que manifiesta serlo de
las Indias, como estaba declarado por SS.MM.

[This coat of arms is composed of three silver castles on a
blue background, referring to the three forts that protect the
entry to the port, and a gold key that represents the key to
the Indies, as was declared by their Majesties.]

José Martín Félix de Arrate, *Llave del Nuevo Mundo*

I. *"Oro quanto ouieren menester": All that glitters*

In 1803 Alexander von Humboldt made a visit to the Zócalo, the principal plaza
of New Spain, where he witnessed for himself the cultural and economic vitality
of Mexico's viceregal capital. Adjacent to the Royal Palace, which housed the
Mining Courts and the Consulate of Commerce, the Casa de Moneda (Mint)
was being built. The Casa de Moneda was a warehouse for vast amounts of silver, which were mined in Mexico during the eighteenth century and sent out
from New Spain to support imperial initiatives in Europe, the Caribbean, and
the Philippines. It loomed large as a symbol of New World riches and of the
institutionalization of the Bourbon Empire in New Spain. There, in front of the
building site, Humboldt gave voice to the wonder that the bricks and mortar
reflection of New World wealth inspired in him: "It is impossible to visit this
building . . . without remembering that more than two thousand million 'pesos
fuertes' [hard coins] have left it in less than three hundred years, and without
reflecting on the powerful influence that these treasures have had on the fate of
the peoples of Europe."[1] Humboldt's words remind us of the symbolic and material importance that the precious minerals of the Americas held throughout
the viceregal period. The date of and setting for his words underscore the complicated network of economic transactions and transmutations in which that
richness was involved by the end of the eighteenth century. What was born as

tesoros (treasure) in the deep veins of the continent ended up converted into *pesos fuertes* (capital) through state intervention, represented on this occasion by the neoclassical facade of the Casa de Moneda under construction.

The possibility of finding new deposits of precious minerals—what Adam Smith would call in 1776 the "sacred thirst of gold"—was one of the principal motives behind the maritime explorations that in the late fifteenth century had culminated in the voyages of Christopher Columbus.[2] Medieval alchemy, with its erroneous claim that one could forgo the mining of precious metals and instead create them through chemical transmutation in the laboratory, had incited a lust for gold that remained unfulfilled. In the wake of this alchemical frustration, Spanish conquistadors would set out into the American interior in search of the mythical cities of El Dorado and Cibola, where they hoped to discover gold in great amounts.

In early accounts written by Spaniards who had traveled to the New World, few words resonate as frequently or as powerfully as "gold." In these accounts (which reflect wishful thinking, to be sure) gold is everywhere—lying on the ground, hidden in riverbeds, and adorning the bodies of the indigenous inhabitants. Columbus alone refers to gold at least sixty-five times in the diary of his first voyage, and his preoccupation with the prospect of finding gold drives his frustrating and frustrated attempts at communication with the people he finds when he makes landfall. On October 13, 1492, Columbus writes: "I was attentive and labored to find out if there was any gold; and I saw that some of them wore a little piece hung in a hole that they have in their noses. And by signs I was able to understand that, going to the south or rounding the island to the south, there was there a king who had large vessels of it and had very much gold."[3] He closes the "Letter to Luis Santangel" by promising to deliver to the Catholic kings, in exchange for additional provisions needed for a second voyage, as much gold as they might ever require. Columbus's predisposition to find gold, inscribed in his contractual obligations to his sovereigns, causes him to misinterpret information he will later receive from the indigenous population.

When Cortés writes to Philip II about his plans to conquer the Aztec city of Tenochtitlán, he boasts to the king: "As of the wealth in gold and silver and precious stones which Your Majesties may judge according to the samples we are sending . . . there must be in this land as much as in that from which Solomon is said to have taken the gold for the temple" (*Letters from Mexico*, 29). Bernal Díaz del Castillo writes of the gold treasure the conquistadors imagine they will find when they discover Moctezuma's secret treasures. He recounts that Cortés presents the Indians with a somewhat rusty gilded helmet, asking whether, "as he wished to know whether the gold of this country was the same as that we find in our rivers, they could return the helmet filled with grains of gold so that he could send it to our great Emperor" (*History of the Conquest*, 55). José de Acosta affirms that "gold was always held to be the chief among all metals, and rightly so, because it is the most durable and incorruptible; for fire, which consumes or diminishes the other metals, improves and perfects it, and gold that has passed through great heat maintains its color and is exceedingly pure" (*Natural and Moral History*, 166).[4] Gold glitters in a long tradition in the European imaginary; whether sprinkled over the earth's surface or hidden deep in its veins, throughout history it has inspired fascination, obsession, and desire.[5]

This background helps to explain why discussions of precious metals, metallurgy, and mining in the Americas have traditionally focused on gold and silver, taking as their point of departure the supposed existence of huge deposits of those metals in Mexico and Peru. Even as golden fantasies gave way to more realistic distinctions between gold found on the surface and gold found deep in the veins of underground mines, and as gold found a companion metal in silver, these two precious metals enjoyed a privileged status as pure value. The fact that gold and silver ornaments were regularly melted down reflects this valorization, and the various accounts of how and where precious metal deposits were found only serves to corroborate their legendary status.[6]

However, viceregal economic discourse reflects the presence of other metals like copper, other mixes or adulterations like bronze, and new mining and metallurgical technologies that emerge in an evolving ecological, sociopolitical, and cultural environment. It has been speculated, for example, that copper was the first metal to be smelted in the Americas, and in the Andean region copper was valued because it altered silver and gold, not only making them stronger but also changing their color and making it reddish.[7] Although gold and silver have a high value in pre-Columbian communities because of their reflective capacity, other metallic mixtures were developed to expand the palette of colors that could be given to ceremonial objects.[8] The variety of methods and techniques used to color the surface of those objects corresponds in the Andean region to the full representation of political rank and power and, ultimately, challenges European notions of the relationship between essence and surface.[9]

The conquistadors' obsession with gold led inevitably to failure and disillusion—at least for most of them—as the grinding, gritty reality of mining precious metals in the New World was brought home to them. By the eighteenth century, a new discursive golden thread becomes discernable, one in which the earlier Columbian discourse of gold has been domesticated. We see this domestication in descriptions of eighteenth-century developments such as the shift in interest from gold and silver to a broad range of other metals, the emphasis on new scientific techniques such as amalgamation or slag mining, and the implications of Bourbon economic reforms for metropolitan communities on the periphery of empire.

These changes had, of course, come gradually over the preceding two centuries as the Spaniards' initial lust for pure gold was displaced by a more complicated engagement with negotiation, exchange, and circulation.[10] Mining, which began in Mexico around 1530 and in the Andes around 1540, also experienced transformations over time. The laborious processes related to mining—excavating, extracting, melting, and amalgamating—imposed themselves on the golden dreams of the conquistadors early on. These processes inevitably had the effect of complicating, contesting, and ultimately rewriting the discourse of gold that had marked the foundational texts of the discovery and conquest of the Americas.[11]

The eighteenth century represents a moment of transition in which an earlier economic discourse based on gold and, to a lesser degree, on silver is converted into a new, more nuanced and mediated discourse. One might even say that the Columbian discourse of gold has been "debased," or domesticated. This discursive shift converges with shifts in the material economy that were already being felt in the late sixteenth and seventeenth centuries. In the eighteenth-century discursive economy, the earlier obsession with precious metals gives way to the economic possibilities of copper and mercury, the use of new technologies such as amalgamation, and the circulation of newly minted coins and goods.[12] The expanding fortunes and strategic importance of viceregal port cities are reflected in the various ways in which their residents lay claim to recognition and reward from the metropolitan center in a new urban twist on the *relación de méritos y servicios* (report of merits and services to the Crown). The cases that I will be discussing in this chapter—amalgamation in the silver mines of Potosí, the copper tailings of El Cobre in Cuba, an urban history written to argue for the considerable merits of eighteenth-century Havana, and, finally, a lost bag of doubloons on the Argentine pampa—all present different domesticating traces of the devaluation of Columbian gold.

II. "Para que tan rica posesión nos dé ventajas": Bourbon economic reforms

Historians have recognized the sense of imperial exhaustion—political, economic, and intellectual—in late seventeenth-century Spain, but they point to the ascent to the throne of Charles III in 1759 as a new beginning.[13] Guided by a pragmatic and dirigiste regime that saw absolutism as the most effective reform strategy, Charles III's reformist administrators applied physiocratic and mercantilist policies in order to resuscitate the colonial economy: the system of *flotas* (convoys) and the Cádiz monopoly were abolished; new taxes were levied; and mining centers (supported by newly established mining academies) opened new domestic markets for agriculture and industry.[14]

If the importance of precious metals during the first two centuries of Spanish presence in the New World is represented by the metaphor of hidden veins laden with silver and gold, then the eighteenth-century metaphor of circulation suggests a new economic paradigm. Precious minerals are no longer hidden treasures but rather commodities to be exchanged and circulated in a widening world. Generally speaking, the eighteenth century was a time of relative material prosperity and demographic growth in Spain and the Americas.[15] The economy was also growing: the eighteenth century saw an increase in mining production due to the high valuation of precious metals in Europe and a general stimulation of commerce due to the mining. America was seen as a market for Spanish goods and a source of raw materials, although it has been argued that the defensive move to stave off possible economic autonomy for the viceroyalties had negative repercussions for both Spain and her territories across the Atlantic.[16]

Given the increasing importance of intra-imperial trade networks, it's important to recognize regional differences, as well as the interdependence of metropolitan and viceregal finances.[17] The significance of criollo contributions to the greater imperial good is something that José Martín Félix de Arrate will stress in *Llave del Nuevo Mundo*. The War of the Spanish Succession had revealed significant weaknesses in Spain's imperial reach, particularly with regard to her navy and the unwieldy *flota* system; while the Treaty of Utrecht in 1713 brought the war to a close, it did little to lessen the threat to Spain's possessions in the Americas from French, British, and Dutch rivals. Economic reforms initiated by Philip V during the first half of the eighteenth century and continued by Charles III therefore had as one of their principal goals defending Spain's transatlantic commerce and protecting and expanding its overseas resources and revenues.[18]

These reforms led to a new and evolving relationship between center and periphery. The colonial state played an active role in the regulation and administration of the late colonial economy, attempting to control the connections between an emerging global market and regional economies in the Americas through a complex network of monopolies, taxes, and regulations.[19] During the second half of the eighteenth century, Spanish territories in the Americas ceased to function like viceroyalties, as they had during the Hapsburg period, when the idea of federated kingdoms and monarchy together permitted some degree of autonomy. They became dominions of a centralized and centralizing royal bureaucracy by means of administrative, political, and economic strategies that reflect what has been called late mercantilism.[20] Conquest and the expansion of empire—both Hapsburg goals—were replaced by the Bourbon consolidation of empire in order to maximize profitability.[21]

At the same time it's important to recognize the tensions between the political and economic liberty implicit in *comercio libre* (free trade) and the centralizing culture of the Spanish Empire.[22] These tensions are reflected in the emergence of regional differences in America, the development of intraregional commerce, and the importance of local agents—criollo functionaries and administrators, *mingas* (paid laborers in the Andean mines), pirates, royal slaves, and local cultural symbols such as the Virgen de la Caridad del Cobre.[23] With the growing importance of transatlantic trade, piracy, contraband, smuggling, and other forms of illegal commerce became central preoccupations for the Bourbon Crown. Individuals and governments alike viewed contraband as both a problem and an opportunity, depending on where they were positioned with regard to Spain's commercial monopoly. Mercury smuggling was extremely prevalent, as I discuss later in this chapter.[24]

During the mid-eighteenth century a document began to circulate that would have enormous repercussions for the Bourbon reform project. In *Nuevo sistema económico para América,* which was written in 1743 but remained

unpublished until 1789, José Campillo y Cosío lays out the key economic issues that underlie my readings in this chapter.[25] Campillo argued that Spain
must take more strategic advantage of her natural and human resources in the
Americas, strengthening intraregional and transatlantic commerce and making
it more agile. He cautioned against the threat of attack by hostile European rivals
and stressed the need for strong military defenses. He proposed the abolition of
the Cádiz monopoly with its high trade tariffs, and he outlined an administrative system based on the creation of new governing bodies (*intendencias*).[26] Furthermore, he argued that the system of *flotas* impeded commercial development
and encouraged smuggling, and should be abolished. Campillo conceived of the
colonies as markets for Spanish goods, thereby obviating the need to develop
local industries. Indigenous populations would be incorporated into society as
potential consumers through *repartimientos de comercio* (trade requirements).

Campillo forcefully addresses what he sees as Spain's pernicious dependency
on the infusion of precious metals sent from the Americas, and he concludes
that precious metals have value only as instruments of exchange. In this view,
which is linked to the mercantilist importance of trade and commerce, the exchange of goods and gold increases a nation's wealth and power, leading to both
growth and trade rivalries. It differs from the view of the physiocrats, who considered precious metals to be a false standard and emphasized instead the land
as the source of all wealth.[27] In Campillo's opinion, the introduction into the
Iberian peninsula of great quantities of bullion had only accelerated inflation
and served as an impediment to economic development, because it hindered
the development of alternative economic forms such as industry and agriculture. Its transport relied, moreover, on the controlled *flota* system, something
that was in direct contradiction with *libre comercio* and invariably incited the
double threat of piracy and contraband, both issues of grave concern.[28]

At the same time, a combination of factors—the high price of precious metals in Europe and the technological advances that led to more efficient mining
processes—contributed to the flourishing of the mining industry. This explains
why Campillo devoted the first chapter of the second part of *Nuevo sistema de
gobierno* to the gold and silver mines of the Americas:

> Their powerful attraction is notorious, and it consists primarily of three things.
> First, the poor quality of the Ministers; second, the lack of skill of those who
> oversee the work; and third, the lack of protection on the government's part;
> and notwithstanding these strong negatives, we see, and I have ascertained,
> that they have produced thousands of millions; and in this can be clearly and
> distinctly seen the richness of their depths, and the shame of not correspond-
> ing on our part to the care, manner, heed, and special attention that should be
> employed in their management and benefit. (192)

To put a stop to the egregious abuses and inefficiencies of mining administration in the Americas, Campillo recommended that the best practices of
European mining be followed.[29] In what follows, we'll see how new scientific

expertise and knowledge were exploited to promote an enlightened and domesticated version of the golden dream.

III. "De la vana y perniciosa aplicación a buscar tesoros escondidos": Mining matters

As I noted earlier, the discourse of gold that Columbus had articulated in his *Diario* gave way slowly but inexorably before the reality that the gold deposits found in the Caribbean and on the mainland were much smaller that what had initially been anticipated.[30] At the same time, silver deposits exceeded all expectations. Peter Bakewell observes, "Indeed, 'mining' in the Spanish American Empire quickly came to mean the extraction of silver. In total value of metal produced, silver probably passed gold during the 1540s, and it remained the prime product of Spanish American mines for the rest of the Spanish colonial period (and beyond it until the late nineteenth century)" (*Mines of Silver,* xv).[31] José de Acosta devotes several chapters to a discussion of the mining and refining of silver ore in Peru, and to the discovery of mercury (or quicksilver) in Huancavelica.[32] Chroniclers such as Pedro Cieza de León, Luis Capoche, and Bartolomé Arzáns record both the discovery in 1545 of the great silver mine at Potosí and the subsequent growth of the lavish and luxury-driven town by the same name.

Early silver mining techniques were relatively primitive and haphazard (involving placer washing and rudimentary smelting), and at first little advantage was taken of new developments in technology.[33] But Bartolomé de Medina's invention of the "patio" process of amalgamation in 1555 revolutionized Andean silver mining and, along with the reorganization of the *mita* (forced labor system based on Inca practice), made possible an explosion in silver production in the Andean region.[34] The process required a series of technological and chemical interventions that were a far cry from the fortuitous discovery of precious metals dreamt of by the conquistadors.[35] Mercury played an essential role in the silver amalgamation process, leading to further refinement of the golden dream.[36] After silver was extracted from subterranean veins, it was crushed, or triturated, first by mallets and then usually by some kind of grinding mill powered by water or animals. The pulverized ore was moistened and mixed with mercury and copper pyrites. This mixture was spread out to dry in open courtyards or patios (hence the name). Finally, the mixture was washed and beaten to separate out the mercury, leaving behind silver in its pure form.[37]

The presence of the great mercury mines of Huancavelica contributed to the expansion of amalgamation. The mercury was taken from Huancavelica to Potosí first by mule, then by ship, and then by mule again across the remaining three hundred miles inland, through deserts and over mountains. The Huancavelica mercury mines exemplify the complex network of economic, political, legal, and administrative considerations that linked the Crown, the metropolis, and the American territories. The viceroy of Peru, Francisco Alvaro de Toledo, described the tandem of Potosí and Huancavelica in 1579 as "the axis on which the wheels of this entire Kingdom turn and the benefits that Your Majesty has from it."[38] Of course, in order for these wheels to turn, it was also necessary to have a market economy and an agricultural sector to support the mining endeavors, all of which were fueled by the exchange of precious metals.[39] The resulting demographic and economic explosion meant that the population of Potosí was connected with other, distant regions in a complex network of roads, markets, posts, and contraband.[40] When, in the eighteenth century, the mines of Almadén surpassed those of Huancavelica as a source of mercury (the latter having experienced a decline in production), the process took yet another transatlantic turn.[41]

The closing decades of the eighteenth century saw renewed efforts to improve the efficiency of mines in Mexico and the Andes. Rather than finding additional sources for precious metals, mining reform was considered the most rational way of increasing revenues (and it had the additional benefit of solidifying local control over the mining industry). Clement G. Motten argues that the 1778 mission of mining engineers and technicians to Mexico, led by Fausto de Elhuyar (who in 1786 had been named director-general of the Royal Mining Corps of Mexico), is an example of the Enlightenment's commitment to knowledge in the service of power and pragmatism, and he points out (making an argument similar to the one that Jorge Cañizares-Esguerra would later make in *How to Write the History of the New World*) that "the transfer of enlightened knowledge . . . turned out to be a reciprocal affair" (*Mexican Silver,* 2).[42] For example, the European mining expert Friedrich Traugott Sonneschmid admitted the superiority of the autochthonous patio method over the *Born* (barrel) process, which represented "the very latest European scientific research on the problem of refining silver ores."[43] Sonneschmid remained in New Spain for over a decade and would later decry the general European rejection of Spanish American metallurgical methods: "It would be well, however, if recognition [of the patio method] were to spread to Europe in order to do justice to this most excellent method which European opinion has treated with considerable scorn."[44]

In the Andean region, a proposal was put forth in 1779 for the establishment of an academy of mining (similar to the one in Mexico) that would bring together local mining functionaries to learn and discuss the newest, most rational mining practices. The first-year class used Alvaro Alonso Barba's *Arte de los metales* (Art of metals) as its primary text, while the second-year class undertook revising and updating Barba's seventeenth-century work chapter by chapter.[45] However, the pressures for Potosí to produce increased revenues left little room for gradual reforms and limited the academy's chance of success. By 1786, it had closed its doors.[46]

Equally important in terms of mining reforms was the issue of ownership of the mines. There is no clear record of when mercury was first discovered in Huancavelica and its environs.[47] Enrique Garcés (a Portuguese merchant who was later praised by Miguel de Cervantes in *La Galatea*) is generally credited with recognizing the significance of the fact that indigenous inhabitants of the region mined cinnabar—*bermellón,* or mercury sulphide, the most common form of mercury ore—for personal adornment.[48] Once news of the mercury mines at Huancavelica began to circulate among the Spaniards, however, it gave rise to foundational legends similar to those that had sprung up regarding Potosí.[49] Furthermore, the discovery of the Huancavelica mine was followed by legal petitions regarding ownership, as supposedly the residents who had pointed out the mercury deposits to the Spaniards then went to the Audiencia de Lima to petition that they be exempted from working in the mines in recognition of their discovery. The local *corregidor* (chief magistrate) almost immediately began to retract these concessions in order to claim the mine as state property.[50]

These legal wranglings took place in a larger context. In an important revision of the existing mining codes, the right to prospect for, own, and operate mines was expanded in 1584 for Spanish subjects, foreigners, and natives.[51] The new code, however, was continually revised, resulting sometimes in clarifications and other times in confusion. Tax reductions were offered for the discovery of mines, and those owning mines were required to keep them "in continuous operation."[52] The Crown's desire to maximize production led to a fairly improvised proliferation of small mines and refineries whose rationalization would be one of the goals of the Bourbon reforms recommended by Campillo and others. At the same time, by never officially making silver mining a state monopoly, the Crown encouraged a system of private entrepreneurship in which "the *mineros* had developed a degree of self-assurance and independence that was rather unusual in the Spanish colonies."[53] Metaphorically speaking, then, what was produced in the Andean region was a kind of economic and demographic amalgamation—a mix of different elements in terms of social class, origin, labor status, and ethnicity that came together to produce a uniform and useful whole, effecting an increase in collective productivity.[54] In the mix the question of who could claim ownership of material and human resources remains a compelling one for criollo historians.

The silver-plated version of the golden dream is reflected in *La historia de la villa imperial de Potosí,* written by Bartolomé Arzáns de Orsúa y Vela during the first decades of the eighteenth century. After a period of expansion and prosperity, silver production in Potosí entered into a time of contraction and decline around the close of the sixteenth century.[55] So at the time Arzáns is writing, Potosí's glory days were long past. Arzáns describes "the famous, greatest, always incredibly rich and never-ending Cerro de Potosí" that reserved its riches until the arrival of the Spanish, announcing with a clap of thunder to the terror-struck Indians who were attempting to mine its veins: "Do not remove the silver from this Hill, because it is for other owners." (*Historia de la villa,* 1:27).[56] The historian explains that when it came time "to give to humans the silver from that rich Hill," discord and rivalries cropped up between the Spaniards who had been, according to the historian, destined by Providence to receive the riches and the Indians who had been living in that area for many years (1:35). Despite indigenous resistance, the Spaniards were eventually successful in imposing their rule and appropriated traditional Andean methods of mineral extraction, modernizing them with new European technological advances.

As he narrates the glories of his *patria chica* (hometown), Arzáns employs what Denise Galarza Sepúlveda has called a criollo moral economy that privileges the Potosinos, descendants of the first colonizers, with respect to all other inhabitants of the region, including peninsulars.[57] But if criollo merit succeeds in transcending economic and political catastrophe, it is because the historian rewrites the history of Potosí, transferring his focus from the mountain with its silver veins to the city with its civil and moral virtues.[58] That is why the narrative perspective of *La historia de la villa imperial de Potosí* foregrounds not silver as a natural resource, but rather the structures of bureaucratic administration and metropolitan merit that grew from it (and in which the historian was a fully engaged participant). The move from essence to process is at the heart of the eighteenth-century domestication of the earlier discourse of gold, as enlightened thinking replaced the focus on mineral wealth itself to a more complex understanding of the value added by human capital and new science.

Legendary accounts of El Dorado or stories of the gold-dusted Chibcha king (whose raft sank in a Colombian lake, taking with it untold treasure) bring together excess and effortlessness: in these stories, gold is everywhere. Although precious metals are elusive, they still hold out a promise to come within one's reach almost magically. The body of a colonial-era indigenous miner, unearthed a number of years ago in the mountains of northern Chile after being buried centuries earlier by a tunnel collapse in a copper mine in the region of Chuquicamata, speaks to a different truth.[59] Surrounded by his tools—an ax, a shovel, and various wooden sticks—the "copper man" (as he has come to be known) bears silent witness to the backbreaking labor and an arduous process of extraction that over time became inextricably linked to the lure of precious metals.

We see a similar reality in the Caribbean, where the copper mines of Cuba have a story to tell that counters the island's earlier role in the propagation of the *leyenda áurea* (golden legend) as first articulated by Columbus in his diary. Cuba also boasts an iconic figure: the Virgen de la Caridad del Cobre (Virgin of the Heart of Copper). The story of the Virgen de la Caridad del Cobre participates in the invention of a local (and, later, national) hagiographic tradition that involves the eighteenth-century rewriting of a colonial story. It represents a construction that is at the same time narrative and bricks and mortar, announcing the emergence of a New World Mariology whose goal is to claim both exceptionalism and legitimization (and whose best-known example is the Virgen de Guadalupe). Both the Cobrera and the Guadalupan figures call into question traditional hierarchies of gender, race and ethnicity, and citizenship, suggesting new possibilities for juridical and economic agency in the eighteenth-century viceroyalty.[60] The Marian icon and the narratives that were produced to inscribe and reinscribe the history of her miraculous apparition circulated in Cuba in a spiritual and institutional economy at a time of great political and economic changes.

Cuba in the eighteenth century represents a peripheral point that was once again becoming a center (as it had been at the beginning of the sixteenth century). After a brief occupation by the British in 1762–1763, Havana enjoyed an expanded military and naval importance, becoming a focus for intra-American commerce in the Caribbean.[61] The town of El Cobre was founded in the eastern part of the island at the end of the sixteenth century after deposits were found there—not of gold or silver, but rather copper, which was used in the manufacture of artillery (one must remember that the Caribbean was the scene for numerous English pirates and, therefore, the site of many Spanish projects for defense and fortification). Throughout the seventeenth century the town continued to grow, along with its social and economic importance. The Spanish Crown appropriated the mines in 1670, creating a local mining community made up of royal slaves and free people of color, setting off an acceleration in the Creolization of and miscegenation in the region, which would be important in the eighteenth century, as María Elena Díaz discusses in her book, *The Virgin, the King, and the Royal Slaves of El Cobre* (51–53).

Campillo recognizes the commercial benefit of these copper mines in *Nuevo sistema de gobierno*:

> The mines whose utility cannot be in doubt and whose costs are without comparison less than those occasioned by silver and gold mines are the copper mines; and since they are so rich and of such superior quality in the Indies, great care must be taken to perfect their benefits, in order to bring to Europe a greater portion of that metal and advance this branch of our commerce, which is so necessary and useful for many things. (200)

It's important to differentiate the royal slaves who worked the copper mines from those caught in the institutionalized plantation slavery that later dominated the sugar and tobacco plantations of the Caribbean.[62] The *cobreros* negotiated and renegotiated their labor conditions with agents of the Crown, appropriating the ideological and legal discourse of the moment to appeal to the king, and they also evoked a religious discourse centered on the figure of the Virgen de la Caridad del Cobre. The activities of the *cobreros* stand out as an eighteenth-century example of the successful manipulation of the viceregal juridical system to defend subaltern rights and privileges.[63] Their success in these negotiations rested on their awareness that labor processes were key to maximizing mining revenues. This represents an important shift from an earlier focus on the pure essence of gold and silver that, according to legend, was waiting for those lucky or worthy enough to find it ("finders keepers").[64]

The *cobreros* brought together various aspects of colonial society: the church; the economy; viceregal economic, legal, and military administration; slavery; and free agency.[65] These so-called "slaves of the king" could ascend in the military hierarchy and were not required to comply with the sumptuary laws that had been established in part to help differentiate between demographic groups. In terms of economic benefits, they had the right to private property and also to the *pedacitos* (tailings) from the copper mines that remained on the surface after the principal quantities of the copper had been extracted.[66] This is key, because those tailings represented not only an important source of income for the *cobrera* community (whose economy in the eighteenth century was based on a combination of agriculture and mining) but also a testimony to the debasement of the Columbian golden dream that I mentioned at the beginning of this chapter.[67] The legal documents from the period contain multiple mentions of debates about the profitability of the mines, whether the tailings constituted part of the legitimate production or were merely *desperdicios* (remains), whether the *cobreros* should pay taxes on the mined or recovered copper, and if a royal slave had the right to prosperity or merely to subsistence. Díaz includes in her book an analysis of various cases related to the copper mines and quotes the *mandador* (foreman) Nicolás Montenegro, who, in a letter written toward the end of the seventeenth century, explained, "Copper is the currency that nowadays moves around in the mines" (*Virgin*, 201).

But there was another type of symbolic capital that circulated in El Cobre and which the *cobreros* also managed to good effect. When in 1670 the Spanish Crown had taken control of the El Cobre copper mines along with the slaves who worked them, its actions heightened tensions between the Creolized *cobreros* who considered El Cobre a kind of *patria chica* and corrupt local administrators, particularly with regard to the question of their obligation to perform forced labor in colonial fortification projects.[68] This system of corvée labor was, like the Indian *repartimientos,* a system that was administered locally.[69] These tensions came to a head in 1677 when, faced with a royal order that a certain number of *cobrero* royal slaves be transferred to Havana to work on fortification projects in the port city, the *cobreros* fled to the mountains. This was not a case of romanticized *cimarrón* flight: the fugitive *cobreros* submitted a petition that, given their legal status as royal slaves, they be exempted from corvée labor obligations.[70] One of the authors of the petition was a royal slave who had achieved the rank of captain and whose name in the document is listed as Capitán Juan Moreno.

The story that emerges is a convergence of nation, religion, and mining around the figure of the Virgen de la Caridad del Cobre. This same Juan Moreno presented in 1697 a notarized declaration in which he swore before colonial authorities that he and two "Indian brothers" had found a Marian effigy floating in the sea: "They recognized and saw the Image of Our Lady the Sainted Virgin with a Baby Jesus in her arms on a small piece of wood, and on that piece of wood in large letters that the aforementioned Rodrigo de Joyos read, it said 'I am the Virgen de la Caridad,' and since her gown was made of cloth they were surprised that it was not wet."[71] The official notarization of Moreno's account was the first step in establishing a historical and authorized account of the cult of the Virgen de la Caridad del Cobre, and all subsequent versions would be based on this document. Many of these circulated extra-officially as a kind of spiritual contraband, as was the case of the account by Onofre de Fonseca, *Historia de la aparición milagrosa de Nuestra Señora de la Caridad del Cobre* (History of the miraculous apparition of Our Lady of Caridad del Cobre; written in 1701, the original manuscript was lost, and it was not until 1830 that an edition was published based on one of the copies that had been in circulation during the previous century).[72] Fonseca was chaplain of the sanctuary of the Virgen de la Caridad del Cobre from 1683 until 1711; he played an important role in the cult's institutionalization, lobbying for its financial autonomy and for the articulation of its success as a reflection of the *cobrero* community during a time of political and economic instability.

It's not possible within the confines of this chapter to study in a detailed manner the different rewritings of the history of the Virgen de la Caridad del Cobre, all of which have to do with the ethnic identity of the men in the canoe.[73] Although Fonseca had mentioned "two Indians and a black man," the illustrations that usually accompanied the various copies of his text frequently showed a black man and two other men—one bearded, as if to suggest a European, and another smooth-cheeked, to suggest that he was indigenous.[74] Morell de Santa Cruz rewrites the story in 1721 with three black *cobreros*. In the nineteenth century it will be rewritten yet again, with a black man, an Indian, and a criollo, reflecting the fact that the Virgen de la Caridad del Cobre had by then become a symbol of the multiracial Cuban nation. What's more, the names of the three men also change: eventually, all are called Juan, emphasizing their collective representation of the entire community. They are known as the "three Juans"—Juan el Blanco, Juan el Negro, and Juan el Mulato. This brief summary allows us to see how the Marian narrative can be at the same time formulaic and improvisational, responding to local conditions as it also translates and maintains a tradition. The Virgen de la Caridad del Cobre participated in that tradition, contributing to the local symbolic capital.[75]

The simple chapel built toward the end of the seventeenth century to house the Marian effigy was replaced in the eighteenth century by a richly adorned sanctuary; at the same time, a narrative tradition was being constructed based on miracles that served to give witness to and authorize the wondrous effigy. The festivals and celebrations of the Virgen de la Caridad del Cobre were of significant economic value to the *cobrero* community, but they also contributed to a wider viceregal spiritual economy.[76] The Virgen de la Caridad del Cobre turned out to be a gold mine, symbolically if not materially. By staking a claim to the Virgen, the *cobreros* consolidated the negotiation of their juridical, political, and economic identity in eighteenth-century Cuba.

Llave del Nuevo Mundo, written by José Martín Félix de Arrate in the mid-eighteenth century (but not published until 1830), attempts to do the same. An urban *relación de méritos, Llave* is a project of reclamation in which the author tallies up the many financial contributions the city of Havana has made to the larger Hispanic imperial project and reiterates the fundamental ties between center and periphery in the Bourbon Empire.

IV. *"Llave del Nuevo Mundo, Antemural de las Indias occidentales": Metropolitan merit*

The lengthy title of Arrate's urban history aptly describes eighteenth-century Havana as "Key to the New World" and "Antemural of the West Indies."[77] Arrate carefully chooses these epithets to highlight Havana's key position as gatekeeper to Spain's Atlantic empire. At the time he is writing, the Caribbean port city was playing an increasingly important role in transatlantic commercial and military networks. Havana had been one of the first colonial outposts in the early sixteenth century, though its importance later diminished as the flow of precious metals from Mexico and Lima shifted Spain's imperial focus toward those cities.[78] Given its location, however, Havana continued to serve as a key stopping point for Spanish ships venturing across the Atlantic; in Sherry Johnson's words, "Taking advantage of its magnificent, bottle-shaped natural harbor, the prevailing winds, and the Gulf Stream, which flows through the Florida Straits, ships laden with treasure and sailing from such mainland ports as Portobelo in Panama and Vera Cruz in Mexico united and revictualed in Havana, and set out on their return journey to Spain" (*Social Transformation,* 19).[79] Indeed, Arrate will explain that the city's coat of arms includes three castles (representing the three forts that guarded the entrance to the port) and a key (*Llave,* 123–24).

As part of the expansion of commerce advocated by Campillo and others (and discussed earlier in this chapter), Spain opened new trade routes in 1765, adding more ports (Havana among them) to the previously authorized triumvirate of Veracruz, Cartagena, and Panama. The British attack on Havana in 1762 was a catalyst for dramatic increases in imperial support in order to fortify the city's defenses, which had proved so ineffective in the face of British forces.[80] These funds largely involved a redirection of Mexican silver shipments, not to the metropolis but rather to Cuba, where they were used to finance work on garrisons and forts, to house and feed troops, for shipbuilding, and for various military operations. The increase in support for defense and commerce (especially for the tobacco and sugar industries) in the closing decades of the eighteenth century led to a corresponding increase in population, further adding to the city's luster; Brading writes, "Protected by massive fortifications, its garrison maintained by an annual subsidy from Mexico, Havana had emerged as a powerful naval base, its resident squadron of warships a major deterrent against the pirate raids that had devastated the Caribbean coastlands a generation earlier" (*First America,* 312). Cuba went from being a peripheral region in Spain's farflung empire to one of its newly emerging centers.[81]

I will argue that Arrate writes his urban history at a pivotal moment, on the eve of the British capture of the city and as economic and social growth begin to redefine the city's relationship with the metropolis.[82] He attempts to act as a broker on behalf of his native city and to secure its credit not only by documenting Havana's geographically strategic location but also by celebrating the residents of Havana as human capital and describing the various secular and ecclesiastical institutions that distinguish the city. There is little mention of mining (either of gold or copper); Arrate's domestication of the discourse of gold eschews precious metals for other, more practical commodities and exchanges.

In the preceding chapters we've seen the ways in which viceregal cities such as Caracas and Quito are the locations for the aspirations and limitations of the eighteenth-century project of domestication as reflected in the writings of José de Oviedo y Baños and Catalina de Jesús Herrera. Oviedo y Baños prefers the orderly foundation and administration of cities to the greed and ambition-driven chaos of conquest. Herrera gives voice to the deep fears of the criollo elite as she envisions the double threat of natural disaster and indigenous rebellion overtaking Quito's ordered urban space. Both accounts are grounded, however, in the same understanding of civic and commercial coexistence as rooted in mutual love and mutual benefits, and in the rational exchange of goods and ideas between center and periphery that undergirds Arrate's history of Havana.[83]

As Patrick O'Flanagan has argued, colonial port cities function in a particular way as gateways for core-periphery relationships, thus making possible different kinds of exchanges that take place in and expand out from the metropolis.[84] In what follows I will explore how Arrate uses Havana's privileged position as key and antemural to Spain's American territories to leverage the city's relationship with the Bourbon Crown, foregrounding the accomplishments and contributions of the residents of Havana.[85] Arrate's portrayal of the city's residents is central to his description of the city itself. Their demonstrated commitment to supporting the Spanish imperial project in the Caribbean is presented as the effect of magnanimous patriotism and a keen awareness of the best interests of the island. Although Havana's stunning geographical location commands center stage initially in Arrate's history, accounting for the city's military and commercial importance, human resources ultimately trump natural resources.[86] This is reflected in Arrate's detailed discussions of the exchanges between Havana's *vecinos* (literally, "neighbors") and the interests of the state—economic, defensive, and religious. Arrate writes, in a sense, as a broker attempting to bring interested parties (Crown and *habaneros*) together with the goal of mutual benefit, and his chapters are constructed rhetorically so as to support an ambitious entrepreneurial project. As Sherry Johnson argues, "Cuba was unique . . . in the ability of the monarchy and Creole elite to reach an accommodation of interest in the fiscal, administrative, and military spheres."[87] This environment of interested accommodation forms the backdrop for Arrate's work.

Unlike some of the other, more peripatetic writers I've been focusing on in these pages (Oviedo y Baños and Azara, for example), Arrate writes as a favorite son of the region he describes. Born in Havana on January 13, 1701, he belonged to a distinguished Havana family and, with the exception of a brief period during which he studied law in Mexico, he spent his entire life on the island. Arrate served in various administrative capacities: he was named *regidor perpetuo* (alderman) of Havana in 1734 and *alcalde ordinario* (civil magistrate) in 1752.[88] He died in Havana on April 23, 1765. In the years prior to his death, Arrate took part in the defense of Havana against British attack.[89] But he wages his most vigorous defense of his birthplace in *Llave del Nuevo Mundo*.[90]

As is the case with many eighteenth-century texts, which are characterized by a particular kind of discursive hybridity, readers have come to differing conclusions about how to define *Llave del Nuevo Mundo* in terms of genre.[91] Raimundo Lazo includes Arrate among early chroniclers of Cuba (*La literatura cubana*, 32–33).[92] Juan Luis Martín, on the other hand, argues that Arrate weaves an entertaining story of a family or neighborhood rather than a history ("José Martín Félix," 43). Arrate is often mentioned along with Ignacio José de Urrutia, Pedro Agustín Morell de Santa Cruz, Nicolás Joseph de Ribera, and Antonio José Valdés as one of Cuba's earliest historians. My own reading will take as its point of departure Julio Le Riverend Brusone's judgment that *Llave del Nuevo Mundo* should be read as an eighteenth-century urban *relación de méritos* ("Carácter y significación," 158).[93]

Llave del Nuevo Mundo was completed in 1761 but remained unpublished until 1830, when it appeared in the *Memorias de la Sección de Historia de la Real Sociedad Patriótica de la Habana* (Memoirs of the History Section of the Royal Patriotic Society of Havana), with an anonymous introduction that has been attributed to Pedro Pasucal Sirgado y Zequeira.[94] The editors of the 1830 edition explain in their introduction that they had searched for an appropriate text to publish as a contribution to Cuban national history and chose *Llave* despite its limited focus on the city of Havana.[95] The work is broken down into forty-nine brief chapters. The first six chapters are devoted to the discovery of Cuba and its early years of colonization; the following chapters include a description of the city and its environs, a discussion of the organization of colonial government, and accounts of various civil and religious institutions.[96] An obligatory deference to earlier foundational histories informs the opening chapters, but as the historian moves forward in time the reader is able to appreciate the significance of more recent events.

Arrate dedicates his history to the illustrious town council of Havana. In a fairly formulaic *excusatio* the author apologizes for the rough and embryonic nature of his text, and he explains his historiographical impulse as a desire that Havana might enjoy the same kind of literary renown as other, less important cities. He expands on this explanation in the prologue. A voracious reader, he reports that he has been disappointed to find very little information about Havana's foundation and subsequent history in the archives, where a relative paucity of documents had been further aggravated by the fire that destroyed much of the city when the French invaded in 1538. As is the case with other eighteenth-century historians (like Oviedo y Baños and Molina), the frustration occasioned by the lack of sources leads to a desire to fill that historiographical gap with an authoritative account.[97] The result is a text that will in turn provide a foundation for later attempts to write the history of Cuba. In these nineteenth- and twentieth-century rewritings, the eighteenth-century perspective is replaced by a more markedly nationalist view, although the earlier preoccupation with Cuba's marginal place in a larger history remains evident.[98]

Arrate takes pride in his meticulous annotation of source materials and marginal notes, although many of the source materials he lists have been lost (or at least not yet recovered).[99] He complains that the publication of the present work (and, indeed, any work) is difficult in Cuba due to the exorbitant cost of paper and the obligation to prepare multiple copies of the manuscript in order to accommodate the censors.[100] Arrate recommends that measures be taken to expand the publishing industry and make it more economical: "If in these parts presses were less costly and easier to acquire, printers would often break a sweat publishing refined works and ingenious writings" (*Llave*, 17).

Arrate begins in 1492 with Columbus's discovery of the island on his first voyage—a beginning that is de rigueur for an eighteenth-century historian. A description of the island's overwhelming natural abundance follows, but this is only a prelude to the later focus on municipal achievements. The city of Havana, the historian proclaims, is "the precious setting for this rich jewel in the Spanish Crown, and the worthy golden center of this Western daisy, as the very wise Orejón, great admirer of her karats, has said" (10). The reader is struck here by the convergence of natural and artificial, and vegetable and mineral, in the metaphors Arrate appropriates from the sixteenth-century chronicler Francisco Dávila Orejón to describe the city. His use of the term *karats* (quilates) to measure the city's merits alerts the reader to the inevitability of comparisons between the island's natural resources and those of other viceregal regions that can lay claim to more ostentatiously brilliant sources of wealth. From Arrate's eighteenth-century vantage point, the shadow of "two very opulent kingdoms of Mexico and Peru" has been cast over his island; the same shadow is cast over the opening pages of his history. Here the historian's strategy is to remind his reader of the role played by the port of Havana in the protection and conservation of Spain's more showy viceregal holdings.[101] This heralds the larger themes of Arrate's history: the importance of Havana as a port city, a role that has become increasingly important in a new and widening Atlantic trade, and the contributions the city's residents make to the maintenance not only of the city itself but also to a larger imperial project. The *vecinos* of Havana are its most valuable domestic product.

When Arrate turns to a consideration of the island's deposits of precious metals, he again seems to be playing defense: "In the wealth of precious metals, although not as opulent as Hispaniola, it is certain that in the early days much gold was extracted from certain locations" (15). Here and elsewhere he is obviously writing in the shadow of the Columbian discourse of gold. He refers to "other regions . . . opulent in minerals" (38).[102] He contests the stated view of Francisco López de Gómara and his contemporaries that the gold found in Cuba was of poor quality compared to Mexican gold. His move from the discussion of gold to a description of the island's copper mines, famous for producing ore to be used in artillery manufacture, represents a first step away from a Cuban discourse of gold toward an appreciation of more common metals whose value lies not so much in their essence as in their utility for manufacturing and trade. Throughout these remarks, Arrate recognizes the growing importance of defense and commerce as the twin engines of the island's economic progress.[103]

In keeping with eighteenth-century thinking on economic issues, Arrate understands labor to be key. In chapter 6 he laments the extermination of the indigenous population of the island. But his concern has less to do with issues of justice than with the vast sums that have been spent to import and support African slave labor: "It is not possible to give an exact account of the enormous quantities of pesos that have left the Island in the commerce and sale of blacks who for more than two centuries have served as laborers on all the plantations, large and small" (40). Arrate's discussion of the pros and cons of indigenous labor versus African slave labor is frequently referenced in later debates in Cuba about plantation slavery. Reading Arrate's points only within this later context, however, minimizes an appreciation of the degree to which the eighteenth-century historian's primary concern is the efficient use of human industry in the exploitation of the island's natural resources, rather than larger moral or ethical questions.[104]

At the close of the chapter, Arrate repeats his main thesis: "This port has been the reason for growth and growth the result of commerce, as 'Key to the New World' and throat [*garganta,* or narrow pass] for all of the West Indies" (40). This introduces the following chapter, which describes the port as the result of a combination of a spectacular geographic configuration and human accomplishment, signaling the move from history to urban panegyric. Commerce, facilitated by the prime location of the port, is the source of all utility and benefits. The port also offers safety and shelter to the victims of the frequent shipwrecks that occur in the region, saving "people and treasures that would without a doubt have been lost had the port not been so close at hand with its assortment of large and small boats that are regularly there and quickly facilitate any rescue expedition or military excursion" (44). Arrate goes so far as to calculate the specific amount of goods, persons, and monies recovered from a precise number of shipwrecked vessels. Here, as in the discussion of slave and indigenous labor, human resources are quantifiable. The reference to shipwrecks introduces a curious kind of argument about Havana's role as both saint and scavenger of the seas and paints a picture of a city benefiting from the turbulence and danger of the waters surrounding it.

Arrate's description of the port leads to a discussion of another driving factor in the local economy: defense.[105] In fact, fortification, shipbuilding, and munitions were perhaps more important in the late colonial period than the plantation crops—sugar and tobacco—that would dominate the nineteenth-century economy.[106] From the seventeenth century onward, most of the funds needed to fortify and defend Cuba came from the Mexico City treasury. Garrisons, fortresses, ships, guns, and gunpowder were all funded by Mexican silver to such a degree that those in New Spain "complained that their silver disappeared into Havana's financial maze."[107]

Arrate emphasizes, however, that all expenses associated with these fortification projects were shouldered by the local population:

> The tranquility of the neighbors and residents of this city must have been disturbed by qualms about some secret disembarkation in their immediate vicinity that, even if there was no intention to attack the plaza, could threaten the nearby plantations and imprison their owners and inhabitants, so it was decided that they would construct two forts, which was done at the expense of those same neighbors who, concerned about their own tranquility and security, contributed happily to the cost, for which His Majesty thanked them, offering to compensate them for this service at a more opportune moment. (57–58)

He describes here a highly rational and civilized process in which the local neighbors, concerned about their own security and peace of mind, decide to construct at their own expense two new forts, an enterprise for which they are duly thanked by the king. The implicit extension of credit to the Spanish Empire will presumably be settled at a future date. The insistence that the local population repeatedly took responsibility for urban improvements benefitting the larger imperial project will become an important leitmotif in *Llave del Nuevo Mundo*. Since, as we have seen, Arrate's work is a *relación de méritos* on behalf of an urban population, he inserts in his text not only a record of Havana's subvention effort in support of its own defensive fortifications but also the fact that the king has recognized those efforts and promised to reimburse them. The *relación de méritos* thus functions as a sort of note to be redeemed at a future date.

Arrate takes every opportunity to reiterate the already-stated royal view of the importance of the port city: "The King and his ministers considered it to be the extremely important key to New Spain and antemural to all the Indies, whose dominion would be in danger if foreigners were to take over Havana" (58). Although he writes before the British attack on Havana, Arrate sagely anticipates the pressing need for more fortification and for increased funds to maintain the troops to be billetted there. In noting that the Crown had provided "military officers and competent garrisons made up of serious members to protect and defend it against the invasions to which it was exposed, because without these necessary provisos the fortifications would be like bodies without souls or lifeless skeletons" (61), he is, in effect, reminding the Crown of its duty and interest in continuing such support. The Crown's imperial infrastructure by itself is worthless—like a body without a soul or a lifeless skeleton—and must be populated by those willing to defend it: namely, the residents of Havana.

The historian, writing from a periphery that is both vulnerable and incredibly strategic, emphasizes that the Crown must protect its vast empire, "without forgetting in its extremely vigilant perspicacity even the most remote towns and least renowned places. . . . It has continually looked out for Havana, which as the most desired city must be given the most attention, and as the most exposed to the designs of enemies is most justified in requesting assistance from the nation" (65).[108] Once again Arrate suggests that he is merely quoting the king himself in his estimation of the need to commit the resources necessary to protect the port city.[109]

Arrate's awareness of narrative order comes to the fore in chapter 15 when he returns to the narrative that he has interrupted in order to describe the port and its fortifications. Behind this interruption, of course, is the need to establish the basis for Havana's urban merit. Comparisons are helpful as well. The historian boasts that Havana has none of the natural drawbacks of other viceregal cities—"neither the earthquakes that assault Lima, nor the floods that afflict Mexico and Jamaica, nor the volcanos that threaten Quito and Guatemala, nor the poisonous snakes and insects that plague other regions of the New World" (74). But he quickly returns to a more mercantilist accounting.

Chapter 18 deals with shipbuilding, which was of utmost importance to the local economy. The protected waters of the harbor are complemented by a shoreline that offers ample space for docks and warehouses, although apparently the Crown was slow to recognize the advantages of a local shipbuilding industry. It fell to Juan Pérez de Oporto, a captain and resident of Havana, who organized a group of merchants to take the initiative and begin building ships in the seventeenth century (*Llave*, 88). Later, Don Agustín de Arriola traveled to Madrid with the goal of lobbying for approval to establish a royal navy yard. After almost a decade, approval was finally granted in 1723.

In arguing for the importance of shipbuilding, Arrate refers specifically to Gerónimo de Ustariz's arguments for the efficacy of building ships in the region, a gesture that serves to bolster his credit as someone familiar with contemporary debates on economic reform. Arrate emphasizes that local timber is best for this enterprise, and is also close at hand. Moreover, Caribbean wood withstands Caribbean temperatures: "Its woods, produced in these climates, are more resistant to excessive heat" (89). Domestic products are best suited to the needs of local industry; homegrown timber provides the best wood for building the ships that will venture out across the seas. Arrate closes with a list of the ships that have been built to date, moving once again from a qualitative argument about Havana's merits to a quantitative one (91).[110] Alexander von Humboldt draws heavily on *Llave del Nuevo Mundo* for his history of Havana's shipbuilding industry in the *Ensayo político sobre la Isla de Cuba* (Political essay on the Island of Cuba, 1836). This is yet another example of the way in which eighteenth-century Spanish American writing serves as primary material for the production of knowledge that is later elaborated and circulated by others. Commenting on the role that shipbuilding and defense played in the economy of the various port cities charged with shipping and defending America's precious metals, Humboldt reminds his reader: "It is well known that Cuba and the Archipelago of the Philippine Islands have for centuries drawn from the treasure of Mexico the sums necessary for their internal administration, and for the preservation of their fortifications, their arsenals, and their navy yards" (*Island of Cuba*, 77).[111]

Given his emphasis on Havana as a port city, Arrate's stance on eighteenth-century debates between mercantilists and physiocrats favors the former. Not surprisingly, therefore, he devotes only a couple of chapters to Havana's surrounding countryside and its potential for agriculture. He barely mentions sugar, and when he turns in chapter 29 to a discussion of the importance of tobacco, his focus is less on the cultivation of the cash crop itself (though tobacco was increasingly important as an item of popular consumption) and more on the successful negotiations of local residents to redefine how tobacco profits would be allocated and taxed (148–49). Arrate provides a succinct recap of the interests of the parties involved in the negotiations (representatives of the Crown, wealthy *vecinos*, tobacco farmers, and merchants). He offers the following summary of these interests, in which he aligns himself with Ustariz: "Not even with respect to these Indies, so rich in gold and silver and so abundant in fruits and products like cochineal, indigo, and others, does Ustariz consider that anything produces the same benefit for His Majesty as tobacco" (151).[112] The economic potential of gold, silver, and other agricultural products pales when compared to the benefit derived from the tobacco trade.

That trade is, of course, part of a larger commercial network. Eighteenth-century Havana's wealth, more generally speaking, is to be found not in precious metals but rather in the plethora of goods to be found for sale in its shops and markets—linen and woolen cloth, silks, gold and silver utensils, and other precious objects intended for daily use (*Llave,* 75). Chapter 19, "On the cleanliness and demeanor of the residents," is the most *costumbrista* of Arrate's chapters.[113] Arrate showers lavish praise on the inhabitants of Havana, concluding with pride that not even those of Mexico City and Lima are their equal, notwithstanding the elegance and opulence of those two cities (93). His descriptions of the finery worn by the women of Havana and the exquisite menus offered at the gatherings of the Havana elite are reminiscent of similar accounts of criollo society in other parts of the viceroyalties.

Arrate's concern that the excess and luxury of these customs impedes the accumulation and conservation of wealth is also familiar (93).[114] Bourbon economic reforms that focused on mercantilist trade and the circulation of goods had the necessary secondary effect of fomenting consumption as well. Eighteenth-century debates over luxury pitted those concerned with individual and public excess against those who argued that consumption was essential for the maintenance of the economic system. Humboldt offers a passionate defense of the benefits of commerce and luxury for the city of Havana: "The increase of commerce—multiplying the friendly ties between nations, opening an immense sphere to the operations of the mind, pouring capital into the lap of agriculture, and creating new wants through the refinements of luxury—presents in itself the remedy for the danger which they believe to exist" (*Island of Cuba,* 190). By inserting this chapter on the moderation and distinction of the criollo residents of Havana between the opening chapters on the city's early history and its natural setting and later chapters describing the urban landscape of secular and ecclesiastical institutions, Arrate emphasizes their role in creating metropolitan merit.

Arrate's frequent use of the term *vecino* to identify the protagonists of his urban history is a constant reminder of the horizontal ties of duty, obligation, and privilege that bound together the residents of Havana. Ideas about the rights and responsibilities related to membership in a community developed on the Iberian Peninsula under Roman rule and were then transferred to the Americas, as Tamar Herzog explains: "Inspired by Roman law as applied and interpreted under Castilian conditions, this rule held that *vecindad* was constituted on its own, at the moment when people acted as if they felt attached to the community" (*Defining Nations,* 18).[115] "Neighbor" is a local concept, based on one's domicile and implying a complex network of interconnection and interdependence. In emphasizing the contributions made by the *vecinos* of Havana to the support not only of their city, but also to that of the larger Spanish republic, Arrate reminds the reader that the same ties of duty and obligation linked all the members of the larger Spanish Empire.

Arrate's position can be read as part of a larger discourse of Creole patriotism outlined in *The First America* by David Brading, who sees Arrate as articulating a traditional defense of American-born Spaniards.[116] We must remember that Arrate's desire to refute the criticisms made by Deán de Alicante Manuel Martí is part of what motivates him to write his history.[117] Arrate's focus on Creole accomplishment certainly reflects the anxieties and resentments of those who felt marginalized by Bourbon reforms of viceregal government.[118] His defense, however, is not so much a call to arms as a calling to account. In presenting a historically based ledger of Cuban contributions to Spain's larger project in the Americas, Arrate speaks for a municipal elite that views itself as fully enfranchised to negotiate the terms of its relationship with the Bourbon Crown.[119]

Thus, Arrate collapses the earlier foundational history of discovery and conquest of the island with more recent events. Preserving traces of heroic discourse, he moves from praising Creole accomplishments and demeanor to offering concrete proof of criollo civic virtue: "The epitome of 'varones ilustres' of all lineages that this city has produced in only two centuries will have its place in this work, because the credit and praise that they have earned with their virtue and devotion to the *patria* will be most sublime among those deserving it" (94).[120] The virtuous credit of Havana's founders has been rewarded by the honors bestowed on the city by a series of Spanish kings and finds its legacy in the positions currently held by criollos (Arrate among them) in Havana's civil administration and legal jurisdiction. He includes a list of governors, *alguaciles* (bailiffs), and other officials, even going so far as to note their salaries, and he also explains the circumstances that have led to his being named to his present post. The narrative pretext is at this point abandoned, and the succeeding chapters amount to little more than lists of names and numbers.[121]

In a volatile and evolving Caribbean economy, Arrate endeavors to set a fixed rate of interest for all exchanges between the Crown and the residents of Havana by locking both into a mutually beneficial relationship. When he discusses the services that his compatriots have lent to the Crown, Arrate is always careful to include the name of the particular citizen or functionary responsible for those services, either administratively or financially. His discussion of the efforts to channel the Chorrera River for the greatest utility to and benefit of the surrounding neighborhoods is typical: "The work continued until Hernán Manrique de Rojas, one of the principal and most affluent residents at that time, took it upon himself under certain capitulations [concessions] with which I'm not completely familiar and which it would be bothersome to explain here" (80). While the initiative of a wealthy individual, Rojas, is key, Arrate also celebrates the collaborative nature of this project. Here the value added to the river's natural course by the enlightened thinking and generous contributions of the locals is made clearly apparent.

Chapter 25 is a meditation on the services that the city and its inhabitants of the city have offered to the Crown; Arrate articulates these using the word *fineza*.[122] He explores the implications of the mutual obligations, founded on both love and responsibility, corresponding to both parties:

Although the gifts and services that the love and recognition of vassals pay as tribute to the sovereignty of their Monarchs are born of an obligation that is as just as it is natural, royal appreciation of their merit is neither diminished nor cancelled by judging them to be voluntary; nor should the same concept of their justly owing them; for such reasons it will not be reprehensible but rather praiseworthy to set forth, if not all, then some of those who have worked since the beginnings of this city as proof of their "fineza" and recognition, since much glory is assigned in understanding who has known how to fulfill that to which he is obliged. (126)

These reflections, coming as they do squarely at the center of *Llave del Nuevo Mundo,* set forth in clear and certain terms the ties that bind Havana and the Crown.

Arrate stresses that Havana's citizens have taken on their obligations voluntarily, choosing to do what they are required or expected to do in defending "this very important port" (126). When the squadron of the infamous pirate Drake threatens the city, men come in from the countryside, with the costs of their lodging and maintenance assumed by the residents (126). Arrate points out that the expenses for the construction of the Cojímar and Chorrera towers were covered by the city, which also contributed men to stand guard and added funds for the towers' maintenance. What's more, the city put up 1,000 pesos for the fabrication of a chain that could be stretched across the mouth of the harbor to close it off in case of attack, and another 4,500 reales for the construction of a gunpowder deposit (127). The residents of Havana built a brigantine to guard its coastal waters and paid for its upkeep without even being asked, having heard of the king's interest in having such a vessel. In the years 1741 and 1742, they contributed funds to supplement the pay received by royal troops in Havana's forts until royal funds arrived from New Spain (131).

Arrate drives home the collective and voluntary contribution of Havana's citizens to Spain's imperial project: "The services they have carried out in times of war have been repeated and considerable, helping with considerable but equal contributions by the *vecinos* to all the public works and fortifications of the plaza . . . without any sovereign measure or intervention, any mild insinuation from those in charge being sufficient for both the town council and the citizens to come together for whatever has been proposed and acknowledged to be convenient for royal purposes" (129). Although his explicit goal is to praise the residents of Havana, Arrate extrapolates from their generous philanthropy a characterization of all New World criollos: "I don't find it hard to believe that this blind obedience and offering of the native sons and neighbors is a particular and almost universal characteristic of all those from this New World" (130).

As we have seen in the previous chapter on Catalina de Jesús Herrera, despite the secularizing impulse of enlightened thinking (exemplified by Campillo's repeated warnings about the power and wealth of the Catholic Church), there existed in the eighteenth century a complex relationship between the church and the Bourbon monarchy.[123] Just as he displaces the power of the state from its metropolitan center to the local Havana citizenry, Arrate also shifts the locus of ecclesiastical authority from the church itself to its parishioners, the *vecinos* who time and time again take on the responsibility of maintaining church property.[124] Arrate again resorts to an enumerative quantification of metropolitan merit as he lists all the religious institutions that have flourished in the city—temples, monasteries, schools, hospitals, and other pious institutions whose coffers contribute to the greater good (167). Arrate (ever mindful of the inevitable comparisons with other viceregal cities), insists that the local saints and virgins who are honored almost daily in festivals taking place around Havana inspire admirable demonstrations of devotion: "If they [the worshippers] might not compete with those of other regions in terms of riches, I believe they equal them in terms of their interest and painstakingness" (167).[125] He later boasts that Havana burns as many votive candles in one month as other viceregal cities burn in a year (231).

Just as he noted individual benefactors when discussing the upkeep and expansion of Havana's administrative and military buildings, Arrate frequently highlights individual acts of generous piety. He notes that although Cuba has gone through hard times that challenged the charitable giving of its residents, the city should be known for the great quantities of money that have been donated to spiritual ends (170). For example, a devout citizen, Don Diego de Salazar, was responsible for financing the much-needed renovations to the church of the Convent of the Purísima Concepción de Nuestra Señora, and Juan Romero, a retired priest, led the way for the renovation of a chapel by raising substantial donations (179). Arrate goes into great detail about the pressing need for such pious philanthropy, noting one case where the decaying foundation of a convent was dissected by deep furrows that regularly flooded with water, further threatening the integrity of the building (178). One might even understand this and other examples as metaphors for the need to build a solid foundation for civic and religious philanthropy—a concern expressed as well by Catalina de Jesús Herrera.

Arrate also writes about Capitán Martín Calvo de Arrieta, who arranged for the convent dowries of five young noblewomen in the Calvo family (169). Captain Calvo de Arrieta's generosity is exemplary but not unusual. In another extended example of the pragmatic piety of Havana's residents, Arrate explains how the need for a convent for "virtuous young noblewomen who have no inclination to matrimony" inspired contributions of more than twelve thousand pesos toward the foundation of the Convent of Santa Clara, and an additional thirty-eight thousand ducats for dowries for the first novitiates (187).[126] Although rural properties provided some additional income, the nuns of Santa Clara "turned to parents and benefactors for support in the way of private incomes [*peculios particulares*]" (Clune, *Cuban Convents*, 9); Arrate remarks on this practice repeatedly.[127] This proved to be a highly successful endeavor: John Clune notes that "on the eve of the British capture and occupation of Havana in 1762, at the height of the Seven Years War, Santa Clara was the largest, wealthiest, and most prestigious female religious community in the Caribbean" (*Cuban Convents*, 5).

If the Bourbon state was concerned that such communities of the "idle religious siphoned off resources that might otherwise have gone into productive enterprises in society," Arrate's text aims to prove the opposite: that religious institutions and individuals in Havana contributed greatly to those state enterprises.[128] This is consonant with religious philanthropy elsewhere in the Spanish viceregalties, where, in the words of Edith Boorstein Couturier, "the possession of wealth brought with it social obligations to help the less fortunate" (*Silver King*, 130).[129] Burns explains that, for elite families in colonial Spanish America, placing a family member in a wealthy convent made financial sense as well: "Where lending institutions were non-existent, having a daughter, sister, or niece in a position of leadership in a religious community made sense: the well-placed nun could tap into one of the few readily available lines of credit, as convents were major sources of investment capital."[130]

I have already commented on the eighteenth-century view of population as a resource not to be squandered. This view is reflected in Arrate's impassioned discussion of the problem of abandoned or orphaned children in Havana and the measures taken by the city's *vecinos* to provide shelter and education for these children (*Llave*, 210). After a detailed explanation of the various subsidies provided by Licenciado D. Francisco de Sotolongo for the Oratorio de San Felipe, Arrate concludes that similar pious works will be necessary to care for and educate Havana's foundlings (211).[131]

Ruth Hill suggests that Arrate and other writers of geographical reports may be minimizing their religiosity in an effort to appear enlightened and modern: "Their piety is simply restrained, separated from their scientific method, as the need to . . . 'grow the economy' outweighs (and often conflicts with) evangelization and the growth of the Church in Havana and other Spanish cities in America" ("Arrate's *La Habana*," 338). I would propose another way of understanding Arrate's discussion of Havana's religious capital. The rhetoric of piety is domesticated, as is evident in his tallying of merit through the lists of convents, monasteries, and benefactors. These chapters reflect a vibrant "spiritual economy" (to use Kathryn Burns's phrase) that established, expanded, and maintained a host of religious institutions that served the public through a constantly negotiated process of Crown support and private financing that paralleled the growth and evolution of the urban center itself.

In order to close the deal he is making about metropolitan merit, Arrate concludes his history with several chapters dedicated to the "considerable honor that comes to this city from the merit and circumstances of the illustrious sons that it has had" (*Llave*, 231). Though he insists that he is not looking for a fight—"I don't bring these points up to quarrel" (235)—Arrate's Creole pride (and resentment) come to the fore in these closing pages. He explains that *indianos* (those who return to the metropolis after long periods of residence in the Americas) often find their professional careers thwarted as the few opportunities that arise go to native-born Spaniards (234).[132] He explains that he has decided to include a compendium of some of the sons of Havana who, with their virtue, education, and effort, have afforded the city so much credit.[133] Once again his narrative thins into a mere enumeration that runs on for several pages before the author reverts to a more overt poetic presence. Arrate concludes *Llave del Nuevo Mundo* with a sonnet, dedicated to the city of Havana, whose final tercet begins by noting how Havana's illustrious sons "bring you credit and exalt you" (251).

What comes across in Arrate's history is the role played by entrepreneurship in Havana's eighteenth-century viceregal economy as individuals and neighborhood groups intervene to play a decisive role in the city's growth and development. As Brading has argued, "The decisive agent behind the economic growth of the Bourbon epoch was an entrepreneurial elite composed of merchants, planters and miners"; to this list we might add "historians" ("Bourbon Spain," 143). Arrate's textual efforts to act as broker on behalf of Havana lead him to use a different sort of currency than that which had circulated in past economic discourse and to argue metropolitan merit on new grounds. Of course, the balance sheet would have to be adjusted after the British invasion of 1762. But Arrate must be credited for arguing in 1761, on the eve of that invasion, that Havana's *vecinos* are worth their weight in gold.

V. "La mejor moneda que por el mundo corre": Coins of the realm

Finally, I'd like to turn to an episode from *El lazarillo de ciegos caminantes* (A guide for blind travelers; 1775) by Alonso Carrió de la Vandera that suggests another problem related to currency, amalgamation, circulation, and negotiation in the eighteenth century.[134] *El lazarillo* is a text that reflects the heterogenous world of the Peruvian viceroyalty and the demographic, administrative, and economic (official and extra-official) factors that came to bear on the world of the Spanish *visitador* (inspector) and his Indian companion, Concolorcorvo, whose travels are chronicled in its pages. *El lazarillo*'s manifest interest in all forms of commerce and exchange—mules, letters, gold bars, and merchandise— corresponds to the transition from the Hapsburg Empire to the Bourbons.[135] If in the eighteenth century, as Anthony Pagden has argued, "commerce replaces conquest; conversation and the voluntary exchange of goods are substituted for war" (*Lords*, 179), one might further argue that in Carrió de la Vandera's text commerce works as a kind of undeclared war—what we might call an example of low-level conflict. The roads traveled by the *visitador* and Concolorcorvo are a battleground in which every exchange is represented as a moment charged with difficulties and complications.

The episode of the lost doubloons is one such moment, and it continues to intrigue me many years after having read the story for the first time. These are the facts of the case: On the royal road between Buenos Aires and Mendoza, a certain Don Juan Antonio Casau lost a sack of doubloons worth 3,200 pesos. The governor, upon hearing of Casau's misfortune, sent a squadron of soldiers to try to recover them. It turned out, however, that a group of horsemen from the pampas (*gauderios,* or gauchos) had found the sack of coins first: "The benighted *gauderios* broke open the sack and distributed among themselves the two thousand pieces of eight, which in the dark of night they took for *pesos dobles,* which is the coin that is commonly seen between Lima and Potosí and Buenos Aires, where only by chance one sees doubloons."[136]

A *peso* is a silver coin, while a *doblon* is made of gold and is therefore much less common.[137] The *gauderios* calculate the value of the purse based on their expectations of what currency might be circulating on the viceregal routes, since in the dark of night they are unable to identify the coins with any degree of certainty. When daylight comes, they are disappointed to ascertain that their booty, in fact, consists of reddish pieces that they immediately assume contain some kind of copper alloy. Instead of correctly identifying the coins, the *gauderios* conclude with a mixture of fear and disappointment that the coins have been debased as divine retribution for their theft: "In the morning they were astonished to see the white color turned to red, believing that God, as punishment for the theft, had reduced the silver pesos to copper coins, and so they handed them over to their wives and sisters, except for a couple of boys, the sons of an honest man who disappeared with more than two thousand pesos."[138] The worthless coins are distributed among their women—a reflection of the fact that neither the coins nor the women are regarded as having much value.[139]

The incident is happily resolved (at least for Juan Antonio Casau) when viceregal authorities recover most, though not all, of the lost doubloons and punish the *gauderios.* But larger questions remain, having to do with circulation and exchange in eighteenth-century Spanish America. Pedro Pérez Herrero explains that the number of coins produced for circulation in the Americas increased dramatically in the eighteenth century (*Comercio y mercados,* 234–37).[140] The proliferation of coinage and the Crown's desire to centralize all aspects of viceregal administration led to a move to regularize and regulate the circulation of coins. Thus, a *real cédula* (royal charter) issued in 1730 calls for the establishment of a "Commission on Coinage and Precious Metals: The Monarch declares that the Commission on Coinage and Precious Metals shall be established for the knowledge and determination of all business, causes and dossiers, civil and criminal . . . in matters having to do with Royal mines, silversmiths, goldsmiths . . . and all others who are involved in the labor of gold and silver and anything else that has to do with gold and silver metal."[141] Both the case of the lost doubloons and the call for the creation of a "Commission on Coinage"— with its overdetermined lists of appropriate matters—reveal the extent to which eighteenth-century economic realities cannot be understood based on earlier discourses that had been articulated for the valorization and circulation of precious metals. Even the proposed name for the bureaucratic office that is to be charged with monitoring questions of value and exchange gives coinage primacy over precious metals.[142]

Michel Foucault in *The Order of Things* proposes that from the Renaissance forward "all wealth is coinable; and it is by this means that it enters into circulation" (175). In the Middle Ages, what was important was the intrinsic value of money: "At that time, 'neither copper, nor silver were minted, but only valued according to their weight'" (169).[143] From the sixteenth century onward, it will be the exchange function that gives value: as Marc Shell observes, "Gold is precious because it is money—not the converse" (*Money, Language, and Thought,* 176).[144] But in the story of the lost doubloons we see that it proves impossible for the *gauderios* to correctly appreciate the value of the metals that have entered into circulation as coins of the realm.[145]

Gonzalo Fernández de Oviedo y Valdés, the indefatigable and exhaustive historian of the natural history of the Americas, had anticipated this difficulty. Before being named royal chronicler, he served as supervisor of mining and gold smelting. In that capacity Oviedo severely critiques Spanish avarice for gold and includes a chapter at the end of his *Sumario*—"On gold mines" (chapter 82)—where he discusses, among other things, the ingenious talent of the Indians for gold-plating copper:

> And since here we are dealing with gold, it seems to me that before moving forward and speaking of other things, I should tell how the Indians are very good at gilding copper coins or gold coins of very low quality; which they do, and they give them such excellent and high color, that it seems that the piece that they gild in this way is of gold of such quality that it might be of twenty-two karats or more. They make this color with certain plants, and in such a way that any silversmith from Spain or Italy, or wherever the most expert ones might be found, would consider those who know how to do this to be expert as well, and very rich with this secret or way of gilding. (165)[146]

The metallurgical process described by Oviedo y Valdés results in the debasement not only of gold (that's where the *gauderios'* confusion comes in) but also the very system by which the hierarchies of value and imperial power are established.[147]

Oviedo y Valdés warns the king, "These double ducats are witnesses that your Majesty spreads throughout the world, and that leave these kingdoms and never return to them; because it is the best coin that today circulates in the world, as it falls into the power of some foreigners, it never leaves it; and if it does return to Spain it is disguised, its karats diminished, and your royal insignia transformed" (*Sumario,* 178). According to the chronicler's admonition, the commercial exchange that is necessary in order to take full advantage of "the innumerable treasures" of the New World brings with it the inevitable alteration—the debasement, even—of the coin of the realm that symbolizes royal power. Like the pieces of what might have been secretly gold plated by the Indians so that no Spanish jeweler will recognize them, these transformed coins are proof of the undeniable challenge that the New World presents for the moral and material taxonomies of the Old World.[148]

The cases discussed in this chapter—the introduction of mercury and amalgamation in Potosí, the royal slaves of the El Cobre copper mines, Arrate's urban *relación de méritos,* and the lost doubloons of the *gauderios* of the Argentine pampas—offer eighteenth-century examples of what Shell has called "the tropic interaction between economic and linguistic symbolization and production" (*Money, Language, and Thought,* 4). The Hispanic eighteenth century must be taken into account as a moment of fluid hierarchies and exchanges constantly negotiated from new ideological and pragmatic imperial perspectives . . . a moment when the narratives of amalgamation, negotiation, and circulation rewrite and domesticate the golden discourse of earlier centuries.

Conclusion

Unfinished Projects, Recuperated Remains

Forget the Alamo.
John Sayles, *Lone Star*

The relationship between the Spanish American Enlightenment, the Enlightenment more generally, and modernity as it has come to be understood today represents a genealogy that is often contested, when it is remembered or acknowledged at all. The closing line of John Sayles's film *Lone Star* (1996)—a provocative and generous exploration of how families and communities tell their stories in a Texas border town—suggests that forgetting history can sometimes be a way of moving forward. And this may help to explain what happens to the eighteenth century in subsequent formulations of Spanish American cultural history: it is forgotten in order to open up a space for new cultural narratives. Carlos Alonso argues that a "narrative of novelty" with roots in the sixteenth century was replaced by a "narrative of futurity" that "created the conditions for a permanent exoticization of the New World—the sort that cannot be undermined or dissolved by actual experience or objective analysis."[1] But I would argue that experience and analysis are precisely where eighteenth-century authors ground themselves; they inhabit a discursive space that is no longer that of novelty but not yet that of futurity, an in-between that must later be actively forgotten. Thus, the domesticating turn that I have argued marks eighteenth-century writing in Spanish America is erased (or, at the very least, subsumed) in nineteenth-century national foundational fictions. Are these eighteenth-century texts, as is commonly thought, too resistant to modernity to be considered relevant? Or do they fall victim to the confusion of an earlier American spirit and an emerging national sentiment, as José Carlos Chiaramonte has suggested?[2] Whatever the answer, it is essential that we rethink the traditional chronology that imposes a seamless continuity on the discontinuities between the colonial period and the formation of Latin American nation-states. We can only do this by remembering the eighteenth century.

The authors I have studied here—Oviedo y Baños, Molina, Azara, Herrera, and Arrate—rewrite the central issues of the colonial period—conquest, Amerindians, nature, God, and gold—on eighteenth-century terms. All reflect a specifically eighteenth-century strain of empire that I have characterized as a project of enlightened domestication; all contribute in some way to the articulation of a new Spanish American epistemology that prioritizes place, presence, and pragmatism, and brings with it new perspectives and new practices. Their project of domesticating empire is built on a foundation of discursive migrations and paradigm shifts that I have traced in each of these chapters.

José de Oviedo y Baños's move from conquest to settlement in *Historia de la conquista y población de la provincia de Venezuela* is reflected both in his title and in his evaluation of the enterprise of conquest itself. Individual conquistadors are portrayed as vain, foolhardy, or greedy, and Oviedo y Baños's portrayal of Lope de Aguirre as the inevitable and disastrous end point of the Spanish fascination with conquest is embedded in the central chapters of the book as a sobering, cautionary tale. Conquest is replaced by the important task of settlement—that is, building and maintaining a viable colonial order—which falls to Oviedo y Baños and his contemporaries.

Juan Ignacio Molina uses earlier accounts of the ferocious and liberty-loving Araucanians (most notably, Ercilla's *La Araucana*) as a point of departure in order to write a domesticated version of Araucanian agency in which the language of diplomacy is substituted for the arts of war. Molina continues his *Compendio de la historia civil del reyno de Chile* up to a present moment in which treaty negotiations with Spanish viceregal authorities demonstrate a new deployment of the Aruacanian tradition of *parlamentos* and a new role for the Araucanians, one that has been prefigured by their portrayal in Molina's history as eloquent and savvy orators.

The Aragonese military engineer Félix de Azara, whose voluminous writings on the flora and fauna of the Río de la Plata provided Darwin with many first-hand observations on New World species, uses the failure of Bourbon Spain's imperial commission to map a new boundary between Spanish and Portuguese territories in the Río de la Plata region, opening a space for a different kind of measuring and measured activity—that of the accidental naturalist. In the process, wonder as a response to natural phenomena is replaced by the imperative of organized curiosity.

Catalina de Jesús Herrera's spiritual autobiography, *Secretos entre el alma y Dios,* reflects the broader context of an eighteenth-century move away from imperial projects of evangelization toward more localized and mundane preoccupations. Herrera rewrites the tradition of female convent writing, emulating New World models such as Rosa de Lima as she narrates her own story and that of her convent home. Written against a backdrop of earthquakes, ecclesiastical intrigues, and the threat of indigenous rebellion, Herrera's spiritual autobiography reflects a hands-on approach to religious authority as well as the aspirations and fears of eighteenth-century Andean criollos.

Finally, José Martín Félix de Arrate's *Llave del Nuevo Mundo* can be read as an account of how the Columbian discourse of gold becomes domesticated—one might even say debased—in the eighteenth-century Caribbean. This is evidenced by a shift in focus from precious metals themselves to the technological processes such as amalgamation and surface mining that make possible the transmutation of gold, silver, and copper into economic commodities. The royal slaves of El Cobre in Cuba exemplify this shift, as their negotiations regarding legal definitions of identity and privilege and their involvement in secondary mining activities such as copper tailings represent a move away from the exalted discourse of the *leyenda áurea*. Arrate's history of Havana reflects a similar move by presenting a ledger sheet of criollo civic and ecclesiastical accomplishment in which an accounting of municipal merit is used to leverage imperial influence.

In these readings I've attempted to demonstrate how these eighteenth-century Spanish American authors were enlightened thinkers who participated fully in a transatlantic exchange of ideas. As Aníbal Quijano notes, the crystallization of modernity that was the Enlightenment occurred simultaneously in Europe and the Americas; Latin Americans not only received ideas and institutions but also shared in their production and circulation (*Modernidad, identidad y utopía,* 13). At the same time these authors, writing from the imperial periphery, articulated a different awareness of the moment and laid out different kinds of projects than those of their European counterparts. They exemplify the production of knowledge to which Walter Mignolo refers when he observes that "knowledge is not something produced from a post-modern non-place. On the contrary, knowledge is always geo-historically and geo-politically located across the epistemic colonial difference" (*Idea of Latin America,* 43).[3]

There are threads that weave these authors together despite differences of time and place and circumstance. One is a marked concern with the reconfiguring of conquest and conflict within an eighteenth-century paradigm. Oviedo y Baños celebrates the foundation of cities as placeholders in the Venezuelan countryside, while Azara calls on Spain to fortify and populate the neutral zones marking the frontier with Brazil that will otherwise fall into the hands of the Portuguese. Molina's Araucanians employ *parlamentos* instead of weapons to negotiate their status, and Arrate congratulates the citizens of Havana for constructing a bulwark for the Spanish Empire in the Caribbean. Mapping works to affirm and challenge imperial boundaries in Molina and Azara; new economic models are emerging in Caracas, Havana, and Quito that are in stark contrast to those in place earlier. These authors also share an ongoing engagement with their local environment and an experience of cross-cultural contact that reflects the changing realities of eighteenth-century Spanish America, and their articulation of that experience is marked by both optimism and ambivalence. In their project of domesticating empire, an emergent identity is defined expansively to include American-born criollos, Spaniards whose longtime residence in the Americas had altered their vantage point and, at least to some degree, an idealized Amerindian population. However, criollo anxieties about mestizos, most explicit in Herrera's *Secretos* but marking other texts as well, prefigure a narrowing of possibilities for full participation in the body politic and an undermining of Enlightenment ideals that will haunt the continent.

In the context of renewed debates about the legacy of the Enlightenment, it is no longer possible to disclaim the relevance of Spanish America for the eighteenth century or of the eighteenth century for Spanish America. Rather, we must put instances of eighteenth-century enlightened thinking on both sides of the Atlantic and in both hemispheres in dialogue with each other again. Doing so will enable us to recognize the degree to which they have always been dependent on one another. As Joshua Lund observes, "The question, then, is not (or no longer): how can a Latin Americanist epistemology stand up to, or even overcome, a Eurocentric tradition that excludes it? Rather, it might be worth asking: how does that Eurocentric tradition depend upon Latin America as its inner exterior that will always fail at 'standing up to it' (whether, to paraphrase Santiago, as deficient economy or deficient intellectual production)?" ("Hybridity, Genre, Race," 123).[4]

The new criollo subjectivity that emerges in the eighteenth century is epistemologically hybrid, manifesting itself as the localized internalization of a dominant discourse.[5] It is a generalized cultural sensitivity that Foucault in his essay "What Is Enlightenment" describes as an "attitude": "And by attitude, I mean a mode of relating to contemporary reality; a voluntary choice made by certain people; in the end, a way of thinking and feeling; a way, too, of acting and behaving that at one and the same time marks a relation of belonging and presents itself as a task" (*Foucault Reader,* 39). Foucault's emphasis on the "task" of Enlightenment squares with the vision of the authors I've discussed here, but this emphasis is later lost from view and becomes, in fact, even suspect in the face of alternative ways of self-fashioning in Spanish America.[6] However, if we "free ourselves from the intellectual blackmail of 'being for or against' the Enlightenment" (as Foucault challenges us to do), we will find that these authors offer a rich, complex, and surprisingly relevant commentary on the Bourbon Spanish Empire in the Americas and its place in the global Enlightenment.[7]

Like de Certeau's shards of history, the whitened bones of the conquistadors, Herrera's convent reliquary, or the copper tailings of El Cobre, the eighteenth century remains to remind us of the past and offer new ways of negotiating the present. Even Azara's precariously preserved specimens resurface in later debates about Darwin's Argentine fossils and their significance for evolutionary theory. It is surely no accident that the remains of several of these authors, after centuries of exile or historical oblivion, were repatriated in the twentieth century, a reminder that the Spanish American eighteenth century still has something to say to us today.[8]

Notes

INTRODUCTION

1. This question was prompted by research for the chapter on eighteenth-century narrative that I was writing at the time for the *Cambridge History of Latin American Literature,* edited by Roberto González Echevarría and Enrique Pupo-Walker.

2. Roberto González Echevarría gives the eighteenth century short shrift in *Myth and Archive,* as does Angel Rama in *The Lettered City;* most attempts to propose a paradigmatic approach to Spanish American modernity do the same.

3. Carrió de la Vandera, *El lazarillo,* 99. The Spanish eighteenth century faces a similar dilemma, as many have observed. Perhaps the starkest categorization of this dilemma comes from Jesús Pérez Magallón: "The eighteenth century in its entirety has become a dead issue, a century excluded from reality and therefore from the canon" ("Enseñar," 133; my translation). See also Deacon, "Spain and Enlightenment," 293–342.

4. See Higgins, *Constructing the Criollo Archive;* Cañizares-Esguerra, *How to Write;* Carrera, *Imagining Identity;* Hill, *Hierarchy, Commerce, and Fraud;* Safier, *Measuring the New World;* Ewalt, *Peripheral Wonders;* Paquette, *Enlightenment, Governance, and Reform;* and Meléndez, *Deviant and Useful Citizens.*

5. Jorge Cañizares-Esguerra's *How to Write the History of the New World,* in which he argues that Spanish and creole historiography on the New World "became first and foremost a reconstruction of self-identity," would be an exception (3).

6. For a wide-ranging collection of essays regarding the place of Hispanism within larger debates on postcolonialism and multiculturalism, see Moraña, *Ideologies of Hispanism.*

7. This is not to suggest a lack of debate on what constitutes that canon. For an early intervention, see the collection of essays edited by Leo Damrosch, *The Profession of Eighteenth-Century Literature.*

8. Recent publications on the European and global Enlightenment provide a larger context for my own project and also point to the gap in the scholarship that *Domesticating Empire* aims to fill. Daniel Carey and Lynn Festa, in the introduction to their coedited collection of essays titled *Postcolonial Enlightenment,* address the role that the Enlightenment has played in "postcolonial critiques of European imperial practices" (v). They have included a number of important essays by scholars of the global eighteenth century (Aravamudan, Nussbaum, Garraway, O'Brien), but none that deal with Spain or Spanish America. In *The Unfinished Enlightenment: Description in the Age of the Encyclopedia,* Joanna Stalnaker examines the French Enlightenment's attempts to describe the world, with particular emphasis on the writings of Buffon, Diderot, d'Alembert, and Rousseau. There is no discussion, however, of how these works intersect with similar attempts written in Spanish. The collection of essays co-edited by Richard Butterwick, Simon Davies, and Gabriel Sánchez Espinosa, *Peripheries of the Enlightenment,* includes one essay on Spain ("An *Ilustrado* in His Province," by Gabriel Sánchez Espinosa), and another on

Mexico ("The *Gazeta de Literatura de México* and the Edge of Reason: When Is a Periphery Not a Periphery?" by Fiona Clark). See also *The Global Eighteenth Century,* edited by Felicity A. Nussbaum. My involvement with the American Society for Eighteenth-Century Studies (ASECS) has provided valuable opportunities to learn about current work on the Enlightenment and has been key to the development of this project.

9.   There is a growing body of scholarship on the hemispheric Americas. Ralph Bauer's *The Cultural Geography of Colonial American Literatures* offers comparative readings of works from colonial and eighteenth-century Anglo- and Spanish America. Bauer's observations about the production and consumption of knowledge in the colonies and the metropolis inform my readings in *Domesticating Empire.* The collection of essays co-edited by Bauer and José Antonio Mazzotti, *Creole Subjects in the Colonial Americas: Empires, Texts, Identities,* is another important contribution to this field.

10. The classic collection of essays edited by A. Owen Aldridge on the Ibero-American Enlightenment takes as its starting point a traditional understanding of the key elements of the European Enlightenment: a commitment to scientific discovery and rejection of superstition, a spirit of critical inquiry, and dedication to social and economic reform (*Ibero-American Enlightenment,* 8). Most contributors to the volume stress the dual importance of reason and experience in understanding and appropriating the world and point to the "intellectual revolution" (to use John Tate Lanning's phrase) that had completely transformed Hispanic academic culture by the end of the century. Although Bourbon administrative reforms were, at heart, profoundly conservative, eighteenth-century thinkers in Spanish America advocated the promotion of useful scientific knowledge and the liberation of philosophic thought from Scholasticism. The bibliography on eighteenth-century Spanish American history is extensive; as a starting point, see Bakewell, *History,* 271–318; Brading, *First America;* Burkholder and Johnson, *Colonial Latin America,* 280–349; Lynch, *Spanish American Revolutions,* 1–37; and Soto Arango, Puig-Samper, and Arboleda, *La Ilustración.* For a representative selection of writings by key thinkers of the Ibero-American Enlightenment, see Chiaramonte, *Pensamiento de la Ilustración.* The bibliography on eighteenth-century Spanish history is equally extensive: see Dominguez Ortiz, *Carlos III* and *Sociedad y estado;* Lynch, *Bourbon Spain;* Sarrailh, *La España ilustrada;* Vaca de Osma, *Carlos III;* and Voltes, *Carlos III.*

11. I do not use "domestication" as synonymous with "domesticity," a concept that informs much recent work on the Anglo-American eighteenth century. "Domesticity" refers to the private domain (houses, women, children, and decorative elements), while "domestication" is understood here as a public project. Of course, both public and private spaces are constructed discursively and intersect in many ways, as Stephanie Hilger has argued ("Public," 394).

12. Not all nineteenth-century nation builders wanted to forget their ties to the colonial past or to sever their connection to the eighteenth century in doing so: for example, Esteban Echeverría in *Dogma Socialista* tries to link colonial regimes with democratic traditions, and Juan María Gutiérrez recuperates the colonial tradition as American rather than Spanish. I am grateful to Hernán Feldman for his observations in this regard.

13. Joshua Lund suggests (following Enrique Dussel) that Latin America, "like any other post-colonial epistemology, has always participated in that genus called 'Western tradition,' but under the terms of a Eurocentric contract that presupposes its status as a constitutive peripherality" ("Hybridity, Genre, Race," 126); it participates in that tradition, "but finds no home there" (129).

14. Charles W. Withers notes that "the Atlantic Enlightenment—understood as negotiated information flow across the space between continental margins and as knowledge made

and received in places on those margins—meant different things to different people in different places" ("Where," 46). That said, Withers's discussion of the Spanish American margins of the Atlantic Enlightenment relies largely on Cañizares-Esguerra and is limited to a fairly brief mention of Spanish American critiques of European commentators on the New World (47).

15. For a reevaluation of the traditional approach to periodization, see the collection of essays edited by Gabriel Paquette, *Enlightened Reform in Southern Europe and its Atlantic Colonies, c. 1750–1830.*

16. Elliott, *Empires,* 307. J. H. Elliott sums up the situation in 1700 as the Hapsburg Empire gave way to the Bourbon Empire: "In principle, a highly regulated transatlantic trading system and a vast body of legislation belatedly codified in the *Recopilación de las leyes de Indias* held Spanish America in a tight metropolitan grip. In practice, the spread of systematized corruption endowed the imperial structure with a flexibility that its rigid framework appeared to belie" (229). For a discussion of the consolidation of Spain's American territories into "an effective imperial framework" under Hapsburg rule, known as the *monarquía española,* see Elliott, 119–30. See also MacLachlan, *Spain's Empire;* Pagden, *Spanish Imperialism;* Pagden, *Lords of All the World;* and Pagden, *Uncertainties of Empire.* For a discussion of Spain's eighteenth-century empire, see Paquette, *Enlightenment, Governance, and Reform.*

17. "Historians would benefit from shifting away from chronological periodization, which largely reflects (geo-)political turning points and dynastic changes. Instead, they might favour a stylistic periodization" (Paquette, "Introduction," 19).

18. See Bauer and Mazzotti, *Creole Subjects.*

19. See Rama, *Lettered City;* see also Carlos Alonso's discussion of Rama's work (*Burden of Modernity,* 38–43).

20. Martínez-San Miguel, "Colonial Writings," 173. This identitarian ambivalence would, of course, no longer be possible post-Independence.

21. For a discussion of Eguiara y Eguren, see Higgins, *Constructing the Criollo Archive,* 23–105. "Bibliotheca" is spelled "Biblioteca" in some editions.

22. There are no mestizo, mulatto, or indigenous authors included in this study, although they are important actors on the eighteenth-century viceregal stage.

23. Eighteenth-century writers in Spanish America see historical narrative "as an arena in which both historian and reader exercise political, emotional, and aesthetic choices; together they create, not an imagined, but an interpretive community engaged in a rhetorical arbitration of their own history" (O'Brien, *Narratives of Enlightenment,* 5).

24. For further discussion, I refer the reader to two essays in *The Cambridge History of Latin American Literature:* Bush, "Lyric Poetry" (375–400); and Luciani, "Spanish American Theater" (401–16).

25. As Gabriel Paquette has argued, "Europe and the Americas, far from being two self-contained political and cultural worlds in the long eighteenth century, can only be understood fully when their histories are fused" ("Introduction," 4–5).

26. Higgins, *Constructing the Criollo Archive,* 13. Higgins argues that in using Baroque aesthetics as the dominant model for theorizing Spanish American coloniality, "modern literary historiography has tended to gloss over the segments of these emergent modes of writing that are articulated with the terms of neoclassical and/or enlightened thought" ("(Post-)Colonial Sublime," 125).

27. Sankar Muthu argues persuasively for a revisionist understanding of Enlightenment thinking about empire: "The Enlightenment era is unique not because of the absence of imperialist arguments, but rather due to the presence of spirited attacks upon the

foundations of empire" (*Enlightenment against Empire,* 4). Moreover, he argues that these attacks went unheeded by later nineteenth-century thinking, when popular notions of progress and nationality tended to characterize the Enlightenment as a "project that ultimately attempted to efface or marginalize difference, a characterization that has hidden from view the anti-imperialist strand of Enlightenment-era political thought" (6).

28. Michael Meranze observes that "the Kantian definition of enlightenment laid down a continual task and made a continuing demand: that critical thought not only reflect upon but engage with its historical moment" ("Critique and Government," 105). Discussing Dussell's reading of Immanuel Kant, Mignolo remarks, "It is notorious, incidentally, that when Kant talks about the Americans he talks about North America, as South America undeniably slides out of the picture" (*Local Histories/Global Designs,* 63). Kant's blindness with regard to the ways in which South American Indians complicate and challenge his racial taxonomies is only one example of how Spanish America has been erased from discussions of the Enlightenment.

29. For a discussion of how the relationship between core and periphery has informed the history of science, see Fiona Clark's exploration of José Antonio Alzate y Ramírez's shifting use of Spanish, American, Hispanic American, and Mexican to describe himself and his intended audience as "indicative of a period in which national identity and the focus of national interests were slowly being transformed by an increasing sense of separateness from the Iberian metropolis" ("*Gazeta de Literatura,*" 256).

30. Clark concludes, "The imperial unity of the Spanish nation was maintained throughout, demonstrating Alzate's belief that the Spanish so-called peripheries were an integral part of this organic whole of the Spanish kingdom and functioned as parts of it" (ibid., 263).

31. Except when otherwise indicated, all translations are my own.

32. See Alonso, *Burden of Modernity,* 28.

33. Dennis Moore, "Beyond Colonial Studies: An Inter-American Encounter" (workshop, Brown University, Providence, RI, November 4–6, 2004).

34. See Subirats, *La ilustración insuficiente.* Pérez-Magallón offers a succinct overview of the limitations of traditional approaches to the Spanish (and, by extension, the Hispanic) eighteenth century in his essay "Enseñar el siglo dieciocho español" (132–34).

35. I am grateful to Dierdra Reber for her insightful comments on this issue.

CHAPTER 1

An earlier version of this chapter appeared as "Oviedo y Baños en tierra de nadie" in *Crítica y descolonización,* edited by Beatriz González Stephan and Lúcia Helena Costigan (Caracas, Venezuela: Academia Nacional de la Historia, 1992). Other versions of this chapter have been presented as follows: "Domesticating Discourse" (Modern Language Association Annual Meeting, Washington, DC, December 2000); "Uncivil Wars" (American Society for Eighteenth-Century Studies Annual Meeting, Colorado Springs, CO, April 2002); and "Bureaucrats and Border Disputes: Domesticating Conquest in Eighteenth-Century Spanish America" (invited lecture, University of Virginia, Charlottesville, December 2004).

1. The *Historia* was first published in Madrid in 1723 and reprinted in Caracas in 1824 by Domingo Navas Spínola. Although there have been numerous editions published in the twentieth century (including a 1987 translation into English by Jeannette Varner), the 1992 Ayacucho edition, based on Navas Spínola's 1824 edition and with a brilliant introduction by Tomás Eloy Martínez and Susana Rotker, is unparalleled. My own reading of the *Historia* is greatly indebted to the insights of Martínez and Rotker. All quotes are drawn from the Ayacucho edition; translations are mine.

2. Oviedo y Baños's dedication of the *Historia* to his brother, "Don Diego Antonio de Oviedo y Baños, Oidor de las Reales Audiencias de la Española, Guatemala y México, del Consejo de su Majestad en el real y supremo de las Indias" (3), rather than to a peninsular luminary, underscores from the outset these local concerns (see Martínez and Rotker, "Prólogo," xxxii).

3. Pedro de Peralta Barnuevo (1664–1743) is the eighteenth-century Spanish American author whose rewriting of conquest, most notably in his epic poem *Lima fundada* and *Historia de España vindicada,* has received the most critical attention. See Gutiérrez, "Pedro de Peralta"; and J. M. Williams, "Popularizing."

4. Book 1 describes the geography of Venezuela, its discovery by Alonso de Ojeda, and the arrival of the Welsers by virtue of the Hapsburg capitulations. Books 2 and 3 narrate a series of battles and conquests. Book 4 tells the story of Lope de Aguirre. Book 5 focuses on Diego de Losada's founding of Caracas. Book 6 returns to the narration of various battles and efforts to found additional cities; it closes with Drake's attack on the city of Santiago.

5. See also Navarro, "Elogio," 551 and Díaz Sánchez, *Evolución de la historiografía,* 18.

6. See also Parra León, who acknowledges Oviedo y Baños's debt to Simón ("Prólogo," xli).

7. Oviedo y Baños explains, "If the curious reader remarks on the infrequent citation of the authors on whom I rely, that is the best proof of the truth of what I write, as I have always been governed by the ancient instruments that I have read and which brevity prevents me from citing, I assure the reader that their authority provides the certainty I need for the events to which I refer" (*Historia,* 11). Ingrid Galster includes a discussion of the plagiarism controversy and a detailed analysis of the parallels between Simón's text and Oviedo y Baños's; see *Aguirre,* 192–98. I will return to the question of Oviedo y Baños's intertextual dialogue with the historiographical tradition later in this chapter.

8. For a more complete biography, see Parra León, "Prólogo"; Morón, "José de Oviedo y Baños"; Varner, "Introduction," xv–xviii; and Galster, *Aguirre,* 188–89.

9. Martínez and Rotker observe, "What mattered to Oviedo y Baños and others of his class was revindicating the right of criollos to exercise through the Cabildos (town councils) political and military authority in cases when there was no governor" ("Prólogo," xxviii; translation mine).

10. Parra León, "Prólogo," xix–xxii; and Morón, *Los cronistas,* 104.

11. This was an extensive document approved in 1680 by Charles II (1665–1700) with the aim of addressing the confusions and contradictions of the existing *Recopilación de leyes de los reynos de las Indias,* "a compilation of individual laws issued over the centuries in response to specific problems [that] constituted historical evidence of the innumerable political contests and accommodations that characterized the Hapsburg state" (MacLachlan, *Spain's Empire,* 119). Needless to say, at a moment when Bourbon administrators were looking to reform existing laws and practices, Oviedo y Baños's efforts to find recourse in the *Nueva recopilación* fell upon deaf ears.

12. For a detailed discussion of this shift, see Paquette's "Colonial Elites and Imperial Governance" (in *Enlightenment, Governance, and Reform,* 127–51).

13. One might argue that this anticipates the *gobernar es poblar* (to govern is to populate) mentality of nineteenth-century writers and statesmen like Domingo Sarmiento and Juan Bautista Alberdi. Both Oviedo y Baños and Molina (the focus of the following chapter) shift the focus of their history from an epic to a civil, or civic, mode.

14. Rojas, *Leyendas históricas,* 223. I will return to the question of this missing second part at the conclusion of this chapter.

15. *Excusatio propter infirmitatem* (literally, "to excuse onself on account of infirmity") was

a rhetorical strategy frequently used by sixteenth- and seventeenth-century Spanish chroniclers writing from the New World to excuse their lack of formal historiographical training.

16. *Adelantado* is a term used to refer to the governor of a border territory under Spanish rule; literally, it means "the one who goes out ahead."

17. Martínez and Rotker use the term "domestication" in this sense when speaking of the sixteenth-century Spaniards' frustrated encounters with New World nature ("Prólogo," xl–xli).

18. Bakewell, *History,* 285.

19. Lombardi continues: "For students of Latin American history whose vision of conquest and settlement is inspired by the Mexican and Peruvian epics, the chronicle of Venezuela's settlement often appears incongruous. Spanish expeditions that failed to conquer relatively poverty-stricken tribes, towns created that disappeared, urban settlements that changed location every so often—these characteristics of early Spanish activity in Tierra Firme seem discordant with the general patterns of conquest and settlement prevalent elsewhere in America" (*Venezuela,* 68).

20. See Lockhart and Schwartz, *Early Latin America,* 283.

21. Lombardi, *Venezuela,* 61.

22. Oviedo y Baños, with the benefit of hindsight, carefully notes a number of missed opportunities in this regard.

23. Lombardi, *Venezuela,* 64. Juan Friede's *Los Welser en la conquista de Venezuela* remains an important—if somewhat biased—resource on this topic. Friede's goal in his exhaustively researched work is to correct the view of the Welsers as prototypically greedy and violent conquistadors, and he points to Oviedo y Baños as one of those responsible for perpetrating this view (*Los Welser,* 14–16).

24. Lombardi sums up the German experiment in these terms: "Towns were founded, Coro securely and Maracaibo precariously; geographic knowledge greatly increased; and Indian hostility substantially intensified. In the subsequent government inquiries, the greatest charge leveled at the German management was their failure to establish towns and create stable forms of Indian control" (*Venezuela,* 66).

25. Hill discusses this issue in *Sceptres and Sciences,* 4–5.

26. Lombardi, *Venezuela,* 73–77. See also Grahn, *Political Economy of Smuggling,* for a dicussion of the informal economy of early Bourbon New Granada.

27. A discussion of the successes and failures of the *Compañia Guipuzcoana* (Caracas Company) in the eighteenth century falls outside the scope of this study, as do the late eighteenth-century political reforms that led to the creation of the Intendancy of Venezuela in 1776 (to consolidate fiscal authority), the Captaincy General of Venezuela in 1777 (to coordinate defense against Spain's enemies), and the Audiencia of Caracas in 1786 (for judicial administration).

28. Hill has explored these issues in a number of essays and, most notably, in *Sceptres and Sciences: Four Humanists and the New Philosophy (ca. 1680–1740).* Anthony Pagden locates this shift even earlier: "By the mid-seventeenth century the declining Spanish position in Europe, the threat which the conquistador elite continued to pose to royal authority in the Americas, and the widespread disapprobation of conquest through Europe (to which the Spaniards were by no means as insensitive as they sometimes claimed) led to a number of attempts to diminish the role of conquest in the ideological image of the origins of the Spanish American colonies" (*Lords,* 101).

29. "The peaceful prince encouraged peace and economic development, stressed education, encouraged research in the sciences and useful arts, promoted an active commerce, and provided for the security and comfort of his subjects. . . . The prince-conquerer, however,

exerted a negative influence" (MacLachlan, *Spain's Empire,* 70). Feijoo addresses the issue of Spanish conquest in a number of essays included in *Teatro crítico universal:* "Glorias de España," "Fábula de las Batuecas," "Situación del gran problema histórico sobre la población de América," and "Españoles americanos." Feijoo's take on the conquest is contradictory. On the one hand he denounces the lust for gold that obscured in many instances Spain's evangelical mission in the Americas; on the other hand, he laments the dissemination of the "Black Legend" by Spain's enemies and points with pride to the fact that the conquest served as an arena for the formation of Spanish heroes.

30. For example, when Oviedo y Baños discusses the death of Bishop Fray Juan de Manzanillo in 1594 and the naming of his successor, Fray Diego de Salinar, in the final chapter of the *Historia,* he states: "Although his arrival in this bishopric did not occur until the year 1598, as he was detained in Spain by the need to attend to certain business dealings, we wish to anticipate the news of his presentation in case there is no opportunity to mention it at a later moment" (324).

31. Pithier and more pragmatic than, for example, the moralizing fulminations of Juan Rodríguez Freyle in *El carnero,* Oviedo y Baños's aphoristic observations remind the reader of Benjamin Franklin's *Poor Richard's Almanack.* My personal favorite is the observation that begins Oviedo y Baños's "Prologue to the reader": "It has always been a tedious and mentally taxing chore to write as one must for publication" (*Historia,* 10). Unfortunately, much of the character of these comments is lost in translation.

32. Fernán Pérez de Guzmán and Hernando del Pulgar each penned collections of brief biographies of exemplary figures from Spanish history: *Generaciones y semblanzas* (Valladolid, 1512) and *Libro de los claros varones de Castilla* (Toledo, 1486), respectively. Juan de Castellanos (1532–1607) wrote the *Elegías de varones ilustres de Indias* in *octavas reales* (royal octaves), drawing on the epic tradition and also on the model of the biographies of illustrious men, such as *Claros varones de Castilla.* Castellanos's text might itself be seen as a distortion of the European model: Marcelino Menéndez Pelayo describes it as a work of "monstrous proportions" (qtd. in Pardo, *Juan de Castellanos,* 65). The monstrousness of Castellanos's poem may suggest that there is inherently something "monstrous" about the enterprise of American heroism itself, as we will see in Oviedo y Baños's portrayal of Lope de Aguirre. For a more positive (and balanced) assessment of Castellanos's work, see Fernández Restrepo, *Un nuevo reino imaginado.*

33. Although Venezuelan colonial history presents a marked contrast with the epic battles for Tenochtitlán and Peru, the basic models of *adelantado* and *capitulaciones* still held: "These rules, designed to limit and direct the efforts of audacious, headstrong men, usually set geographical boundaries to the enterprise, imposed a time limit on the initiation of the expedition, stipulated the activities permitted, and specified the preparations required" (Lombardi, *Venezuela,* 60).

34. In what is perhaps the basest anecdote of conquistador folly, Oviedo y Baños describes how Diego de Paradas is killed while slipping away from his companions to relieve himself: "Obliged by a bodily evacuation—fatal carelessness that cost him his life!" (*Historia,* 223).

35. I maintain Oviedo y Baños's Hispanicized versions of these Welser names here (as does Varner in her English translation): Utre (Hutten); Spira (Speyer); Fedreman (Federman or Federmann).

36. See also Oviedo y Baños's account of Don Pedro, who loses his life in pursuit of El Dorado (*Historia,* 255–56).

37. An *encomendero* is someone who has been designated to receive free labor and tribute from the Indians in exchange for their protection and indoctrination in Christianity.

38. The historian prefaces this anecdote with a lengthy apology in which he defends the ve-

racity of the incredible tale he is about to tell, invokes the topic of great deeds forgotten by history, and compares Garci González to Cortés (*Historia,* 292–93).

39. The apparent success of this bluffing tactic raises the interesting question of how well, if at all, the Indians understood Spanish, particularly a phrase shouted out in the heat of battle. Nevertheless, Oviedo y Baños's evident admiration for Garci González's cunning speaks volumes.

40. Martínez and Rotker offer a thought-provoking characterization of Garci González as hero, though they note that he is unsuccessful in founding cities ("Prólogo," xxxviii–xxxix).

41. The fatal consequences of the decisions made by unwise leaders is a frequent topic in colonial historiography (Pánfilo de Narváez's disastrous expedition to Florida comes immediately to mind as an example).

42. *Cacica* is the feminine form of *cacique;* both terms refer to someone who enjoys political power and respect in an indigenous community.

43. Although race, occupation, and status functioned in colonial Spanish America in more fluid ways than has often been acknowledged, Jane E. Mangan notes that "mestizo identity became increasingly synonymous with illegitimacy as well as other negative characteristics that defined mixed-race society (that is, non-Indians and non-Spaniards)" ("Market of Identities," 72). For an extended discussion, see the volume in which Mangan's essay appears: Fisher and O'Hara, *Imperial Subjects.*

44. For more on the El Dorado myth, see Friede, *Los Welser,* 99–106; Pastor, "Lope de Aguirre the Wanderer," 97n1; and Ramos Pérez, *El mito del Dorado.*

45. "The Welsers devoted all their energies and resources to a frantic and ultimately frustrated search for El Dorado, the mythical king and his fabulous civilization" (Lombardi, *Venezuela,* 65–66).

46. Privately, Utre was more likely to express misgivings; see Friede, *Los Welser,* 357, on the letter he writes to his brother back in Germany. Ivonne del Valle studies a similar gap between public writing and familial correspondence by eighteenth-century Jesuits in New Spain in *Escribiendo desde los márgenes.*

47. In chapter 4 of *Naufragios,* as Cabeza de Vaca and his shipwrecked companions begin to explore the mainland, they ask the indigenous inhabitants about corn and gold (86).

48. Martínez observes that Oviedo y Baños makes frequent use of necrological notes (Oviedo y Baños, *Historia,* 199n10). Castellanos includes Utre in his *Elegías de varones ilustres de Indias.* Eighteenth-century epic poetry often includes similar necrological passages.

49. Oviedo y Baños's description of this failed expedition is yet another account of a disastrous Spanish mission (*Historia,* 267).

50. I would therefore disagree with Lombardi's assertion that the main actors in Oviedo y Baños's history are "no longer seduced by dreams of El Dorado's kingdom" (*Venezuela,* 66).

51. Oviedo y Baños includes another lengthy necrology for García de Paredes, who is killed in an Indian ambush after having been named governor of Popayán. His feats are eulogized in a passage that spans from his death to birth and back to his death and that makes particular note of his decision to leave behind the incendiary chaos of Pizarro's Peru in order to pursue his destiny in the New Kingdom of Venezuela (*Historia,* 207).

52. See Pagden, "Identity Formation," 56–60; and Pastor, *Armature of Conquest.*

53. Friede maintains that anyone connected with the Welsers becomes a target for Oviedo y Baños's hostility (*Los Welser,* 16). Utre, whose somewhat ambiguous portrayal in the *Historia* I have already discussed, is an exception.

54. Friede, *Los Welser,* 21–23; and Martínez and Rotker, "Prólogo," xxviii.

55. Lombardi, *Venezuela,* 65–66; and Bakewell, *History,* 102–3.

56. Oviedo y Baños later repeats this condemnation of the Welsers' attitude toward the province of Venezuela: "They viewed it without affection, considering it something borrowed; they paid no heed to its conservation nor did they attempt its development, as they tended only to make the most of the opportunity while it lasted, without considering that the methods they used were most efficient for its destruction" (*Historia,* 108). *Repartimientos* were rewards within the Spanish system of forced labor; *encomiendas* were grants of labor and tribute rights given by the Spanish crown.

57. Again, see Hill, *Sceptres and Sciences,* 4–5.

58. In one of his few specific references to earlier historiography, Oviedo y Baños notes that the abuses committed by the Welsers and their Spanish surrogates like Carvajal were so numerous and egregious that "Don Fray Bartolomé de las Casas in his book on the *Destrucción de las Indias* called this province unhappy and wretched; and it undoubtedly was" (108). For a discussion of the reception of Las Casas in the eighteenth century, see Slade and Stolley, "On the *Brevísima,*" 92–98.

59. José Rabasa explores the use of violence as spectacle in *Writing Violence;* for a discussion of spectacle as a representation of viceregal power in the Americas, see Cañeque, *King's Living Image.*

60. Hulme, "Introduction," 4; see also Jáuregui, "El plato más sabroso" and *Canibalia;* Avramescu, *Intellectual History of Cannibalism;* Cottom, *Cannibals and Philosophers;* and Still, *Enlightenment Hospitality.* Montaigne's essay "Des cannibales" is, of course, one of the earliest and best-known reflections on cannibalism in the Americas.

61. Jorge Cañizares-Esguerra reminds us that "revived accounts of American cannibalism provided ammunition for many parties engaged in furious ideological struggles over alternate visions of human nature" (*How to Write,* 27). Oviedo y Baños's treatment of the topic strikes me as surprisingly evenhanded and curiously removed from these struggles, though it must be acknowledged that he is writing early in the eighteenth century, before later debates about the New World Black Legend were fully engaged.

62. Daniel Cottom suggests that there are two lines of representation of cannibalism, one epitomized by Las Casas, "in which cannibalism ceases to be barbaric in and of itself," and another "in which the brutality of cannibalism becomes a starting point for critical reflection, followed in the tradition set forth by Montaigne" (*Cannibals and Philosophers,* 176).

63. As Peter Hulme explains with reference to Edgar Rice Burroughs's *Tarzan of the Apes,* the "primal scene of 'cannibalism' as 'witnessed' by Westerners is of its aftermath rather than its performance. At the center of the scene is the large cooking pot, essential utensil for cannibal illustrations; and surrounding it is the 'evidence' of cannibalism: the discarded human bones. . . . There is no more typical scene in the writing about cannibalism in whatever genre than that in which a witness stumbles across the remains of a cannibal feast" ("Introduction," 1–3).

64. Later in the *Historia* the city of Valencia is threatened by repeated invasions by the Caribs, who are greatly feared owing to their appetite for human flesh. The Spaniards who organize a counterattack come upon what Oviedo y Baños describes as a typical cannibal scene: "They found laid out in an orderly fashion on barbecue grills about two hundred heads, that the Caribs had left there, from Indians that they had taken prisoner and were sacrificing in their drunken feasts in order to satiate with their bodies the bestial inclination to fill themselves up with human flesh" (300). For a discussion of the portrayal of Caribs and Arawaks as cannibals, see Hulme, *Colonial Encounters,* 45–87.

65. Utre writes in the letter to his brother from which I quoted earlier: "It's horrifying what kinds of creatures the Christians had to eat during this journey, like snakes, toads, lizards, vipers, worms, plants, roots and many other things, and bad food, some even devouring human flesh, against nature. A Christian was found cooking with herbs a quartered Indian boy" (qtd. in Friede, *Los Welser*, 357–58).

66. When he learns of their transgression, Spira initially plans to punish the men with death but commutes the sentence, as he is short on soldiers. Divine justice intervenes, however: Oviedo y Baños reports that all four men die shortly thereafter, in separate but clearly providentially directed accidents (*Historia*, 68).

67. This is a familiar tale of transculturation through domesticity—one which we have seen in Bernal Díaz's account of Gonzalo Guerrero and which is parodied in the closing cannibal scene in the Brazilian film *How Tasty Was My Little Frenchman* (1971).

68. See Martínez and Rotker, "Prólogo," xxxvi–xxxvii. They note that Simón includes the story of Francisco Martín as a point of departure for a long sermon criticizing anthropophagy, while for Oviedo y Baños it reflects the misfortunes of power.

69. Lombardi agrees that from the early 1550s on, "jurisdictional disputes between rival conquistadors, each with a royal authorization that could be interpreted to cover the same territory, kept the precarious Iberian towns in Cubagua and on the mainland coast in intermittent turmoil" (*Venezuela*, 62). What interests me here is not so much the sixteenth-century historical situation as the way it is represented by the eighteenth-century historian.

70. On more than one occasion, Oviedo y Baños refers to the conquest of Peru in negative terms, as we shall see in the discussion of Lope de Aguirre.

71. As in the case of Rodríguez Freyle (and unlike what we see with Cortés and Bernal Díaz), later historians are no longer protagonists of the history they narrate but rather arbitrators or administrators of it. Oviedo y Baños's concerns about administrative disorder grew out of personal experience; I will explore their implications at the conclusion of this chapter.

72. Another crisis arises in Coro when, following the death of Governor Henrique Rembolt, the two *alcaldes* to whom interim governance is entrusted until a new governor can be named squabble between themselves and contradict each other's orders to such a degree that the city is reduced to great confusion and "monstrous disorder in which all one saw were injustices, bribery, and violence" (Oviedo y Baños, *Historia*, 87). Happily, once a new governor is named, order is restored. The quarrelsome *alcaldes* flee one night under the cover of darkness, never to be heard from again.

73. Given this generally negative depiction of conquest, it's interesting to note that eighteenth-century Spanish theater often appropriated the topic of the discovery and conquest (and particularly the figure of Cortés) in service of an imperialist ideology. See Llanos, *(Re)descubrimiento y (re)conquista;* and Hill, "Hierarchy and Historicism."

74. The story of Lope de Aguirre has captured the imagination of critics, novelists (among them Ramón Sender, Miguel Otero Silva, and Abel Posse), and filmmakers. It has been suggested that Ramón del Valle Inclán found inspiration for his novel *Tirano Banderas* (1926) in the figure of Aguirre (Pastor, *Armature of Conquest*, 305n103). Werner Herzog's film *Aguirre, the Wrath of God* (1972) focuses on Aguirre's megalomaniacal battle against nature in retelling the story of the ill-fated rebellion as an analogy for Hitler and German fascism. See also Castro Arenas, "Lope de Aguirre"; Kirschner and Manchón, "Lope de Aguirre"; Larrazábal Henríquez, "Lope de Aguirre"; and Waller, "Aguirre." Beatriz Pastor argues that all the different accounts of the Aguirre rebellion reflect a crisis of the conquistador model and substitute a discourse of rebellion for an earlier discourse

of failure (*Armature of Conquest,* 153–204). Evan L. Balkan revisits the Aguirre story to argue for his revolutionary role (*Wrath of God*). For a recent overview of the figure of Aguirre in Latin American historical novels, see B. L. Lewis, *Miraculous Lie;* see also Galster, *Aguirre.*

75. Burkholder and Johnson, *Colonial Latin America,* 58; and Barrientos, "Aguirre y la rebelión," 93.

76. The *Oxford English Dictionary,* 3rd ed., defines a "delinquent" as one who fails in duty or obligation (i.e., a defaulter); more generally, a delinquent is one guilty of an offence against the law (i.e., an offender). But the word has also taken on the connotation of being late or overdue .

77. Pagden observes that "the history of the Spanish dependencies in America was marked from the beginning by always unsuccessful, often ludicrous attempts by overambitious men, deprived of what they regarded as their rights as vassals, to create independent states for themselves" ("Identity Formation," 54).

78. There is an earlier moment in book 3 that functions as a farcical foreshadowing of Lope de Aguirre's revolt: the rebellion organized by Miguel, one of the eighty African slaves brought in by Governor Juan de Villegas in the mid-1550s to help work the gold mines in the Barquisimeto Valley. The rebellion, which breaks out when Miguel resists a whipping by grabbing a sword and escaping, expands to involve 180 former slaves, a fortified village, and the formal coronation of a king and queen (Oviedo y Baños, *Historia,* 120–23). When Miguel and his band attack the city of Nueva Segovia, its inhabitants request support from neighboring towns and organize a counterattack. The rebellion quickly falls apart once Miguel is killed, and Oviedo y Baños closes the chapter, "ending in tragedy what began as farcical majesty" (124).

79. It's interesting to compare Oviedo y Baños's account of Aguirre's rebellion with that of Pedro Simón. Simón was a Franciscan friar living in Bogotá and Tunja who traveled throughout Venezuela in 1612–1613 and later wrote the *Primera parte de las noticias historiales* (corresponding to Venezuela) in 1627 (parts 2 and 3 were not published until the nineteenth century, and only then in fragmentary form). Oviedo y Baños refers the reader to Simón's account on several occasions (*Historia,* 156; see also 156n3). Galster includes a detailed comparison of Oviedo y Baños's account with that of Simón (*Aguirre,* 188–98). In Simón's account, it is Ursúa whose story takes center stage; Aguirre is not initially portrayed as the leader of the rebellion. Most striking is Simón's portrayal of the governor of Margarita. While both Simón and Oviedo y Baños make reference to the governor's greediness, only Simón goes so far as to suggest that it borders on malfeasance or even treason.

80. "He had ordered that black taffeta flags with red swords be made, which were at the same time insignias of his evilness and public signs of his heartlessness, the emblem and colors that his tyranny had as its coat of arms manifesting all the ravages and deaths" Aguirre had perpetrated (Oviedo y Baños, *Historia,* 168). Patricia Seed explores similar rituals of Spanish conquest in *Ceremonies of Possession in Europe's Conquest of the New World.*

81. The legal definition of *hubris* for the ancient Greeks initially included specific reference to the mutilation of a corpse.

82. Oviedo y Baños mentions Aguirre's former occupation on an earlier occasion: "Taming horses and mules was how he spent his time in Peru" (*Historia,* 165). He seems especially offended by the irony that someone who had worked as a muleteer (literally, a "tamer" of mules) was so unbridled in his own actions.

83. Galster, *Aguirre,* 195. Aguirre also writes to Provincial Fray Francisco de Montesinos (see Pastor, *The Armature of Conquest,* 195).

84. At this point Aguirre commits his final and most heinous crime, stabbing his own daughter to death so that she will not face the indignity of capture by Spanish authorities (Oviedo y Baños, *Historia,* 197).

85. This may explain Herzog's decision to end his film with Lope de Aguirre adrift on a raft in the Amazon, accompanied only by chattering monkeys and his feverish delusions. That imaginative rewriting is, after all, much more suggestive than what actually happened: the suppression of the rebellion by colonial authorities and Aguirre's ignominious assassination at the hands of his own Marañones. Myth and madness are compelling for the filmmaker, but not for the eighteenth-century historian. See Pastor, *Armature of Conquest,* 194–204.

86. For a discussion of colonial cities, see Kagan, *Urban Images;* Kinsbruner, *Colonial Spanish-American City;* and Hoberman and Socolow, *Cities and Societies.* Oviedo y Baños sums up Caracas as "one of the best cities of those that make up the expansive empire of the Americas" (*Historia,* 238).

87. Galster, *Aguirre,* 188.

88. Lombardi proposes that the particular characteristic of the mode of settlement in Venezuela is "a carefully articulated urban system . . . invented, imposed, and developed during the years from 1500 to 1650" (*Venezuela,* 5). See also his discussion of the founding of El Tocuyo and a number of other cities (66–68).

89. In book 3 the historian narrates the founding of Borburata (chap. 7), Barquisimeto (chap. 8), Valencia (chap. 9), and, finally, the discovery of Caracas (chap. 10).

90. Even Arístides Rojas, a vehement partisan of Simón's primacy as Venezuelan history's founding father, agrees that the conquest of Caracas is one of the few topics that Oviedo y Baños does not take from Simón (*Leyendas históricas,* x).

91. Martínez and Rotker also read Losada as the antithesis of Aguirre ("Prólogo," xxxviii).

92. Martínez suggests that Oviedo y Baños, sensitive about his own position as a relative newcomer to Caracas, includes these names in hopes of currying favor among his eighteenth-century Mantuan/Caracan readers (Oviedo y Baños, *Historia,* 216n1).

93. See Martínez for more information regarding the date (Oviedo y Baños, *Historia,* 231n3).

94. See Lombardi for a discussion of Caracas and other Venezuelan cities in the seventeenth and early eighteenth centuries (*Venezuela,* 66–85).

95. As we will see in Chapter 5, Arrate will do the same in his *Llave del Nuevo Mundo.*

96. Galster, *Aguirre,* 188.

97. For more on the "dispute of the New World," see Gerbi, *Dispute.*

98. For example, in discussing the foundation of Maracaibo in 1571, Oviedo y Baños permits himself an observation about the subsequent development of that port city: "If we Spaniards knew how to take advantage of the opportunities encompassed by the beauty of the lagoon, its shores would be continuous gardens and a kingdom might have been populated on its banks: the repeated invasions by pirates have been sufficient cause to forestall its growth" (*Historia,* 272).

99. See chapters 12 and 13 (ibid., 247–54).

100. The initial dispute was a complicated one involving the manner in which *regidores* and *alcaldes* were to be appointed, and it led to open conflict between Governor Don Luis de Rojas and the inhabitants of Caracas. The crisis continued under the administration of the new governor, Diego de Osorio. Here Oviedo y Baños uses the word *vecinos* (neighbors) to identify those who by virtue of having established their domicile in the city are considered engaged citizens of the urban area; see Herzog, *Defining Nations.*

101. José Carlos Chiaramonte discusses the important political role played by cities in the Americas, given their distance from the metropolitan centers of power in Europe, and

notes that during the first half of the eighteenth century the sale of offices strengthened the hold of the local oligarchy in viceregal centers ("Modificaciones del pacto imperial," 88–92).

102. Arcila Farías, *Reformas económicas,* 38.

103. The author makes another reference to a second volume when speaking of the miraculous image of Nuestra Señora de Coromoto (*Historia,* 323).

104. The notes, which Oviedo y Baños took during his research at the Ayuntamiento de Caracas, correspond to the years 1568–1703 and were published on the occasion of Caracas's quatricentenary as *Tesoro de noticias e índice general de las cosas más particulares que se contienen en los Libros Capitulares de esta ciudad de Caracas desde su fundación hecho por el theniente general Don Joseph de Oviedo y Baños siendo rexidor de ella, el año de mil setecientos y tres, habiendo por orden del mui noble e ilustre cavildo de esta dicha ciudad, reconocido y visto todos los libros y papeles de su archivo* (Treasury of news and general index of the most salient things contained in the Capitular Books of this city of Caracas since its foundation prepared by the general lieutenant Don Joseph de Oviedo y Baños as its regidor, in the year 1703, having by order of the most noble and illustrious Cabildo of this said city reviewed and seen all the books and papers contained in its archive). See Rojas for a discussion of the fate of these documents (*Leyendas históricas,* 230–32).

105. See Ralph Bauer's discussion in *The Cultural Geography of Colonial American Literatures* on the division of intellectual labor and production in the early Americas as a kind of "epistemic mercantilism." Bauer writes, "The poetics of this mercantilist production of knowledge demanded a division of intellectual labor between imperial peripheries and centers, the effacement of colonial subjects, and the transparency of colonial texts as the providers of 'raw facts'" (4).

106. Oviedo y Baños is caught between several competing claims: that he was a plagiarist or, at best, an insufficiently original historian; that he was a founding father of Venezuelan history; and even that he was an incipient novelist, as Planchart suggests ("Oviedo y Baños"). See also Hermano Nectario María's *Historia de la conquista y fundación de Caracas,* which is highly critical of Oviedo y Baños. For a more positive view, see Raimundo Lazo's judgment in *Historia de la literatura hispanoamericana* (383–84).

107. Rojas, *Leyendas históricas,* 224. See also Planchart's "Oviedo y Baños y su *Historia de la conquista y población de la provincia de Venezuela*" in *Discursos pronunciados,* in which he discusses the possibility that the manuscript might still be found in Spain. More recently, Martínez and Rotker made an exhaustive but unsuccessful archival search for any trace of the work ("Prólogo," xxviii).

108. Rojas, *Leyendas históricas,* 235–36. *El carnero* is the colloquial title of Freyle's *Conquista y descubrimiento del nuevo reino de Granada* (*The Conquest of New Granada*).

109. Both Rojas and Morón cite a handwritten note found in the margins of a copy of the 1723 edition of *Historia* stating that the second volume was never published out of consideration for certain families who had taken offense at the actions of Bishop Don Fray Mauro de Tovar (Morón, *Los cronistas,* 125; Rojas, *Leyendas históricas,* 232). See also Martínez and Rotker, "Prólogo," xxix.

110. Note that the issue of the *Revista Iberoamericana* (166–67, 1994) devoted to Venezuelan literature included nothing on colonial Venezuela.

111. Who first spotted land is itself a contested issue. See Phillips and Phillips, *Worlds of Christopher Columbus,* 152–54; and Stolley, "Death by Attrition."

112. For example, book 4 (which narrates Aguirre's rebellion and which I have argued may be seen as the center of Oviedo y Baños's *Historia*) is framed at the beginning and end by discussions of administrative succession.

113. Burkholder and Johnson discuss the mixed results of eighteenth-century administrative

reforms, noting that political and economic pressures were reflected in the increased frequency of sales of *audiencia* appointments and a reduction in the number of criollo appointees (*Colonial Latin America,* 281–83). Chiaramonte notes that the second half of the eighteenth century saw increasing efforts to limit the direct or indirect power of prominent criollo families in local government ("Modificaciones del pacto imperial," 96–97). See also Lynch, *Bourbon Spain,* 336–41.

114. For a discussion of eighteenth-century Venezuela, see Salcedo-Bastardo, "Prólogo."

115. Pagden has observed that "the criollo of the eighteenth century, though still grounding his claims to possess both independent political rights and an identity separate from the peninsular Spaniards in his associations with the origins of the colony, was now, in keeping with a general eighteenth-century distrust of heroism, appealing to a genealogy based upon a history of service and development rather than one of arms and bloodshed" ("Identity Formation," 61–62).

CHAPTER 2

Earlier versions of this chapter were presented in lectures at the Virginia-Carolina-Georgia Conference on Colonial Latin American History (Atlanta, GA, March 1998); the American Society for Eighteenth-Century Studies Annual Meeting (Notre Dame, IN, April 1998), the Modern Language Association Annual Meeting (San Francisco, CA, December 1998), at the symposium "Beyond Colonial Studies: An Inter-American Encounter" (Providence, RI, November 2004), and at the University of Wisconsin (Madison, October 2009).

1. Picunches (Cunchos), Araucanians, and Uilliches (Huillichies) were all linguistic subgroups of a larger group called the Mapuche, from *mapu* (land) and *che* (people), who subsisted through a combination of agriculture, hunting, and gathering in the west-central area of what is now Chile (see Villalobos, *Vida fronteriza,* 27–28; and Bengoa, *Historia del pueblo mapuche,* 20–21). José de Acosta classifies Araucanians as "bárbaros de segunda clase" (barbarians of the second class, or category) but erroneously concludes that the Araucanians had formed part of a larger Inca empire (Antei, *La invención,* 29); Peter Bakewell notes that "the Inca, indeed, called the Picunche 'wild wolves' on account of their unwillingness to serve the state and the crudeness of their agriculture" (*History,* 38). By the eighteenth century, their reputation extended beyond the Hispanic world; in his *History of the Discovery and Settlement of America* (1777), William Robertson writes of the territory that now constitutes Chile: "The Incas had established their dominion in some of its northern districts; but in the greater part of the country, its gallant and high spirited inhabitants maintained their independence" (342).

2. Padden, "Cultural Adaptation," 70; and Bengoa, *Historia del pueblo mapuche,* 34. Valdivia was later ambushed, killed, and reportedly eaten by the Indians of Tucapel in a trap prepared by the legendary Lautaro (Padden, "Cultural Adaptation," 76; and Bengoa, *Historia del pueblo,* 34).

3. In 1882 the Araucanians were "pacified" into the Chilean republic. (S. Lewis, "Myth," 1). Mapuche (as the Araucanians later called themselves) resistance movements in Chile continued throughout the late nineteenth and twentieth centuries and are in evidence even today. For a discussion of present-day Mapuches, see Bengoa, *Historia de un conflicto.*

4. TePaske, "Integral," 37.

5. This boundary was established in 1641 by the Treaty of Quillín. Rivers often function as natural and political boundaries; see Chapter 3 of this text on Félix de Azara's mapping of the boundary between Spanish and Portuguese territory in the Río de la Plata region.

6. All quotes are from the 1795 Spanish edition; translations are mine.

7. Molina uses the term "Araucanian" to refer both to the specific indigenous group and, in a significant slippage I will discuss later, to a more general Chilean indigeneity. In this chapter I have adopted Molina's usage of "Araucanian," even as I acknowledge its contested nature from the nineteenth century to the present in Chile; see Boccara, *Los vencedores,* 15, and Boccara, "Etnogénesis," 427.

8. Michel-Rolph Trouillot has observed, "Just as utopia itself can be offered as a promise or as a dangerous illusion, the savage can be noble, wise, barbarian, victim, or aggressor, depending on the debate and the aims of the interlocutor" ("Anthropology," 33).

9. For further reflections on writing Indian-white history, see Calvin Martin's *The American Indian and the Problem of History.*

10. Vanita Seth explores this issue in *Europe's Indians: Producing Racial Difference, 1500–1900.* Because she focuses on Europeans who write about America and India, however, Seth overlooks the role that criollos writing from Spanish territories in the New World played in the production of knowledge about racial difference and the role that Amerindians in the Spanish viceroyalties played—at least occasionally—as "authors of their history" and "architects of their temporal condition" (113).

11. D. Weber, *Bárbaros,* 6.

12. Ronan, *Juan Ignacio Molina,* 60n13.

13. D. Weber, *Bárbaros,* 54.

14. Domestication, as I have explored earlier, involves taming and making familiar or utilitarian that which has previously been regarded as strange, alien, or savage.

15. José Bengoa recognizes Molina's importance as a predecessor of nineteenth-century criollo independence movements in Chile, which aspired to found a new nation that was neither Indian nor Spanish (*Conquista y barbarie,* 122).

16. Charles Ronan, who has contributed significantly to our understanding of the Spanish American Jesuits with his scholarship on Clavigero, Molina, and others, offers an exhaustive bio-bibliographical summary in *Juan Ignacio Molina: The World's Window on Chile.*

17. Don Augustín de Molina Vasconcelos y Navejas responded enthusiastically to Philip V's request for specimens from the Americas for the natural history museum being built in Madrid by sending a number of Chilean plants, minerals, and animals (Ronan, *Juan Ignacio Molina,* 6).

18. Ibid., 22–30. Ronan draws heavily from the Chilean scholar Walter Hanisch Espíndola for his discussion of these events. Hanisch has written extensively on the exiled Chilean Jesuits, Molina in particular. In recognition of a long career devoted to memorializing Molina as a Chilean humanist, historian, naturalist, bibliographer, and constitutionalist, Hanisch was invited in 1991 by the Chilean government to christen the *Abate Molina,* a 430-ton ship commissioned for oceanographic research by the Chilean navy and named in honor of the eighteenth-century historian and naturalist (ibid., 142).

19. Ibid., 24.

20. Molina benefited from the Spanish Crown's decision to double the pension of Jesuit writers who produced accounts favorable to Spain (Hanisch, "Juan Ignacio Molina," 240).

21. Molina reconciles his geographical allegiances by equating Chile and Italy in the preface to the *Compendio de la historia civil* (iv). At the time of his death, Molina had several portraits hanging on the walls of his apartments, among them one of Ignatius de Loyola and another of Benjamin Franklin—a minor detail, but one that speaks to the cosmopolitan character of the Hispanic Enlightenment (Ronan, *Juan Ignacio Molina,* 236).

22. There is a vast bibliography on Jesuits in Spain and the Americas: see Mörner, *Expulsion*

of the Jesuits; Gagliano and Ronan, *Jesuit Encounters;* Batllori, *La cultura hispano-italiana;* Egido, Burrieza Sánchez, and Revuelta González, *Los jesuitas en España;* Santos, *Los jesuitas en América;* Tietz, *Los jesuitas españoles expulsos;* Negro and Marzal, *Un reino;* and Bernier, Donato, and Lüsebrink, *Jesuit Accounts.* For a discussion of Jesuit contributions to scientific knowledge, see Millones Figueroa and Ledezma, *El saber.*

23. The publication history of Molina's various works is complicated, as is often the case with the writings (in Spanish, Italian, and Latin) of the exiled Jesuits. For a complete bibliography, see Ronan, *Juan Ignacio Molina,* 270–71. Molina's writings on natural history, which have received the bulk of critical attention to date, will not be the focus of my reading.

24. Ronan, *Juan Ignacio Molina,* 36.

25. For example, the 1788 *Compendio de la historia geográfica, natural y civil del reyno de Chile* opens with a brief preface by the author in which he proclaims the great interest that American flora, fauna, and civilization have awakened in European readers (iii). Molina's willingness to cite European travelers is somewhat unusual; perhaps he was willing to do so because "Chile had traditionally fared well in most European travel accounts . . . a land whose climate most learned travelers found benign, and whose original Araucanian inhabitants were portrayed as courageous republican warriors" (Cañizares-Esguerra, *How to Write,* 253; see also Arias, "Geografía, imperio," 342–43).

26. For a discussion of the spirited debates between Molina and Salvador Gilij that took place between 1780 and 1784, see Gerbi, *Dispute,* 227–29.

27. Raimundo Lazo considers Olivares, Molina, and their Jesuit contemporaries as members of a transitional generation, between colony and revolution, although in his view, Molina's works, written in Italian, should be studied not as part of Chilean literary history but rather the history of ideas in Europe (Lazo, *Historia de la literatura hispanoamericana,* 322–23; see also Hanisch, *Juan Ignacio Molina: Sabio de su tiempo*).

28. In a marketing strategy common to eighteenth-century publishers, both volumes of the *Saggio* were announced for sale to early subscribers for a bargain price, even though the second volume had not yet been completed at the time the first volume appeared. Fellow Jesuit historian Francisco Javier Clavigero, also exiled and living in Bologna, was among the original purchasers (Ronan, *Juan Ignacio Molina,* 58).

29. Despite his reliance on the Linnaean scheme, Molina acknowledges the limitations of using superficial similarities for purposes of categorization and vehemently rejects Cornelius de Pauw's view of the Amerindian as degenerate.

30. See Acosta, *Natural and Moral History of the Indies,* translated by Frances López Morillas, edited by Jane E. Mangan, with an introduction and commentary by Walter D. Mignolo; see also Pagden, *Fall of Natural Man.*

31. Pagden argues that Acosta "did believe—and the *Historia* was written to demonstrate the truth of his case—that the history of the 'real' but remote Indian world could illuminate the historical process itself and that by studying such a seemingly alien society his European readers might come to understand something about the natural behaviour of all human communities including their own" (*Fall of Natural Man,* 150).

32. In tracing this move, I'm less interested in the degree to which Molina's account of the Araucanians is historically accurate (in other words, in Molina's rigor as historian and ethnographer) than in how he structures his narrative in accordance with the preoccupations of his age.

33. Gerbi argues that exiled Jesuits played a key role in debates about geographical determinism that had been sparked much earlier in Europe by Buffon. In Spain the decision in 1777 by the Academy of History to translate Robertson's *History of America* served to

further galvanize these debates. However, after a damning review of Robertson's history published by an anonymous reviewer, the translation project was abandoned (Cañizares-Esguerra, *How to Write,* 170–82); see also Ronan, *Juan Ignacio Molina,* 143–63.

34. In evaluating Molina's contribution to the dispute, Gerbi focuses on Molina's natural history rather than the later civil history and acknowledges that "one notes a new feeling of attachment to country, some sort of embryonic and minuscule physical patriotism that finds more immediate and spontaneous expression in the exile" (*Dispute,* 217).

35. At one point Molina protests that "Paw [sic] has written about the Americas and their inhabitants with the same liberty with which he might have written about the moon" (*Compendio de la historia geográfica,* xvi–xvii).

36. Gerbi, *Dispute,* 212–16.

37. Ronan, *Juan Ignacio Molina,* 150.

38. Pagden, *Spanish Imperialism,* 91. Molina's arguments echo those made by fellow Jesuits Francisco Javier Clavigero and Juan de Velasco, who wrote about Mexico and Quito, respectively, in a concerted effort to contest de Pauw and other enlightened critiques of the New World; see Navia Méndez-Bonito, "Las historias naturales."

39. Pagden, *Spanish Imperialism,* 98–101.

40. Ferguson's *An Essay on the History of Civil Society* (1767) includes a chapter titled "The History of Rude Nations." The author, one of the most important representatives of the Scottish Enlightenment, embraces the classical and republican figure of the citizen-soldier and defends "military valour as a cornerstone of civic virtue" (Oz-Salzberger, "Introduction," x; see also Cañizares-Esguerra, *How to Write,* 51). Molina was very interested in contemporary philosophical debates and was familiar with Robertson's work, but his biographer notes that with regard to Ferguson and Smith, "strange as it may seem, nowhere does he mention either of these authorities in his writings" (Ronan, *Juan Ignacio Molina,* 214).

41. In describing the state of the inhabitants of Chile prior to the arrival of the Spaniards, Molina argues that they had already reached the third agricultural stage. Molina wrote an unpublished essay, "On the gradual propagation of the human race in the different parts of the world" (Ronan, *Juan Ignacio Molina,* 196), which Hanisch argues is based on his reading of Adam Smith ("Juan Ignacio Molina," 234).

42. Here, Molina is echoing Acosta's classification of the different types of barbarians (Pagden, *Fall of Natural Man,* 162–64), although the Araucanians, who enjoy stable republics and a system of laws but lack writing, resist Acosta's typology.

43. Withers, *Placing the Enlightenment,* 137. See Withers for a discussion of the relationship between geographical knowledge and enlightened thinking about human development (138).

44. This is similar to Oviedo y Baños's view of the need to perfect the conquest by moving beyond it to settlement, discussed in the previous chapter.

45. Molina concludes the *Compendio de la historia geográfica* with a "Brief Dictionary of Chilean words relative to the objects described in this work," anticipating the role that language will play in his representation of the Araucanians in the *Compendio de la historia civil* (xix). Language is one of the topics he debates with his fellow Jesuit Gilij.

46. Outram, *Enlightenment,* 63.

47. Dorinda Outram revises her original discussion of Enlightenment thinking about cosmopolitanism and difference for the second edition of *The Enlightenment* (2005; first published in 1995).

48. Herder, "Yet Another Philosophy of History" (qtd. in Outram, *Enlightenment,* 59).

49. This is Gayatri Chakavorty Spivak's argument in "Can the Subaltern Speak?"

50. See Outram, *Enlightenment,* 47–59; see also Baker and Reill, *What's Left of Enlightenment?*

51. Eze, *Race and the Enlightenment,* 35. "Division of races closely followed the geographical division of the earth into four continents. . . . The Enlightenment imagination had become dominated by the picture of great continental land masses, each, apparently, with its own color of humans" (Hudson, "From 'Nation' to 'Race,'" 255). Kant quotes Molina on the existence of blue-eyed, blond Indians—a curious detail that troubles this picture (Hanisch, "Juan Ignacio Molina," 290).

52. Rojas Mix, "La idea," 95.

53. See Pagden's chapter "From Noble Savages to Savage Nobles: The *Criollo* Uses of the Amerindian Past" in *Spanish Imperialism,* 91–116; and Phelan, "Neo-Aztecism" (760–70).

54. See Steve Lewis's "Myth and the History of Chile's Araucanians" for an overview of this narrative; see also Villalobos, *Vida fronteriza,* 63–67.

55. The bibliography on *La Araucana* is extensive. See Davis, who argues for a "divided subjectivity" in the epic (*Myth and Identity*); Fuchs on Othering and empire in *Mimesis and Empire;* Padrón on geography in *The Spacious Word;* and Melczer on the "divided heroic vision" in "Ercilla's Divided Heroic Vision" (216–21). Various critics have remarked on the ways in which *La Araucana* calls into question Philip II's imperial project while at the same time celebrating it: Barbara Fuchs speaks of "imperial fractures" (*Mimesis and Empire,* 36–49), while Ricardo Padrón points to "a critical counter-cartography of imperial design" (*Spacious Word,* 186).

56. Despite the author's attempts to create the impression that his verses were penned in the heat of battle, *La Araucana* was probably written during a three-month period Ercilla spent in prison after a minor altercation. The first part (fifteen cantos) was published in 1569, the second part (also fifteen cantos) in 1578, and the final section (a mere seven cantos) in 1589.

57. Robert Charles Padden notes, "Historians and anthropologists seem to be under a strange compulsion to use this poem as a prime documentary source" ("Cultural Adaptation," 86n30). Molina also invokes "the celebrated Ercilla" in more general terms (*Compendio de la historia civil,* 75); see also Ronan, *Juan Ignacio Molina,* 46, 61.

58. Ronan, *Juan Ignacio Molina,* 61. The 1808 English translation of Molina's history included an appendix with extensive fragments of Ercilla's poem, also translated into English.

59. For a discussion of the concept of nobility in service in Ercilla's epic, see Elizabeth B. Davis's *Myth and Identity in the Epic of Imperial Spain.* Davis argues that since Ercilla's Araucanians are portrayed as having warriors and caciques but no king, and as eloquent but torn by internal strife, they can claim no complex form of government that would justify their occupying a more advanced place in a scheme of stadial history (41). See also Padrón, *Spacious Word,* 215–18; Pastor, *Armature of Conquest,* 257–62; and Fuchs, *Mimesis and Empire,* 35–63.

60. Gordon M. Sayre explores the representation of indigenous resistance in *The Indian Chief as Tragic Hero.*

61. Unlike the "cannibals" and "savages" of other colonial texts, the Araucanians not only hold onto their name but—thanks in part to Ercilla's eponymous epic—they become synonymous with the history of colonial Chile. This explains later attempts in the eighteenth and nineteenth centuries to appropriate their story as a foundational fiction, as well as recent efforts to reclaim the name "Mapuche" and undo the earlier heroicizing (and domesticating) move.

62. "Contra el método común de los Geógrafos" comes from the 1788 Spanish translation of Molina's *Compendio de la historia geográfica.* The author explains in the preface his

decision to include in the present edition the same map that had been incorporated into the 1782 publication in Italian. For a discussion of the viceregal peripheral regions, see D. Weber, *Spanish Frontier.*

63. Santa Arias explores the construction of a criollo cartographic imaginary by Molina and other eighteenth-century Jesuits. She discusses the same textual fragments I refer to in my own reading of Molina's cartographic practices, with a particular focus on the manipulation and ornamentation of the maps included in different editions ("Geografía, imperio," 338–40). See also Ronan, *Juan Ignacio Molina,* 50n91 and 61–62n18; and Hanisch, "Juan Ignacio Molina," 63–66.

64. Matthew Edney has argued that in the eighteenth century geographical knowledge was "deeply concerned with the legitimation, reproduction, and the perpetuation of a given social order" ("Reconsidering Enlightenment Geography," 166). See also Gregory, *Geographical Imaginations;* Gagliano and Ronan, *Jesuit Encounters;* Livingstone and Withers, *Geography and Enlightenment;* Withers, *Placing the Enlightenment;* Harley, *New Nature of Maps;* and Arias and Meléndez, *Mapping Colonial Spanish America. Geography and Enlightenment* includes two essays on Humboldt but none on Hispanic thinkers and scientists. If "the situated nature of scientific knowledge" is central to enlightenment thinking about geography (Livingstone and Withers, *Geography and Enlightenment,* vii), then how to account for their absence in these pages?

65. Harley, *New Nature of Maps,* 57. Harley discusses the relationship between maps, knowledge and power, with particular emphasis on the various ways in which what he calls "hidden structures"—map geometry, silences or omissions, and the cartographic representation of hierarchical tendencies—influence how maps are produced and read (52–81). I will return to these questions in the following chapter on Félix de Azara.

66. I am mindful of Edney's contention that although the Enlightenment brought a shift away from narrative accounts and memoirs as validations of scientific data, it would be a mistake to conclude that science completely replaces other discourses ("Reconsidering Enlightenment Geography," 193).

67. Molina repeats a similar assertion at the beginning of the *Compendio civil* regarding Inca attempts to conquer the various tribes that lived to the south: "Thus, Chile has remained since then divided into two parts, one free and the other subject to foreign domination" (11). His collapsing of pre-Hispanic and Spanish colonial history here is striking.

68. Arias provides a useful summary of Molina's manipulation of maps ("Geografía, imperio"). The Madrid editions of 1788 and 1798 included three maps: the map originally published in the anonymous *Compendio della storia,* a second titled "Map of one part of Chile," and a third map titled "General map of the border of Arauco in the Kingdom of Chile." Nicolás de la Cruz y Bahamonde, translator and editor of the Spanish edition, added fifteen drawings of plazas and forts, as well as three charts illustrating the sizes of militias, troops, and missions (Molina, *Compendio de la historia civil,* 343–44). See also Ronan, *Juan Ignacio Molina,* 50n91 and 61–62n18; and Hanisch, "Juan Ignacio Molina," 63–66.

69. Arias, "Geografía, imperio," 341. Arias notes the editorial changes in the maps included in subsequent editions (343–44).

70. Arias, "Geografía, imperio," 344.

71. At one point Molina complains that he has been unable to include a general map of Chile because the friend who had promised to send it to him has died. Instead, he has opted to include a revised version of a map of Araucanian territory that had been included in a recent edition of Ercilla's *La Araucana* (Hanisch, "Juan Ignacio Molina: Sabio," 239).

72. This move anticipates in curious and obviously unintended ways the "Upside-Down

Map of Latin America" that became popular in the 1970s, adorning the office doors of many professors of Latin American history and literature—a visual reconceptualization that challenged hierarchical relationships long taken for granted.

73. Pratt, *Imperial Eyes,* 132.

74. Craib, "Cartography and Power," 10.

75. Ibid.

76. In her discussion of indigenous cartography in the *relaciones geográficas* (official responses to a sixteenth-century royal questionnaire whose aim was to elicit a general description of Spain's territories in the Indies), Barbara Mundy studies how "the dazzling story of possession is trailed by the dark shadow of dispossession" (*Mapping,* xx).

77. See J. G. Johnson's "Ercilla's Construction and Destruction."

78. Wertheimer, *Imagined Empires,* 9.

79. This is known as *correr la flecha,* or "running the arrow" (Molina, *Compendio de la historia civil,* 69).

80. D. Weber, *Bárbaros,* 78. Weber notes that "as Spaniards had deepened their knowledge of independent Indians over the course of two-and-a-half centuries, so too had independent Indians become more sophisticated in their understanding of Spaniards" (53).

81. Weber sees militarized horse culture as a key factor in indigenous acculturation (ibid., 81).

82. Francisco Núñez de Pineda y Bascuñán's *Cautiverio feliz* (1673) is an extensive and generally sympathetic account of the author's brief captivity among the Araucanians.

83. As we have seen, Oviedo y Baños also relates Spain's Gothic history to barbarism.

84. Sergio Villalobos discusses the importance of trade between Araucanians and Spaniards during the early phases of the conquest, particular with regard to iron tools and weapons, alcohol, and horses (*Vida fronteriza,* 117–24).

85. See Alvarez de Miranda, *Palabras e ideas,* 211–69.

86. Hudson, "From 'Nation' to 'Race,'" 257. For a discussion of how earlier definitions of "nation" were reformulated in the early nineteenth century, see Chiaramonte, *El mito,* 19–24.

87. Qtd. in Verdesio, *Forgotten Conquests,* 58.

88. Ivonne del Valle discusses the implications of translation for missionary practices in border regions of eighteenth-century New Spain in *Escribiendo desde los márgenes.*

89. For a discussion of Enlightenment views on rhetoric, see Bizzell and Herzberg, *Rhetorical Tradition,* 637–69.

90. Other Jesuit writers at the time argued that acculturated Amerindians were better lawyers than Spaniards because they were masters of Latin and rhetoric. Antonio de Ulloa in the *Noticias americanas* suggested that Spanish viceregal administrations should focus on teaching Spanish to Amerindians, as language was a key step in making them useful and productive vassals. In Molina's view, the Araucanians' predisposition to language and oratory, well documented in book 2, gives them a significant advantage in this process.

91. In *Declaring Independence: Jefferson, Natural Language and the Culture of Performance,* Jay Fliegelman explains that as part of what was called "the elocutionary revolution," eighteenth-century theorists sought to identify and understand a "natural common language that would be a corollary to natural law, a language that would permit universal recognition and understanding" through the performative display of feelings and thoughts (2).

92. Sandra M. Gustafson has studied these issues at length in *Eloquence Is Power* and *Imagining Deliberative Democracy.*

93. The "Quechua Renaissance" of the eighteenth century, a process in which Quechua became homogenized (although not necessarily hegemonic), is part of the background for Molina's views on indigenous language, although it will not be my focus in this chapter. See Mannheim, *Language of the Inka.*

94. Ronan, *Juan Ignacio Molina,* 74–75.

95. Cañizares-Esguerra discusses these issues in a chapter on "Changing European Interpretations of the Reliability of Indigenous Sources" (*How to Write,* 60–129).

96. "The question of language is central to all eighteenth-century discussions of the development of society. Robertson shares with [Adam] Smith and [Jean-Jacques] Rousseau the essentially Lockean idea that social institutions could not develop without the advent of abstract vocabulary to convey general ideals, and that abstract vocabulary, since all words are only symbols of ideas, can only develop as a consequence of a more complex social experience" (O'Brien, *Narratives of Enlightenment,* 159).

97. Molina had earlier included a "Breve Diccionario de vocablos Chileños relativos á los objetos descriptos en esta obra" in the *Compendio de la historia geografica* (xix).

98. Historians who have studied seventeenth- and eighteenth-century *parlamentos* include Guillaume Boccara, Rolf Foerster, Leonardo León, Luz María Méndez y Beltrán, and Sergio R. Villalobos.

99. Dialogue was very important in the teaching of European languages; French, Spanish, Italian, and English grammar books often dealt with grammar first and then included representative dialogues to illustrate grammatical structures. Andres Febrés, one of Molina's Jesuit colleagues, included a bilingual dialogue in *Gramática araucana o sea arte de la lengua general de los indios de Chile* (1765), presenting the Araucanian and Spanish on opposite pages (Foerster, *Jesuitas y Mapuches,* 17). Other examples are José Joaquín Granados y Gálvez's *Tardes americanas* (Mexico, 1778), written as a series of dialogues between Spaniard and Indian (Tudisco, "America in Some Travelers," 11), and *Dialogues avec un sauvage* (1703), written by Louis-Armand de Lom d'Arce, Baron de Lahontan (Garraway, "Of Speaking Natives," 211–20). .

100. Patricia Seed explores national differences in encounters between Europeans and Amerindians in *Ceremonies of Possession.* See also David Weber on gifting and treaty making (*Bárbaros,* 178–220).

101. David Weber discusses this shift at length, concluding that "a bad peace was less costly and more effective than either offensive or defensive war" (*Bárbaros,* 176).

102. Describing the battles that follow, Molina draws on Ercilla's account of Caupolicán, Tucapel, and Galbarino in *La Araucana.* He notes a curious convergence of New World and Old World history, remarking that this battle occurs the same day that the Spanish defeated the French in San Quintín (*Compendio de la historia civil,* 173).

103. Molina provides further details of Dutch efforts to challenge the Spanish presence in Chile (*Compendio de la historia civil,* 288–89).

104. Araucanians thought strategically about their alliances with these mestizos, who, Molina complained, "were the most terrible enemigos of the name Spaniard" (ibid., 258). His complaint, not uncommon at the time, reflects the degree to which the growing numbers of mestizos in eighteenth-century Spanish America unsettled ethnic and racial categories and complicated assumptions about political hierarchies. For further discussion of mestizos in Araucanian territory, see D. Weber, *Bárbaros,* 246–47; Hill, "Towards"; Hill, "Categories"; and Hill, "Entering and Exiting Blackness." See also Fisher and O'Hara, *Imperial Subjects.*

105. D. Weber, *Bárbaros,* 161. This was even more difficult when the Indians had foreign allies: "Bourbon officer-administrators, who believed they needed to pacify Indians in

order to develop frontier regions, recognized that they needed the loyalty of those Indians to defend the empire against foreigners" (ibid., 142).

106. The editorial decision to capitalize "Congress" may indicate a certain degree of institutional status afforded to the Araucanian recipients of the king's missive, who may or may not have considered themselves to be a fully constituted political body.

107. This "unforeseen accident," as Molina characterizes it, raises a number of interesting questions about captives and sovereignty hinging on whether the women and children have been baptized or not, as those who had already been Christianized were judged to be deserving of protection by the governor and could not be returned (*Compendio de la historia civil*, 265–66). For a discussion of captivity narratives, see D. Weber, *Bárbaros*, 224–28; Adorno (on Gonzalo Guerrero and Cabeza de Vaca), *Polemics of Possession*, 220–78; and Voigt, *Writing Captivity*.

108. The reader of Molina's *Compendio de la historia civil* might wonder whether there is an implicit comparison between the historian's account of the modulated deliberations of the Araucanians and the tumultuous events that had convulsed Spanish territories in Peru during the second half of the sixteenth century.

109. *Reducciones* are the settlement towns created by the large-scale relocation of the indigenous population, either by secular authorities or missionaries. Foerster references the nineteenth-century Chilean historian Diego Barros Arana's discussion in *Historia jeneral de Chile* (General history of Chile; 1884) of the role that Jesuit missionaries played in advocating for the treaty (*Jesuitas y Mapuches*, 182–87).

110. Claudia Zapata Silva quotes the Mapuche intellectual R. Marhiquewun/Marhikewun's assessment of the symbolic importance of this treaty, while noting that his version of a heroic, idealized past in some ways converges with recent military versions of national history ("Identidad, nación y territorio," 493).

111. Spaniards often convinced themselves "that a single individual spoke for an entire people" (D. Weber, *Bárbaros*, 210), while Amerindians often expected treaties to be repeated with a whole series of individuals, leading to considerable ambiguity about which version of a given treaty prevailed. For a discussion of how European ideas regarding sovereignty and claims to dominion affected Spanish treaty negotiations with Amerindians, see D. Weber, *Bárbaros*, 207–11. Weber notes that geographically defined borders such as the one marked by the BíoBío River often complicated treaty negotiations, which varied in practice depending on local conditions.

112. "The numbers of Spaniards involved in the Indian trade probably grew in the late XVIII as the Bourbons brought new economic vitality to previously neglected areas and made trade their preferred mode of Indian control" (ibid., 230).

113. Molina later notes that the Araucanians honored these provisions of the Treaty of Quillín, despite Dutch efforts to enlist their aid (*Compendio de la historia civil*, 289).

114. Araucanians worried that the treaty facilitated the construction of new Spanish forts and settlements along the frontier. Moreover, they resented the abusive authority of the "capitanes de amigos" (Indian agents) who served as missionary escorts (Molina, *Compendio de la historia civil*, 293; see also D. Weber, *Bárbaros*, 231).

115. The eighteenth century sees the arrival of a growing number of Europeans—French merchants, who from 1707 to 1717 dominate trade, as well as enlightened scientists who journey to the region to make botanical and astronomical observations. Molina makes specific mention of both groups in his *Compendio de la historia civil* (292).

116. See D. Weber, *Bárbaros*, 280 n22, for an interesting discussion of the frontier, which he defines as a "meeting place of peoples in which geographical and cultural borders aren't clearly defined." Weber also explores this concept in *The Spanish Frontier in North America*.

117. A similar conscription order for constructing fortress walls in the city of Havana led the royal slaves of El Cobre in eighteenth-century Cuba to revolt; see Díaz, *Virgin,* and "Conjuring Identitites." For a discussion of mid-eighteenth-century Chile, including the disastrous attempt by the Jesuits in 1752 to bring Araucanians into their *reducciones,* see Foerster, *Jesuitas y Mapuches,* 317–25.

118. Missionaries, "who had no defect other than that of being Spaniards," were not to be harmed (Molina, *Compendio de la historia civil,* 297).

119. Following the 1766 revolt, Viceroy Amat rejected plans to expand the missions and continue an offensive war in Chile, as he believed both were doomed to failure (D. Weber, *Bárbaros,* 153).

120. David Weber enumerates the competing demands on Spanish military resources during the late eighteenth century: war with England from 1779 to 1783, followed by continued tensions and a blockade from 1796 to 1808; war with France from 1792 to 1795; the Tupac Amaru rebellion in Peru from 1780 to 1781; and the popular uprising known as the *comunero* revolt that occurred in New Granada from 1780 to 1782 (*Bárbaros,* 161).

121. Note the governor's pragmatic emphasis on utility here. The Chilean historian Sergio Villalobos uses a periodization of the Araucanian wars to argue that by the eighteenth century, conflict was no longer the defining factor in Araucanian-Spanish relations, as commerce, *parlamentos,* and a growing number of "capitanes de amigos" served as vehicles for communication and cross-cultural contact ("Guerra y paz," 10–11, 19).

122. Villalobos notes that even when eighteenth-century *parlamentos* did not lead to peace, they enabled a wide-ranging discussion between Indians and criollos ("Guerra y paz," 18–19). In "Parlamentos y afuerinos," Leonardo León discusses how Spanish and Mapuche leaders came together for *parlamentos* in the late eighteenth century to address tensions along the BíoBío River frontier region caused by growing numbers of mestizo outlaws, or *afuerinos* (outsiders).

123. The editor/translator of the Spanish edition added copious notes to this section that offer suggestions for commercial development.

124. For example, when he speaks of "Chilean language," Molina means a transliterated Araucanian language whose lexicon and syntax he compares to Greek, Italian, and Castilian.

125. Colonial historians focus on the Hapsburg imperial phase of the conquest and settlement of Spanish America. Moreover, David Weber argues that, with the exception of the 1767 Jesuit expulsions and the Tupac Amaru Andean revolts in 1780–1781, "most historians of Spanish-Indian relations have overlooked the impact on Indians of Bourbon Spain's enlightened reforms" (*Bárbaros,* 11).

126. De Certeau's concept of the *événement* (literally, "event"), involving the difference between historical writing and performed discourse, is helpful here (*Writing of History,* xvi). De Certeau is concerned not just with what happens but also how it is passed down or transmitted. *Parlamentos* are the trace not of a forgotten or idealized past but rather of an ongoing present. They make history as much as they narrate it. In discussing *parlamentos* Molina speaks from the (absent) third person of the historian, but he brings to life "the simulation of living speech conveyed by discourse" (Certeau, *Writing of History,* xx).

127. See David Weber on power as horizontal negotiation (*Bárbaros,* 281–82 n35). See also Dillehay on Araucanian history "as a blueprint for encoding and acting on changing geopolitical and interethnic relations along a Spanish frontier" (*Monuments, Empires, and Resistance,* 9).

128. David Weber defines frontiers as "zones of interaction between two different cultures—as places where the cultures of the invader and of the invaded contend with one another and with their physical environment to produce a dynamic that is unique to time and

place. . . . Frontiers represent both place and process" (*Spanish Frontier,* 11). As Rolena Adorno explains in *The Polemics of Possession,* she first used the term "zona de contacto" in 1987 "to evoke the notion of a colonial society in which the simple line between Spaniard and Andean that defined native experience at the moment of conquest no longer existed with such clarity" (23). Mary Louise Pratt further develops the notion of "contact zone" in *Imperial Eyes* as "the relations among colonizers and colonized, or travelers and 'travelers,' not in terms of separateness, but in terms of co-presence, interaction, interlocking understandings and practices, and often within radically asymmetrical relations of power" (8).

129. Eric Wertheimer observes, "While some 'pasts' are elevated to national prestige, others are marginalized or 'fused' out of the national imaginary. The past *is* 'usable' insofar as it can be forgotten, denied, changed, found somewhere else" (*Imagined Empires,* 7). For a discussion of "usable pasts," see Haberly, "Form and Function"; Antei, *La invención;* and Woll, *Functional Past.*

130. For example, Clavigero's account of ancient Mexico ends with the fall of Tenochtitlán in 1521, and his passion for Mexican antiquity did not extend to an interest in the reality of eighteenth-century indigenous life.

131. Outram, *Enlightenment,* 78.

132. This is a problem, as I have discussed elsewhere, for exiled Jesuits who were prohibited by the 1767 expulsion edict from writing about their own exile (Stolley, "East from Eden").

133. They might be considered an example of Srinivas Aravamudan's "tropicopolitan," "the colonized subject who exists both as a fictive construct of colonial tropology *and* actual resident of tropical space, object of representation *and* agent of resistance" (*Tropicopolitans,* 4).

134. Ronan, *Juan Ignacio Molina,* 208.

135. "With the stroke of a pen, Araucanians became Chileans, their status as a separate people erased along with their historic boundary at the Biobío" (D. Weber, *Bárbaros,* 265).

136. Molina's remains were returned to Chile in 1966.

137. A. J. Bauer, *Goods, Power, History,* 156.

138. For a discussion of current-day Mapuche intellectuals, see Zapata Silva, "Identidad, nación y territorio."

CHAPTER 3

These ideas in this chapter were originally set forth in papers delivered at various conferences: "Bureaucrats and Border Disputes: Domesticating Conquest in Eighteenth-Century Spanish America" (invited lecture, University of Virginia, Charlottesville, December 2004); "Border Disputes, Loose Canons, and Criollo Subjects" (Modern Language Association Annual Meeting, Washington, DC, December 2005); "Contestar al imperio/contestar la colonia: El discurso transatlántico/dieciochesco de la emancipación" (Latin American Studies Association Convention, Montreal, Canada, September 2007); "Scientific Americans: Eighteenth-Century Natural History through a Transatlantic Lens" (Symposium: "Re-Defining Transatlantic Hispanic Studies," Louisiana State University, Baton Rouge, April 2008); "Writing Back to Empire: Negotiating Eighteenth-Century Spanish America" (invited lecture, University of Oregon, Eugene, April 2008); "Scientific Americans: Negotiating Nation and Natural History in Eighteenth-Century Expeditions to Spanish America" (Latin American Studies Association Convention, Rio de Janeiro, Brazil, June 2009); and "Bordering on Empire: Félix de Azara's *Memoria sobre el estado rural del Río de la Plata y otros informes*" (Early American Borderlands Conference, St. Augustine, FL, May 2010). I would like to thank the organizers and audience at each of these events for their valuable feedback and suggestions.

1. The viceroyalty of the Río de la Plata had been established in 1776 to solidify Spanish control over the commercial potential of the Southern Cone region, particularly with regard to the Portuguese in Brazil and trade routes with Lima (Bakewell, *History,* 286).

2. There are many figures whose writings could have been the focus of this chapter—José Antonio Alzate y Ramírez, José Hipólito Unanúe y Pavón, José Eusebio Llano Zapata, José Gumilla, and Francisco José de Caldas, among others.

3. José Carlos Chiaramonte sounds a note of caution about collapsing together enlightenment culture, localism, and nationalist sentiment (*Pensamiento de la Ilustración,* 18–19). This is not to argue against David Brading's very persuasive case for the importance of Creole patriotism in *The First America* and elsewhere, but rather to emphasize that it is but one facet of an extraordinarily complex political, social, and philosophical environment in eighteenth-century Spanish America.

4. As Ralph Bauer notes, "Of paramount importance in this geo-political conflict over imperial centralization was the question of how knowledge could be centrally produced and controlled in the centrifugal cultural dynamics of outwardly expanding geo-political systems" (*Cultural Geography,* 3).

5. See J. C. González, "Apuntes bio-bibliográficos," vii–cxiv; Galera Gómez, *Descripción general del Paraguay,* 7–35; Asín, *Aragón y América,* 133–47; Beddall, "Isolated Spanish Genius;" Furlong, *Naturalistas argentinos;* and the publications of Enrique Alvarez López listed in the Bibliography. Asín lists Azara's date of birth as 1746.

6. Nicolás de Azara is considered by many to be one of the most important figures of the Spanish Enlightenment; see Asín, *Aragón y América,* 133; Corona Baratech, *José Nicolás de Azara;* and Arregui Martínez, "Un diplomático aragonés," 861–927.

7. Galera Gómez, *Descripción general del Paraguay,* 11.

8. C. A. Walckenaer includes in his notes to the 1809 French edition of the *Voyages dans l'Amérique méridionale* a detailed description of Azara's injury (Azara, *Voyages,* 15). Azara seems to have suffered from celiac disease or a gluten allergy: Julio César González quotes at length from a letter Azara wrote in 1806 explaining the reasons behind his decision to forgo eating bread—a decision made easier by the fact that in the South American territories where he had spent so many years bread was not part of the local diet ("Apuntes bio-bibliográficos," xvi).

9. Antonio Lafuente and Nuria Valverde note the considerable overlap between military and scientific activity in eighteenth-century Spain (*Los mundos,* 14).

10. This border dispute had its origins in fourteenth-century disputes over the Canary Islands that were further complicated in 1494 by the Treaty of Tordesillas and remained unresolved in 1777, despite the intervening passage of a number of treaties, including the Treaty of Utrecht (1713), the Treaty of Permuta (1750), and the Treaty of El Pardo (1777). See J. C. González, "Apuntes bio-bibliográficos," ix–x; and Asín, *Aragón y América,* 136–37.

11. See Asín, *Aragón y América,* 138–39, for a discussion of the commercial possibilities that resulted from the 1778 *Reglamento y aranceles para el comercio libre de España e Indias* (Regulations and tariffs on free trade between Spain and the Indies), aimed at rationalizing contraband by increasing penalties for foreigners and opening possiblities for Spaniards in the export of hides. Azara's arrival in the Río de la Plata region occurred at a moment when both his personal career trajectory and the possibilities of imperial expansion seemed promising (ibid., 140).

12. The border was divided into five sections, with different administrators responsible for surveying each one (Asín, *Aragón y América*, 137–38; and J. C. Gónzalez, "Apuntes bio-bibliográficos," xxi–xxii).

13. Azara adds, "The Portuguese weren't ready, lacking horses, mules, and wagons, and they were anxious and suspicious" (qtd. in J. C. González, "Apuntes bio-bibliográficos," xx).

14. The particulars of the various phases of Azara's commission fall outside the scope of this chapter but are discussed in detail by Julio César González in "Apuntes bio-bibliográficos," xxii–lxxv. See also Rodolfo R. Schuller's prologue to Azara's *Geografía física y esférica* (ix–lxxii).

15. Qtd. in J. C. González, "Apuntes bio-bibliográficos," lxxiii. Fearful of the risks of a transatlantic crossing, particularly in wartime, Azara left all his correspondence, manuscripts, and instruments with Don Pedro Cerviño (González, "Apuntes bio-bibliográficos," lxxv). This may explain why Victor von Hagen reports that Azara's manuscripts were confiscated (*Green World,* 132).

16. Beddall, "Isolated Spanish Genius," 236–38. Barbara Beddall is a biologist whose essays on Azara appeared in the *Journal of the History of Biology,* where one suspects they found limited readership among Hispanists.

17. Rousseau and Porter, *Ferment of Knowledge,* 4.

18. Qtd. in Buesa Olivar, "Sobre Cosme Bueno," 341.

19. This complaint (or boast?) is reminiscent of José Gumilla's claim that he has spent "over thirty years eating American bread" (qtd. in Ewalt, "Crossing Over," 11).

20. While the portrait of the Hispanic scientific genius as an anomalous and isolated figure has particular currency in the Hispanic context, the myth of a general Hispanic hostility or indifference to science has been challenged recently. See Bedall, "Isolated Spanish Genius"; Glick and Quinlan, "Félix de Azara"; Deans-Smith, "Special Section"; Cañizares-Esguerra, *Nature, Empire, and Nation;* and Bleichmar, De Vos, Huffine, and Sheehan, *Science in the Spanish and Portuguese Empires.*

21. The first was a two-volume study published in Madrid in 1802 (it had appeared in French the previous year: *Essais sur l'histoire naturelle des quadrupèdes de la province du Paraguay;* an English translation was published in 1838). Azara's study of birds was published in a three-volume edition in Madrid (1802–1805).

22. "Azara requested that his manuscript not be published until he returned from some additional journeys, but this request, delayed perhaps by the troubled political situation, arrived too late. José Nicolás, by now in Paris, had given the document to the French scholar M. L. E. Moreau de Saint-Mery, who had returned from exile in the United States in November 1799. Moreau translated the work and published it in 1801 under the title *Essais sur l'histoire naturelle des quadrupèdes de la province du Paraguay.* Apparently encountering acrimonious opposition to Azara's criticisms of Buffon, Moreau defended his role in translating the text" (Bedall, "Isolated Spanish Genius," 253). See also Torre Revello, *El momento histórico,* 574.

23. The *Viajes* were a translation into Spanish of a French 1809 edition by C. A. Walckenaer of another copy of the manuscript of *Descripción e historia (Voyages dans l'Amérique méridionale)*; see also Buesa Olivar, "Sobre Cosme Bueno," 344.

24. *Memoria sobre el tratado de límites de la América* (Memorial on the American border treaty) was first published in 1847, in a volume that also contained a number of Azara's letters and memoranda. *Memoria sobre el estado rural de Río de la Plata y otros informes* was published in Argentina in 1943 with an extensive bio-bibliographical introduction by Julio César González; this publication brought together a number of Azara's writings: *Memoria sobre el estado rural del Río de la Plata; Memoria sobre el tratado de límites de*

la América; Correspondencia oficial e inédita (Official and unpublished correspondence); *Informe acerca de un reconocimiento de las guardias y fortines que guarnecen la línea de frontera de Buenos Aires* (Report on a reconnaissance of the sentry posts and forts protecting the border of Buenos Aires); and *Informes sobre varios proyectos de colonización del Chaco* (Report on various colonization projects in the Chaco), among others. In quoting from the 1943 collection, I will refer to it as *Memoria.*

25. Galera Gómez, *Descripción general del Paraguay,* 9; and Glick and Quinlan, "Félix de Azara," 76–77. Despite Azara's relative notoriety among his contemporaries, Victor von Hagen was not stretching the point when he noted in 1948 that "the name of Félix de Azara is perhaps utterly new to all save a few zoologists" (*Green World,* 131). Von Hagen included an excerpt titled "The Wild Horses of the Pampas," taken from the 1837 English edition of *The Natural History of the Quadrupeds of Paraguay and the River La Plata,* in his anthology *The Green World of the Naturalists* (133–44).

26. One might contrast the isolation Azara feels with the nostalgia that permeates the writings of exiled Jesuits like Juan Ignacio Molina, who had to labor far from their objects of study.

27. For an exhaustive discussion, see Gerbi, *Dispute* and *Nature.* Azara received in Buenos Aires a Spanish translation of Buffon's *Historia natural* from his friend Martín Boneolds Pedro Cervigno that served as a guide for his own study and reflection (Galera Gómez, *Descripción general del Paraguay,* 10n2).

28. Alvarez López goes on to argue that Azara's work exercised a profound—albeit forgotten—influence on the work of nineteenth-century European naturalists, including Darwin. I will return to the question of Azara and Darwin at the close of the chapter.

29. Ewalt calls our attention to the appropriation of the Spanish-born Gumilla as "the voice of Venezuelan-ness" by the Venezuelan critic Ciriaco Morón, a gesture that "points to the late eighteenth- and early nineteenth-century appropriations of Gumilla in Colombia and Venezuela as the national took precedence over the Spanish Viceroyalty of New Granada" ("Crossing Over," 26n42).

30. Soto Arango characterizes the vision of criollo scientists as clearly separated from that of their European counterparts, using Bernard Lavallé's discussion of the process of creolization as her point of departure (in Soto Arango, Puig-Samper, and González-Ripoll, *Científicos Criollos,* 9–10). As I argued in the Introduction, I think that it's helpful to rethink the issue of criollo identity in more nuanced ways.

31. José Celestino Mutis's life and work challenged narrow nationalist categories in the same way that Azara's does. Like the Aragonese engineer, Mutis traveled widely and collaborated with scientists from all over Europe and the Americas. He led the botanical expedition that contributed to the founding of Madrid's botanical garden and is remembered as the creator of botanical iconography in the Hispanic World. See Amaya, *Celestino Mutis.* The *Actas del Simposium CCL Aniversario Nacimiento de Joseph Celestino Mutis,* edited by Paz Martín Ferrero, reflects nationalist traditions in both Spain and Colombia and reminds us of the extent to which national rivalries, occasionally transcended in the eighteenth century in the interest of scientific pursuits, still hold sway today.

32. Lowood, "New World," 298. The degree to which the New World initially influenced European natural history is a topic for debate. Henry Lowood concludes that "the European discovery of America was for natural history, as indeed for other scholarly subjects of the sixteenth century, at most a marginal event" ("New World," 317). Antonio Barrera-Osorio argues to the contrary in *Experiencing Nature.*

33. Walter Mignolo notes in his introduction to the English translation of José de Acosta's *Historia natural y moral de las Indias* (1590) that "understanding nature, for Acosta, was

not just a question of describing minerals, plants, and animals but of understanding the order of the universe and the chain of being" (xviii).

34. Qtd. in Findlen, *Possessing Nature,* 4. "In stressing that knowledge was to be found in the world, and not merely in texts, Bacon opened the floodgates: his call for the collection of *new* facts and observations stimulated an expectation of constant revision of current doctrines, making the concept of a stable encyclopaedia more problematic than it had ever been" (Yeo, *Encyclopaedic Visions,* 10); See also Hill, *Sceptres and Sciences,* for an assessment of Bacon's influence in the transition to enlightened science in the Hispanic World (4–6).

35. Feijoo, "Historia natural," in *Teatro crítico universal* (volume 2, discourse 2, section 10, paragraph 72). Travel books "made imperial expansion meaningful and desirable to the citizenries of the imperial countries" and "gave European publics a sense of ownership, entitlement and familiarity with respect to the distant parts of the world that were being explored, invaded, invested in, and colonized" (Pratt, *Imperial Eyes,* 3).

36. David Livingstone reminds us of the close ties between voyaging, natural history, and regional geography and discusses what he calls the "Kantian turn"—a detheologizing of natural history and geography (*Geographical Tradition,* 114–19). See Neil Safier's *Measuring the New World: Enlightenment Science and South America* for a discussion of enlightened knowledge about Spanish America.

37. See Findlen, *Possessing Nature,* 394–99. For a discussion of Gumilla's *Orinoco ilustrado* as wondercabinet, see Ewalt, *Peripheral Wonders.* Susan Scott Parrish's *American Curiosity* is a wide-ranging exploration of natural history in Anglo-America.

38. Linnaeus's *Systema Naturae* (1735) proposed an elegant and practical binomial nomenclature combining species and genus that is used by naturalists to this day. Lisbet Koerner discusses the longstanding enmity between Linnaeus and Buffon, quoting Linnaeus's pronouncement on his rival: "He isn't particularly learned, but as he is rather eloquent, that seems to count for something" ("Purposes of Linnaean Travel," 119; see also her *Linnaeus: Nature and Nation*). For a discussion of how Linnaean classification was deployed in the Hispanic world, see Lafuente and Valverde, "Linnaean Botany," 134–47; Martínez Sanz, *Relaciones científicas,* 157–59; and Pratt, *Imperial Eyes,* 24–26.

39. "The eighteenth-century classificatory systems created the task of locating every species on the planet, extracting it from its particular, arbitrary surroundings (the chaos), and placing it in its appropriate spot in the system (the order-book, collection, or garden) with its new written, secular European name" (Pratt, *Imperial Eyes,* 31).

40. Koerner places Linnaean localism within the broader context of tensions between global modernizers and local modernizers (*Linnaeus,* 191).

41. Antonio Rumeu de Armas contrasts the defeatist attitude prevalent in late seventeenth-century Spain (which prevented it from joining the revolution in scientific thinking exemplified by Descartes, Newton, Galileo, and others) with the eighteenth-century *novatores* (new thinkers) who were determined to bring Spanish science in from the periphery (*Ciencia y tecnologia*). See also Hill, *Sceptres and Sciences;* and Pérez Magallón, *Construyendo la modernidad.*

42. For a discussion of how official information about the New World was solicited and processed by Spanish Bourbon rulers, see Marchena, "Su Majestad quiere saber," 151–85. Marchena cautions that the long-term effects of the many royal requests for information from the Americas were negligible, suggesting that the transatlantic exchange during the Spanish Enlightenment can be summed up by the shipping of a Panamanian tiger and a couple of talking parrots from a New Spain convent to Madrid (185).

43. For discussions of eighteenth-century science in the Hispanic world, see Soto Arango, Puig-Samper, Bender, and González-Ripoll, *Recepción y difusión;* Lafuente and Sala Catalá, *Ciencia colonial en América;* Lafuente and Valverde, "Linnaean Botany"; Martínez Sanz, *Relaciones científicas;* and Sellés, Peset, and Lafuente, *Carlos III.* The collection of essays edited by Luis Millones Figueroa and Domingo Ledezma, *El saber de los Jesuitas, historias naturales y el Nuevo Mundo,* includes several essays on eighteenth-century Jesuit science. Susan Deans-Smith edited a special section titled "Nature and Scientific Knowledge in the Spanish Empire" for the *Colonial Latin American Review.* See also Castro-Gómez, *La hybris.*

44. Iris H. W. Engstrand, in *Spanish Scientists in the New World,* gives a succinct overview in her introduction of eighteenth-century science in Spain before moving to a discussion of two important late eighteenth-century Spanish expeditions: the Royal Scientific Expedition to New Spain (1785–1800) and Alejandro Malaspina's voyage (1789–1794). See also Arias Divito, *Las expediciones científicas;* Galera Gómez, *La ilustración española;* and Lafuente and Mazuecos, *Los caballeros.*

45. The relatively sedate circumstances of Azara's expedition contrast strikingly with the more scandalous and conflict-filled fate of the La Condamine expedition. That disastrous expedition did result in a great deal of writing, however, and in this regard it is similar to Azara's commission (Pratt, *Imperial Eyes,* 16–23).

46. Livingstone, *Geographical Tradition,* 129; and Pratt, *Imperial Eyes.* This may also be understood as "a rise of internationalist cosmopolitanism in the arts and sciences in the circum-Atlantic world that operated largely in eighteenth-century civil or 'polite' society beyond the reach of political institutions" (R. Bauer, "Atlantic Triangulations," 8).

47. Pratt describes the background for these developments: "Bourgeois forms of subjectivity consolidated themselves, a new territorial phase of capitalism propelled by searches for raw materials began, coastal trade extended inland, and nations began to seize overseas territory in order to prevent its being seized by rival European powers" (*Imperial Eyes,* 11).

48. New Creoles were frequently implicated in the eighteenth-century involvement in Spain's "second conquest," which "attempted to centralize the political administration over the newly conquered territories in order to channel the economic profits to be reaped from the exploitation of the New World in ways most profitable to the imperial metropole" (R. Bauer, *Cultural Geography,* 3).

49. See Brading on Creole patriotism in *First America.*

50. In the collection of essays edited by William Clark, Jan Golinski, and Simon Schaffer, *The Sciences in Enlightened Europe,* the Iberian and Ibero-American world is (once again) absent. Spain appears in the index only once, under the heading "Spain, flight of Aublet to" (563). There are relatively few pages devoted to Spain and Spanish America in Jonathan Israel's massive three-volume work on the Enlightenment. I point this out not to minimize the important contribution made by these scholars to our understanding of the eighteenth century, but rather to attempt to put the Hispanic world on the eighteenth-century map.

51. See Millones Figueroa and Ledezma, *El saber.*

52. Roberto González Echevarría proposes that the paradigm for the nineteenth-century novel was established by scientific travel narratives such as those written by Darwin and Humboldt: "If the first discoverers and settlers appropriated Latin America by means of legal discourse, these new conquistadors did so with the aid of scientific discourse, which allowed them to name again (as if for the first time) the flora and fauna of the new world" (*Myth and Archive,* 96). In *Myth and Archive* (as in most attempts to describe the

trajectory of Spanish American literary and cultural history), the eighteenth century is largely absent.

53. Unlike what was happening in England and Anglo-America, landscaping and gardens seem not to be a concern in the Spanish viceregal world. For a discussion of American gardens in the eighteenth century, see Leighton, *American Gardens;* see Stephanie Ross on the history and aesthetics of the eighteenth-century English landscape garden in *What Gardens Mean.*

54. David Livingstone has studied Jefferson's presidency and the ways in which it brought together civic, imperial, and scientific ambitions, noting in particular his patriotic, utilitarian, and empiricist enthusiasms and his "personal fascination with the brute geography of the continent" as reflected in *Notes on the State of Virginia* (*Geographical Tradition,* 144–45). Although Azara does not share Jefferson's background as a large-scale plantation and slave owner, there are intriguing similarities in their shared interest in the substitution of a Georgic rhetoric of settlement for the complexities of colonial conquest. Azara's focus on settlement emerges in his bureaucratic correspondence.

55. Dictionaries and encyclopedias, so important to the eighteenth-century epistemological project, may also be understood as ways of collecting, organizing, and exhibiting information; Antonio de Alcedo y Bejarano's *Diccionario geográfico-histórico de las Indias Occidentales o América* (1786) is an example from the Hispanic world. For a broad overview, see Yeo, *Encyclopaedic Visions.*

56. In measuring the water flow, Azara used the cubic *toesa* or toise—an early French unit of measurement equal to 1.949 meters.

57. Unlike Gumilla, Azara's rhetoric of wonder is markedly secular; see Ewalt, "Father Gumilla, Crocodile Hunter?," 306–7. Galera Gómez argues nevertheless that Azara espouses an unequivocally creationist position with regard to the earth's origins (*Descripción general,* 18). I would agree, but I would add that Azara's reconciliation of science and faith is typical of many Catholic enlightened thinkers.

58. See Higgins's essay, "(Post-)Colonial Sublime: Order and Indeterminacy in Eighteenth-Century Spanish American Poetics and Aesthetics." Higgins uses Rafael Landívar's *Rusticatio mexicana* as a point of departure for discussing "the generally effaced discursive formation of the sublime in Spanish-American literary discourse" (119). See Bush's *Routes of Modernity* for a discussion of the links between eighteenth- and nineteenth-century Spanish American poetry.

59. Higgins, "(Post-)Colonial Sublime," 124.

60. Margaret Ewalt has argued that Gumilla's textual wondercabinets represent an eighteenth-century variant of the classical *admiratio-scientia* paradigm ("Father Gumilla, Crocodile Hunter?," 305); see also her *Peripheral Wonders.* Albanese sees the wondercabinet as a "protoinstitutional site of epistemological contention" (*New Science, New World,* 44). Lorraine Daston and Katharine Park offer an overview in *Wonders and the Order of Nature, 1150–1750,* exploring how *Wunderkammern* functioned by "provocatively subverting or straddling the boundaries of familiar categories" (273).

61. Azara is more a zoologist than a botanist, unlike some of his contemporaries, although he does devote two chapters of the *Viajes* to a discussion of "wild plants" and "cultivated plants." There is abundant bibliography on enlightenment botany: see Delaporte, *Nature's Second Kingdom;* Schiebinger and Swan, *Colonial Botany;* Shtier, "Dream"; and R. L. Williams, *Botanophilia in Eighteenth-Century France.* In a curious note L. C. Arboleda refers to two different branches of New World botany: *conquistadora,* which conquers through Linnaean taxonomy, and *conservadora,* which emphasizes the virtuous use of botanical economy ("La ciencia," 308).

62. Beddall notes, "When he spoke of communication with the birds and wild beasts, he meant it literally, for he often kept live animals caged or free in his room, or occasionally in a corral" ("Isolated Spanish Genius," 233). The numerous examples that can be found in both *Apuntamientos . . . páxaros* and *Apuntamientos . . . quadrúpedos* suggest that Azara was a kind of Aragonese Doctor Doolittle. His utilitarian approach to his animals is a far cry from the fascination with exotic animals that characterized eighteenth-century France and that Louise Robbins explores in *Elephant Slaves and Pampered Parrots.*

63. Don Pedro Blas Noseda helps Azara in a failed experiment to domesticate an *agüará-güazú,* or large fox. The first animal dies after eating the raw beef the two friends feed it, and a second animal has similar difficulties. They decide to try a diet of roasted meat with a third animal, but that is equally unsuccessful, and the animal eventually escapes (*Apuntamientos . . . quadrúpedos,* 266–67).

64. The *relaciones geográficas* are another example; see Mundy, *Mapping.*

65. Paula De Vos studies how "several aspects of the collections—the administrators assigned to oversee collecting, the collection of actual physical specimens in addition to descriptions and drawings, and the search for new commodities—reflect these aims and illustrate the importance that natural history played in the political economy of Bourbon Spain" ("Natural History," 210). See Calatayud Arinero, *Pedro Franco Dávila.*

66. Asín, *Aragón y América,* 143–44; see also Walckenaer, "Advertencia," 30–34; and Beddall, "Isolated Spanish Genius."

67. Julio César González notes that the instruments needed for the mathematical operations of the delegation were not available in Buenos Aires ("Apuntes bio-bibliográficos," xii). The improvised nature of Azara's expedition stands in sharp contrast to the heroic figure of Humboldt, who is often portrayed surrounded by an array of scientific instruments. Marie-Nöelle Bourguet asks, "How did it happen that, in the course of the eighteenth century, it became a requisite for naturalist-travelers to carry instruments and make measurements along the way, as well as to collect and classify samples? To what kind of botanical programme would numbers and measurements add some epistemological value? In turn, to what extent did these quantifying practices contribute to reshaping the travelers' encounter with nature and their perception of it?" ("Landscape with Numbers," 97). I will return to Humboldt at the close of this chapter.

68. Azara does, however, insist on having a junior officer accompany him, to whom he imparts instructions on mapping techniques (*Viajes,* 1:68).

69. For examples of this kind of illustration, consider John James Audubon's well-known drawings of birds or the lesser-known watercolors that make up the bulk of Baltasar Martínez Compañón's nine-volume *Trujillo del Perú.* For a discussion of the latter, see Meléndez's *Deviant and Useful Citizens.* For a discussion of illustrations in the reports of eighteenth-century Spanish scientific expeditions, see Pedro Robles, "Las expediciones científicas," 407–25. See Bleichmar, "Painting as Exploration," for a discussion of the botanical illustrations that resulted from Mutis's Royal Botanical Expedition; see also Bleichmar's *Visible Empire.*

70. Later editions did include drawings and other illustrations; see Beddall, "Un Naturalista Original," 38.

71. Neil Safier understands measurement as a metaphor for the activities of enlightened scientists: "They were measuring in the traditional sense, but they were also weighing and evaluating in a far more metaphorical vein: by observing indigenous cultures, by assaying plants and minerals, and by assessing historical truths" (*Measuring the New World,* 8).

72. In their introduction to the collection of essays titled *Instruments, Travel and Sci-*

ence: Itineraries of Precision from the Seventeenth to the Twentieth Century, the editors Marie-Nöelle Bourguet, Christian Licoppe, and H. Otto Sibum point to the moment in which science became "an instrumental activity" in the seventeenth century: "Both geographical distance and cultural diversity came to be regarded as obstacles to scientific practices when they would not allow for meaningful comparisons. Instruments, measures and data were meant to travel and provide templates for standardisation and accountability to varied experiences and encounters made in far-flung sites" (3).

73. Regis, *Describing Early America,* 17.

74. Measurement thus works as a Derridean supplement and replaces the original object that either remains in its natural habitat or becomes unrecognizably deteriorated because of the rigors of transatlantic travel.

75. Buffon began publishing his *Histoire naturelle, genérale et particuliere* in 1749, although publication of the forty-four volumes was not completed until 1804, sixteen years after the author's death.

76. Azara describes 448 species of birds, more than half of which had never before been heard of in Europe. He identified two new animal species that were named after him: the aguarichay (*Canis azarae*) and the micuré (*Didelphis azarae*); see Asín, *Aragón y América,* 143. Azara's legacy as a naturalist embraces both the Adamic naming function of early Spanish explorers and the new Linnean taxonomy.

77. Later, when Azara was in Paris, he discovered a number of errors related to his earlier criticisms of Buffon and corrected them in various subsequent publications (Beddall, "Isolated Spanish Genius," 254).

78. For example, he writes of the French naturalist's explanation of American deer: "From what has been said it can be deduced that Buffon's judgment is mistaken in believing that the deer and roebucks of America are the same as in Europe; but I excuse him because the indications and descriptions that exist of them are so incomplete, obscure, and lacking of any special characteristics that they do not seem to have been done by trained Travelers and Naturalists, and that means that all must guess at what they wanted to say" (*Apuntamientos . . . quadrúpedos,* 50).

79. For an overview of Azara's ideas on Buffon, see Alvarez López, *Félix de Azara,* 70–75.

80. See Gregory, *Geographical Imaginations,* 13–15, on the complications of the "travelling theory" metaphor in this context.

81. For further reading on cartography and mapping, see Akerman, *Imperial Map;* Burnett, *Masters of All;* Edney, *Mapping an Empire;* Gagliano and Ronan, *Jesuit Encounters;* Gregory, *Geographical Imaginations;* Livingstone, *Geographical Tradition;* Livingstone and Withers, *Geography and Enlightenment;* and Thrower, *Maps and Civilization.* While the extremely useful collection of essays edited by Livingstone and Withers, *Geography and Enlightenment,* emphasizes the importance of thinking about "geographies" in the plural, it contains no essays specifically focused on Latin America (there are, however, two essays on Humboldt).

82. Francisco Javier Asín cautions, however, that Azara copied sections of his maps of the Paraná and Paraguay Rivers from other sources (*Aragón y América,* 140–41).

83. See also Galera Gómez, *Descripción general,* 12.

84. Landscape, which looms large in other eighteenth-century contexts, is less of an issue for Spanish American geography, at least until the nineteenth century. See Mitchell, *Landscape and Power;* Schama, *Landscape and Memory;* and Cosgrove and Daniels, *Iconography of Landscape.*

85. Another way of thinking about Azara as a practical geographer is in the context of Kant's distinction between rational sciences and empirical sciences, "the latter dealing with the world of experience and the senses and therefore subsuming both the natural and the

human sciences" (Livingstone, *Geographical Tradition*, 114); see also Bowen, *Empiricism and Geographical Thought*, 206–8 and Warf and Arias, *Spatial Turn*, 54–55.

86. "Established as a technological fix for the Enlightenment's epistemological ideals, triangulation engendered a significant shift in cultural conceptions of space and geography. Enlightenment encyclopedism, the rational reconciliation of conflicting viewpoints, was reconfigured to a new ideology of systematic and disciplined observation (Edney, "Reconsidering Enlightenment Geography,"191). See also Edney, "Irony of Imperial Mapping."

87. Unlike the systematic science that Santiago Castro-Gómez discusses in *La hybris del punto cero,* Azara's scientific practice is admittedly accidental and improvisational.

88. Edney, "Reconsidering Enlightenment Geography," 176. Given the frustrations and tensions experienced by Azara's delegation, one might also characterize their project in terms of a Lacanian "méconnaissance"—that is, a misunderstanding or misrecognition of the borders proposed in negotiations with the Portuguese (Turnball, "Travelling Knowledge," 274).

89. In one letter, Azara writes, "In order to make myself understood, I am adding a little map, which even though it is not exact in terms of the course of the smaller rivers, is sufficiently exact to explain my ideas" (*Memoria,* 157).

90. Regis, *Describing Early America,* 26.

91. Asín, *Aragón y América,* 136. The exceptions to this relative lack of activity in the region, of course, were the Jesuit missions, which became a hotly contested issue in the border negotiations, partly because of the admitted anticlericalism of Sebastião José de Carvalho e Melo, the Marquis de Pombal, as well as his vigorous defense of Portuguese commercial interests. See Maxwell, *Pombal,* 51–55, 125–27. For a consideration of this issue from the Jesuit point of view, see Astrain, *Jesuitas, guaraníes y encomenderos.*

92. Akerman, *Imperial Map,* 1.

93. Safier adds, "In other words, imperial rivalries make for bad maps" ("Confines," 134).

94. See my earlier note on the contents of *Memoria sobre el estado rural de Río de la Plata y otros informes.*

95. Commenting on the confusion on the maps between the Yaguarey, Igurey, and Yaguari Rivers, Azara remarks, "Effectively, it's easy to recognize that the name *Igurey* is altered and corrupted, since it means nothing in Guarany, while the names *Yaguarey* and *Yaguari* do" (*Memoria,* 115). Here he draws not only on his cartographic expertise but also on his familiarity with local indigenous language.

96. Azara's complaint hinges on his understanding of the word *caudaloso,* whose inherent contradictions are less obvious in English translation. One might say that any river must be "large," as a small river would be considered a stream or a brook.

97. Another interesting aspect of Azara's correspondence are the letters Azara writes to Don Joaquín de Alós, the governor of Paraguay who (as we have seen) later became embroiled in controversy with the Aragonese engineer. These are included in the *Memoria* as *Correspondencia oficial e inédita.*

98. Ralph Bauer describes Byrd's mission in these terms: "The American landscape resists the utopian reason of the Line, as local knowledge of the landscape conflicts with the logo-centrism of imperial geography" (*Cultural Geography,* 194).

99. Pratt, *Imperial Eyes,* 35. In fact, there seems to be no mention of Azara's ever having used a weapon to do anything other than hunt during the duration of his stay in the Río de la Plata region. Azara does issue a memorandum calling for the formation of urban militia in Paraguay, noting that most farmers have never held a firearm or even a sword (*Memoria,* 301).

100. See also Baulny, "La colonización."

101. Juan Marchena notes that the urgent question for eighteenth-century political functionaries in the Spanish Bourbon court was whether reform measures were proving to be
successful ("Su Majestad quiere saber," 155).

102. See Pratt's discussion of the difference between "contact zone" and frontier in the revised
introduction to the second edition of *Imperial Eyes* (8); I refer the reader to my earlier
discussion of how Adorno, Pratt, and Weber understand these terms (Chapter 2, n128).

103. Azara cautions, "We should do everything possible so that there is not neutral terrain, or
to reduce its width as much as possible" (*Memoria*, 30).

104. Azara is the author of a number of reports on various colonization projects proposed for
the Chaco region, and he is fairly critical of earlier colonizing attempts by both secular
administrators and ecclesiastics (*Memoria*, 187–207).

105. Gustavo Verdesio discusses Azara's portrayal of the Amerindians of the Río de la Plata,
in *Forgotten Conquests*, 99–109; see also his *La invención del Uruguay*, 51–63. Verdesio
characterizes Azara as an encyclopedist whose duality of thought regarding the Amerindians is striking: "On the one hand, he constructs the Other based on the assumptions
and categories of his episteme; on the other, he is an observer interested in the Other's
way of life, regardless of his own assumptions" (*Forgotten Conquests*, 102).

106. David Weber quotes Azara in the epigraph to his chapter "Trading, Gifting, and Treat-
ing": "The reduction of the savage nations can only be carried out by three means: the
first is through commerce and friendly relations, the second is through force, and the
third is through persuasion" (*Bárbaros*, 178). Azara devotes numerous chapters of the
second volume of his *Viajes* to the Amerindian groups of the Río de la Plata, although he
emphasizes that he does not presume expertise in this area. Fiercely anticlerical, Azara
offers a stinging critique of the Jesuit *reducciones*.

107. Azara's proposals here reflect the view of enlightened thinkers like William Robertson
and Adam Ferguson on stadial human development, which I discussed in Chapter 2.

108. See Azara's "Informe acerca de un reconocimiento de las guardias y fortines," written in
Buenos Aires on July 31, 1796 (*Memoria*, 167–81).

109. The phrase, of course, is Juan Bautista Alberdi's famous maxim.

110. Azara was extremely interested in issues of populations and census figures and viewed
population growth as a means of consolidating Spanish control over the Río de la Plata
region.

111. However, Azara is adamant with regard to the evils of slavery. In Azara's view, slave trading was an issue that complicated the border negotiations, as it underscored fundamental differences between the Portuguese and the Spanish (*Memoria*, 20).

112. Azara includes a description of the cattle herders who work the pampas of Paraguay and
Buenos Aires (*Viajes* 2:186–95). Azara's observations regarding their table manners and
eating habits are particularly pointed: "They sit on their heels or on the skull of a cow or
horse. They don't eat vegetables or salad, saying that they're grass, and they make fun of
Europeans, who eat like horses and use oil, another thing that they find very repugnant.
They eat absolutely nothing other than beef grilled the way the Charrúa Indians do it
and without salt. They have no set time for eating, and they clean their mouth with the
blade of their knife and their hands on their pants or their boots" (*Viajes*, 2:191). His
comments have much in common with accounts offered by Alonso Carrió de la Vandera
in *El lazarillo* and, later, by Sarmiento.

113. *Proyectismo* (projectism) emerges in eighteenth-century Spain and Spanish America as
an enlightened approach to political and economic reform projects; the term also refers
to the writings—plans, propositions, memoranda—that describe the proposed projects.

114. Asín, *Aragón y América*, 145; and Baulny, "La colonización," 239–42. Olivier Baulny, who

analyzes the eventual fate of the Batoví colony in light of nineteenth-century develop-ments, includes a number of letters written by Azara to Miguel de Lastarria.

115. Buesa Olivar, "Sobre Cosme Bueno" 332–72.

116. In her introduction to *La naturaleza en disputa: Retóricas del cuerpo y el paisaje en América Latina,* Gabriela Nouzeilles characterizes Enlightenment descriptions of na-ture as fundamentally imperialist (25); she makes specific mention of Hume, Voltaire, Raynal, de Pauw, and Humboldt but overlooks Azara, Gumilla, and their Spanish and criollo contemporaries. This leads to an overly Eurocentric view of eighteenth-century natural history in Latin America in what is otherwise an excellent collection of essays devoted principally to the nineteenth and twentieth centuries.

117. See Roy Porter's characterization of Foucault's misreading of the epistemological break around 1800 and the resulting over-emphasis on romantic geographers such as Hum-boldt ("Afterword," 415–31).

118. Like Azara, Humboldt is also to some extent an accidental South American naturalist. His expedition to the Orinoco with Aimé Bonpland (and the voluminous publications that resulted from their five years in South America from 1799 to 1804) came about when their plans for a Nile River trip were interrupted by the Napoleonic invasion of North Africa (Pratt, *Imperial Eyes,* 12). Humboldt's life and works have occasioned enormous scholarly interest. See Pratt, *Imperial Eyes* 109–40; Ochoa, *Uses of Failure;* and Pérez-Mejía, *Geography of Hard Times.*

119. It's telling that when Gabriela Nouzeilles sums up the so-called dispute of the New World, she points to Humboldt as a figure who links earlier discovery tropes with an emerging Romantic sensibility (*La naturaleza en disputa,* 25–26). Pratt concurs: "Hum-boldt remained the single most influential interlocutor in the process of reimagining and redefinition that coincided with Spanish America's independence from Spain" (*Imperial Eyes,* 109).

120. Pratt, *Imperial Eyes,* 126.

121. Ewalt reminds us of Humboldt's appropriation of Gumilla's writings on the Orinoco (*Peripheral Wonders,* 180–88). She notes that Humboldt was "regarded as a 'rediscoverer' of South America," but he "in fact compiled knowledge from Amerindians, criollos, and clerics who continue to be insufficiently cited, as their contributions to modernity have been eclipsed by Humboldt's international fame" (181). See also Cañizares-Esguerra, "How Derivative Was Humboldt?"

122. In *The Voyage of the Beagle,* Darwin wrote, "As the force of impressions generally de-pends on preconceived ideas, I may add, that all mine were taken from the vivid descrip-tions in the Personal Narrative of Humboldt (qtd. in Stepan, *Picturing Tropical Nature,* 7). For a discussion of Azara's importance to Darwin, see Beddall, "Un Naturalista Original," 22n13; and Baulny, *Félix de Azara.*

123. Darwin makes additional references to Azara on the migration of vultures (*Voyage of the Beagle,* 73); on whether or not Pampas Indians used bows and arrows (119); on destruc-tive thunderstorms in the vicinity of Buenos Aires (76); on skunks, about whom "Azara says the smell can be perceived at a league distant; more than once, when entering the harbour of Monte Video, the wind being off shore, we have perceived the odour on board the Beagle" (95); and on hydrophobia, or rabies (365; here Darwin also refers to "Dr Unanúe's account of hydrophia in Arequipa in 1807").

124. Beddall, "Un Naturalista Original," 47. For a discussion of the relationship between color and domestication, see Alvarez López, "Azara y Darwin," 69–70.

125. Darwin references Azara on the feral dogs of La Plata (*Variation,* 1:27) and on the crossing of domestic and wild cats in Paraguay (*Variation,* 1:46). He relays details from

the French edition of Azara's *Apuntamientos . . . quadrúpedos:* "Azara relates that in Paraguay horses are occasionally born, but are generally destroyed, with hair like that on the head of a negro" (1:55); later, Darwin adds that "according to Azara horses are often born in Paraguay with curly hair; but as the natives do not like them, they are destroyed. On the other hand, Azara states that a hornless bull, born in 1770, was preserved and propagated its race" (2:189). Darwin also notes that "Azara, who wrote towards the close of the last century, states that in the interior parts of South America, where I should not have expected that the least care would have been taken of poultry, a black-skinned and black-boned breed is kept, from being considered fertile and its flesh good for sick persons" (2:243). For a discussion of the development of critical race theories in nineteenth-century Spanish America, see Hill, "Categories and Crossings," 1–6.

126. Azara's observations on the relationship between cattle ranching, cattle husbandry, and plant species are relevant given later debates about how to modernize the economies of the newly independent nations of the Río de la Plata region. For example, in the late nineteenth century, Uruguayan cattle ranchers engaged in vigorous debates about modernizing the cattle industry in which Darwinian theories regarding crossing and selection played an important role. Curiously, Thomas Glick's extensive discussion of these debates in "The Reception of Darwinism in Uruguay" includes no mention of Darwin's frequent references to Azara's writing in order to corroborate his own observations. For further discussion of criollo cattle ranching, see Higgins on Landívar's *Rusticatio, Constructing,* 200–206. For a discussion of how local flora and fauna were "seriously affected by the introduction of animals of European origin" in the Río de la Plata region, see Verdesio, "Original Sin."

127. There is no mention of Azara in the collections of essays on this fascinating debate. See Gómez, *La piedra del escándalo;* Glick, Puig-Samper, and Ruiz, *El Darwinismo;* and Alvarez López, "Azara y Darwin."

128. Simon Schaffer, in his afterword to *Visions of Empire: Voyages, Botany, and Representations of Nature,* questions the generally accepted dichotomy between interest and curiosity as a way of approaching European imperial exploration (335–36).

129. De Vos, "Natural History," 210.

130. Castro-Gómez, *La hybris,* 16. In *Science in Action,* Bruno Latour looks at the way that science is produced in an uneven relationship between colony and metropolis. See John Gascoigne's discussion of Latour's "centers of calculation," through which the natural world is conceptualized in a way that supports Western hegemony through systematic appropriation and the building of networks ("Ordering of Nature," 108); see also Gómez, *La piedra del escándalo,* 15–16.

CHAPTER 4

A much earlier version of this chapter was presented in October 1997 at the Conference on Women Writers of Early Modern Spain and Colonial Latin America, hosted by the University of Virginia. I am grateful to the following colleagues who offered valuable suggestions at that time: Jennifer Eich, Kathleen Myers, María Mercedes Carrión, Stacey Schlau, and Fernando Iturburu. My essay titled "Llegando a la primera mujer: Catalina de Jesús Herrera y la invención de una genealogía femenina en el Quito del Siglo XVIII" appeared in the *Colonial Latin American Review* in 2000. My essay titled "Las pesadillas criollas en *Secretos entre el alma y Dios* (c. 1760) de Catalina de Jesús Herrera" appeared in *Guaraguao* in 2011; editors Mario Campana and Raquel Chang-Rodríguez offered valuable suggestions that have also informed this chapter. My work on Herrera would have been impossible without the generous collaboration of Peter Bakewell and Frank Graziano, who managed to track down a copy of the 1954 published version of Herrera's *Autobiografía* during a visit to the Convent of Santa Catalina in

Quito in the summer of 1997. In response to Frank's persistent queries, the nuns surrendered via the convent turnstile a musty copy of Herrera's autobiography, which he then sent to me. All quotations from the *Secretos* are taken from this 1954 edition; the translations are mine.

1. Pérez Pimentel, *Diccionario biográfico del Ecuador,* 2:101.

2. Paniagua Pérez, "El monacato," 275; and Muriel, *Las mujeres,* 279. The Convent of Santa Catalina was founded in 1593 by Doña María Siliceo, who provided an initial endowment of twelve thousand pesos and later secured a commitment of royal funds for the purchase of wine, candles, oil, and medicines (Paniagua Pérez, "El monacato," 274–76). In 1613 the convent moved to its current location. See also Vargas, *Historia de la provincia,* 188–90. For a detailed description of a Dominican convent in colonial New Spain, see Muriel, *Conventos de monjas,* 317–28.

3. Vargas, *Historia de la iglesia,* 363.

4. Herrera explains that her brother tormented her by repeatedly postponing the day when she might don the Dominican habit and enter the convent (*Secretos,* 38), and she describes the lengths to which she had to go to acquire the "six kilos [*medio arroba*] of candle wax that one gave in order to profess" (94). According to the historian Asunción Lavrin, "The amount of money required as dowry changed over time and varied from area to area. In the sixteenth and seventeenth centuries dowries ranged from 1,000 to 2,000 pesos. Inflation and the greater financial requirements of convents in the late seventeenth century resulted in an increase up to 3,000 pesos, and by the end of the colonial period some convents were demanding 4,000 pesos" ("Female Religious," 177). Herrera's story differs markedly from the *vocation forcée* (forced vocation) narratives that were popular in eighteenth-century France, in which a critique of despotism's denial of individual rights is constructed through a gendered critique of convent life (Choudhury, *Convents and Nuns,* 11).

5. Vargas, *Sor Catalina,* 24–31. Kathryn Burns explains, "Nuns might speak with visitors only during certain hours of the day and in the presence of an *escucha,* a listener delegated to monitor every conversation at the grille and to report any improprieties to her superior for disciplinary action" (*Colonial Habits,* 102).

6. As in the case of Sor Juana Inés de la Cruz, what little we know of the life of Catalina de Jesús Herrera—with the exception of a few brief notes and official documents preserved in the convent archives—comes from her own autobiographical writings. My reading of the *Secretos entre el alma y Dios* relies on the foundational research on colonial Spanish American convents done by Asunción Lavrin and Josefina Muriel; on the groundbreaking volume *Untold Sisters,* coedited by Electa Arenal and Stacey Schlau; and on subsequent work by Kathryn Burns, María Mercedes Carrión, Margaret Chowning, Clark Colahan, Jennifer Eich, Kristen Ibsen, Stephanie Kirk, Kathryn McKnight, Kathleen Myers, Kathleen Ross, Elisa Sampson Vera Tudela, Stacey Schlau, Sherry Velasco, and Alison Weber. Mariselle Meléndez devotes a chapter of her book *Deviant and Useful Citizens: The Cultural Production of the Female Body in Eighteenth-Century Peru* to a discussion of Sor María Josefa de la Santísima Trinidad's *Historia de la Fundación del Monasterio de Trinitarias Descalzas de Lima* (1783); I will return to what Meléndez calls "religious patriotism" later in this chapter. Herrera's work is to date largely unknown to readers outside of Ecuador (even those familiar with the wealth of scholarly work that has been done on convent writing in the past two decades); she is regularly overlooked even in recent attempts to expand the canon, no doubt because of the lack of a current edition of the *Secretos.* Diana Serrano's doctoral dissertation, "Catalina de Jesús Herrera," is a welcome (although not easily accessible) addition to the bibliography.

7. Herrera describes the inspiration for the title in these words: "Once again you animated

me, oh my God, as I was thinking and saying to myself: Oh, to order me to write when there is nothing new to write anymore, now that everything has been said! And when I eventually write all that God has done with me, what title should I give those writings when all titles have already been given to other books and there is none left for this one? Then You snatched my soul for a brief instant, Lord, and said clearly and distinctly: The title for these writings will be: Secrets between the Soul and God" (*Secretos*, 82).

8.   The *Autobiografía* was reprinted in 1954.

9.   There are a few tantalizing references to Herrera in histories of colonial Ecuador and institutional histories of the Dominican order. Victor Manuel Albornoz, Pablo Herrera and Remigio Crespo Toral included fragments of the *Secretos* in their *Prosistas de la República*, and José Ignacio Checa y Barba was also familiar with the text (Vargas, *Sor Catalina*, 8); see also Pérez Pimentel, *Diccionario biográfico del Ecuador*, 2:103 and 4:287–89; Lavrin, "Female Religious," 185; and Muriel, *Las mujeres*, 279–84. In noting that the autobiography contains much useful information about religious and secular life in the second half of the eighteenth century, Vargas acknowledges the myriad ways in which convents participated in and influenced life outside their walls (*Historia de la iglesia*, 363).

10.   In addition to Herrera's text, the volume *Letras de la Audiencia de Quito* includes the *Vida prodigiosa de la Venerable Virgen Juana de Jesús . . .* , written by Francisco Xavier Antonio de Santa María (Lima, 1756); "La Azucena de Quito que brotó el florido campo de la Iglesia . . . la V. Virgen Mariana de Jesús Paredes y Flores . . . ," written by Father Padre Jacinto Morán de Butrón (Madrid, 1724); and the previously unpublished "La perla Mystica escondida en la concha de la humildad," written by Gertrudis de San Ildefonso in collaboration with her spiritual director Fray Martín de la Cruz.

11.   Qtd. in Jerves, "Introducción," 11.

12.   Roger Chartier notes the divide between "a private, cloistered, solitary reading, considered to be one of the essential elements for constituting a sphere of private life, and the collective reading—both disciplined and rebellious—of communitarian spaces" (*Order of Books*, 17).

13.   As do many other critics who have put forth paradigms for reading Latin American literature, Jean Franco here moves from baroque religiosity to nineteenth-century nationalism, overlooking the eighteenth century.

14.   Teresa of Avila (1515–1582), Spanish mystic, theologian, and religious reformer, is remembered, with John of the Cross, as the founder of the Discalced Carmelite Order. The *Libro de fundaciones* was written during the years 1573–1582 as an account of her efforts to found new convents that would adhere to reformist principles.

15.   Taylor observes that the decorated altars and elaborately clothed saints represent a late colonial "spiritual capital" as Bourbon administrative reforms filtered down to parish churches in eighteenth-century Mexico (*Magistrates of the Sacred*, 3).

16.   The traditional view had been that the Enlightenment led to "either an absolute decline in religious belief, or a radical shift in its meaning and content"; Outram concisely summarizes recent assessments of those claims (*Enlightenment*, 111). See also Roy Porter on Enlightenment views on religion (*Enlightenment*, 31).

17.   Regarding Bourbon anticlericalism, see Noel, "Clerics and Crown," 123; and Taylor, *Magistrates of the Sacred*, 13–23.

18.   Noel, "Clerics and Crown," 120. For additional discussion, see Bradley and Van Kley, *Religion and Politics*, 27–29.

19.   The role of Jesuits in the eighteenth-century Hispanic world, up to and through their 1767 expulsion from Spanish territories, has generated a wealth of scholarship; see Batl-

lori, *La cultura hispano-italiana;* Mörner, *Expulsion of the Jesuits;* and Tietz, *Los jesuitas españoles expulsos.* See also Bernier, Donato, and Lüsebrink, *Jesuit Accounts.*

20. Noel cautions that "interiorization and simplication of faith never signified dechristianization, and virtually all Spaniards remained loyally Catholic" ("Clerics and Crown," 128). I would argue that the same is true for criollos.

21. Karen Melvin suggests that in eighteenth-century New Spain, "prelates' calls to modernize religious practice went largely unheeded by their flocks, and baroque forms of Catholicism continued to prevail" (*Building Colonial Cities,* 8).

22. Noel, "Clerics and Crown," 123-24.

23. Peter Bakewell notes that "though by the early eighteenth century Tepeyac was the prime pilgrimage site in Mexico, it was only after 1746, when the Mexican bishops and cathedral chapters proclaimed Our Lady of Guadalupe to be the patroness of New Spain, that her cult became colony-wide" (*History,* 254). For an extensive discussion of criollo advocacy for the Guadalupe cult, see Lafaye, *Quetzalcóatl y Guadalupe.*

24. For a wide-ranging collection of essays reflecting the ways in which Old World hagiographic conventions and traditions were transplanted or reinvented in the New World, see Greer and Bilinkoff, *Colonial Saints.* See also Morgan, *Spanish American Saints.*

25. Taylor, *Magistrates of the Sacred,* 19.

26. See del Valle, *Escribiendo desde los márgenes,* for a discussion of the challenges faced by Jesuit missionaries in the hinterlands of eighteenth-century New Spain.

27. See O'Hara, *Flock Divided,* 56-58; and del Valle, *Escribiendo desde los márgenes,* 40-42.

28. Sampson Vera Tudela, *Colonial Angels,* 84-85. Elisa Sampson Vera Tudela argues that, despite the traditional view of convents as "'colonial' in the most derogatory sense," they functioned as spaces where women participated in the emergence of a modern sensibility (85). She also notes that "in strict economic terms the eighteenth century was a period of expansion and success for many convents, in stark opposition to the situation of many male religious orders and their institutions" (87).

29. See Note 6 in this chapter for a list of scholars of convent writing. For the following overview of female confessional autobiography, I draw on Kathleen Myers's introductory overview in *Neither Saints Nor Sinners* (3-19) and Kathryn McKnight's chapter, "The Genre of the Vida Espiritual," in *The Mystic of Tunja* (17-59). The bibliographic essay Myers includes at the conclusion of her *Word from New Spain,* "Autobiographical Writing in Spanish American Convents, 1650-1800," is especially useful (209-14).

30. Myers tracks the evolution of the *vida* from informal notes, known as "cuentas de conciencia," taken in anticipation or in lieu of oral confession (*Neither Saints Nor Sinners,* 9-11).

31. Ibid., 14.

32. McKnight, *Mystic of Tunja,* 2, 19. McKnight's discussion of Madre Castillo is particularly useful for my own reading of Herrera, as both are eighteenth-century nuns living in the viceregal periphery.

33. Melvin, "Potential Saint Thwarted," 172.

34. Bynum is referring here to the medieval period, but her observations are relevant for this discussion of spiritual autobiography in the eighteenth century.

35. Herrera's mother also teaches her to read: "My mother kept me busy learning to read, with which I had no difficulty, because of my interest in knowing fables and history, of which I was much enamored, and they told me that one learned those things in books" (*Secretos,* 26).

36. In Spanish the phrase "to give birth" is often translated as *dar a luz*—literally, to present to the light.

37. Alison Weber offers an astute analysis of the ambivalence demonstrated by Teresa regarding paternal authority (its exemplary nature notwithstanding): "Much of her psychological history can be seen as a repeated 'leaving home'—as a response to her continued need to rebel or break affective ties with successive authority figures" (*Teresa of Avila,* 124). In Teresa's case, as in Herrera's, the decision to leave the family home leads ultimately to a project of building a monastic home that is both bricks and mortar and textual.

38. Rodolfo Pérez Pimentel offers a somewhat contradictory commentary, noting both his virtue and his violent character (*Diccionario biográfico del Ecuador,* 2:101). Muriel (drawing on a Dominican account) repeats the obligatory praise of Herrera's parents (*Las mujeres,* 279).

39. Myers discusses this process in the case of María de San José: "Removing these auto-biographical writings from their original context and adapting them as official Church documents used for edifying ends has often muted the personal voice found in these writings so that they could be read as formulaic devotional texts" (*Word from New Spain,* 3).

40. Herrera mentions this moment again later (*Secretos,* 294).

41. For a discussion of conjugal violence in late eighteenth-century Ecuador, see León Galarza, *La primera alianza,* 115–46.

42. Sor Juana does the same in her famous poem "Hombres necios."

43. Burns, *Colonial Habits,* 101–5. For a discussion of the reforms that were enacted in an attempt to correct monastic excess and disorder in seventeenth- and eighteenth-century Peru, see C. Martin, *American Indian,* 230–42. Lavrin studies ecclesiastic reforms in eighteenth-century New Spain, but much of what she observes also pertains to the viceroyalty of Peru ("Ecclesiastical Reform"). Vargas lists the specific measures taken to reform the Convent of Santa Catalina (*Sor Catalina,* 26–28).

44. Mariselle Meléndez includes numerous examples of the "corporeal rhetorics" of the nuns of the Monasterio de Trinitarias Descalzas de Lima (*Deviant and Useful Citizens,* 100–123). She concludes, "The extreme transformations suffered by these nuns' bodies highlight the awareness that they all possessed with regard to the potential symbolic power of their bodies. They were cognizant of the legibility of their own corporeality and how fellow nuns and other religious authorities would read them" (117).

45. For example, according to her biographer, Mariana de Jesús Paredes y Flores requested mortification by her fellow nuns by asking them to stone her (Rodríguez Casteló, *Letras de la Audiencia,* 63).

46. Herrera includes several other incidents that might be read as suggesting covert or overt lesbianism. She is frightened by repeated visits of an "alma in pena" (lost soul) who turns out to be a deceased nun who seeks Herrera's forgiveness for having spoken ill of Herrera to their prelate (*Secreto,* 133–34). The nun complains that she has been unable to resolve this issue, accusing Herrera of having broken convent rules by sharing a bed with another nun (134). Although the conversation turns on the nature of true forgiveness, repeated references to Herrera's sleeping arrangements suggest a more complicated context. See J. Brown, *Immodest Acts,* 6–20.

47. Fernando Cervantes explores eighteenth-century diabolism in the closing chapter and epilogue of *The Devil in the New World* (125–61). He proposes that exiled Jesuit Francisco Javier Clavigero's *Historia antigua de México* (1780–1781), which became a foundational text for Mexican criollo consciousness, represents a watershed moment in which the devil is effectively exorcized from the *patria's* past.

48. Kathleen Ross argues persuasively that similar stories of *escarmiento* (punishment)

included by Carlos de Sigüenza y Góngora in *Parayso Occidental* (1684) reflect a pater-
nalistic discourse whose goal is to control and circumscribe his female protagonists (*Baroque Narrative,* 138). Herrera, on the other hand, employs these narratives to highlight
her own privileged relationship with God.

49. José María Vargas devotes an entire chapter to listing these confessors with detailed
    biographic and bibliographic information (*Sor Catalina,* 32–50).

50. In the 1954 edition, direct discourse is indicated typographically by the use of italics,
    which I reproduce in quoting here.

51. Another example is the series of questions Herrera directs to God, who patiently an-
    swers them one by one (*Secretos,* 168).

52. Vargas recognizes the role that Saint Augustine and Teresa play as models for Herrera,
    but he insists that *Secretos*'s structure as a constant colloquy between God and the author
    is unique (*Sor Catalina de Jesús,* 54–55).

53. For Herrera, writing about earlier moments of doubt and torment is tantamount to
    experiencing them all over again: "Because each time that I write about one of my tri-
    als, my soul returns to the same torment as when it first experienced them" (*Secretos,*
    80–81).

54. Like Sor Juana, Herrera anxiously desires to learn how to write and teaches herself, with
    the help of God: "Lord, you helped me to learn how to write" (*Secretos,* 22).

55. Herrera later repeats her understanding of this bargain in which God has given her
    license to omit from her narrative many examples of her own sins and errors: "But since
    You want me to show the benefits that I have received from You, and hide my sins, your
    Will be done" (*Secretos,* 84).

56. Melvin notes that unlike monastic communities, whose members withdrew from the
    world, mendicant orders in the Americas aspired "to follow a life of both contemplation
    and work in the world, to become, in a phrase the friars borrowed from the gospel of
    Luke, 'both Marthas and Marys'" (*Building Colonial Cities,* 9).

57. New World hagiography raises "questions of colonial identity and protonationalism," as
    Alan Greer and Jodi Bilinkoff point out in their introduction to *Colonial Saints: Discov-
    ering the Holy in the Americas 1500–1800* (iv).

58. Electa Arenal and Stacey Schlau explain that in addition to the practice of *imitatio
    Christi,* religious women often found female models to imitate (*Untold Sisters,* 303–8).

59. Rosa of Lima's importance as a New World saint validated the general sense of Lima's
    primacy over other cities in the Andean region. Ronald Morgan discusses this relation-
    ship in *Spanish American Saints and the Rhetoric of Identity, 1600–1810.* In chapter 5,
    "Hagiography in Service of the Patria Chica," he argues that *quiteño* aspirations to vice-
    regal importance led to a campaign in the late seventeenth and early eighteenth century
    on behalf of Mariana de Jesús that culminated in the publication of *La azucena de Quito*
    (117). This work, first published in 1702 and again in 1724, undoubtedly forms part of
    the backdrop for Herrera's campaign to promote her own convent.

60. Herrera includes additional mentions of Rosa of Lima in *Secretos,* 350–52.

61. For a discussion of mystical eroticism as it related to Rosa de Lima, see Graziano,
    Wounds of Love, 14–15, 196.

62. In another striking example of Herrera's efforts to affirm autochthonous religiosity, the
    author explains how she was cured of an attack of dysentery when a nun rubbed her
    stomach with what Herrera first thought was a relic from the cross (*Secretos,* 300). As
    it turned out, the nun was using a branch from a tobacco plant. Herrera explains her
    confusion and the resultant cure by attributing both to God's performance of a miracle
    of transubstantiation (300). The miraculous cure is thus expanded to elevate a quintes-

sentially New World plant to the category of relic. For a discussion of tobacco consumption by an eighteenth-century Peruvian nun, see Meléndez, *Deviant and Useful Citizens*, 103–4.

63. Here and elsewhere Herrera plays with the confusion of names (Catalina, Catarina).

64. Herrera describes an early encounter with a group of Carmelite nuns on their way to found a convent in Trujillo; the choice of convent is associated here with a foundational gesture (*Secretos,* 24). Herrera later recounts that her brother at one point shows her a hidden cave that she marks with a cross to signal the creation of a holy space of her own (43).

65. Burns, speaking of relations between Peruvian convents at the same time, refers to the "subtle boundary not on any map: the imperceptible border separating the spiritual economy of Arequipa from that of Cuzco," and the resulting differentiation between local nuns and "forasteras" (*Colonial Habits,* 71). Herrera describes the rivalries between different monastic orders and explains how she finally came to choose a Dominican convent (*Secretos,* 69–74). Jenny Londoño López provides an overview of the convents of Quito (*Angeles o demonios?,* 235–80), including the Franciscan Convento de la Inmaculada Concepción, the largest and oldest in the city with more than 100 nuns and over a thousand Indians and servants (*Angeles o demonios?,* 241).

66. Arenal and Schlau note that the elaborate crowns of flowers or jewels seen in the portraits of illustrious (or "flowery") nuns reflect not only spiritual qualities but also the material wealth of their convents (*Untold Sisters,* 294).

67. This identification between lost or scattered remains of an exemplary nun and convent history appears also in Carlos de Sigüenza y Góngora's *Parayso Occidental,* although in Sigüenza's account inter-convent rivalry, which is the prime motivation for Herrera's expedition, does not play a role (K. Ross, *Baroque Narrative,* 129). Sor María Josefa de la Santísima Trinidad includes an example of the incorruptibility of the cadaver of a nun in her *Historia de la Fundación del Monasterio de Trinitarias Descalzas de Lima* (Meléndez, *Deviant and Useful Citizens,* 115–16).

68. Herrera walks a fine line here in explaining how the plot was sanctioned so as not to suggest any disobedience on her part. Supposedly a priest (who remains unnamed) assured two other nuns that there was no harm in opening the tomb. He cautioned them, however, to do it secretly (*Secretos,* 163).

69. In his essay "A Variant: Hagio-Graphical Edification" (included in *The Writing of History,* 269–83), Michel de Certeau describes hagiographic discourse as a monument or "tautological tomb" that is located "at the outer edge of historiography" (269).

70. In addition to Sor Juana's remains, there is also another, recently buried body, a minor detail that does not derail the expedition.

71. The theft of the shoe reminds the reader that nuns' bodies, like those of other sainted figures, represent a coming together of sanctity and materiality that has powerful symbolic implications. This helps to explain why relics figure so prominently in Catholic religious practice from medieval times to the present; they become particularly significant in the context of New World hagiography, as we shall see at the close of this chapter. Meléndez includes a fascinating account of a power struggle over the remains of one of the nuns of the Monasterio de Trinitarias Descalzas in Lima that erupts when "the priests forcibly seized the dead body from the arms of the nuns who were carrying it" (*Deviant and Useful Citizens,* 107). Both the nuns and the priests sought to claim the remains as "a symbol of worship and religious prestige" (107).

72. See J. H. Elliott, *Empires of the Atlantic,* 178. Pilgrimage may be understood as a liminal phenomenon involving "release from mundane structure; homogenization of status; simplicity of dress and behavior; communitas; ordeal; reflection on the meaning of basic

religious and cultural values; ritualized enactment of correspondences between religious paradigms and shared human experiences," and "movement from a mundane center to a sacred periphery which suddenly, transiently, becomes central for the individual" (Turner and Turner, *Image and Pilgrimage*, 34).

73. Part 2 of *Secretos* begins with a markedly negative vision that Herrera has of her own convent: "I lifted my eyes to see the walls of my Convent and Church, and instead of happiness my heart was covered with a great darkness, as if to erase my desire to be a nun" (88). It ends with the excavation of the remains of Sor Juana.

74. Nina Scott provides an annotated catalog of these women in her essay "'La gran turba de las que mercieron nombres': Sor Juana's Foremothers in 'La respuesta a Sor Filotea.'"

75. "At a time when many monasteries were facing a period of crisis and decay, documenting the history of a monastery became a crucial tool to justify the intrinsic and necessary existence of the monastery as a religious and social institution" (Meléndez, *Deviant and Useful Citizens*, 85).

76. According to Burns, the phrase suggests "the inextricability of the material and the sacred, relying on a very old sense of 'economy' as the managing of a house (Greek *oikos*) and pointing to the spiritual goals orienting such activity" (*Colonial Habits*, 3).

77. Lavrin, "Female Religious," 167–72; Sampson Vera Tudela, "Voyages," 197. Sampson Vera Tudela also reminds us that spiritual autobiographies were necessarily "narrative[s] of the quotidian," marked by "division and conflict" (*Colonial Angels*, 89).

78. González Suárez, *Historia general*, 4:283.

79. Ibid., 4:284. These complaints are similar to ones that Herrera would later register in her autobiographical narrative.

80. Ibid., 4:285.

81. Ibid., 4:287.

82. Ibid., 4:288.

83. Ibid., 4:289.

84. Margaret Chowning in *Rebellious Nuns* describes a period of intense rebellion (1759–1772) in a Capuchin convent in eighteenth-century Mexico that mirrors what happened at the Convent of Santa Catalina. She argues that convent reform efforts were an attempt to "stand in answer to eighteenth-century 'enlightened' critics" (6).

85. Sampson Vera Tudela, "Illustrating Sainthood," 97.

86. For an account of how an eighteenth-century priest in New Spain used miracles to reinforce his own position, see Taylor, "Between Nativitas," 97–100.

87. Lavrin discusses the struggle over *vida común* in eighteenth-century New Spain in *Brides of Christ*, 275–309. See also Meléndez's discussion of religious reform in Peruvian monasteries (*Deviant and Useful Citizens*, 86–90).

88. Vargas, *Historia de la provincia*, 191.

89. Vargas, *Historia de la iglesia*, 391.

90. P. Herrera, *Ensayo*, 61.

91. Ibid., 62.

92. Muriel, *Las mujeres*, 281.

93. Herrera's family had also experienced a number of calamities that beset Guayaquil in the early years of the eighteenth century, including a fire that destroyed much of the city in 1705, an epidemic that ravaged its inhabitants in 1708, and an attack by pirates in 1709 (Vargas, *Sor Catalina*, 17).

94. At another point Herrera announces, "My inclination was far reaching, because all I desired was to go to Lima to throw myself at the feet of the Archbishop so that he would send me to the Convent of Santa Rosa, never to return" (*Secretos*, 295).

95. Muriel, *Las mujeres*, 282; and Vargas, *Sor Catalina*, 89. The rebuilding was sponsored

by a generous patron, the Marqués de Selva Alegre (Vargas, *Historia de la iglesia,* 392). Charles Walker's *Shaky Colonialism* offers a fascinating account of efforts to rebuild Lima after the 1746 earthquake.

96. Corrales would become Herrera's most important spiritual guide. Herrera records with relief that God obviously did not intend for her to pursue a solitary spiritual journey. Clearly conscious of her hagiographic models, she notes that, unlike María Egipcíaca, who was left alone in the desert, "I am not a saint" (*Secretos,* 318).

97. Vargas, *Sor Catalina,* 88. In his essay, "A Variant: Hagio-Graphical Edification," de Certeau reads hagiography as "a geography of the sacred," or "a composition of places . . . whose aim is to return after/through a series of displacements to a founding place" (*Writing of History,* 280–81).

98. The narrative achieves this despite the fact that Herrera does not control the disposition of the notebooks themselves and expresses on several occasions great anxiety regarding their fate (*Secretos,* 340, 472).

99. At one point, when Herrera wonders if God will punish Quito for its sins, God warns her to flee (*Secretos,* 325). On several other occasions, Herrera personally takes credit for having persuaded God not to smite either her convent or the city of Quito (263). Here, too, there are local models. Mariana de Jesús Paredes y Flores supposedly gave up her life in 1645 when Quito was threatened by earthquakes. Inspired (or perhaps exasperated) by a long-winded sermon in which a Jesuit priest theatrically offered his own life in order to placate the divine ire that was believed to be causing so many tremors and volcanic eruptions, Mariana is said to have shouted out, "My God, take my life so that these troubles will cease in Quito." She died soon after and was canonized in 1950 (Pérez Pimentel, *Diccionario biográfico del Ecuador,* 5:220; and González Suárez, *Historia general,* 4:222). For a discussion of atonement, see Graziano on Rosa of Lima's vicarious expiation, in *Wounds of Love,* 133–48.

100. For a comprehensive discussion of eighteenth-century political and economic turmoil in Ecuador, see Andrien, *Kingdom of Quito,* 165–89. Kenneth Andrien gives particular attention to the Quito insurrection of 1765, which surely would have loomed large for Herrera as she penned her autobiography.

101. Vargas suggests that atmospheric changes led to these prolonged periods of drought and flooding, as well as repeated epidemics of fever and pox (*Historia de la iglesia,* 232–33); he also points out that the economic crisis put into motion a complex interaction in which more and more people entered convents and monasteries, with detrimental results for the observance of religious life (347–48).

102. According to Andrien, "In many provinces, such long-term structural changes merged with unique local problems to produce economic dislocation, social tensions and political unrest, affecting the entire populace" ("Economic Crisis," 130). Andrien offers a detailed analysis of the political and economic tensions of the period from 1690 to 1778 (*Kingdom of Quit0,*165–89). For a discussion of how Bourbon reform measures affected colonial elites, see Milton, *Many Meanings of Poverty.*

103. McFarlane, "Rebellion," 283, 305–6.

104. Jorge Cañizares-Esguerra notes Juan de Velasco's admiration for Amerindian and white elites and his virulent critique of Andean mestizos (*How to Write,* 251). Herrera would have concurred with Velasco regarding the prevalence of vices typically associated with mestizos, such as drunkenness, idleness, and lying.

105. *Convivencia* is a term used to refer to the coexistence of Christians, Jews, and Muslims in medieval Spain. I use it advisedly here to suggest all its attendant complexity of stability and tension.

106. John Leddy Phelan explains, "Although they belonged to the 'república de los españoles' and in law enjoyed the same rights of Whites, the castes [individuals of mixed ancestry] were in fact socially inferior to those of European descent" (*Kingdom of Quito,* 237). *Castas* enjoyed some upward mobility and, in rare cases, were either able to "pass" or to be legally recognized as white through what what known as *la cédula de gracias al sacar* (an official decree of legitimation issued by the Council of the Indies). In other words, it was possible to "buy" whiteness from the Crown. Those who secured a *cédula de gracias al sacar* tended to be economically privileged and represented a relatively small number of Indians, mestizos, blacks, and mulattoes.

107. Richard Kagan discusses the Aristotelian concept of the city as a locus of civilized life, "the instrument through which Roman *civilitas* would replace the *rusticitas* of the barbarian" (*Urban Images,* 27). For additional discussion of the late colonial city, with particular reference to Mexico City, see Carrera, *Imagining Identity,* 106–25.

108. Gauderman, *Women's Lives,* 4.

109. Gauderman, *Women's Lives,* 5; and Phelan, *Kingdom of Quito,* 238. See also Fisher and O'Hara, *Imperial Subjects,* 3–9.

110. Francisco Javier Eugenio de Santa Cruz y Espejo's satire *El nuevo luciano de Quito* (The new Luciano of Quito), which began circulating in manuscript form in 1779, gives some sense of the general climate of fear and uncertainty that prevailed at the time Herrera was writing *Secretos.* Espejo, a mestizo who despite his humble beginnings became an important physician, committed social reformer, and widely read satirist, participated actively in enlightened circles in late eighteenth-century Quito. Ultimately he was persecuted for his liberal beliefs and imprisoned shortly before his death in 1795. See J. G. Johnson, *Satire in Colonial Spanish America,* 139–54.

111. The same might be said of Félix de Arrate's *Llave del Nuevo Mundo* (the subject of the next chapter), which reflects the preoccupations of Havana's criollo population in the years leading up to the British invasion of that port city.

112. Herrera refers in *Secretos* to "that great Plague" that struck the city in October 1759 (387), and in succeeding chapters she recounts a number of the terrifying visions she experienced during this period in reaction to the general atmosphere of fear, disease, and death.

113. There are numerous minor grammatical errors in this passage, reflecting perhaps Herrera's lack of schooling or the haste and even fearfulness with which she wrote these personal missives.

114. Another vision reflects a more positive and intimate experience of racial mixing: it features the *negrita* slave who had accompanied Herrera in the monastery and died of typhoid fever. The girl appears to Herrera and speaks of spending four years in purgatory. In the vision she wears a large emerald around her neck and, in response to Herrera's somewhat indignant query, she explains that God had given her such a beautiful jewel in recognition of "the good will with which she had left her parents and homeland to come to be in my company, cloistered" (*Secretos,* 160).

115. For a discussion of how *limpieza de sangre* (the concept of blood purity) plays out in the Mexican context as eighteenth-century concerns about *mestizaje* (particularly about corruption of Spanish lineage by black blood), see Martínez, *Genealogical Fictions.* The author notes that in eighteenth-century Mexico "colonial officials expressed . . . concerns about the rising incidence of mestizaje and in particular about Spanish lineages being corrupted by black blood" (243). See also Carrera, *Imagining Identity,* 9–15.

116. See Jouve Martín, *Esclavos.* José Ramón Jouve Martín looks at slavery, literacy, and

colonialism in late seventeenth-century Lima in order to explore the official and extra-official negotiations of blacks, mulattoes, and *zambos* with the lettered city.

117. Regarding the question of indigenous languages and missionary efforts, see D. Weber, *Bárbaros,* 93–102; and del Valle, *Escribiendo desde los márgenes,* 75–82.

118. See Gauderman, *Women's Lives,* 1–5; Minchom, *People of Quito,* 17–23; and Andrien, *Kingdom of Quito,* 37–44.

119. See Hill, "Entering and Exiting Blackness," 43–50.

120. See Herzog, "Meaning of Territory," 163.

121. Later, these criollo fears will be rewritten in a nineteenth-century Ecuadoran foundational myth of *mestizaje,* described by Erika Silva in *Los mitos de la Ecuatorianidad* as a belief in an ethnic and cultural whitening of the Ecuadoran population and the resulting identity crisis of a mestizo nation that denies its *mestizaje* (17–18).

122. Herrera's view differs from that of other eighteenth-century observers of native cultures, like José Antonio de Alzate y Ramírez, who "drew a distinction between 'pure' Indians, who were supposedly found in the countryside, and those 'less-than-pure' Indians of the cities" (O'Hara, *Flock Divided,* 98).

123. For a discussion of *casta* painting, see Katzew, *Casta Painting;* and Carrera, *Imagining Identity.*

124. There is more than a hint of anthropophagical anxiety here, although it is not developed. Carlos Jáuregui proposes that savages and cannibals function in the eighteenth century as an ambivalent sign of the heterogeneity and fragmentation that threatened the whitening and unifying aspirations of the criollo Enlightenment ("El plato más sabroso," 223).

125. Matthew O'Hara discusses various aspects of Bourbon secularization in New Spain in *A Flock Divided,* including measures to eliminate the use of indigenous languages: "Some Spaniards thought that Indian languages posed an even greater challenge to cross-cultural communication in the eighteenth century than at the time of the conquest. . . . The king found the linguistic environment frightfully complex and unacceptable" (63).

126. Herrera does not control the disposition of her notebooks and expresses on several occasions great anxiety regarding their fate (*Secretos,* 340, 472).

127. Pablo Herrera quotes extensively from accounts of the 1768 earthquake, describing the general state of danger and terror (*Ensayos,* 66). It is interesting to note here the nineteenth-century historian's collapsing of geological and moral disorder, though his indictment of the colonial system leads him to condemn criollos and Indians alike (unlike Catalina Herrera's vision of a criollo elite at the mercy of both earthquakes and rebellious Indians). The historian's apocalyptic images—stones raining from the heavens, midday darkness, a terrorized population—are similar to what Catalina Herrera describes.

128. Juan Pablo Dabove writes, "The Latin American lettered city is haunted by monsters. These monsters turn the lettered city's noble dreams into nightmares" (*Nightmares,* 1). As we read Herrera's epistolary narratives, we can identify eighteenth-century stirrings of Dabove's teratology.

129. Franco, *Plotting Women,* 13.

130. Vargas, *Sor Catalina,* 31, 47, 63, 95.

131. Rubial García, "Icons of Devotion," 49. As Alan Greer and Jodi Bilinkoff observe, "For persons of European descent born in one of the American colonies, or Creoles, saints and their cults proved instrumental in their efforts to prove that their homeland, while only recently Christianized, was just as blessed and beloved by God as was the Old World. The holy persons, images, relics, and spaces found in the colonies could be

construed as 'sites of divine presence and favor,' and imagined as both causes and effects of America's greatness" (*Colonial Saints*, xviii). For a discussion of relics in the post-Tridentine Church, see Bouza Alvarez, *Religiosidad contrarreformista*, 32–46.

132. We have seen a similar homecoming in the case of the exiled Jesuit Molina.

133. In 1903, as a delegation of ecclesiastical authorities watched, the remains of the two nuns were deposited in a new shared resting place in the convent (Vargas, *Sor Catalina*, 112–14).

134. This is what Kathryn McKnight refers to, speaking of Madre Castillo in the Colombian literary tradition, as "a reverent glorification of the national mystic" (*Mystic of Tunja*, 7).

CHAPTER 5

These ideas in this chapter were originally set forth in papers delivered at various conferences: "Amalgamación, negociación e intercambio: La economía discursiva del XVIII hispanoamericano" (invited lecture, "La Ilustración hispánica: Un diálogo transatlántico; Simposio Internacional conmemorativo del trigésimo aniversario de *Dieciocho*." Charlottesville, VA, University of Virginia. March, 2008; later published in *Dieciocho at 30 Treinta años de Dieciocho*. Anejos 4: 149–69); "Writing Back to Empire in Eighteenth-Century Cuba: The Virgen de la Caridad del Cobre" (invited lecture, Symposium on Race and the Americas, Southeast Modern Language Association Annual Meeting, Charlotte, NC, November 2006). I would like to thank the organizers and audience at each of these events for their valuable feedback and suggestions.

1. Humboldt, *Ensayo político sobre el reino*, 457 (my translation); qtd. in Marichal, *La bancarrota*, 15.

2. Smith, *Wealth of Nations*, 421 (qtd. in Bernstein, *Power of Gold*, 131). Adam Smith's reference to the "sacred thirst of gold" points, perhaps unwittingly, to the way in which the Spanish search for gold converged with an equally important imperial project, that of religious conversion of the indigenous population.

3. Columbus, *Diario*, 71. The editor-translators have included a concordance; see page 456 for the entry on *oro* (gold). Peter Hulme discusses two discursive threads that are evident in the *Diario*: "Gold was not simply the one element common to both the Oriental discourse and the discourse of savagery; it was in each case the pivotal term around which the others clustered" (*Colonial Encounters*, 22).

4. José de Acosta goes on to describe the gold produced in the Indies, and the various ways of obtaining gold nuggets, gold dust, and gold mixed with other metals (*Natural and Moral History*, 167–69).

5. See Bernstein, *Power of Gold*; and Campos, "West of Eden." Peter Bernstein's book is a fascinating romp that goes from Moses to Richard Nixon; Edmund Valentine Campos offers a reading of the work of Richard Eden, well-known in the fifteenth century in England for his translation of an Italian text on metallurgy that he titled *The Booke of Metals*.

6. Bartolomé Arzáns de Orsúa y Vela's account of the Spanish discovery of Potosí in his *Historia de la villa imperial de Potosí* is one example.

7. Heather Lechtman discusses the different mixtures of copper, gold, and silver, concluding, "Copper was nevertheless the vehicle through which the real achievements in Andean metallurgy took place, and it was on the threshold of assuming a much more important role in Andean life when Andean civilization was cut down by Spanish invaders in search of the land's rich gold and silver deposits" (*America's Vanished Metalsmiths*, 18).

8. "These efforts resulted in the purposeful manufacture of binary and ternary alloys of

copper, silver, and gold, and in a remarkable set of metallurgical and electrochemical procedures for gilding and silvering objects made of copper" (Lechtman, *America's Vanished Metalsmiths,* 15).

9.   One might even posit that such American realities might have led to a reconsideration of Kantian racial categories based on color; that is, the association of Asia with yellow, Africa with black, America with red, and Europe with white. See Greer, Mignolo, and Quilligan, *Rereading the Black Legend;* and Eze, *Race and the Enlightenment, 5.*

10.   Elvira Vilches's *New World Gold* explores how sixteenth-century attitudes and anxieties about gold and money developed in response to the opportunities and disruptions of the imperial enterprise of the Americas: "Concerns about rising prices, the growth of financial markets, and the outflow of bullion returned time and again to the Indies, which were seen as both the source of infinite wealth and a threat to the benefits it was supposed to provide" (11).

11.   A. García-Baquero González suggests that economic historians themselves fall prey to the fascination of gold and silver, overlooking other influences on the economy of the early Americas ("American Gold and Silver," 120).

12.   At the 2000 Modern Language Association annual meeting in Washington, DC (for a session titled "Articulating New Histories and New Identities in Colonial Spanish America," chaired by Mariselle Meléndez), Antony Higgins presented a paper, "Circulating Letters: Archive and Market in the *Lazarillo de ciegos caminantes,*" in which he discussed culturalist and materialist currents in colonial studies. Higgins's untimely death prevented him from developing these ideas, but they are fundamental to my reading in this chapter.

13.   In what follows, I attempt only to provide an introduction to the key economic issues that inform my reading of the eighteenth-century domestication of the discourse of gold. It goes without saying that these issues are complex, and the attendant bibliography extensive. For a more comprehensive discussion of Bourbon economic reforms, see Arcila Farías, *Reformas económicas;* Bakewell, *History;* Bitar Letayf, *Economistas españoles;* Brading, "Bourbon Spain"; Fisher, "Estructuras comerciales"; Johnson and Tándeter, *Essays;* Marichal, *La bancarrota;* Paquette, *Enlightenment, Governance, and Reform;* Pérez Herrero, *Comercio y mercados,* 227–17; and TePaske, "Integral to Empire."

14.   "Thus the Bourbon epoch constituted a relatively brief period of equipoise between the external and domestic sectors of the economy in which, if the rising curve of silver production certainly helped to finance the revival of the military power of the Crown and allowed the colonies to import greater quantities of fine cloth from Europe, it also generated a considerable range of employment which in turn created a lively market for domestic industry and agriculture . . . [a] complex and variegated internal economy which allowed the emergence of an equally complex and distinctive colonial society" (Brading, "Bourbon Spain," 156).

15.   This includes the recovery of the indigenous population—12.6 million—and a growing mestizo population.

16.   Clement Motten describes the effect of New World precious metals on the Spanish economy: "This influx of treasure caused a price revolution which culminated in 1601, but, in an effort to counterbalance sharply declining receipts of American gold and silver during the next fifty years, vellon, or copper money, was coined to such an extent that an even more ruinous inflation was precipitated. Secondly, the influx of treasure tended to make Spain a profitable market for the rest of Europe at the expense of Spanish industry and agriculture" (*Mexican Silver,* 3).

17.   The increasing importance of local economies and intra-imperial networks led to a confusing patchwork of policies. The *Recopilación de leyes de los reynos de las Indias,*

published by the Consejo de Indias in 1681, includes many Hapsburg-era documents on a wide range of economic issues; there is no similar compendium for the Bourbon period (TePaske, "Economic Texts," 120–21).

18. Lynch, *Bourbon Spain,* 142–45; and Pérez Herrero, *Comercio y mercados,* 220–234.

19. Andrien and Johnson, *Political Economy,* 3.

20. González Adánez, "From Kingdoms to Colonies," 113. As later became apparent, the success of the Bourbon reforms had as one consequence the alienation of the criollo elite, who took advantage of moments of crisis to fortify their own economic position and develop their own bureaucratic and military organization.

21. Anthony Pagden explains, "The problem was how to make profitable an empire which had grown up piecemeal, which, under the Hapsburgs, had only ever been a collection of semi-independent states related to each other through the person of the monarch himself, into an economically efficient, politically compliant unit" (*Uncertainties of Empire,* 3).

22. Pagden, "Heeding Heraclides," 328.

23. "By the eighteenth century, however, the regional balance of commercial activity had shifted away from the Mesoamerican and Andean cultural heartlands out towards frontier zones once inhabited by roving tribes or down to the tropical coasts and islands of the Caribbean and Pacific" (Brading, "Bourbon Spain," 143); see also TePaske, "Integral to Empire," 29–41.

24. "Illegal trading in foreign goods and the smuggling of untaxed gold, silver, and mercury were to be persistent, interrelated practices in the viceregalties of New Spain, New Granada, and Peru throughout the eighteenth century" (Hill, *Hierarchy, Commerce, and Fraud,* 108). See Jacob Price's analysis of the relationship between official and illicit commerce for port cities ("Summation"); for a discussion of piracy in the colonial period, see Gerassi-Navarro, *Pirate Novels,* 1–68; and Lane, *Pillaging the Empire,* 181–92.

25. The full title reads: *Nuevo sistema de gobierno económico para América: Con los daños y males que hoy tiene, de lo que participa copiosamente España; Y remedios universales para que la primera tenga considerables ventajas y la segunda mayores intereses* (New system of economic governance for America: With the dangers and problems that it faces today, in which Spain participates fully; And universal remedies so that the former might enjoy considerable advantages and the latter greater profit). Campillo is only one (although arguably the best known) of a group of ministers emerging out of the physiocratic and mercantilist paradigm whose thinking was enormously influential during the first half of the eighteenth century. The members of the group, known as the "proyectistas," also included Gerónimo de Ustariz, Gaspar de Jovellanos, Pedro Rodríguez de Campomanes, and Bernardo Ward. Campillo's interest in maximizing the benefits of Spanish possessions in the Americas is reflected in "Para que tan rica posesión nos dé ventajas," the quote that serves as subheading for this section (*Nuevo sistema,* 63).

26. According to Lynch, Campillo sums up the prevailing economic concerns as "improvement of transatlantic communications; fiscal change; establishment of trading companies; and administrative reform" (*Bourbon Spain,* 147).

27. For a succinct overview of the mercantilist and physiocratic models in eighteenth-century Spain, see Bitar Letayf, *Economistas españoles,* 3–9. In his *Viajes por la América meridional,* Azara offers suggestions for the reform of the economic model of the Río de la Plata region (2:199–202). See also his *Memoria sobre el estado rural del Río de la Plata y otros informes,* where the author makes a physiocratic argument for the advantages of an economy based on agriculture and livestock, as opposed to the limitations of a mining-based economy.

28. González Adánez, "From Kingdoms to Colonies," 113. Pagden notes the undeniable ten-

sion between the political liberties implicit in *comercio libre* and the political culture of a closed and unified Spanish Empire ("Heeding Heraclides," 328).

29.   Campillo y Cosio, *Nuevo sistema de gobierno,* 199. Although Campillo's main focus was on the inefficient administration of the American mines, correcting labor abuses was also part of the reform agenda, since written denunciations had fueled the fires of the so-called Black Legend. Campos attributes the wide dissemination and popularity in the seventeenth and early eighteenth centuries of the writings of Bartolomé de las Casas to the fact that "mining, then, became one of the most powerful tropes of genocide and the site of particularly vehement colonial critique" ("West of Eden," 258).

30.   The title of this section comes from Feijoo's "De la vana y perniciosa aplicación a buscar Tesoros escondidos" (in *Cartas eruditas y curiosas*). Although he is speaking here specifically about false rumors of Moorish gold buried on the Iberian peninsula, Feijoo's general lack of enthusiasm for mining as a productive economic activity reflects the eighteenth-century enlightened reservations regarding mining that we have already discussed with regard to Campillo. For a discussion of the value of the *quinto* (the royal fifth paid to the Crown) in the mid-eighteenth century, see Motten, *Mexican Silver,* 12–14. For a discussion of Humboldt's extensive explanation of the long-standing obsession with gold and silver mining in the New World in chapter 9 of his *Political Essay on the Kingdom of New Spain,* see Prieto, *Mining,* 35–36. The degree to which gold and silver are still understood at the time Humboldt is writing as the default standard for all mining is reflected in this explanation.

31.   For an overview of mining in eighteenth-century Spanish America, see Lavallé, Naranjo, and Santamaría, *La América Española,* 15–36; see also Bakewell, "Mining."

32.   See book 4, chapters 5–13, of Acosta's *Natural and Moral History of the Indies.* Acosta writes, "The reason why silver holds second place among metals is that it is closest to gold in being more durable than any other and less affected by fire, lends itself to being treated and worked better, and even surpasses gold in shining more and ringing clearer" (170).

33.   "Consequently, in 1802, Humboldt found the mining art of New Spain still in its infancy and many miners still using old-fashioned tools exactly like those which had served German miners in the time of Charles V" (Motten, *Mexican Silver,* 14). José Eusebio Llano Zapata also discusses silver mining in the first volume of his *Memorias histórico, físicas, crítico, apologéticas de la América meridional* (156–71).

34.   Amalgamation is a method for refining silver that dates back to the classical period, although its first large-scale use was in the New World after the development of "patio" amalgamation (Bakewell, "Mining," 115–17). See Agricola, *De re metallica* (1556), for an early account. A curious footnote: Herbert Hoover (a mining engineer who later became president of the United States) published in collaboration with his wife a facsimile edition of *De re metallica* for which he wrote an introduction that included comments on Alvaro Alonso Barba's 1640 discussion of amalgamation (Prieto, *Mining,* xi).

35.   Peter Bakewell reminds us of the improvisational and experimental nature of these technological advances ("La minería," 60).

36.   The two classic studies on the Huancavelica mercury mines are by Guillermo Lohmann-Villena (*Las minas de Huancavélica*) and Arthur P. Whitaker (*The Huancavelica Mercury Mine*). At the time there was limited awareness of the pernicious effects of exposure to mercury.

37.   Prieto, *Mining,* 78. This was sometimes also called "beneficio en frío" (Motten, *Mexican Silver,* 22). The bibliography on mining in viceregal America is extensive: see Bakewell, "Mining"; Bargalló, *La amalgamación;* Buechler, *Gobierno, minería y sociedad;* Motten, *Mexican Silver;* and Prieto, *Mining.* "Technological Change in Potosí: The Silver Boom

of the 1570s," an essay by Bakewell, is particularly relevant for this discussion of techno-logical advances in mining (*Mines of Silver,* 75–95).

38. Quoted in Lohmann-Villena, *Las minas de Huancavélica,* 5.

39. Although Arzáns in *La historia de la villa imperial de Potosí* does not deal with the spe-cific details of the mining industry, the Potosino new world that is reflected in the pages of his history is populated by mayors and *corregidores,* bishops and sinners, Indians and *azogueros*—all of them relying on the economic benefits of amalgamation.

40. Johnson and Socolow, "Colonial Centers," 64. Ruth Hill studies legitimate and illegiti-mate commerce in precious metals in chapter 3 of *Hierarchy, Commerce, and Fraud,* giv-ing particular attention to the question of contraband mercury (113). Guillermo Lohm-ann-Villena also acknowledges the complicity in mercury smuggling of unscrupulous administrators who sought to recover their costs without paying the royal *quinto* (*Las minas de Huancavélica,* 470). A curious intersection of the texts and contexts discussed in this book can be noted here: after completing his travels with the La Condamine ex-pedition, Antonio de Ulloa was later named governor of Huancavelica and charged with increasing mercury production and eliminating corruption.

41. Bakewell, "Mining," 63. For a discussion of the ecological and human costs of Andean mercury mining, see Robins, *Mercury, Mining and Empire.*

42. Carlos Prieto includes a panegyric overview of colonial architectural and other cultural achievements related to mining and mining wealth, pointing to the "elegant and impres-sive" School of Mining (built in 1797 in Mexico City) to train mining engineers (*Mining,* 116–27). José de Gálvez's 1765 visit led to the foundation in 1777 of the Royal Mining Court and later to the School of Mining in México (Motten, *Mexican Silver,* 59).

43. Motten, *Mexican Silver,* 53. The *Gazeta de México* played an important role in public discussions of mining technology. The cool reception initally afforded the German mining experts can be explained in part by the publication in the *Gazeta de México* of a letter Elhuyar had written criticizing the *mineros* of New Spain, leading to a lively debate, chronicled in a number of issues published in 1784, among Alzate, Bartolache, and a number of other eighteenth-century Mexican *ilustrados* (Motten, *Mexican Silver,* 55).

44. Qtd. in Prieto, *Mining,* 80.

45. Buechler, *Gobierno, minería y sociedad,* 85.

46. The final payment to the faculty was made in 1784 (ibid., 97).

47. Acosta is apparently the first Spanish author to treat the subject of mercury mines in Alto Perú (Lohmann-Villena, *Las minas de Huancavélica,* 20). Fernando Montesinos in his *Anales del Peru* (1566) elaborates on the story (Lohmann-Villena, *Las minas de Huancavélica,* 22–23); the Inca Garcilaso describes them as well in the *Comentarios reales.*

48. Prieto, *Mining,* 79.

49. Lohmann-Villena, *Las minas de Huancavélica,* 21–23. The various versions of the legend all involve indigenous informants who share their knowledge of the mines with Amador de Cabrera. Garcés had found smaller deposits earlier; see Portela, "El beneficio."

50. Lohmann-Villena, *Las minas de Huancavélica,* 31–38.

51. The *Ordenanzas del Nuevo Cuaderno,* approved in 1584 by Philip II in an attempt to consolidate all mining codes, were not updated until 1783. They stipulated that Spanish subjects and natives as well as foreigners were entitled to discover or work in any silver mines, both those already discovered or to be discovered (Prieto, *Mining,* 91; see also Motten, *Mexican Silver*).

52. Motten, *Mexican Silver,* 15.

53. Ibid., 17.

54. We might consider the *chicha* (corn-based alcoholic beverage) economy to be yet an-

other manifestation of this commercial and social amalgamation; see Mangan, *Trading Roles.*

55. The manuscript of the *Historia,* which covers the years 1545 to 1735, was unfinished at the time of Arzáns's death in 1736; his son Diego added eight chapters.

56. Arzáns explains (without any apparent etymological authority) that the name Potosí comes from the Quechua word meaning "it gave off a loud thunderous noise" (*Historia de la villa,* 1:27).

57. See Galarza Sepúlveda's doctoral thesis, "City, Myth, and Morality in Bartolome Arzáns's *Historia de la villa imperial de Potosi:* A Criollo Project," and her article "Of Legends and Lack."

58. One of the most striking examples of this narrative maneuver is the story of the first criollo child born in Potosí, who managed to survive despite the hostile climate and altitude—a Potosino Christ who was born on December 25 (Arzáns, *Historia de la villa,* 1:193).

59. West, "Aboriginal Metallurgy," 49.

60. See Lafaye, *Quetzalcóatl y Guadalupe;* Brading, *Mexican Phoenix;* and the collection of essays edited by Greer and Bilinkoff, *Colonial Saints.*

61. TePaske, "Integral to Empire," 38.

62. Scholars of the eighteenth century are well aware of the obvious contradictions inherent in the flowering of slavery at a time when human rights were articulated and celebrated; see Festa, "Tropes and Chains," 322; and S. Johnson, *Social Transformation,* 9. Royal slaves were able to engage in small-scale farming in the countryside or, in the case of the *cobreros,* mining; many served in the militia.

63. Díaz, *Virgin,* 10. The "patria chica" of El Cobre "may have represented one way available to people of African descent to reimagine, remap, and root their identities within the societies of the New World in a nondiasporic manner" (11).

64. See Buechler, *Gobierno, minería y sociedad,* 16–19, on the *azogueros'* negotiation of their role in the Andean economy. Of course, there are numerous examples of mining entrepreneurship already in place by the mid-seventeenth century; Bakewell explores one such example in *Silver and Entrepreneurship.*

65. Díaz, *Virgin,* 8.

66. Speaking of the Potosí silver mines, Campillo asks, "What expense has not been wasted in those mines through the ignorance of their Directors, and what treasures must there be in the tailings and scraps that they must have thrown away as useless?" (*Nuevo sistema de gobierno,* 197).

67. According to the 1709 account of the priest Don Juan Antonio Pérez, "To subsist, some of them ingeniously search for copper grains among the tailings that remain from the time of the mines; and they also extract it industriously from the rocks that had been thrown away during the searches leading to the discovery of [new] veins of copper" (Díaz, *Virgin,* 202). *Cobreros* also mined copper from the river that ran through the town; Díaz emphasizes that women were largely responsible for mining in El Cobre (203).

68. During the Bourbon era the old *encomienda* system of local labor was gradually broadened to include voluntary and paid labor (Brading, "Bourbon Spain," 142).

69. Diaz, *Virgin,* 244.

70. Ibid., 74.

71. Portuondo Zúñiga, *La Virgen,* 299. One of the models for the *cobrera* Virgin is the Spanish Virgen de la Caridad de Illescas.

72. Díaz lists the following versions of the story of the Virgen de la Caridad del Cobre: 1703, Onofre de Fonseca's manuscript; 1766, Julián José Bravo's manuscript; 1782, Bernardo

Ramírez's transcription, probably of Fonseca's text; and 1829, Paz y Ascanio's revision of Ramírez's text, which became the first published version (*Virgin*, 129–37).

73. One version adds an episode dating from the time of the conquest and narrates the conversion of a cacique to Catholicism by means of the same effigy later found by Juan Moreno and his companions (Díaz, *Virgin*, 136). The 1766 account written by Julián José Bravo (after the earthquake that occurred in that same year) changes the name of one of the Indians to Juan Diego, thus echoing the Guadalupan legend; it reflects the criollo patriotic fervor of the moment and includes accounts of many miracles supposedly performed by the Virgen de la Caridad del Cobre in order to protect the island residents from threats of naval attack by the British.

74. Portuondo Zúñiga, *La Virgen*, 256.

75. Díaz, *Virgin*, 98.

76. Ibid., 142–45.

77. Arrate explains that the work's title comes from a 1634 royal *cédula* that refers to the city as both *llave* (key) and *antemural* (a type of gateway fortification) (*Llave*, 8).

78. "Once the island cycle of exploration, settlement, and exploitation of available mineral resources and Indian labor in the early sixteenth century had run its course, Cuba and the surrounding islands were almost abandoned" (S. Johnson, *Social Transformation*, 19).

79. Although Johnson focuses on the final decades of the century, following the British attack on Havana, she begins with an overview of the city of Havana in the 1760s that draws heavily on Arrate's account (*Social Transformation*, 18–38). See also Kuethe, "Havana," 13–39.

80. "However, until its shocking fall to British forces, the city did not enjoy the royal attention lavished upon more prosperous cities, such as the mining centers of Mexico and Peru" (S. Johnson, *Social Transformation*, 19). Other developments that occurred after 1761, when Arrate completed *Llave del Nuevo Mundo*, fall outside the scope of the present study but include the successful negotiation in 1765 by the residents of Havana of a liberalization of trade policy (whose extension throughout the other viceregalties was stymied by the Esquilache rebellion in Madrid). Thanks in part to these negotiations, Havana "retained but expanded its historic function as a way station and entrepot" (Kuethe, "Havana," 27). Arrate writes before the 1767 expulsion of the Jesuits, before José de Gálvez's tenure as minister of the Indies began in 1776, and before Charles III's death in 1788.

81. Clune, *Cuban Convents*, 15. By the end of the eighteenth century, Cuba's fiscal expansion had eclipsed that of the Río de la Plata region (TePaske, "Integral to Empire," 31–32).

82. See Le Riverend Brusone, "Carácter y significación"; Le Riverend Brusone, "Prólogo," xix; Naranjo Orovio and Mallo, *Cuba*; and Parcero Torre, *La pérdida*, 15–38.

83. José Cuello reminds us of the importance of municipal governments for the success of Bourbon reforms ("Economic Impact," 301).

84. A transoceanic economy based on commerce and defense was something Havana shared with other Atlantic port cities such as Philadelphia and Rio de Janeiro. There were, of course, several factors unique to Havana, among them the large slave and free black population and the role played by sugar and tobacco, all of which would become increasingly important in the late eighteenth and early nineteenth centuries. See Knight and Liss, *Atlantic Port Cities*.

85. Patrick O'Flanagan's use of the term "gateway" mirrors Arrate's foregrounding of "llave" and "antemural" in the title of his history (*Port Cities*, 12).

86. Allan Kuethe, while acknowledging the military and commercial significance of Havana's strategic location, emphasizes the human factor implicit in "*habanero* entrepreneurial and political skills" ("Havana," 25).

87. S. Johnson, *Social Transformation*, 12.

88. Juan Luis Martín (who has written an effusive tribute to Arrate, situating him in a distinguished Cuban family history) suggests that Arrate (like Oviedo y Baños) suffered frustrations in his career common to many criollos ("José Martín Félix," 41).

89. The bibliography on Arrate is fairly limited, although he does merit brief mentions in a number of works presenting a panoramic view of Cuban literary history. See Almodóvar Múñoz, *Antología crítica,*123–40; Henríquez Ureña, *Antología cubana;* Lazo, *La literatura cubana;* and Le Riverend Brusone, "Carácter y significación."

90. As Julio Le Riverend Brusone notes, the fact that Arrate is a member of the municipal oligarchy helps to explain his hyperbolic praise of his native city and his vigorous defense of its criollo inhabitants ("Carácter y significación," 327); see also Almodóvar Muñoz, who argues that the work should be read as a reflection of the classist interests of the eighteenth-century Havana oligarchy (*Antología crítica,* 125).

91. In addition to the *Llave del Nuevo Mundo,* Arrate wrote a number of poems and a play (which has never been located). According to Juan Luis Martín, Arrate was included in Eguiara y Eguren's *Bibliotheca Mexicana* (1755), although Eguiara does not seem to have known about *Llave* ("José Martín Félix," 51).

92. See Hill's "Arrate's *La Habana.*" She argues that *Llave del Nuevo Mundo* "appears to be the earliest extant report of Cuba written by a Cuban, although both a religious history and a general history of Cuba preceded it" (329), and she seems to be suggesting that there might be a royal questionnaire lurking in the background of Arrate's project. She cautions, however, that Arrate's writing of his report, much in the manner of a civil servant, should not be mistaken for the freelance and speculative reformism that characterized eighteenth-century "proyectistas" (329). According to Raimundo Lazo, Arrate's local focus reflects an emerging Cuban patriotism (*La literatura cubana,* 33).

93. Le Riverend Brusone, "Carácter y significación," 158.

94. *Llave del Nuevo Mundo* was later reprinted in *Los tres primeros historiadores de la Isla de Cuba,* along with works by Urrutia and Valdés (Habana, 1876), and in later editions in 1949 and 1964. According to Le Riverend Brusone, the mid-eighteenth century is the founding moment of Cuban historiography ("Prólogo," xii). Onofre de Fonseca, discussed earlier in this chapter, might also be included here.

95. According to Le Riverend Brusone, Arrate is an avowed propagandist for his native city ("Comentarios," 337); for Lazo, the "cubanness" of Arrate's work is its most significant element (*La literatura cubana,* 408). Their comments are a reflection of the degree to which allegiance to city and allegiance to nation are joined.

96. As Le Riverend Brusone acknowledges, the history is organized according to a clear plan (despite its unwieldy title and the reader's first impression of arbitrariness and disorder): geography, economy, government, civil and ecclesiastical institutions, and culture ("Prólogo," xiv).

97. We see a similar line of reasoning in the writings of Oviedo y Baños, Molina, and even Herrera—the sense of belatedness and a somewhat aggrieved awareness of one's exclusion from history.

98. In the 1830 publication of *Llave,* the editors' defensive posture vis-à-vis Cuban history comes across in their introduction, which was reprinted as part of the 1949 edition (xxxiii).

99. Juan Luis Martín includes an annotated list of the works and authors that Arrate consulted ("José Martín Félix," 55–60).

100. Arrate might be seen here as joining a chorus of writers (beginning with Fray Ramón Pané and including Alejo Carpentier's narrator in *Los pasos perdidos*) who lament the shortage of paper in the New World that often frustrates their attempts to write.

101. This remark comes as part of a discussion of previous writers who have praised Cuba

and to whom Arrate feels indebted. The list includes Gil González, Juan Díaz de la Calle, Pedro Cuber, Father Francisco de la Florencia, and Francisco Dávila Orejón (*Llave*, 7).

102. Arrate refers later to Havana's role in "the subsistence of the vast empire of the Indies, as opulent for its riches as their recovery is difficult due to distance" (*Llave*, 59). The 1949 editor adds a note to explain that the failure to sufficiently fortify and staff the fort would turn out to be an important factor in the success of the British attack in 1762—events that fall beyond the scope of Arrate's history.

103. Copper was used for similar practical purposes in Mexico, and locally mined copper sulphate played a key role in the amalgamation processes in Mexico and the Andes from the late-sixteenth century onward, as I noted earlier. I discuss the role of copper in coinage at the conclusion of this chapter.

104. According to Le Riverend Brusone, Arrate recognized that slavery had certain advantages in resolving labor shortages and felt strongly that the benefits of conversion to Christianity mitigated some of slavery's harsher implications but never dealt directly with the question of its legitimacy ("Comentarios," 333–34). David Brading notes Arrate's laments regarding the extinction of Cuba's indigenous population and the resulting need to employ African slave labor (*First America*, 312–13). See also Hill's reading of Arrate's "joining of the indigenous population and fiscal issues" ("Arrate's *La Habana*," 336).

105. Chapter 9 discusses the importance of walls and fortifications, chapter 10 is a detailed description of the Castillo del Morro, and chapter 11 focuses on the fortification of the plaza.

106. "Economic studies overwhelmingly concentrate on the spread of sugar cultivation and its impact domestically and internationally . . . and with few exceptions, Cuban historiography has been held hostage to studies of sugar, slavery, colonialism, and dependence" (S. Johnson, *Social Transformation*, 1).

107. Kuethe, "Havana," 24. "The Mexican *situado* (subsidy) rose from 437,000 pesos in the 1750s to an annual average around 1,485,000 pesos from 1763–1769" (S. Johnson, *Social Transformation*, 42). See also Marichal and Souro Mantecón, "Silver and *Situados*."

108. Arrate repeats his point about Havana's key role in protecting Spain's other possessions in the Americas (*Llave*, 65).

109. There is a long tradition in colonial historiography of an author's careful manipulation of royal prerogatives and duties, of which Las Casas's prologue to the *Brevísima relación* is an excellent example.

110. Humboldt includes a similar, expanded list of ships built in Havana (*Island of Cuba*, 85–89).

111. Humboldt continues, "Havana has been the naval port of Mexico, as I have stated in another work, and received annually (until 1808) from its treasury more than one million eight hundred thousand dollars" (*Island of Cuba*, 77). But later developments lessened Havana's dependence on Mexico, leading Humboldt to observe, "The Abbé Raynal has said, at a time when its agriculture contributed, in sugar and coffee, barely two millions to the commerce of the world, 'The island of Cuba alone may be worth a kingdom to Spain'" (179).

112. Arrate's frequent references to Gerónimo de Ustariz throughout *Llave* reflect the fact that eighteenth-century economic practices and projects were part of a grand scheme to reform and invigorate the Spanish transatlantic economy. Arrate's focus on seventeenth- and eighteenth-century events distinguishes his work from that of his contemporary Urrutia (who only deals with the sixteenth century); we see a similar preoccupation in Oviedo y Baños and Molina.

113. *Costumbrismo* is a nineteenth-century literary genre that emerged in Spain and Spanish America, focusing on detailed descriptions of regional or national customs.

114. "The eighteenth century was the period when the debate as to the meaning and value-laden status of luxury came into prominence" (Berry, *Idea of Luxury,* 126). For a discussion of the role that "civilizing goods" played in eighteenth-century Spanish America's material culture, see A. J. Bauer, *Goods, Power, History,* 85–128.

115. See Herzog, *Defining Nations,* for an exploration of how notions of citizenship and *vecindad* developed over time in response to local circumstances in medieval and early modern Spain, and in colonial Spanish America.

116. "To clinch his argument, he recalled that in 1702 the concurrent deaths of the bishop and governor in Havana had left all the chief positions of command in the city held by creoles, men who at a time of great threat from British forces, had distinguished themselves and kept the island firmly on the side of King Philip" (Brading, *First America,* 312).

117. Le Riverend Brusone, "Comentarios," 339. See chapter 27 on the Royal Pontifical University of San Jerónimo where Arrate, in response to Martí's remarks about the lack of teachers and poor quality of the instruction, lists a number of the university's distinguished alumni (*Llave,* 143).

118. Juan Luis Martín also sees Arrate as vigorously defending criollo prerogatives ("José Martín Félix," 41–42). Hill insists, however, "There is no hint of a Creole identity that goes beyond regional pride in Arrate's *La Habana descripta*" ("Arrate's *La Habana,*" 332).

119. Sherry Johnson agrees that the Cubans' receptivity to empire—more accommodating than that of other viceregal criollos—stemmed from their sense that "their best hope for commercial success and political power was to remain part of the Spanish Empire" (*Social Transformation,* 6).

120. Arrate continues his argument about the unbroken lineage that links the nobles who first founded the city of Havana with its current residents (*Llave,* 99). Although these comments correspond to his larger project of celebrating Havana, Arrate is clearly prickly about a more specific insult to the residents of the city—a romance written by the Marqués de S. Andrés—to which he alludes in these pages.

121. I am referring to chapters 21 and 22. I am indebted to Brittany Anderson for fruitful conversations about the rhetoric of enumeration that characterizes much eighteenth-century writing.

122. *Fineza,* a seventeenth-century concept that means "delicacy or subtlety of manipulation or discrimination; refinement, refined grace," figures frequently in the writings of Sor Juana Inés de la Cruz (Tavard, *Juana,* 139; see also Paz, *Sor Juana,* 517).

123. Despite the conventional view of the eighteenth century as a secular age, Carlos Marichal notes the key role of ecclesiastical institutions in maintaining the Bourbon economy in New Spain (*La bancarrota,* 27).

124. For a discussion of the importance of parish religion in eighteenth-century New Spain, see Taylor, *Magistrates of the Sacred;* see also Farriss, *Crown and Clergy.*

125. Arrate includes a long list of these festivals in chapter 45. Of course, the Virgen de la Caridad del Cobre would be one of the most important of these. Juan Luis Martín suggests that Arrate uses Marian devotion in the Americas as a capital claim ("José Martín Félix," 48); I would concur.

126. See chapter 37, "Del monasterio de religiosas de Santa Clara." See also Clune, *Cuban Convents.*

127. John J. Clune quotes Bishop Augustín Morell de Santa Cruz, who wrote in 1765 that private benefactors of the Convent of Santa Clara provided it with financial assistance "far beyond what their means allowed" (qtd. in *Cuban Convents,* 9). The bishop had been charged several years earlier with assessing the conditions in the convent with particular

regard to compliance with rules and constitution. In his report he noted many instances of excess and disorder, including entertaining visitors and family in private cells, gossiping, indulging in sweets instead of conforming with communal meals, and not wearing their veils when going out in the Havana heat—complaints similar to those we discussed in the previous chapter (Clune, *Cuban Convents,* 24–29).

128. Clune, *Cuban Convents,* 19. According to Nancy Farriss, Charles III "evaluated the Church and the clergy in terms of their contribution to economic progress and maintenance of empire" (*Crown and Clergy*).

129. In *The Silver King,* Edith Bourstein Couturier discusses the "spiritual dimensions of material wealth" as understood in eighteenth-century Mexico; see also Burns, *Colonial Habits;* and Taylor, *Magistrates of the Sacred.*

130. Qtd. in Clune, *Cuban Convents,* 12.

131. For a discussion of eighteenth-century reforms related to minors, see O. González, "Down and Out."

132. Arrate notes somewhat defensively, "I am also obligated by the desire to show that these climates are not as barren of good men or virtuous gentlemen as is said, nor do the offspring of Castilians become bastardized here like good seeds in sterile earth" (*Llave,* 232). He adds that *indianos* often find that they are blocked from ascending to positions of power and influence in Spain; he may be using the term *indianos* to refer to American-born Spaniards.

133. Arrate divides his list into (1) ecclesiastics; (2) individuals in the areas of literature, university, and law; and (3) military personnel. Last to be listed—in a separate category—are his brothers, Santiago and Manuel de Arrate (*Llave,* 250).

134. Meléndez, in *Raza, género e hibridez,* and Hill, in *Hierarchy, Commerce, and Fraud,* have made essential contributions to the critical bibliography on Carrió de la Vandera.

135. David Weber discusses the importance of commerce in local interactions between indigenous and viceregal functionaries in *Bárbaros.*

136. Carrió de la Vandera, *El lazarillo,* 266.

137. Since every European colonial territory had its own currency, exchanges and conversions were complicated. However, Spanish gold—pieces of eight, or the "peso"—remained the standard, as one contemporary observer explained in 1782: "The various coins which have circulated in America have undergone different changes in their value, so that there is hardly any which can be considered as a general standard, unless it be Spanish dollars" (US secretary of finance Robert Morris, January 15, 1782, qtd. in McCusker, *Money and Exchange,* 3).

138. Carrió de la Vandera, *El lazarillo,* 266.

139. Hill discusses the metaphorical resonance of Concolorcorvo's name, noting that color in a rhetorical and poetical sense can mean embellishment, trope, or figure; she emphasizes that "the semantics of color included simulation, or feigning, and the *Diccionario de la lengua castellana* in Carrió's time associated *color* with dissimulation" (*Hierarchy, Commerce, and Fraud,* 244).

140. Pérez Herrero, *Comercio y mercados,* 234–37.

141. 1730 real cédula, in *Cedulario americano,* ed. Muro Orejón, xxv–xxvi.

142. A similar situation existed in late sixteenth-century Spain: "With the fiscal crisis of the 1590s, the Crown flooded the country with worthless copper. The transparency of gold and silver pieces remained, but the balance between commodity money and fiat money . . . collapsed. As unsound money drove away wholesome coins, and copper's legal value increased, the ground of value became a matter of deep anxiety" (Vilches, *New World Gold,* 8). Vilches notes that in the Indies, "the quest for gold is continually haunted by the fear that gold might not be as pure as it appeared" (133).

143. Foucault is quoting here from an anonymous compendium: "Money was a fair measure because it signified nothing more than its power to standardize wealth on the basis of its own material reality as wealth" (in *Order of Things*, 169).

144. "First, the value of things will no longer proceed from the metal itself; it establishes itself by itself, without reference to the coinage, according to the critera of utility, pleasure, or rarity" (Shell, *Money, Language, and Thought*, 176). With respect to coins that enter into circulation carrying the seal of the prince of the state to authorize their value, Marc Shell asks if these still have value once the inscription marking them as official circulating coinage has disappeared, and he affirms that they do: "However much they may lose their status as coins, they are still substantial metal commodities" (15).

145. In this context it's fascinating to remember that Garcés, who was in charge of initial attempts to mine mercury at Huancavelica, initially confused the mercury there with another base metal, given the lack of reddish color with which he has always associated the metal (see Lohmann-Villena, *Las minas de Huancavélica*, 11–23).

146. There is also a very brief chapter about gold in the "Book of deposits" included in Oviedo y Valdés's *Historia general y natural* (Enguita Utrilla, "El oro de las Indias," 274).

147. In "Precious Metals," M. J. Sallnow argues that in the pre-Hispanic central Andes, gold and silver treasure was not for trade or exchange, but rather for the symbolic display of state treasure or as personal adornment.

148. See the fascinating exchange of e-mail posts in a thread titled "18th Century coins," which took place in July 2000 on the H-LatAm discussion network (*h-latam@h-net.msu.edu*). Contributors included Jovita Baber, David Weiland, and Robert Patch. See also Burzio, *Diccionario*.

CONCLUSION

1. Alonso, *Burden of Modernity*, 8.

2. Chiaramonte, *El mito*, 7.

3. The authors I've examined in this book might be considered examples of what Mignolo calls "border thinking"—that is, what is known from the perspective of imperial borders.

4. Lund is referring here to Silviano Santiago's classic essay, "Latin American Discourse: The Space In-Between."

5. Lund calls for a rereading of Latin America in terms of its historical specificity and "in its dialectical relations with Eurocentrism" ("Hybridity, Genre, Race," 116).

6. This is true despite the unfinished nature of so many of the projects launched during the Hispanic eighteenth century—Juan Bautista Muñoz's *Historia del Nuevo Mundo* and Eguiara y Eguren's *Bibliotheca mexicana* being only two examples. For a discussion of Muñoz, see Cañizares-Esguerra, *How to Write*, 190–203; Slade, "Enlightened Architextures"; and Stalnacker, *Unfinished Enlightenment*.

7. "What Is Enlightenment" (*Foucault Reader*, 15). In *Enlightenment against Empire*, Sankar Muthu writes, "It is high time, then, that we pluralize our understanding of 'the Enlightenment' both for reasons of historical accuracy and because, in doing so, otherwise hidden or understudied moments of Enlightenment-era thinking will come to light" (264).

8. This was the case with Molina and Herrera. After several earlier attempts proved unsuccessful, the remains of exiled Jesuit Francisco Javier Clavigero were also repatriated in 1970 amid lavish homecoming ceremonies; one particularly enthusiastic report announced, "Clavijero Returns Alive" (Worthen, "Mexican Historian Returns Home," 457). For a discussion of similar instances of reburials in the history of the United States, see Kammen, *Digging Up the Dead*.

Bibliography

Acosta, José de. *Natural and Moral History of the Indies.* Edited by Jane E. Mangan. Introduction by Walter D. Mignolo. Translated by Frances López Morillas. Durham, NC: Duke University Press, 2002.

Adorno, Rolena. *The Polemics of Possession in Spanish American Narrative.* New Haven, CT: Yale University Press, 2007.

Agricola, Georgius. *De re metallica.* Translated from the first Latin edition of 1556 by Herbert Clark Hoover and Louis Henry Hoover. New York, NY: Dover, 1950.

Aguirre Anaya, Carlos, and Marcela Dávalos, eds. *Los espacios públicos de la ciudad: Siglos XVIII y XIX.* Mexico City, Mexico: Casa Juan Pablo/Instituto de Cultura de la Ciudad de México, 2002.

Akerman, James R., ed. *The Imperial Map.* Chicago, IL: University of Chicago Press, 2009.

Albanese, Denise. *New Science, New World.* Durham, NC: Duke University Press, 1996.

Albornoz, Víctor Manuel, Pablo Herrera, and Remigio Crespo Toral, eds. *Prosistas de la República.* Puebla, Mexico: J. M. Cajica, 1959.

Aldridge, Owen, ed. *The Ibero-American Enlightenment.* Urbana: University of Illinois Press, 1971.

Alfageme, C., and N. Almazán. *Féliz de Azara, ingeniero y naturalista.* Huesca, Spain: Instituto de Estudios Altoaragoneses, CSIS, 1987.

Almodovar Muñoz, Carmen. *Antología crítica de la historiografía cubana (época colonial).* Havana, Cuba: Editorial Pueblo y Educación, 1986.

Alonso, Carlos J. *The Burden of Modernity: The Rhetoric of Cultural Discourse in Spanish America.* New York, NY: Oxford University Press, 1998.

Alvarez Cuartero, Izaskun. "Las Sociedades Económicas de Amigos del País en Cuba (1787–1832): Una aportación al pensamiento ilustrado." In Naranjo Orovio and Mallo Gutiérrez, *Cuba,* 35–43. Madrid, Spain: Doce Calles, 1991.

Alvarez de Miranda, Pedro. *Palabras e ideas: El léxico de la ilustración temprana en España (1680–1760).* Madrid, Spain: Real Academia Española, 1992.

Alvarez López, Enrique. "Azara y Darwin." *Revista de Indias* 83 (1961): 63–93.

———. "Comentarios y anotaciones acerca de la obra de don Félix de Azara. *Miscelánea Americana* (Instituto Gonzalo Fernández de Oviedo) 3 (1952): 9–62.

———. "Ensayo acerca de las ideas biológicas de Azara." *Boletín de la Sociedad Española de Historia Natural* 8 (1933): 19–49.

———. "Félix de Azara, precursor de Darwin." *Revista de Occidente* 43 (1934): 149–66.

———. *Félix de Azara: Siglo XVIII.* Madrid, Spain: M. Aguilar, n.d.

Amaya, José Antoni. *Celestino Mutis y la Expedición Botánica.* Madrid, Spain: Debate, 1986.

Anderson, Benedict. *Imagined Communities: Reflections on the Origins and Spread of Nationalism.* London, UK: Verso, 1983.

Andrien, Kenneth J. "Economic Crisis, Taxes and the Quito Insurrection of 1765." *Past and Present* 129 (1990): 104–31.

———. *The Kingdom of Quito, 1690–1830: The State and Regional Development.* Cambridge, UK: Cambridge University Press, 1995.

Andrien, Kenneth J., and Lyman L. Johnson, eds. *The Political Economy of Spanish America in the Age of Revolution, 1750–1850.* Albuquerque: University of New Mexico Press, 1994.

Anés Alvarez, Gonzalo. *La Corona y America en el siglo de las Luces.* Madrid, Spain: Marcial Pons/Asociación Francisco López de Gómara, 1994.

Antei, Giorgio. *La invención del reino de Chile: Gerónimo de Vivar y los primeros cronistas chilenos.* Bogotá, Colombia: Caro y Cuervo, 1989.

Appiah, Kwame Anthony. *Cosmopolitanism: Ethics in a World of Strangers.* New York, NY: Norton, 2006.

Aravamudan, Srinivas. *Tropicopolitans: Colonialism and Agency, 1688–1804.* Durham, NC: Duke University Press, 1999.

Arboleda, L. C. "La ciencia y el ideal de ascenso social de los criollos en el virreinato de la Nueva Granada." In Lafuente and Sala Catalá, 285–316.

Arcila Farías, Eduardo. *Reformas económicas del siglo XVIII en Nueva España.* 2 vols. 1955. Mexico City: Sep/Setentas, 1974.

Arciniegas, German. *Latin America: A Cultural History.* New York, NY: Knopf, 1968.

Arenal, Electa, and Stacey Schlau. *Untold Sisters: Hispanic Nuns in Their Own Works.* Albuquerque: University of New Mexico Press, 1989.

Arias, Santa. "Geografía, imperio e iglesia bajo la huella de la Ilustración: Conciencia criolla y los espacios del imaginario cartográfico jesuita durante el siglo XVIII." In *Poéticas de lo criollo: La transformación del concepto "criollo" en las letras hispanoamericanas (siglo XVI al XIX),* edited by Juan M. Vitulli and David M. Solodkow, 331–52. Buenos Aires, Argentina: Corregidor, 2009.

Arias, Santa, and Mariselle Meléndez, eds. *Mapping Colonial Spanish America: Places and Commonplaces of Identity, Culture, and Experience.* Lewisburg, PA: Bucknell University Press, 2002.

Arias Divito, Juan Carlos. *Las expediciones científicas españolas durante el siglo XVIII: Expedición botánica de Nueva España.* Madrid, Spain: Cultura Hispánica, 1968.

Arrate, José Martín Félix de. *Llave del Nuevo Mundo.* Mexico City: Fondo de Cultura Económica, 1949.

Arregui Martínez, Luis. "Un diplomático aragonés: Don José Nicholeas de Azara y su intervención en la extinción de la Compañía de Jesus." *Universidad: Revista de cultura y vida universitaria* October–December 1934: 861–927.

Arrom, José Juan. "La Virgen del Cobre: Historia, leyenda y símbolo sincrético." In *Certidumbre de América,* 2nd ed., 184–214. Madrid, Spain: Gredos, 1971.

Arzáns de Orsúa y Vela, Bartolomé. *Historia de la villa imperial de Potosí.* Edited by Lewis Hanke and Gunnar Mendoza. 3 vols. Providence, RI: Brown University Press, 1965.

Asín, Francisco Javier. *Aragón y América.* Madrid, Spain: MAPFRE, 1992.

Astrain, Antonio. *Jesuitas, guaraníes y encomenderos: Historia de la Compañía de Jesús en el Paraguay.* Asunción: Centro de Estudios Paraguayos "Antonio Guasch," 1995.

Avramescu, Catalin. *An Intellectual History of Cannibalism.* Princeton, NJ: Princeton University Press, 2009.

Azara, Félix de. *Apuntamientos para la historia natural de los páxaros del Paraguay y del Río de la Plata.* 3 vols. Madrid, Spain: 1802–1805.

———. *Apuntamientos para la historia natural de los quadrúpedos del Paraguay y Río de la*

Plata. 2 vols. Madrid, Spain: 1802. Translation of *Essais sur l'histoire naturelle des quadru-pèdes de la province du Paraguay.* 2 vols. Paris, France: 1801; 1838.

———. *Descripción e historia del Paraguay y del Río de la Plata.* 2 vols. Madrid, Spain: 1847.

———. *Descripción general del Paraguay.* Edited by Andrés Galera Gómez. Madrid, Spain: Alianza, 1990.

———. *Diario de un reconocimiento de guardias.* In *Colección de obras y documentos relativos a la historia antigua y moderna de las provincias del Río de la Plata.* Vol. 6, edited by Pedro de Angelis. Buenos Aires, Argentina: Imprenta del Estado, 1837.

———. *Geografía física y esférica de las provincias del Paraguay y Misiones guaraníes.* Prologue by Rodolfo R. Schuller. Montevideo, Uruguay: Anales del Museo Nacional de Montevideo/Talleres A. Barreiro y Ramos, 1904.

———. *Memoria sobre el estado rural de Río de la Plata y otros informes.* Introduction by Julio César González. Buenos Aires, Argentina: Bajel, 1943.

———. *Viajes por la América meridional.* 2 vols. Madrid, Spain: Espasa Calpe, 1941.

———. *Voyages dans l'Amérique méridionale.* Edited by C. A. Walckenaer. Notes by G. Cuvier and M. Sonnini. 4 vols. Paris, France: Dentu, 1809.

Baker, Keith Michael, and Peter Hanns Reill, eds. *What's Left of Enlightenment? A Postmodern Question.* Stanford, CA: Stanford University Press, 2001.

Bakewell, Peter. *A History of Latin America: 1450 to the Present,* 2nd ed. Oxford, UK: Blackwell, 2004.

———. *Miners of the Red Mountain: Indian Labor in Potosí, 1545–1650.* Albuquerque: University of New Mexico Press, 1984.

———, ed. *Mines of Silver and Gold in the Americas.* Vol. 10 of *An Expanding World: The European Impact on World History, 1450–1800.* Burlington, VT: Ashgate, 1997.

———. "Mining in Colonial Spanish America." In Bethell, *Cambridge History,* 2:105–51.

———. *Silver and Entrepreneurship in Seventeenth-Century Potosí: The Life and Times of Antonio López de Quiroga.* 1988. Dallas, TX: Southern Methodist University Press, 1994.

Balkan, Evan L. *The Wrath of God: Lope de Aguirre, Revolutionary of the Americas.* Albuquerque: University of New Mexico Press, 2011.

Barba, A[lvaro] A[lonso]. *Arte de los metales en que se enseña el verdadero beneficio de los de oro y plata por azogue: El modo de fundirlos todos y cómo se han de finar y apartar unos de otros.* 1640. New York, NY: Wiley, 1923.

Barbier, Jacques A. "Imperial Policy towards the Port of Veracruz, 1788–1808: The Struggle between Madrid, Cádiz and Havana Interests." In *The Economies of Mexico and Peru during the Late Colonial Period, 1760–1810,* edited by Nils Jacobsen and Hans-Jürgen Puhle, 240–51. Berlin, Germany: Colloquium Verlag, 1986.

Bargalló, Modesto. *La amalgamación de los minerales de plata en Hispanoamérica colonial.* Mexico City: Compañía Fundidora de Fierro y Acero de Monterrey, 1969.

Barker, Francis, Peter Hulme, and Margaret Iversen, eds. *Cannibalism and the Colonial World.* Cambridge, UK: Cambridge University Press, 1998.

Barrera, Antonio. "Local Herbs, Global Medicines: Commerce, Knowledge, and Commodities in Spanish America." In Smith and Findlen, *Merchants and Marvels,* 163–81. New York, NY: Routledge, 2002.

Barrera-Osorio, Antonio. *Experiencing Nature: The Spanish American Empire and the Early Scientific Revolution.* Austin: University of Texas Press, 2006.

Barrientos, Juan José. "Aguirre y la rebelión de los marañones." *Cuadernos Americanos: Nueva Época* 2.8 (1988): 92–115.

Batllori, Miguel. *La cultura hispano-italiana de los jesuitas expulsos: Españoles, hispanoamericanos, filipinos, 1767–1814.* Madrid, Spain: Gredos, 1966.

Bauer, Arnold J. *Goods, Power, History: Latin America's Material Culture.* Cambridge, UK:
    Cambridge University Press, 2001.

Bauer, Ralph. "Atlantic Triangulations: Teaching the Eighteenth-Century Americas across
    Imperial Boundaries." *Dieciocho* 30.1 (2007): 7–31.

———. *The Cultural Geography of Colonial American Literatures.* Cambridge, UK: Cambridge
    University Press, 2003.

Bauer, Ralph, and José Antonio Mazzotti, eds. *Creole Subjects in the Colonial Americas: Em-
    pires, Texts, Identities.* Chapel Hill: University of North Carolina Press; Williamsburg, VA:
    Omohundro Institute of Early American History, 2009.

Baulny, Olivier. "La colonización de la Banda Oriental vista a través del epistolario de Félix
    de Azara (cartas inéditas a Miguel de Lastarria)." *Investigaciones y Ensayos* 10 (1968):
    239–63.

———. *Félix de Azara, un aragonais précurseur de Darwin.* Paris, France: Marrimpouey
    Jeune, 1968.

Beddall, Barbara. "The Isolated Spanish Genius—Myth or Reality? Félix de Azara and the
    Birds of Paraguay." *Journal of the History of Biology* 16.2 (1983): 225–58.

———. "'Un Naturalista Original': Don Félix de Azara, 1746–1821." *Journal of the History of
    Biology* 8.1 (1975): 15–66.

Bender, John, and Michael Marrinan, eds. *Regimes of Description: In the Archive of the Eigh-
    teenth Century.* Stanford, CA: Stanford University Press, 2005.

Bengoa, José. *Conquista y barbarie: Ensayo crítico acerca de la conquista de Chile.* Santiago,
    Chile: Ediciones SUR, 1992.

———. *Historia de un conflicto: El estado y los mapuches en el siglo XX.* Santiago: Editorial
    Planeta Chilena, 1999.

———. *Historia del pueblo mapuche: Siglo XIX y XX.* 1985. Santiago, Chile: LOM Editores,
    2000.

Bernier, Marc André, Clorinda Donato, and Hans-Jürgen Lüsebrink, eds. *Jesuit Accounts of the
    Colonial Americas: Intercultural Transfers, Intellectual Disputes, and Textualities.* Toronto,
    Canada: University of Toronto Press, forthcoming.

Bernstein, Peter L. *The Power of Gold: The History of an Obsession.* New York, NY: Wiley, 2000.

Berry, Christopher J. *The Idea of Luxury: A Conceptual and Historical Investigation.* Cam-
    bridge, UK: Cambridge University Press, 1994.

Betancor, Orlando. "Matter, Form, and the Generation of Metals in Alvaro Alonso Barba's *Arte
    de los metales.*" In "Science in Translation: The Commerce of Facts and Artifacts in the
    Transatlantic Spanish World," edited by Miruna Achim, special issue, *Journal of Spanish
    Cultural Studies* 8.2 (2007): 117–33.

Bethell, Leslie, ed. *The Cambridge History of Latin America.* 2 vols. Cambridge, UK: Cam-
    bridge University Press, 1984.

Bickham, Troy. *Savages within the Empire: Representations of American Indians in Eighteenth-
    Century Britain.* Oxford, UK: Oxford University Press, 2005.

Bitar Letayf, Marcelo. *Economistas españoles del siglo XVIII: Sus ideas sobre la libertad de com-
    ercio con Indias.* Madrid, Spain: Ediciones Cultura Hispánica, 1968.

Bizzell, Patricia, and Bruce Herzberg, eds. *The Rhetorical Tradition from Classical Times to the
    Present.* Boston, MA: St. Martin's Press, 1990.

Black, Jeremy. *Europe and the World: 1650–1830.* New York, NY: Routledge, 2001.

Bleichmar, Daniela. "Painting as Exploration: Visualizing Nature in Eighteenth-Century Colo-
    nial Science." *Colonial Latin American Review* 15.1 (2006): 81–104.

———. *Visible Empire: Botanical Expeditions and Visual Culture in the Hispanic Enlighten-
    ment.* Chicago, IL: University of Chicago Press, 2012.

Bleichmar, Daniela, Paula S. De Vos, Kristin Huffine, and Kevin Sheehan, eds. *Science in the Spanish and Portuguese Empires, 1500-1800.* Stanford, CA: Stanford University Press, 2009.

Boccara, Guillaume. "Etnogénesis Mapuche: Resistencia y restructuración entre los indígenas del Centro-Sur de Chile (siglos XVI–XVIII)." *Hispanic American Historical Review* 79.3 (August 1999): 425–61.

———. *Los vencedores: Historia del pueblo Mapuche en la época colonial.* Santiago, Chile: Linea Editorial IIAM, 2007.

Bolaños, Alvaro Félix, and Gustavo Verdesio, eds. *Colonialism Past and Present: Reading and Writing about Colonial Latin America Today.* Albany: State University of New York Press, 2002.

Bonilla, Heraclio, ed. *El sistema colonial en la América Española.* Barcelona, Spain: Crítica, 1991.

Bourguet, Marie-Noëlle. "Landscape with Numbers: Natural History, Travel and Instruments in the Late Eighteenth and Early Nineteenth Centuries." In Bourguet, Licoppe, and Sibum, *Instruments, Travel and Science,* 96–125.

Bourguet, Marie-Noëlle, Christian Licoppe, and H. Otto Sibum, eds. *Instruments, Travel and Science: Itineraries of Precision from the Seventeenth to the Twentieth Century.* London, UK: Routledge, 2002.

Bouza Alvarez, José Luis. *Religiosidad contrarreformista y cultura simbólica del barroco.* Madrid, Spain: Consejo Superior de Investigaciones Científicas, 1990.

Bowen, Margarita. *Empiricism and Geographical Thought: From Francis Bacon to Alexander von Humboldt.* Cambridge, UK: Cambridge University Press, 1981.

Brading, David A. "Bourbon Spain and Its American Empire." In *The Cambridge History of Latin America,* 1:389–439. Cambridge, UK: Cambridge University Press, 1984.

———. *The First America: The Spanish Monarchy, Creole Patriots, and the Liberal State, 1492–1867.* Cambridge, UK: Cambridge University Press, 1993.

———. *Mexican Phoenix: Our Lady of Guadalupe: Image and Tradition across Five Centuries.* Cambridge, UK: Cambridge University Press, 2003.

———. *Miners and Merchants in Bourbon Mexico, 1763–1810.* Cambridge, UK: Cambridge University Press, 1971.

Bradley, James E., and Dale K. Van Kley, eds. *Religion and Politics in Enlightenment Europe.* Notre Dame, IN: University of Notre Dame Press, 2001.

Briones Toledo, Hernán. *El abate Juan Ignacio Molina: Ensayo crítico introductorio a su vida y obra.* Santiago, Chile: Andrés Bello, 1968.

Brokaw, Galen. *A History of the Khipu.* Cambridge, UK: Cambridge University Press, 2010.

———. "Toward Deciphering the Khipu." *Journal of Interdisciplinary History* 35.4 (2005): 571–89.

Brown, Judith C. *Immodest Acts: The Life of a Lesbian Nun in Renaissance Italy.* Oxford, UK: Oxford University Press, 1986.

Brown, Kendall W. "La recepcion de la tecnologia minera española en las minas de Huancavelica, siglo XVIII." In *Saberes andinos: Ciencia y tecnología en Bolivia, Ecuador y Peru,* edited by Marcos Cueto, 59–90. Lima: Instituto de Estudios Peruanos, 1995.

Buechler, Rose Marie. *Gobierno, minería y sociedad: Potosí y el "Renacimiento" Borbónico (1776–1810).* 2 vols. La Paz: Biblioteca Minera Boliviana, 1989.

Buesa Olivar, Tomás. "Sobre Cosme Bueno y algunos de sus coetáneos." In *Homenaje a Fernando Antonio Martínez,* 332–72. Bogotá, Colombia: Instituto Cara y Cuervo, 1979.

Buisseret, David. "Jesuit Cartography in Central and South America." In Gagliano and Ronan, *Jesuit Encounters,* 113–62.

Burkholder, Mark A. "Bureaucrats." In Hoberman and Socolow, *Cities and Society,* 77–103.

————. *Politics of a Colonial Career: José Baquíjano and the Audiencia of Lima.* 2nd ed. Wilmington, DE: Scholarly Resources, 1990.

Burkholder, Mark A., and D. S. Chandler. *From Impotence to Authority: The Spanish Crown and the American Audiencias, 1687–1808.* Columbia: University of Missouri Press, 1977.

Burkholder, Mark A., and Lyman L. Johnson. *Colonial Latin America.* 5th ed. New York, NY: Oxford University Press, 2004.

Burnett, D. Graham. *Masters of All They Surveyed: Exploration, Geography, and a British El Dorado.* Chicago, IL: University of Chicago Press, 2000.

Burns, Kathryn. *Colonial Habits: Convents and the Spiritual Economy of Cuzco, Peru.* Durham, NC: Duke University Press, 1999.

————. *Into the Archive: Writing and Power in Colonial Peru.* Durham, NC: Duke University Press, 2010.

Burzio, Humberto F. *Diccionario de la moneda hispanoamericana.* Santiago, Chile: Fondo Histórico y Bibliográfico José Toribio Medina, 1956.

Bush, Andrew. "Lyric Poetry in the Eighteenth and Nineteenth Centuries." In González Echevarría and Pupo-Walker, *Cambridge History of Latin American Literature,* 1:375–400.

————. *The Routes of Modernity: Spanish American Poetry from the Early Eighteenth to the Mid-Nineteenth Century.* Lewisburg, PA: Bucknell University Press, 2002.

Butterwick, Richard, Simon Davies, and Gabriel Sánchez Espinosa, eds. *Peripheries of the Enlightenment.* Oxford, UK: Voltaire Foundation, 2008.

Bynum, Caroline Walker. "' . . . And Woman His Humanity': Female Imagery in the Religious Writing of the Later Middle Ages." In *Gender and Religion: On the Complexity of Symbol,* edited by Caroline Walker Bynum, Steven Harrell, and Paula Richman, 257–88. Boston, MA: Beacon, 1986.

————. *Holy Feast and Holy Fast.* Berkeley: University of California Press, 1987.

Byrne, James M. *Religion and the Enlightenment from Descartes to Kant.* Louisville, KY: Westminster John Knox Press, 1996.

Cabeza de Vaca, Alvar Núñez. *Naufragios.* Edited by Juan Francisco Maura. Madrid, Spain: Cátedra, 1989.

Calatayud Arinero, Mária de los Angeles. *Pedro Franco Dávila, primer director del Real Gabinete de Historia Natural fundado por Carlos III.* Madrid, Spain: Consejo Superior de Investigaciones Científicas, 1988.

Calloway, Colin G. *New Worlds for All: Indians, Europeans, and the Remaking of Early America.* Baltimore, MD: Johns Hopkins University Press, 1997.

Campal, Esteban. *Azara y su legado al Uruguay.* Montevideo, Uruguay: Ediciones de la Banda Oriental, 1969.

Campillo y Cosio, José del. *Nuevo sistema de gobierno económico para la América.* 1743. Edited by Manuel Ballesteros Gaibrois, 1789. Oviedo, Spain: Grupo Editorial Asturiano, 1993.

Campomanes, Pedro Rodríguez, conde de. *Reflexiones sobre el comercio español a Indias.* Edited by Vicente Llombart Rosa, 1762. Madrid, Spain: Instituto de Estudios Fiscales, 1988.

Campos, Edmund Valentine. "West of Eden: American Gold, Spanish Greed, and the Discourse of English Imperialism." In Greer, Mignolo, and Quilligan, *Rereading the Black Legend,* 247–69.

Campuzano, Luisa, ed. *Mujeres latinoamericanas: Historia y cultura, siglos XVI al XIX.* Havana, Cuba: Fondo Editorial Casa de las Américas, 1997.

Cañeque, Alejandro. *The King's Living Image: The Culture and Politics of Viceregal Power in Colonial Mexico.* New York, NY: Routledge, 2004.

Cañizares-Esguerra, Jorge. "The Devil in the New World: A Transnational Perspective." In Cañizares-Esguerra and Seeman, *Atlantic in Global History,* 21–37.

———. "How Derivative Was Humboldt? Microcosmic Nature Narratives in Early Modern Spanish American and the (Other) Origins of Humboldt's Ecological Sensibilities." In Schiebinger and Swan, *Colonial Botany,* 148–65.

———. *How to Write the History of the New World: Histories, Epistemologies, Identities, in the Eighteenth-Century Atlantic World.* Stanford, CA: Stanford University Press, 2001.

———. "Iberian Colonial Science." *Isis* 96 (2005): 64–70.

———. *Nature, Empire, and Nation: Explorations of the History of Science in the Iberian World.* Stanford, CA: Stanford University Press, 2006.

———. "New World, New Stars: Patriotic Astrology and the Invention of Indian and Creole Bodies in Colonial Spanish America, 1600–1650." *American Historical Review* 104.1 (1999): 33–68.

———. *Puritan Conquistadors: Iberianizing the Atlantic, 1550–1700.* Stanford, CA: Stanford University Press, 2006.

Cañizares-Esguerra, Jorge, and Erik R. Seeman, eds. *The Atlantic in Global History, 1500–2000.* Upper Saddle River, NJ: Pearson Prentice Hall, 2007.

Carey, Daniel, and Lynn Festa, eds. *Postcolonial Enlightenment.* Oxford, UK: Oxford University Press, 2009.

Carrera, Magali. *Imagining Identity in New Spain: Race, Lineage, and the Colonial Body in Portraiture and Casta Paintings.* Austin: University of Texas Press, 2003.

Carrió de la Vandera, Alonso. *El lazarillo de ciegos caminantes.* Edited by Emilio Carilla. Barcelona, Spain: Labor, 1973.

Carrión, María M. *Arquitectura y cuerpo en la figura autorial de Teresa de Jesús.* Barcelona, Spain: Anthropos, 1994.

Casanova Guarda, Holdenis. *Las rebeliones auracanas del siglo XVIII: Mito y realidad.* Temuco, Chile: Universidad de la Frontera, 1987.

Castellanos, Juan de. *Un nuevo reino imaginado: Las elegías de varones ilustres de Indias.* Edited by Luis Fernando Restrepo. Bogotá, Colombia: Intituto Colombiano de Cultura Hispánica, 1999.

Castillo Martos, Manuel. *Minería y metalurgía: Intercambio tecnólogico y cultural entre América y Europa durante el período colonial español.* Seville, Spain: Muñoz Moya y Montraveta, 1994.

Castro Arenas, Mario. "Lope de Aguirre o el punto de vista del soldado." In *Homenaje a Luis Alberto Sánchez,* edited by Robert G. Mead, 143–62. Madrid, Spain: Insula, 1983.

Castro-Gómez, Santiago. *La hybris del punto cero: Ciencia, raza, e ilustración en la Nueva Granada.* Bogotá, Colombia: Pontificia Universidad Javeriana, 2005.

Certeau, Michel de. *Heterologies: Discourse on the Other.* Minneapolis: University of Minnesota Press, 1986.

———. *The Writing of History.* Translated by Tom Conley. New York, NY: Columbia University Press, 1988.

Cervantes, Fernando. *The Devil in the New World: The Impact of Diabolism in New Spain.* New Haven, CT: Yale University Press, 1994.

Chartier, Roger. *The Order of Books: Readers, Authors and Libraries in Europe between the Fourteenth and Eighteenth Centuries.* Stanford, CA: Stanford University Press, 1994.

Chiaramonte, José Carlos. *La Ilustración en el Río de la Plata: Cultura eclesiástica y cultura laica durante el Virreinato.* 2nd ed. Buenos Aires, Argentina: Sudamericana, 2007.

———. *El mito de los orígenes en la historiografía latinoamericana.* Buenos Aires, Argentina: Facultad de Filosofía y Letras-Universidad de Buenos Aires, 1993.

————. "Modificaciones del pacto imperial." In *Inventando la nación: Iberoamérica, siglo XIX*, edited by Antonio Annino and François-Xavier Guerra, 85–113. Mexico City: Fondo de Cultura Económica, 2003.

————, ed. *Pensamiento de la Ilustración: Economía y sociedad iberoamericanas en el siglo XVIII*. Caracas, Venezuela: Ayacucho, 1979.

Choudhury, Mita. *Convents and Nuns in Eighteenth-Century French Politics and Culture*. Ithaca, NY: Cornell University Press, 2004.

Chowning, Margaret. *Rebellious Nuns: The Troubled History of a Mexican Convent, 1752–1863*. Oxford, UK: Oxford University Press, 2006.

Church, G. E. "La Plata Region in the Eighteenth Century." *Geographical Journal* 27.3 (1906): 296–297.

Clark, Fiona. "The *Gazeta de Literatura de México* and the Edge of Reason: When Is a Periphery Not a Periphery?" In Butterwick, Davies, and Sánchez Espinosa, *Peripheries*, 251–64.

Clark, William, Jan Golinski, and Simon Schaffer, eds. *The Sciences in Enlightened Europe*. Chicago, IL: University of Chicago Press, 1999.

Clavigero, Francisco Javier. *Historia antigua de México*. Mexico City: Porrúa, 1987.

————. *The History of Mexico*. New York, NY: Garland, 1979.

Clune, John J., Jr. *Cuban Convents in the Age of Enlightened Reform (1761–1807)*. Gainesville: University Press of Florida, 2008.

Coatsworth, John H. "The Mexican Mining Industry in the Eighteenth Century." In Bakewell, *Mines of Silver and Gold*, 263–82. .

Colahan, Clark. *The Visions of Sor María de Agreda: Writing, Knowledge and Power*. Tucson: University of Arizona Press, 1994.

Colás, Alejandro. *Empire*. Cambridge, UK: Polity, 2007.

Collier, Simon. *Ideas and Politics of Chilean Independence, 1808–1833*. Cambridge, UK: Cambridge University Press, 1967.

Columbus, Christopher. *The Diario of Christopher Columbus's First Voyage to America 1492–1493*. Translated by Oliver Dunn and James E. Kelley, Jr. Norman: University of Oklahoma Press, 1989.

Conley, Tom. *The Self-Made Map: Cartographic Writing in Early Modern France*. Minneapolis: University of Minnesota Press, 1996.

Corona Baratech, Carlos E. *José Nicolás de Azara: Un embajador español en Roma*. Zaragoza, Spain: Institución Fernando el Católico (CSIS), 1948.

Cortés, Hernán. *Letters from Mexico*. Translated and edited by Anthony Pagden. Introduction by J. H. Elliott. New Haven, CT: Yale University Press, 1986.

Cosgrove, Denis E., and Stephen Daniels, eds. *The Iconography of Landscape: Essays on the Symbolic Representation, Design, and Use of Past Environments*. Cambridge, UK: Cambridge University Press, 1988.

Cottom, Daniel. *Cannibals and Philosophers: Bodies of Enlightenment*. Baltimore, MD: Johns Hopkins University Press, 2001.

Couturier, Edith Boorstein. *The Silver King: The Remarkable Life of the Count of Regla in Colonial Mexico*. Albuquerque: University of New Mexico Press, 2003.

Craib, Raymond B. "Cartography and Power in the Conquest and Creation of New Spain." *Latin American Research Review* 35.1 (2000): 7–36.

Cro, Stelio. *The Noble Savage: Allegory of Freedom*. Waterloo, Canada: Wilfrid Laurier University Press, 1990.

Cuello, José. "The Economic Impact of the Bourbon Reforms and the Late Colonial Crisis of Empire at the Local Level: The Case of Saltillo, 1777–1817." *Americas* 44.3 (1988): 301–23.

Cueto, Marcos, ed. *Saberes andinos: Ciencia y tecnología en Bolivia, Ecuador y Peru.* Lima: Instituto de Estudios Peruanos, 1995.

Dabove, Juan Pablo. *Nightmares of the Lettered City: Banditry and Literature in Latin America, 1816–1929.* Pittsburgh, PA: University of Pittsburgh Press, 2007.

Damrosch, Leo, ed. *The Profession of Eighteenth-Century Literature: Reflections on an Institution.* Madison: University of Wisconsin Press, 1992.

Daniels, Christine, and Michael V. Kennedy, eds. *Negotiated Empires: Centers and Peripheries in the Americas, 1500–1820.* New York, NY: Routledge, 2002.

Darwin, Charles. *The Origin of Species and The Voyage of the Beagle.* New York, NY: Everyman's Library, 2003.

———. *Variations of Animals and Plants under Domestication.* 2 vols. In *The Works of Charles Darwin,* vols. 19–20, edited by Paul H. Barrett and R. B. Freeman. London, UK: William Pickering, 1988.

———. *The Voyage of the Beagle.* In *Origin,* 1–517.

Daston, Lorraine, and Katharine Park. *Wonders and the Order of Nature, 1150–1750.* New York, NY: Zone Books, 1998.

Davis, Elizabeth B. *Myth and Identity in the Epic of Imperial Spain.* Columbia: University of Missouri Press, 2000.

Deacon, Philip. "Spain and Enlightenment." In *The Cambridge History of Spanish Literature,* edited by David T. Gies, 293–42. Cambridge, UK: Cambridge University Press, 2004.

Deans-Smith, Susan. "Special Section: Nature and Scientific Knowledge in the Spanish Empire." *Colonial Latin American Review* 15.1 (2006): 29–38.

de Certeau, Michel. *See under* Certeau, Michel de.

Delaporte, François. *Nature's Second Kingdom: Explorations of Vegetality in the Eighteenth Century.* Translated by Arthur Goldhammer. Cambridge, MA: MIT Press, 1982.

del Valle, Ivonne. *Escribiendo desde los márgenes: Colonialismo y jesuitas en el siglo XVIII.* Mexico City: Siglo XXI, 2009.

De Vos, Paula S. "Natural History and the Pursuit of Empire in Eighteenth-Century Spain." *Eighteenth-Century Studies* 40.2 (2007): 209–39.

———. "Research, Development and Empire: State Support of Science in the Later Spanish Empire." *Colonial Latin American Review* 15.1 (2006): 55–79.

Díaz, María Elena. "Conjuring Identities: Race, Nativeness, Local Citizenship, and Royal Slavery on an Imperial Frontier (Revisiting El Cobre, Cuba)." In Fisher and O'Hara, *Imperial Subjects,* 197–224.

———. *The Virgin, the King, and the Royal Slaves of El Cobre: Negotiating Freedom in Colonial Cuba, 1670–1780.* Stanford, CA: Stanford University Press, 2000.

Díaz del Castillo, Bernal. *The History of the Conquest of New Spain.* Edited by David Carrasco. Albuquerque: University of New Mexico Press, 2008.

Díaz Sánchez, Ramón. *Evolución de la historiografía en Venezuela.* Caracas, Venezuela: Ediciones del Ministerio de Educación, Dirección de Cultura y Bellas Artes, 1956: 3–19.

———. "Historia de una historia: José Agustín Oviedo y Baños, pionero de nuestra cultura." *Revista Nacional de Cultura* (Caracas) 2.25 (1941): 3–18.

Dillehay, Tom D. *Monuments, Empires, and Resistance: The Araucanian Polity and Ritual Narratives.* Cambridge, UK: Cambridge University Press, 2007.

Dobado González, Rafael. "El monopolio estatal del mercurio en Nueva España durante el siglo XVIII." *Hispanic American Historical Review* 82.4 (2002): 685–718.

Domínguez Ortiz, Antonio. *Carlos III y la España de la Ilustración.* 1988. Madrid, Spain: Alianza, 2005.

———. *Sociedad y estado en el siglo XVIII español.* 1976. Barcelona, Spain: Ariel, 1990.

Dussel, Enrique. *The Invention of the Americas: Eclipse of "the Other" and the Myth of Modernity*. New York, NY: Continuum, 1995.

Earle, Rebecca. "Creole Patriotism and the Myth of the 'Loyal Indian.'" *Past and Present* 172 (2001): 125–45.

Edney, Matthew H. "The Irony of Imperial Mapping." In Akerman, *Imperial Map,* 11–45.

———. *Mapping an Empire: The Geographical Construction of British India, 1765–1843*. Chicago, IL: University of Chicago Press, 1997.

———. "Reconsidering Enlightenment Geography and Map Making: Reconnaissance, Mapping, Archive." In Livingstone and Withers, *Geography and Enlightenment,* 165–98.

Egido, Teófanes, Javier Burrieza Sánchez, and Manuel Revuelta González, eds. *Los jesuitas en España y en el mundo hispánico*. Madrid, Spain: Marcial Pons, 2004.

Eguiara y Eguren, José de. *Prologos a la "Biblioteca mexicana."* Edited by Agustín Millares Carlo. Mexico City: Fondo de Cultura Económica, 1984.

Elliott, J. H. *Empires of the Atlantic World: Britain and Spain in America 1492–1830*. New Haven, CT: Yale University Press, 2006.

Engstrand, Iris H. W. *Spanish Scientists in the New World*. Seattle: University of Washington Press, 1981.

Enguita Utrilla, José María. "El oro de las Indias: Datos léxicos en la *Historia general y natural de Fernández de Oviedo*." In *América y la España del siglo XVI: Homenaje a Gonzalo Fernández de Oviedo, Cronista de Indias,* edited by Francisco de Solano y Fermín del Pino, 1:273–94. Madrid, Spain: Instituto Gonzalo Fernández de Oviedo, 1982.

Ercilla, Alonso de. *La Araucana*. Edited by Marcos A. Morínigo and Isaías Lerner. 2 vols. Madrid, Spain: Castalia, 1987.

Espinosa, Januario. *El abate Molina, uno de los precursores de Darwin*. Santiago, Chile: Zig-Zag, 1946.

Ewalt, Margaret R. "Crossing Over: Nations and Naturalists in *El Orinoco Ilustrado;* Reading and Writing the Book of Orinoco Secrets." *Dieciocho* 29.1 (2006): 7–31.

———. "Father Gumilla, Crocodile Hunter? The Function of Wonder in *El Orinoco Ilustrado*." In Millones Figueroa and Ledezma, *El saber de los jesuitas,* 305–33.

———. *Peripheral Wonders: Nature, Knowledge, and Enlightenment in the Eighteenth-Century Orinoco*. Lewisburg, PA: Bucknell University Press, 2008.

Eze, Emmanuel Chukwude, ed. *Race and the Enlightenment: A Reader*. Oxford, UK: Blackwell, 1997.

Farriss, Nancy M. *Crown and Clergy in Colonial Mexico, 1759–1821: The Crisis of Ecclesiastical Privilege*. London, UK: Athlone, 1968.

Febrés, Andrés. *Gramática araucana o sea arte de la lengua general de los indios de Chile*. 1765. Edited by Juan M. Lársen. Buenos Aires, Argentina: Juan A. Alsina, 1884.

Feijoo, Benito Jerónimo. *Cartas eruditas y curiosas*. Edited by Agustín Millares Carlo. Madrid, Spain: Espasa Calpe, 1944.

———. *Teatro crítico universal*. Edited by Agustín Millares Carlo. 3 vols. Madrid, Spain: Espasa Calpe, 1941.

———. *Teatro crítico universal*. 1728. Biblioteca Feijoniana, *www.filosofia.org/feijoo.htm*.

Ferguson, Adam. *An Essay on the History of Civil Society*. Edited by Fania Oz-Salzberger. 1767. Cambridge, UK: Cambridge University Press, 1995.

Fernández-Armesto, Felipe. *The Americas: A Hemispheric History*. New York, NY: Modern Library, 2003.

Fernández de Oviedo y Valdés, Gonzalo. *Historia general y natural de las Indias*. Edited by Juan Pérez de Tudela Bueso. 5 vols. Biblioteca de Autores Españoles. Madrid, Spain: Atlas, 1959.

————. *Sumario de la natural historia de las Indias.* Edited by Alvaro Baraibar. Madrid, Spain: Iberoamericana; Frankfurt, Germany: Vervuert, 2010.

Fernández-Armesto, Felipe. *The Americas: A Hemispheric History.* New York, NY: Modern Library, 2003.

Fernández Restrepo, Luis, ed. *Un nuevo reino imaginado: Las elegías de varones ilustres de Indias de Juan de Castellanos.* Bogotá: Instituto Colombiano de Cultura Hispánica, 1999.

Festa, Lynn. "Tropes and Chains: Figures of Exchange in Eighteenth-Century Depictions of the Slave Trade." In Wells and Stewart, *Interpreting Colonialism,* 322–44.

Findlen, Paula. *Possessing Nature: Museums, Collecting, and Scientific Culture in Early Modern Italy.* Berkeley: University of California Press, 1994.

Fisher, Andrew B., and Matthew D. O'Hara, eds. *Imperial Subjects: Race and Identity in Colonial Spanish America.* Durham, NC: Duke University Press, 2009.

Fisher, John R. "Estructuras comerciales en el mundo hispánico y el reformismo borbónico." In *El reformismo borbónico: Una visión interdisciplinar,* edited by Augustín Guimerá, 109–43. Madrid, Spain: CSIC/Alianza Universidad, 1996.

————. "El impacto del comercio libre en América durante el último cuarto del siglo XVIII." In Fontana and Bernal, *El "comercio libre,"* 29–38.

————. "Mining and Imperial Trade in Eighteenth-Century Spanish America." In Flynn, Giráldez, and Glahn, *Global Connections,* 123–31.

————. "Silver Production in the Viceroyalty of Peru, 1776–1824." In Bakewell, *Mines of Silver,* 283–301.

Fliegelman, Jay. *Declaring Independence: Jefferson, Natural Language and the Culture of Performance.* Stanford, CA: Stanford University Press, 1993.

Flynn, Dennis O., Arturo Giráldez, and Richard von Glahn. *Global Connections and Monetary History, 1470–1800.* Burlington, VT: Ashgate, 2003.

Foerster, Rolf. *Jesuitas y Mapuches, 1593–1767.* Santiago, Chile: Universitaria, 1996.

Fontana, Josep, and Antonio Miguel Bernal, eds. *El "Comercio Libre" entre España y América Latina, 1765–1824.* Madrid, Spain: Fundación Banco Exterior, 1987.

Fontecilla Larrain, Arturo. "En torno a la personalidad del Abate Molina." *Revista chilena de historia y geografía* 23 (1932): 71–82.

Foucault, Michel. *The Foucault Reader,* edited by Paul Rabinow. New York, NY: Pantheon, 1984.

————. *The Order of Things: An Archaeology of the Human Sciences.* New York, NY: Vintage Books/Random House, 1973. Translation of *Les Mots et les Choses.* Paris, France: Gallimard, 1966.

Fourney, Diane R. "Ideas of Enlightenment." *Eighteenth-Century Studies* 37.4 (2004): 689–92.

Fox, Christopher, Roy Porter, and Robert Wokler, eds. *Inventing Human Science: Eighteenth-Century Domains.* Berkeley: University of California Press, 1995.

Franco, Jean. *Plotting Women: Gender and Representation in Mexico.* New York, NY: Columbia University Press, 1989.

Frías Núñez, Marcelo. *Tras El Dorado vegetal: José Celestino Mutis y la Real Expedición Botánica del Nuevo Reino de Granada (1783–1808).* Seville, Spain: Diputación de Sevilla, 1994.

Friede, Juan. *Los Welser en la conquista de Venezuela.* Caracas, Venezuela: Edime, 1961.

Fuchs, Barbara. *Mimesis and Empire: The New World, Islam, and European Identities.* Cambridge, UK: Cambridge University Press, 2001.

Furlong, Guillermo. *Naturalistas argentinos durante la dominación hispánica.* Buenos Aires, Argentina: Huarpes, 1948.

Gaceta de México. Facsimile edition. Mexico City: Rolston-Gain, 1983.

Gagliano, Joseph A., and Charles E. Ronan, eds. *Jesuit Encounters in the New World: Jesuit Chroniclers, Geographers, Educators and Missionaries in the Americas, 1549–1767.* Rome, Italy: Institutum Historicum, 1997.

Galarza Sepúlveda, Denise. "City, Myth, and Morality in Bartolome Arzáns's *Historia de la villa imperial de Potosi:* A Criollo Project." Diss., Emory University, 2002.

———. "Of Legends and Lack: The Economy of Criollo Discourse in the *Historia de la villa imperial de Potosí.*" *Revista de Estudios Hispánicos* 43.1 (2008): 3–29.

Galera Gómez, Andrés, ed. *Descripción general del Paraguay,* by Féliz de Azara. Madrid, Spain: Alianza, 1990.

———. *La ilustración española y el conocimiento del Nuevo Mundo.* Madrid, Spain: Centro de Estudios Históricos/Consejo Superior de Investigaciones Científicas, 1988.

Galster, Ingrid. *Aguirre o La posteridad arbitraria: La rebelión del conquistador vasco Lope de Aguirre en historiografía y ficción histórica (1561–1992).* 1996. Bogotá, Colombia: Editorial Universidad de Rosario/Editorial Universidad Javeriana, 2011.

García-Baquero González, A. "American Gold and Silver in the Eighteenth Century: From Fascination to Accounting." In Flynn, Giráldez, and Glahn, *Global Connections,* 107–21.

García-Bedoya, Carlos. "El discurso andino en el Perú colonial: Los textos del renacimiento inca." In *Asedios a la heterogeneidad cultural: Libro de homenaje a Antonio Cornejo Polar,* edited by José Antonio Mazzotti and U. Juan Zevallos Aguilar, 197–216. Philadelphia, PA: Asociación Internacional de Peruanistas, 1996.

Garner, Richard L. "Long-Term Silver Mining Trends in Spanish America: A Comparative Analysis of Peru and Mexico." In Bakewell, *Mines of Silver,* 225–62.

Garraway, Doris L. "Of Speaking Natives and Hybrid Philosophers: Lahontan, Diderot, and the French Enlightenment Critique of Colonialism." In Carey and Festa, *Postcolonial Enlightenment,* 207–39.

Gascoigne, John. "The Ordering of Nature and the Ordering of Empire: A Commentary." In Miller and Reill, *Visions of Empire,* 107–13.

Gauderman, Kimberly. *Women's Lives in Colonial Quito: Gender, Law, and Economy in Spanish America.* Austin: University of Texas Press, 2003.

Gerassi-Navarro, Nina. *Pirate Novels: Fictions of Nation Building in Spanish America.* Durham, NC: Duke University Press, 1999.

Gerbi, Antonello. *The Dispute of the New World: The History of a Polemic, 1750–1900.* 1955. Pittsburgh, PA: University of Pittsburgh Press, 1973.

———. *Nature in the New World: From Christopher Columbus to Gonzalo Fernández de Oviedo.* Pittsburgh, PA: University of Pittsburgh Press, 1985.

Glick, Thomas F. "The Reception of Darwinism in Uruguay." In Glick, Puig-Samper, and Ruiz, *Reception of Darwinism,* 29–52.

Glick, Thomas F., Miguel Angel Puig-Samper, and Rosaura Ruiz, eds. *The Reception of Darwinism in the Iberian World: Spain, Spanish America, and Brazil.* Dordrecht, Netherlands: Kluwer, 1999. Also publ. as *El Darwinismo en España e Iberoamérica.* Mexico City: Universidad Nacional Autónoma de México, 1999.

Glick, Thomas F., and David M. Quinlan. "Félix de Azara: The Myth of the Isolated Genius in Spanish Science." *Journal of the History of Biology* 8.1 (1975): 67–83.

Godlewska, Anne Marie Claire. "Commentary: The Fascination of Jesuit Cartography." In Gagliano and Ronan, *Jesuit Encounters,* 99–111.

Golinski, Jan. *Making Natural Knowledge: Constructivism and the History of Science.* Cambridge, UK: Cambridge University Press, 1998.

Gómez, Leila, ed. *La piedra del escándalo: Darwin en Argentina (1845–1909).* Buenos Aires, Argentina: Simurg, 2008.

Gómez de Vidaurre, Felipe. *Historia geográfica, natural y civil del reino de Chile.* 1789. Edited by José Toribio Medina. Santiago, Chile: Ercilla, 1889.

González, Julio César. "Apuntes bio-bibliográficos de don Félix de Azara: Bibliografía. Iconografía." In Azara, *Memoria,* vii–cxiv.

González, Ondina. "Down and Out in Havana: Foundlings in Eighteenth-Century Cuba." In *Minor Omissions: Children in Latin American History and Society,* edited by Tobias Hecht, 102–13. Madison: University of Wisconsin Press, 2002.

González, Ondina, and Bianca Premo, eds. *Raising an Empire: Children in Early Modern Iberia and Colonial Latin America.* Albuquerque: University of New Mexico Press, 2007.

González Adánez, Noelia. "From Kingdoms to Colonies: The Enlightened Idea of America in Charles III's Spain." In Wells and Stewart, *Interpreting Colonialism,* 113–24.

González Echevarría, Roberto. *Myth and Archive: A Theory of Latin American Narrative.* Cambridge, UK: Cambridge University Press, 1990.

González Echevarría, Roberto, and Enrique Pupo-Walker, eds. *The Cambridge History of Latin American Literature.* Vol. 1, *Discovery to Modernism.* Cambridge, UK: Cambridge University Press, 1996.

González Suárez, Federico. *Historia general de la república del Ecuador,* Vol. 4. Quito, Ecuador: Imprenta del Clero, 1890–1903.

Goodman, Dena. "Difference: An Enlightenment Concept." In Baker and Reill, *What's Left,* 29–147. Stanford, CA: Stanford University Press, 2001.

Graffigny, Françoise de. *Letters of a Peruvian Woman.* Translated by Jonathan Mallinson. Oxford, UK: Oxford University Press, 2009.

Grahn, Lance R. *The Political Economy of Smuggling: Regional Informal Economies in Early Bourbon New Granada.* Boulder, CO: Westview Press, 1997.

Grases, Pedro. *De la imprenta en Venezuela y algunas obras de referencia.* 1967. Caracas, Venezuela: Ediciones de la Facultad de Humanidades y Educación, 1979.

Graziano, Frank. "Santa Rosa de Lima y el cuerpo sacrificial." In Moraña, *Mujer y cultura,* 195–99.

———. *Wounds of Love: The Mystical Marriage of Saint Rose of Lima.* Oxford, UK: Oxford University Press, 2004.

Greer, Allan, and Jodi Bilinkoff, eds. *Colonial Saints: Discovering the Holy in the Americas, 1500–1800.* New York, NY: Routledge, 2003.

Greer, Allan, and Kenneth Mills. "A Catholic Atlantic Enlightenment." In Cañizares-Esguerra and Seeman, *Atlantic,* 3–20.

Greer, Margaret R., Walter D. Mignolo, and Maureen Quilligan, eds. *Rereading the Black Legend: The Discourses of Religious and Racial Difference in the Renaissance Empires.* Chicago, IL: University of Chicago Press, 2007.

Gregory, Derek. *Geographical Imaginations.* Cambridge, MA: Blackwell, 1994.

Gunckel Lüer, Hugo. *Bibliografía moliniana.* Santiago, Chile: Andrés Bello, 1980.

———. "De cómo el abate Molina vió y describió los chilenos." *Boletín de la Universidad de Chile* 80–81 (1967): 41–44.

Gustafson, Sandra M. *Eloquence Is Power: Oratory and Performance in Early America.* Williamsburg, VA: Omohundro Institute of Early American History and Culture; Chapel Hill: University of North Carolina Press, 2000.

———. *Imagining Deliberative Democracy in the Early American Republic.* Chicago, IL: University of Chicago Press, 2011.

Gutiérrez, Renee. "Pedro de Peralta as Philosopher-Conqueror: A *Maestre de Campo* in the Republic of Letters." *Dieciocho* 32.2 (2009): 307–32.

Haberly, David T. "Form and Function in the New World Legend." In *Do the Americas Have a*

Common Literature?, edited by Gustavo Pérez Firmat, 42–61. Durham, NC: Duke University Press, 1990.

Haenke, Thaddaeus Peregrinus. *Descripción del reyno de Chile.* 1789–1794. Santiago, Chile: Nascimento, 1942.

Hanisch, Walter. *El arte de cocinar de Juan Ignacio Molina.* Providencia, Chile: Imprenta de la Universidad Católica, 1976.

———, ed. *Juan Ignacio Molina: Historia natural y civil de Chile.* Santiago, Chile: Universitaria, 1978.

———. *Juan Ignacio Molina: Sabio de su tiempo.* Caracas, Venezuela: Andrés Bello, 1974.

———. "Juan Ignacio Molina: Sabio de su tiempo." *Montalban* (UCAB) 3 (1974): 205–308.

Harley, J. B. *The New Nature of Maps: Essays in the History of Cartography.* Edited by Paul Laxton. Baltimore, MD: Johns Hopkins University Press, 2001.

Henríquez Ureña, Max. *Antología cubana de las escuelas.* Santiago, Cuba: Archipélago, 1929.

———. *Panorama histórico de la literatura cubana.* 2 vols. Havana, Cuba: Arte y Literatura, 1978.

Heredia Herrera, Antonio. *La renta del azogue en Nueva España (1709–1751).* Seville, Spain: Escuela de Estudios Hispano-Americanos de Sevilla/Consejo Superior de Investigaciones Científicas, 1978.

Herr, Richard. *The Eighteenth-Century Revolution in Spain.* Princeton, NJ: Princeton University Press, 1958.

Herrera, Catalina de Jesús. *Secretos entre el alma y Dios.* 1758–1760. Published in 1950 as *Autobiografía de la Vble. Madre Sor Catalina de Jesús Herrera: Religiosa de Coro del Monasterio de Santa Catalina de Quito,* transcribed by Alfonso A. Jerves. Reprint, Quito, Ecuador: Editorial Santo Domingo, 1954.

———. "Secretos entre el alma y Diós." In *Letras de la Audiencia de Quito (Período Jesuítico),* edited by Hernán Rodríguez Casteló, 117–35. Caracas, Venezuela: Ayacucho, 1984.

Herrera, Pablo. *Ensayo sobre la historia de la literatura ecuatoriana.* Quito, Ecuador: Imprenta del Gobierno, 1860.

Herzog, Tamar. *Defining Nations: Immigrants and Citizens of Early Modern Spain and Spanish America.* New Haven, CT: Yale University Press, 2003.

———. "The Meaning of Territory: Colonial Standards and Modern Questions in Ecuador." In *Globality and Multiple Modernities: Comparative North American and Latin American Perspectives,* edited by Luis Roniger and Carlos H. Waisman, 162–82. Brighton, UK: Sussex Academic Press, 2002.

Higgins, Antony. *Constructing the Criollo Archive: Subjects of Knowledge in the "Rusticatio mexicana" and the "Bibliotheca mexicana."* West Lafayette, IN: Purdue University Press, 2000.

———. "(Post-)Colonial Sublime: Order and Indeterminancy in Eighteenth-Century Spanish American Poetics and Aesthetics." In Bolaños and Verdesio, *Colonialism Past and Present,* 119–49.

Hilger, Stephanie M. "The Public, the Private, and the In-Between: Revisiting the Debate on Eighteenth-Century Literature." *Eighteenth-Century Studies* 39.3 (2006): 394–97.

Hill, Ruth. "Arrate's *La Habana Descripta* and the Modernization of the Geographical Report (ca. 1750–1769)." *Revista Hispánica Moderna* 49 (1996): 329–40.

———. "Bourbon Castile and Other 'Antiquities': Memory, Conquest and Tradition in Luzán's Occasional Poetry." *Journal of Spanish Cultural Studies* 4.1 (2003): 95–110.

———. "Bourbon Cultural Management and the State of Eighteenth-Century Studies." Paper presented at the 23rd International Congress of the Latin American Studies Association, Washington, DC, September 6–8, 2001.

———. "Categories and Crossings: Critical Race Studies and the Spanish World." *Journal of Spanish Cultural Studies* 10.1 (2009): 1–6.

———. "Conquista y modernidad, 1700–1766: Un enfoque transatlántico." In *Fénix de España: Modernidad y cultura propia,* edited by Pablo Fernández Albaladejo, 57–71. Madrid, Spain: Marcial Pons, 2006.

———. "De la *Historia literaria de España* al *Teatro histórico, jurídico y político de Cuba* (Modernidad historiográfica y Subjectividad Ilustrada en dos Archivos Transatlánticos)." In *La literatura ciencia cierta,* edited by Leopoldo Bernucci and Tamara Williams, 258–77. Madrid, Spain: Juan de la Cuesta, 2010.

———. "Entering and Exiting Blackness: A Color Controversy in Eighteenth-Century Spain." *Journal of Spanish Cultural Studies* 10.1 (2009): 43–58.

———. "Hierarchy and Historicism in Orbea's *La conquista de Santa Fe de Bogotá.*" *Latin American Theater Review* 39.1 (2005): 115–34.

———. *Hierarchy, Commerce, and Fraud in Bourbon Spanish America: A Postal Inspector's Exposé.* Nashville, TN: Vanderbilt University Press, 2005.

———. *Sceptres and Sciences in the Spains: Four Humanists and the New Philosophy (ca. 1680–1700).* Liverpool, UK: Liverpool University Press, 2000.

———. "Towards an Eighteenth-Century Transatlantic Critical Race Theory." *Literature Compass* 2 (2006): 1–12.

Hinnant, Charles H. "Gifts and Wages: The Structures of Exchange in Eighteenth-Century Fiction and Drama." *Eighteenth-Century Studies* 42.1 (2008): 1–18.

Hoberman, Louisa Schell, and Susan Socolow, eds. *Cities and Societies in Colonial Latin America.* Albuquerque: University of New Mexico Press, 1986.

Hudson, Nicholas. "From 'Nation' to 'Race': The Origin of Racial Classification in Eighteenth-Century Thought." *Eighteenth-Century Studies* 29.3 (1996): 247–64.

Huffine, Kristin. "Raising Paraguay from Decline: Memory, Ethnography, and Natural History in the Eighteenth-Century Accounts of the Jesuit Fathers." In Millones Figueroa and Ledezma, *El saber de los jesuitas,* 279–302.

Hulme, Peter. *Colonial Encounters: Europe and the Native Caribbean, 1492–1797.* London, UK: Methuen, 1986.

———. "Introduction: The Cannibal Scene." In Barker, Hulme, and Iverson, *Cannibalism,* 1–38.

Humboldt, Alexander von. *Ensayo político sobre el reino de la Nueva España.* Edited by Juan Antonio Ortega y Molina. Mexico City: Porrúa, 1973.

———. *Ensayo político sobre la Isla de Cuba.* Havana, Cuba: Oficina del Historiador de la Ciudad, 1959.

———. *The Island of Cuba.* Translated by J. S. Thrasher. Introduction by Luis Martínez-Fernández. Princeton, NJ: Markus Wiener Publishers; Kingston, Jamaica: Ian Randle Publishers, 2001.

———. *Personal Narrative of Travels to the Equinoctial Regions of the New Continent, during the Years 1799–1804.* New York, NY: AMS, 1966.

Hyland, Sabine. *The Jesuit and the Incas: The Extraordinary Life of Padre Blas Valera, S.J.* Ann Arbor: University of Michigan Press, 2003.

Iacono, Alfonso M. "The American Indians and the Ancients of Europe: The Idea of Comparison and the Construction of Historical Time in the 18th Century." In *European Images of the Americas and the Classical Tradition,* vol. 1 of *The Classical Tradition and the Americas,* edited by Wolfgang Haase and Meyer Reinhold, 658–81. Berlin, Germany: Walter de Gruyter, 1994.

Ibsen, Kristine. *Women's Spiritual Autobiography in Colonial Spanish America.* Gainesville: University Press of Florida, 1999.

Israel, Jonathan I. *Democratic Enlightenment: Philosophy, Revolution, and Human Rights, 1750–1790*. Oxford, UK: Oxford University Press, 2011.

———. *The Enlightenment Contested: Philosophy, Modernity, and the Emancipation of Man, 1670–1752*. Oxford, UK: Oxford University Press, 2006.

———. *Radical Enlightenment: Philosophy and the Making of Modernity, 1650–1750*. Oxford, UK: Oxford University Press, 2001.

Jaffe, Catherine M., and Elizabeth Franklin Lewis, eds. *Eve's Enlightenment: Women's Experience in Spain and Spanish America, 1726–1839*. Baton Rouge: Louisiana State University Press, 2009.

Jahoda, Gustav. *Images of Savages: Ancient Roots of Modern Prejudice in Western Culture*. London, UK: Routledge, 1999.

Jáuregui, Carlos. *Canibalia: Canibalismo, calibanismo, antropofagia cultural y consumo en América Latina*. Madrid, Spain: Iberoamericana; Frankfurt, Germany: Vervuert, 2008.

———. "'El plato más sabroso': Eucaristía, plagio diabólico, y la traducción criolla del caníbal." *Colonial Latin American Review* 12.2 (2003): 199–230.

———. "Saturno caníbal: Fronteras, reflejos y paradojas en la narrativa sobre el atropófago." *Revista de Crítica Literaria y Cultural* 51 (2000): 9–39.

Jerves, Alfonso A. "Introducción." In Herrera, *Autobiografía*, 5–11.

Jiménez Berguecio, Julio. *El Abate Molina: Humanista clásico y sabio cristiano (escritos inéditos)*. Santiago: Universidad Católica de Chile, 1974.

Johnson, Julie Greer. "Ercilla's Construction and Destruction of the City of Concepción: A Crossroads of Imperialist Ideology and the Poetic Imagination." In Arias and Meléndez, *Mapping*, 237–50.

———. *Satire in Colonial Spanish America: Turning the New World Upside Down*. Austin: University of Texas Press, 1993.

Johnson, Lyman L., and Susan Migden Socolow, "Colonial Centers, Colonial Peripheries, and the Economic Agency of the Spanish State." In Daniels and Kennedy, *Negotiated Empires*, 59–77.

Johnson, Lyman L., and Enrique Tándeter, eds. *Essays on the Price History of Eighteenth-Century Latin America*. Albuquerque: University of New Mexico Press, 1990.

Johnson, Sherry. *The Social Transformation of Eighteenth-Century Cuba*. Gainesville: University Press of Florida, 2001.

Jouve Martín, José Ramón. *Esclavos de la ciudad letrada: Esclavitud, escritura y colonialismo en Lima (1650–1700)*. Lima, Peru: Instituto de Estudios Peruanos, 2005.

Juan, Jorge, and Antonio de Ulloa. *Viaje a la América meridional*. Madrid, Spain: Historia 16, 1990.

———. *A Voyage to South America*. Translated by John Adams. Introduction by Irving A. Leonard. Tempe: Center for Latin American Studies, Arizona State University, 1975.

Kagan, Richard L. *Urban Images of the Hispanic World, 1493–1793*. New Haven, CT: Yale University Press, 2000.

———. "Urban Views." In *Guide to Documentary Sources for Andean Studies, 1530–1900*, edited by Joanne Pillsbury, 1:315–29. Norman: University of Oklahoma Press, 2008.

Kammen, Michael. *Digging Up the Dead: A History of Notable American Reburials*. Chicago, IL: University of Chicago Press, 2010.

Katzew, Ilona. *Casta Painting: Images of Race in Eighteenth-Century Mexico*. New Haven, CT: Yale University Press, 2004.

———, ed. *New World Orders: Casta Painting and Colonial Latin America*. New York, NY: Americas Society, 1996.

Keyes, Frances Parkinson. *The Rose and the Lily*. New York, NY: Hawthorn, 1961.

Kinsbruner, Jay. *The Colonial Spanish-American City: Urban Life in the Age of Atlantic Capitalism.* Austin: University of Texas Press, 2005.

Kirschner, Teresa J., and Enrique Manchón. "Lope de Aguirre como signo político polivante." *Revista Canadiense de Estudios Hispánicos* 18.3 (1994): 405–16.

Knight, Franklin W. "El Caribe en la época de la Ilustración, 1788–1837." In Piqueras, *Las Antillas,* 3–26.

Knight, Franklin W., and Peggy K. Liss, eds. *Atlantic Port Cities: Economy, Culture, and Society in the Atlantic World, 1650–1850.* Knoxville: University of Tennessee Press, 1991.

Koerner, Lisbet. *Linnaeus: Nature and Nation.* Cambridge, MA: Harvard University Press, 1999.

———. "Purposes of Linnaean Travel: A Preliminary Research Report." In Miller and Reill, *Visions of Empire,* 117–52.

Kuethe, Allan J. *Cuba, 1753–1815: Crown, Military, and Society.* Knoxville: University of Tennessee Press, 1986.

———. "Havana in the Eighteenth Century." In Knight and Liss, *Atlantic Port Cities,* 13–39.

Lafaye, Jacques. *Quetzalcóatl y Guadalupe: La formación de la conciencia nacional en México.* Mexico City: Fondo de Cultura Económica, 1999.

Lafuente, Antonio, and Antonio Mazuecos. *Los caballeros del punto fijo: Ciencia, política y aventura en la expedición geodésica hispanofrancesa al vierreinato del Perú en el siglo XVIII.* Madrid, Spain: Serval, 1987.

Lafuente, Antonio, and José Sala Catalá, eds. *Ciencia colonial en América.* Madrid, Spain: Alianza, 1992.

Lafuente, Antonio, and Nuria Valverde. "Linnaean Botany and Spanish Imperial Biopolitics." In Schiebinger and Swan, *Colonial Botany,* 134–47. Philadelphia: University of Pennsylvania Press, 2005.

Lafuente, Antonio, and Nuria Valverde, eds. *Los mundos de la ciencia en la Ilustración española.* Madrid, Spain: Fundación Española para la Ciencia y la Tecnologiá, 2003.

Lane, Kris. "Gone Platinum: Contraband and Chemistry in Eighteenth-Century Colombia." *Colonial Latin American Review* 20.1 (2011): 61–79.

———. *Pillaging the Empire: Piracy in the Americas, 1500–1750.* Armonk, NY: M. E. Sharpe, 1998.

Larrazábal Henríquez, Osvaldo. "Lope de Aguirre, Príncipe de la libertad, una novedosa novela de Miguel Otero Silva." *Revista Iberoamericana* 166–67 (1994): 469–75.

Latour, Bruno. *Science in Action: How to Follow Scientists and Engineers through Society.* Cambridge, MA: Harvard University Press, 1987.

Lavallé, Bernard. *Las promesas ambiguas: Ensayos sobre el criollismo colonial en los Andes.* Lima: Pontifica Universidad Católica del Perú/Instituto Riva-Agüero, 1993.

Lavallé, Bernard, Consuelo Naranjo, and Antonio Santamaría, eds. *La América Española (1763–1898): Economía.* Madrid, Spain: Editorial Síntesis, 2002.

Lavrin, Asunción. *Brides of Christ: Conventual Life in Colonial Mexico.* Stanford, CA: Stanford University Press, 2008.

———. "La celda y el siglo: Epístolas conventuales." In Moraña, *Mujer y cultura,* 139–59.

———. "Ecclesiastical Reform of Nunneries in New Spain in the Eighteenth Century." *Americas* 22.2 (1965): 182–203.

———. "Female Religious." In Hoberman and Socolow, *Cities,* 165–95.

Lazo, Raimundo. *La literatura cubana: Esquema histórico (desde sus orígenes hasta 1966).* Havana, Cuba: Editorial Universitaria, 1967.

———. *Historia de la literatura hispanoamericana.* Mexico City: Porrúa, 1965.

Lechtman, Heather. *America's Vanished Metalsmiths.* Santiago: Museo Chileno de Arte Precolombino, 1992.

Leighton, Ann. *American Gardens in the Eighteenth Century: "For Use or for Delight."* Boston, MA: Houghton Mifflin, 1976.

León, Leonardo. "Parlamentos y afuerinos en la frontera mapuche del río Bío-Bío (Chile), 1760–1772." *Fronteras de la Historia* 11 (2006): 83–114.

Leonard, Irving A. *Books of the Brave.* Berkeley: University of California Press, 1992.

León Galarza, Natalia. *La primera alianza: El matrimonio criollo; Honor y violencia conyugal, Cuenca, 1750–1800.* Quito, Ecuador: Nueva Editorial, 1997.

Le Riverend Brusone, Julio J. "Carácter y significación de los tres primeros historiadores de Cuba." *Revista Bimestre Cubana* 65.1–3 (1950): 152–80.

———. "Comentarios en Torno a las ideas Sociales de Arrate." *Revista Cubana* 17.2 (1943): 326–41.

———. "Prólogo." In Arrate, *Llave del Nuevo Mundo,* vii–xxvi.

Lewis, Bart L. *The Miraculous Lie: Lope de Aguirre and the Search for El Dorado in the Latin American Historical Novel.* Lanham, MD: Lexington Books, 2003.

Lewis, Steve. "Myth and the History of Chile's Araucanians." *Radical History Review* 58 (1994): 112–41.

Lezama Lima, José. *La expresión americana.* Madrid, Spain: Alianza, 1969.

Livingstone, David. *The Geographical Tradition: Episodes in the History of a Contested Enterprise.* Oxford, UK: Blackwell, 1992.

Livingstone, David, and Charles W. J. Withers, eds. *Geography and Enlightenment.* Chicago, IL: University of Chicago Press, 1999.

Llano Zapata, José Eusebio. *Memorias histórico, físicas, crítico, apologéticas de la América meridional.* Edited by Ricardo Ramírez, Antonio Garrido, Luis Millones Figueroa, Victor Peralta, and Charles Walker. Lima: IFEA/Pontificia Universidad Católica del Perú/Universidad Nacional Mayor de San Marcos, 2005.

Llanos M., Bernardita. *(Re)descubrimiento y (re)conquista de América en la Ilustración española.* New York, NY: Peter Lang, 1994.

Lockhart, James, and Stuart B. Schwartz. *Early Latin America.* Cambridge, UK: Cambridge University Press, 1983.

Lohmann-Villena, Guillermo. *Las minas de Huancavélica en los siglos XVI y XVII.* 1949. Lima: Fondo Editorial de la Pontificia Universidad Católica del Peru, 1999.

Lombardi, John V. "Foreword." In Oviedo y Baños, *Conquest and Settlement,* ix–xiii.

———. *Venezuela: The Search for Order, the Dream of Progress.* New York, NY: Oxford University Press, 1982.

Londoño López, Jenny. *Angeles o demonios? Las mujeres y la iglesia en la Audiencia de Quito.* Quito, Ecuador: Centro para el Desarrollo Social/Universidad Estatal de Bolívar, 1995.

Lowood, Henry. "The New World and the European Catalog of Nature." In *America in European Consciousness, 1493–1750,* edited by Karen Ordahl Kupperman, 295–323. Williamsburg, VA: Omohundro Institute of Early American History and Culture; Chapel Hill: University of North Carolina Press, 1995.

Luciani, Frederick. "Spanish American Theater of the Eighteenth Century." In González Echevarría and Pupo-Walker, *Cambridge History of Latin American Literature,* 401–16.

Lund, Joshua, "Hybridity, Genre, Race." In *Revisiting the Colonial Question,* edited by Mabel Moraña and Carlos A. Jáuregui, 113–37. Madrid, Spain: Iberoamericana, 2008.

Lynch, John. *Bourbon Spain, 1700–1808.* Oxford, UK: Blackwell, 1989.

———. *The Spanish American Revolutions, 1808–1826.* 2nd. ed. New York, NY: Norton, 1986.

Lyon, John, and Phillip R. Sloan, eds. *From Natural History to the History of Nature: Readings from Buffon and His Critics.* Notre Dame, IN: Notre Dame University Press, 1981.

Macchi, Fernanda. "Imágenes de los Incas en el siglo XVIII." Diss., Yale University, 2003.

———. *Incas ilustrados: Reconstrucciones imperiales en la segunda mitad del XVIII.* Madrid, Spain: Iberoamericana, 2009.

———. "*Mille et une heures, contes péruviens:* Una lectura oriental de los *Comentarios Reales de los Incas.*" *Dieciocho* 30.2 (2007): 365–86.

MacLachlan, Colin M. *Spain's Empire in the New World: The Role of Ideas in Institutional and Social Change.* Berkeley: University of California Press, 1988.

Mangan, Jane E., ed. *Natural and Moral History of the Indies.* By José de Acosta. Introduction by Walter D. Mignolo. Translated by Frances López Morillas. Durham, NC: Duke University Press, 2002.

———. "A Market of Identities." In Fisher and O'Hara, *Imperial Subjects,* 61–80.

———. *Trading Roles: Gender, Ethnicity, and the Urban Economy in Colonial Potosí.* Durham, NC: Duke University Press, 2005.

Mannheim, Bruce. *The Language of the Inka since the European Invasion.* Austin: University of Texas Press, 1991.

Manning, Susan, and Francis D. Cogliano, eds. *The Atlantic Enlightenment.* Burlington, VT: Ashgate, 2008.

Maravall, José Antonio. *Estudios de la historia del pensamiento español (siglo XVIII).* Edited by María Carmen Iglesias. Madrid, Spain: Biblioteca Mondadori, 1991.

Marchena F., Juan. "Su Majestad quiere saber: Información oficial y reformismo borbónico en la América de la Ilustración." In Soto Arango, Puig-Samper, Bender, and González-Ripoll, *Recepción y difusión,* 151–85.

María, Hermano Nectario. *Historia de la conquista y fundación de Caracas.* Madrid, Spain: Cuatricentenario de Caracas, 1966.

Marichal, Carlos. *La bancarrota del virreinato: Nueva España y las finanzas del Imperio español, 1780–1810.* Mexico City: Fondo de Cultura Económica, 1999.

Marichal, Carlos, and Matilde Souro Mantecón. "Silver and *Situado*s: New Spain and the Financing of the Spanish Empire in the Caribbean in the Eighteenth Century." *Hispanic American Historical Review* 74.4 (1994): 587–616.

Marrer, Leví. *Cuba: Economía y sociedad.* Madrid, Spain: Editorial PLAYOR, 1980.

Marshall, P. J., and Glyndwr Williams. *The Great Map of Mankind: Perceptions of New Worlds in the Age of Enlightenment.* Cambridge, MA: Harvard University Press, 1982.

Martin, Calvin, ed. *The American Indian and the Problem of History.* New York, NY: Oxford University Press, 1987.

Martín, Juan Luis. "José Martín Félix de Arrate y Mateo de Acosta, el primero que se sintió cubano." *Revista de la Biblioteca Nacional* (Havana) 1.4 (1950): 32–60.

Martínez, María Elena. *Genealogical Fictions: Limpieza de Sangre, Religion, and Gender in Colonial Mexico.* Stanford, CA: Stanford University Press, 2008.

Martínez, Tomás Eloy, and Susana Rotker. "Prólogo." In Oviedo y Baños, *Historia,* ix–xlviii.

———. "Oviedo y Baños: La fundación literaria de la nacionalidad venezolana." In *Las colonias del Nuevo Mundo: Discursos imperiales,* 77–130. Tucumán, Argentina: Instituto Interdisciplinario de Estudios Latinoamericanos/Facultad de Filosofía y Letras/Universidad Nacional de Tucumán, 1999.

Martínez Ruiz, Enrique, and Magdalena de Pazzis Pi Corrales. *Ilustración, ciencia y técnica en el siglo XVIII español.* Valencia, Spain: Universitat de Valencia, 2008.

Martínez-San Miguel, Yolanda. "Colonial Writings as Minority Discourse?" In Bauer and Mazzotti, *Creole Subjects,* 162–90.

———. *From Lack to Excess: "Minor" Readings of Latin American Colonial Discourse.* Lewisburg, PA: Bucknell University Press, 2008.

————. *Saberes americanos: Subalternidad y epistemología en los escritos de Sor Juana.* Pittsburgh, PA: Instituto Internacional de Literatura Iberoamericana, 1999.

Martínez Sanz, José Luis. *Relaciones científicas entre España y América.* Madrid, Spain: MAPFRE, 1992.

Martín Ferrero, Paz, ed. *Actas del Simposium CCL Aniversario Nacimiento de Joseph Celestino Mutis.* Cádiz, Spain: Diputación de Cádiz, 1986.

Maxwell, Kenneth R. "Hegemonies Old and New: The Ibero-Atlantic in the Long Eighteenth Century." In *Colonial Legacies: The Problem of Persistence in Latin American History,* edited by Jeremy Adelman, 69–90. New York, NY: Routledge, 1999.

————. *Pombal, Paradox of the Enlightenment.* Cambridge, UK: Cambridge University Press, 1995.

Mazzotti, José Antonio. "The Dragon and the Seashell: British Corsairs, Epic Poetry and Creole Nations in Viceregal Peru." In Bolaños and Verdesio, *Colonialism Past and Present,* 197–214.

McCusker, John J. *Money and Exchange in Europe and America, 1600–1775: A Handbook.* Chapel Hill: University of North Carolina Press, 1978.

McFarlane, Anthony. "The Rebellion of the Barrios: Urban Insurrection in Bourbon Quito." In *Reform and Insurrection in Bourbon New Granada and Peru,* edited by John R. Fisher, Allan J. Kuethe, and Anthony McFarlane, 197–254. Baton Rouge: Lousiana State University Press, 1990.

McKnight, Kathryn Joy. *The Mystic of Tunja: The Writings of Madre Castillo, 1671–1742.* Amherst: University of Massachusetts Press, 1997.

Melczer, William. "Ercilla's Divided Heroic Vision: A Re-Evaluation of the Epic Hero in 'La Araucana.'" *Hispania: A Journal Devoted to the Teaching of Spanish and Portuguese* 56.1 (1973): 216–21.

Meléndez, Mariselle. *Deviant and Useful Citizens: The Cultural Production of the Female Body in Eighteenth-Century Peru.* Nashville, TN: Vanderbilt University Press, 2011.

————. "Eighteenth-Century Spanish America: Historical Dimensions and New Theoretical Approaches." *REH* 35.3 (2001): 615–32.

————. *Raza, género e hibridez en "El lazarillo de ciegos caminantes."* Chapel Hill: University of North Carolina Press, 1999.

Melvin, Karen. *Building Colonial Cities of God: Mendicant Orders and Urban Culture in New Spain.* Stanford, CA: Stanford University Press, 2012.

————. "A Potential Saint Thwarted: The Politics of Religion and Sanctity in Late Eighteenth-Century New Spain." In *Studies in Eighteenth-Century Culture,* edited by Jeffrey S. Ravel and Linda Zionkowski, 36:169–85. Baltimore, MD: Johns Hopkins University Press, 2007.

Méndez y Beltrán, Luz María. "La organización de los parlamentos de indios en el siglo XVIII." In *Tres siglos y medio de vida fronteriza,* with contributions by Sergio Villalobos R. et al., 9–64. Santiago: Ediciones Universidad Católica de Chile, 1982.

Meranze, Michael. "Critique and Government: Michel Foucault and the Question 'What Is Enlightenment?'" In Baker and Reill, *What's Left,* 102–12.

Merrim, Stephanie. *Early Modern Women's Writing and Sor Juana Inés de la Cruz.* Nashville, TN: Vanderbilt University Press, 1999.

Mieres, Antonio. *Tres autores en la Historia de Baralt.* Caracas: Universidad Central de Venezuela, 1966.

Mignolo, Walter. "Commentary: José de Acosta's *Historia natural y moral de las Indias;* Occidentalism, the Modern/Colonial World, and the Colonial Difference." In Acosta, *Natural and Moral History,* 451–523.

————. *The Idea of Latin America.* Malden, MA: Blackwell, 2005.

———. "Introduction." In Acosta, *Natural and Moral History* xvii–xxviii.

———. *Local Histories/Global Designs: Coloniality, Subaltern Knowledges, and Border Thinking.* Princeton, NJ: Princeton University Press, 2000.

———. "The Movable Center: Geographical Discourses and Territoriality During the Expansion of the Spanish Empire." In *The Latin American Cultural Studies Reader,* edited by Ana del Sarto, Alicia Ríos, and Abril Trigo, 263–90. Durham, NC: Duke University Press, 2004.

Miller, David Philip, and Peter Hanns Reill, eds. *Visions of Empire: Voyages, Botany, and Representations of Nature.* Cambridge, UK: Cambridge University Press, 1996.

Millones Figueroa, Luis, and Domingo Ledezma, eds. *El saber de los jesuitas, historias naturales y el Nuevo Mundo.* Frankfurt, Germany: Vervuert; Madrid, Spain: Iberoamericana, 2005.

Milton, Cynthia E. *The Many Meanings of Poverty: Colonialism, Social Compacts, and Assistance in Eighteenth-Century Ecuador.* Stanford, CA: Stanford University Press, 2007.

Minchom, Martin. *The People of Quito, 1690–1810: Change and Unrest in the Underclass.* Boulder, CO: Westview Press, 1994.

Mira, Guillermo. "Plata y tecnología en la América española del siglo XVIII: Una aproximación a los cambios productivos bajo la Ilustración." In *Ciencia colonial en América,* edited by Antonio Lafuente and José Sala Catalá, 253–71. Madrid, Spain: Alianza, 1992.

Mitchell, W. J. T., ed. *Landscape and Power.* Chicago, IL: University of Chicago Press, 2002.

Molina, Juan Ignacio. *Compendio de la historia civil del reyno de Chile: Parte segunda traducida y aumentada con varias notas por Nicolás de la Cruz y Bahamonde.* Madrid, Spain: Imprenta de Sancha, 1795.

———. *Compendio de la historia geográfica, natural y civil del reyno de Chile: Primera parte traducida al español por Domingo Joseph de Arquellada Mendoza.* Madrid, Spain: Antonio de Sancha, 1788.

———. *Epistolario de Juan Ignacio Molina, S.J.* Edited by Charles E. Ronan and Walter Hanisch. Chicago, IL: Loyola University Press; Santiago, Chile: Universitaria, 1979.

———. *The Geographical, Natural, and Civil History of Chili.* 2 vols. Middletown, CT: I. Riley, 1808.

———. *Historia natural y civil de Chile.* Edited by Walter Hanisch. Santiago, Chile: Universitaria, 1978.

Montaigne, Michel de. *The Complete Essays.* New York, NY: Penguin, 1993.

Montesquieu, Charles de Secondat, Baron de. *The Spirit of Laws.* Littleton, CO: F. B. Rothman, 1991.

Moraña, Mabel, ed. *Ideologies of Hispanism.* Nashville, TN: Vanderbilt University Press, 2005.

———. *Mujer y cultura en la colonia hispanoamericana.* Pittsburgh, PA: Instituto Internacional de Literatura Iberoamericana, 1996.

Morell de Santa Cruz, Pedro Agustín. *Historia de la isla y catedral de Cuba.* Havana: Imprenta "Cuba Intelectual," 1929.

Morgan, Ronald J. *Spanish American Saints and the Rhetoric of Identity, 1600–1810.* Tucson: University of Arizona Press, 2002.

Mörner, Magnus, ed. *The Expulsion of the Jesuits from Latin America.* New York, NY: Knopf, 1965.

Morón, Guillermo. *Los cronistas y la historia.* Caracas, Venezuela: Ediciones del Ministerio de Educación, 1957.

———. "José de Oviedo y Baños." In *Los cronistas y la historia,* 85–153.

———. *José de Oviedo y Baños (1671–1783).* Caracas, Venezuela: Ediciones de la Fundación Eugenio Mendoza, 1958.

Morse, Richard. "Introducción a la historia urbana de Hispanoamérica." In *Estudios sobre la ciudad iberoameriana,* 9–53. Madrid, Spain: Consejo Superior de Investigaciones Científicas, 1983.

Motten, Clement G. *Mexican Silver and the Enlightenment.* New York, NY: Octagon/Farrar, Straus and Giroux, 1972.

Mundy, Barbara. *The Mapping of New Spain: Indigenous Cartography and the Maps of the Relaciones Geográficas.* Chicago, IL: University of Chicago Press, 2000.

Muriel, Josefina. *Conventos de monjas en la Nueva España.* Mexico City: Editorial Santiago, 1946.

———. *Las mujeres de Hispanoámerica: Epoca colonial.* Madrid, Spain: MAPFRE, 1992.

Muro Orejón, Antonio, ed. *Cedulario americano del siglo XVIII.* Seville, Spain: Escuela de Estudios Hispano-Americanos de Sevilla y de la Cátedra de Historia del Derecho Indiano de la Universidad de Sevilla, 1977.

Muthu, Sankar. *Enlightenment against Empire.* Princeton, NJ: Princeton University Press, 2003.

Mutis, José Celestino. *Archivo epistolar.* 2 vols. Edited by Guillermo Hernández de Alba. Bogotá, Colombia: Kelly, 1968.

———. *Viaje a Santa Fe.* Edited by Marcelo Frías Núñez. Madrid, Spain: Historia 16, 1990.

Myers, Kathleen Ann. "The Addressee Determines the Discourse: The Role of the Confessor in the Spiritual Autobiography of Madre María de San Joseph (1656–1719)." *Bulletin of Hispanic Studies* 69 (1992): 39–47.

———. "El discurso espiritual en la fundación del Convento de la Soledad: La crónica de la Madre María de San José (1656–1719)." In Moraña, *Mujer y cultura,* 123–38.

———. "'Miraba las cosas que desía': Convent Writing, Picaresque Tales, and the *Relación autobiográfica* by Ursula Suárez (1666–1749)." *Romance Quarterly* 40.3 (1993): 156–72.

———. *Neither Saints Nor Sinners: Writing the Lives of Women in Spanish America.* Oxford, UK: Oxford University Press, 2003.

———. "'Redeemer of America': Rosa de Lima (1586–1617), the Dynamics of Identity, and Canonization." In Greer and Bilinkoff, *Colonial Saints,* 251–71.

———. *Word from New Spain: The Spiritual Autobiography of Madre María de San José (1656–1719).* Liverpool, UK: Liverpool University Press, 1993.

Myers, Kathleen Ann, and Amanda Powell, eds. *A Wild Country out in the Garden: The Spiritual Journals of a Colonial Mexican Nun.* Bloomington: Indiana University Press, 1999.

Naranjo Orovio, Consuelo, and Tomás Mallo Gutiérrez, eds. *Cuba, la perla de las Antillas: Actas de las I Jornadas sobre "Cuba y su Historia."* Madrid, Spain: Doce Calles/Consejo Superior de Investigaciones Científicas, 1994.

Navallo, Tatiana. Review of Millones Figueroa and Ledezma, *El saber de los jesuitas. Dieciocho* 29.1 (2006): 136–39.

Navarro, Nicolás E. "Elogio de Oviedo y Baños y Conmemoración de los cronistas que historiaron cosas de Venezuela." *Boletín de la Academia Nacional de la Historia* (Caracas) 22.88 (1939): 551–57.

Navia Méndez-Bonito, Silvia. "Las historias naturales de Francisco Javier Clavigero, Juan Ignacio de Molina y Juan de Velasco." In Millones Figueroa and Ledezma, *El saber,* 224–50.

———. "Juan de Velasco's Natural History: Differentiating the Kingdom of Quito." In *How Far Is America from Here? Selected Proceedings of the First World Congress of the International American Studies Association, 22–24 May 2003,* edited by Theo D'Haen, Paul Giles, Djelal Kadir, and Lois Parkinson Zamora, 359–67. Amsterdam, Netherlands: Rodopi, 2005.

———. "Presence of an Incipient Pre-Nationalist Consciousness in Juan de Velasco's 'Natural History.'" Diss., University of Massachusetts, 2002.

Negro, Sandra, and Manuel M. Marzal, eds. *Un reino en la frontera: Las misiones jesuitas en la América colonial*. Quito, Ecuador: Ediciones ABYA-YALA/Pontificia Universidad Católica del Perú, 2000.

Nesvig, Martin Austin, ed. *Local Religion in Colonial Mexico*. Albuquerque: University of New Mexico Press, 2006.

Noel, Charles C. "Clerics and Crown in Bourbon Spain, 1700–1808: Jesuits, Jansenists, and Enlightened Reformers." In Bradley and Van Kley, *Religion and Politics*, 119–53.

Nouzeilles, Gabriela, ed. *La naturaleza en disputa: Retóricas del cuerpo y el paisaje en América Latina*. Buenos Aires, Argentina: Paidós, 2002.

Nussbaum, Felicity A., ed. *The Global Eighteenth Century*. Baltimore, MD: Johns Hopkins University Press, 2003.

Nussbaum, Felicity A, and Laura Brown, eds. *The New Eighteenth Century: Theory, Politics, English Literature*. New York: Methuen, 1987.

O'Brien, Karen. *Narratives of Enlightenment: Cosmopolitan History from Voltaire to Gibbon*. Cambridge, UK: Cambridge University Press, 1997.

Ochoa, John A. *The Uses of Failure in Mexican Literature and Identity*. Austin: University of Texas Press, 2004.

O'Flanagan, Patrick. *Port Cities of Atlantic Iberia, c. 1500–1900*. Aldershot, UK: Ashgate, 2008.

O'Hara, Matthew D. *A Flock Divided: Race, Religion, and Politics in Mexico, 1749–1857*. Durham, NC: Duke University Press, 2010.

Olivares, Miguel de. *Historia militar, civil y sagrada de Chile: Colección de Historiadores de Chile y documentos relativos a la Historia Nacional*. Vol. 4. Santiago, Chile: Imprenta del Ferrocarril, 1864.

Onís, Harriet de, ed. "José de Oviedo y Baños." In *The Golden Land*, 80–84. New York, NY: Knopf, 1948.

O'Phelan Godoy, Scarlett, ed. *El Perú en el siglo XVIII: La era borbónica*. Lima: Pontificia Universidad Católica del Perú, 1999.

Outram, Dorinda. *The Enlightenment*. 2nd ed. Cambridge, UK: Cambridge University Press, 2005.

———. *Panorama of the Enlightenment*. Los Angeles, CA: J. Paul Getty Museum, 2006.

Ovando-Sanz, Guillermo. *La academia de minas de Potosí*. La Paz: Banco Central de Bolivia/Academia Boliviana de la Historia, 1975.

Oviedo y Baños, José de. *Los Belzares, el Tirano Aguirre, Diego Losada*. Caracas, Venezuela: Monte Avila, 1972.

———. *The Conquest and Settlement of Venezuela*. Translated by Jeannette Johnson Varner. Foreword by John V. Lombardi. Berkeley: University of California Press, 1987.

———. *Historia de la conquista y población de la provincia de Venezuela*. Edited by Pedro Grases. Caracas, Venezuela: Ariel, 1967.

———. *Historia de la conquista y población de la provincia de Venezuela*. Edited by Tomás Eloy Martínez. Prologue by Tomás Eloy Martínez and Susana Rotker. Caracas, Venezuela: Ayacucho, 1992.

———. *Tesoro de noticias e índice general de las cosas más particulares que se contienen en los Libros Capitulares de esta ciudad de Caracas desde su fundación*. Caracas: Ministerio de Educación, 1967.

Oviedo y Valdés, Gonzalo Fernández de. *See* Fernández de Oviedo y Valdés, Gonzalo.

Oz-Salzberger, Fania. "Introduction." In Ferguson, *Essay*, vii–xxv.

Padden, Robert Charles. "Cultural Adaptation and Militant Autonomy among the Araucanians of Chile." In *The Indian in Latin American History: Resistance, Resilience, and Acculturation,* edited by John E. Kicza, 69–88. Wilmington, DE: Scholarly Resources, 1993.

Padrón, Ricardo. *The Spacious Word: Cartography, Literature, and Empire in Early Modern Spain.* Chicago, IL: University of Chicago Press, 2004.

Pagden, Anthony. *The Fall of Natural Man: The American Indian and the Origins of Comparative Ethnology.* Cambridge, UK: Cambridge University Press, 1982.

———. "The Forbidden Food: Francisco de Vitoria and José de Acosta on Cannibalism." *Terrae Incognitae* 13 (1981): 17–29; rpt. in *Uncertainties of Empire.*

———. "Heeding Heraclides: Empire and Its Discontents, 1619–1812." In *Spain, Europe and the Atlantic World: Essays in Honour of John H. Elliott,* edited by Richard L. Kagan and Geoffrey Parker, 316–33. Cambridge, UK: Cambridge University Press, 1995.

———. "Identity Formation in Spanish America." In *Colonial Identity in the Atlantic World, 1500–1800,* edited by Nicholas Canny and Anthony Pagden, 51–93. Princeton, NJ: Princeton University Press, 1987.

———. *La Ilustración y sus enemigos: Dos ensayos sobre los orígenes de la modernidad.* Edited and translated by José María Hernández. Barcelona, Spain: Ediciones Península, 2002.

———. *Lords of All the World: Ideologies of Empire in Spain, Britain and France, c.1500–c.1800.* New Haven, CT: Yale University Press, 1995.

———. *Spanish Imperialism and the Political Imagination.* New Haven, CT: Yale University Press, 1990.

———. *The Uncertainties of Empire: Essays in Iberian and Ibero-American Intellectual History.* Burlington, VT: Ashgate, 1994.

Paniagua Pérez, Jesús. "El monacato femenino en la Audiencia de Quito." In *El monacato femenino en el imperio español: Homenaje a Josefina Muriel; Memoria del II Congreso Internacional,* coordinated by Manuel Ramos Medina, 273–87. Mexico City: Centro de Estudios de Historia de México, 1995.

Paquette, Gabriel B., ed. *Enlightened Reform in Southern Europe and Its Atlantic Colonies, c. 1750–1830.* Burlington, VT: Ashgate, 2009.

———. *Enlightenment, Governance, and Reform in Spain and Its Empire, 1759–1808.* New York, NY: Palgrave Macmillan, 2008.

———. "Introduction: Enlightened Reform in Southern Europe and its Atlantic Colonies in the Long Eighteenth Century." In Paquette, *Enlightened Reform,* 1–20.

Parcero Torre, Celia María. *La pérdida de la Habana y las reformas borbónicas en Cuba (1760–1773).* Madrid, Spain: Junta de Castilla y León/Consejería de Educación y Cultura, 1998.

Pardo, Isaac J. *Juan de Castellanos: Estudio de las "Elegías de varones ilustres de Indias."* 2nd ed. Caracas, Venezuela: Academia Nacional de la Historia, 1991.

Parra León, Caracciolo. "Prólogo: D. José de Oviedo y Baños." In *Analectas de Historia Patria,* iv–xlvi. Caracas, Venezuela: Parra León Hermanos/Editorial Sur América, 1935.

Parrish, Susan Scott. *American Curiosity: Cultures of Natural History in the British American Atlantic World.* Williamsburg, VA: Omohundro Institute of Early American History; Chapel Hill: University of North Carolina Press, 2006.

Parry, J., and M. Bloch. "Introduction: Money and the Morality of Exchange." In Parry and Bloch, *Money,* 1–32.

Parry, J., and M. Bloch, eds. *Money and the Morality of Exchange.* Cambridge, UK: Cambridge University Press, 1989.

Pastor, Beatriz. *The Armature of Conquest: Spanish Accounts of the Discovery of America, 1492–1589.* Stanford, CA: Stanford University Press, 1992. Translation of *Discursos narrativos de la conquista: Mitificación y emergencia.* 2nd ed. Hanover, NH: Ediciones del Norte, 1988.

———. "Lope de Aguirre el loco: La voz de la soledad." *Revista de crítica literaria latinoamericana* 14.28 (1988): 159–73.

———. "Lope de Aguirre the Wanderer: Knowledge and Madness." *Dispositio* 11.28–29 (1986): 85–98.

Pauw, Cornelius de. *Recherches philosophiques sur les Américains.* 2 vols. Paris, France: Chez J. G. Baerstecher, 1772.

Paz, Octavio. *Children of the Mire: Modern Poetry from Romanticism to the Avant-Garde.* Translated by Rachel Phillips. Cambridge, MA: Harvard University Press, 1991.

———. *Sor Juana, or The Traps of Faith.* Translated by Margaret Sayers Peden. Cambridge, MA: Harvard University Press, 1990.

Pearce, Adrian J. "Huancavelica 1700–1759: Administrative Reform of the Mercury Industry in Early Bourbon Peru." *Hispanic American Historical Review* 79.4 (1999): 669–702.

Pedro Robles, Antonio E. de. "Las expediciones científicas a América a la luz de sus imágenes artístico-científicas." In *Ciencia, vida y espacio en Iberoamérica,* edited by José Luis Peset, 3:407–25. Madrid, Spain: Consejo Superior de Investigaciones Científicas, 1989.

Pérez Beato, Manuel. "Bibliografía cubana del siglo XVIII." *Revista Bibliográfica Cubana* 2.7 (1938): 41–55.

Pérez Herrero, Pedro. *Comercio y mercados en América latina colonial.* Madrid, Spain: MAPFRE, 1992.

Pérez Magallón, Jesús. *Construyendo la modernidad: La cultura española en el tiempo de Los Novatores (1675–1725).* Madrid: Consejo Superior de Investigaciones Científicas/Instituto de la Lengua Española, 2002.

———. "Enseñar el siglo dieciocho español: Contexto, problemas, instrumentos." *Dieciocho* 30.1 (2007):131–40.

Pérez-Mejía, Angela. *A Geography of Hard Times: Narratives about Travel to South America, 1780–1849.* Translated by Dick Cluster. Albany, NY: State University of New York Press, 2004. Translation of *La geografía en los tiempos difíciles: Escritura de viajes a Sur América durante los procesos de independencia, 1780–1849.* Medellín, Colombia: Universidad de Antioquía, 2002.

Pérez Murillo, María Dolores, Jesús María de la Casa Rivas, and Antonio Dueñas Olmo. "El interés por la historia natural en la época de Carlos III según los fondos documentales del Archivo General de Indias." In Martín Ferrero, *Actas del Simposium,* 59–67.

Pérez Pimentel, Rodolfo. *Diccionario biográfico del Ecuador.* 5 vols. Guayaquil, Ecuador: Universidad de Guayaquil, 1987–1988.

Peset, José Luis, ed. *Ciencia, vida y espacio en Iberoamerica.* 3 vols. Madrid, Spain: Consejo Superior de Investigaciones Científicas, 1989.

Phelan, John Leddy. *The Kingdom of Quito in the Seventeenth Century: Bureaucratic Politics in the Spanish Empire.* Madison: University of Wisconsin Press, 1967.

———. "Neo-Aztecism in the Eighteenth Century and the Genesis of Mexican Nationalism." In *Culture in History: Essays in Honor of Paul Radin,* edited by Stanley Diamond, 760–70. New York, NY: Octagon, 1981.

Phillips, William D., Jr., and Carla Rahn Phillips. *The Worlds of Christopher Columbus.* Cambridge, UK: Cambridge University Press, 1992.

Pineda y Bascuñán, Francisco Núñez de. *Cautiverio Feliz.* 2 vols. Edited by Mario Ferreccio Podestá and Raïssa Kordic Riquelme. Santiago, Chile: RIL Editores, 2001.

Piqueras, José A. *Las Antillas en la era de las luces y la revolución.* Madrid, Spain: Siglo XXI, 2005.

Planchart, Julio. "Oviedo y Baños y su *Historia de la conquista y población de la provincia de Venezuela.*" In *Discursos pronunciados en la recepción del Señor Julio Planchart como in-*

dividuo de número de la Academia Nacional de la Historia el 15 de marzo de 1941, 5–57. Caracas, Venezuela: Tipografía Americana, 1941. Reprinted (with some minor revisions) in *Temas críticos,* 207–48. Caracas, Venezuela: Ministerio de Educación Nacional, 1948.

Pocock, H. R. S. *The Conquest of Chile.* New York, NY: Stein and Day, 1967.

Portela, Eugenio. "El beneficio de los minerales de plata en la América colonial." In *Ciencia, vida y espacio en Iberoamérica,* coordinated by José Luis Peset, 2:153–83. Madrid, Spain: Consejo Superior de Investigaciones Científicas, 1989.

Porter, Roy. "Afterword." In Livingstone and Withers, *Geography and Enlightenment,* 415–31.

———. *The Enlightenment.* 2nd ed. New York, NY: Palgrave, 2001.

Portuondo, José Antonio. "Los comienzos de la literatura cubana (1510–1790)." In *Panorama de la literatura cubana,* 7–85. Havana: Universidad de la Habana/Centro de Estudios Cubanos, 1970.

Portuondo Zúñiga, Olga. *La Virgen de la Caridad del Cobre: Símbolo de cubanía.* Santiago, Cuba: Oriente, 1995.

Pratt, Mary Louise. *Imperial Eyes: Travel Writing and Transculturation.* 2nd ed. New York, NY: Routledge, 2008.

Price, Jacob M. "Summation: The American Panorama of Atlantic Port Cities." In Knight and Liss, *Atlantic Port Cities,* 262–76.

Prieto, Carlos. *Mining in the New World.* New York, NY: McGraw-Hill, 1973.

Quijano, Aníbal. *Modernidad, identidad y utopía en América latina.* Quito, Ecuador: El Conejo, 1990.

Quispe-Agnoli, Rocío. "Escritura femenina en los conventos coloniales: Control y subversión." In Campuzano, *Mujeres latinoamericanas,* 161–68.

Rabasa, José. *Writing Violence on the Northern Frontier.* Durham, NC: Duke University Press, 2000.

Rama, Angel. *The lettered city.* Edited and translated by John Charles Chasteen. Durham, NC: Duke University Press, 1996.

Ramos Pérez, Demetrio. *El mito del Dorado: Génesis y proceso.* Caracas, Venezuela: Academia Nacional de la Historia, 1973.

Raynal, Abbé [Guillaume-Thomas-François]. *Historia política de los establecimientos untramarinos de las naciones europeas.* Madrid, Spain: Antonio de Sancha, 1784–1790.

———. *A History of the Two Indies: A Translated Selection of Writings from Raynal's "Histoire philosophique et politique des établissements des Européens dans les Deux Indes."* Edited by Peter Jimack. Burlington, VT: Ashgate, 2006.

Regis, Pamela. *Describing Early America: Bartram, Jefferson, Crèvecoeur, and the Rhetoric of Natural History.* DeKalb: Northern Illinois University Press, 1992.

Ribera, Nicolas Joseph de. *Descripción de la isla de Cuba.* Edited by Hortensia Pichardo Viñals. Havana: Instituto Cubano del Libro, 1973.

Robbins, Louise E. *Elephant Slaves and Pampered Parrots: Exotic Animals in Eighteenth-Century Paris.* Baltimore, MD: Johns Hopkins University Press, 2002.

Robertson, William. *The History of the Discovery and Settlement of America.* 1777. New York, NY: Harper, 1829.

Robins, Nicholas A. *Mercury, Mining and Empire: The Human and Ecological Cost of Colonial Silver Mining in the Andes.* Bloomington: Indiana University, 2011.

Rodríguez Casteló, Hernán, ed. *Letras de la Audiencia de Quito (Período Jesuítico).* Caracas, Venezuela: Ayacucho, 1984.

Rojas, Arístides. *Leyendas históricas de Venezuela.* Caracas, Venezuela: Imprenta de la Patria, 1890.

Rojas Mix, Miguel. "La idea de la historia y la imagen de América en el abate Molina." *Revista de Filosofía* (Universidad de Chile) 10.1 (1963): 67–97.

Romero, José Luis. *Latinoamérica: Las ciudades y las ideas.* 4th ed. Buenos Aires, Argentina: Siglo XXI, 1986.

Ronan, Charles E. *Juan Ignacio Molina: The World's Window on Chile.* New York, NY: Peter Lang, 2002.

Ronan, Charles E., and Walter Hanisch, eds. *Epistolario de Juan Ignacio Molina.* Chicago, IL: Loyola University Press; Santiago, Chile: Universitaria, 1979.

Ross, Kathleen. *The Baroque Narrative of Carlos de Sigüenza y Góngora: A New World Paradise.* Cambridge, UK: Cambridge University Press, 1993.

Ross, Stephanie. *What Gardens Mean.* Chicago, IL: University of Chicago Press, 1998.

Rousseau, G. S., and Roy Porter, eds. *The Ferment of Knowledge: Studies in the Historiography of Eighteenth-Century Science.* Cambridge, UK: Cambridge University Press, 1980.

Rubial García, Antonio. "Icons of Devotion: The Appropriation and Uses of Saints in New Spain." In *Local Religion in Colonial Mexico,* edited by Martin Austin Nesvig, 91–117. Albuquerque: University of New Mexico Press, 2006.

———. *La santidad controvertida: Hagiografía y conciencia criolla alrededor de los venerables no canonizados de Nueva España.* Mexico City: UNAM/Fondo de Cultura Económica, 1999.

Rumeu de Armas, Antonio. *Ciencia y tecnología en la España ilustrada: La Escuela de Caminos y Canales.* Madrid, Spain: Turner, 1980.

Rusher, William A. *The Ambiguous Legacy of the Enlightenment.* Lanham, MD: University Press of America, 1995.

Safier, Neil. "The Confines of the Colony. Boundaries, Ethnographic Landscapes, and Imperial Cartography in Iberoamerica." In Akerman, *Imperial Map,* 133–83.

———. "Los jardines de París y las anotaciones al Inca Garcilaso: *La Histoire des Incas* (1744), entre crónica y exposición museológica." In *Lecturas y ediciones de crónicas de Indias: Una propuesta interdisciplinar,* edited by Ignacio Arellano and Fermín del Pino Díaz, 461–75. Madrid, Spain: University of Navarra/Iberoamericana; Frankfurt, Germany: Vervuert, 2004.

———. *Measuring the New World: Enlightenment Science and South America.* Chicago, IL: University of Chicago Press, 2008.

Said, Eduard. *Culture and Imperialism.* London, UK: Vintage, 1993.

Saínz, Enrique. *La literatura cubana de 1700 a 1790.* Havana: Letras Cubanas, 1983.

Salazar Simarro, Nuria. "Los conventos femeninos y la configuración urbana: un arquitecto del siglo XVIII." In Campuzano, *Mujeres latinoamericanas,* 175–83.

Salcedo-Bastardo, José Luis. "Prólogo." In *Venezuela en el Siglo de las Luces,* edited by Carmen Mena García, 7–10. Seville, Spain: Muñoz Moya y Montraveta, 1995.

Sallnow, M. J. "Precious Metals in the Andean Moral Economy." In Parry and Bloch, *Money,* 209–31.

Sampson Vera Tudela, Elisa. *Colonial Angels: Narratives of Gender and Spirituality in Mexico, 1580–1750.* Austin: University of Texas Press, 2000.

———. "Illustrating Sainthood: The Construction of Eighteenth-Century Spanish American Hagiography." In Jaffe and Lewis, *Eve's Enlightenment,* 84–100.

———. "Voyages in the New World Cloister: The Representation of Travel in the Hagiographic Literature of New Spain." *History and Anthropology* 9.2–3 (1996): 191–206.

Santiago, Silviano. *The Space In-Between: Essays on Latin American Culture.* Durham, NC: Duke University Press, 2001.

Santos, Angel. *Los jesuitas en América.* Madrid, Spain: MAPFRE, 1992.

Sarrailh, Jean. *La España ilustrada de la segunda mital del siglo XVIII.* 4th ed. Mexico City: Fondo de Cultura Económica, 1992.

Saugnieux, Joël, ed. *Foi et Lumieres dans l'Espagne du XVIIIe siecle.* Lyon, France: Presses Universitaires de Lyon, 1985.

Sayre, Gordon M. *The Indian Chief as Tragic Hero: Native Resistance and the Literatures of America, from Moctezuma to Tecumseh.* Chapel Hill: University of North Carolina Press, 2005.

————. *Les Sauvages Américains: Representations of Native Americans in French and English Colonial Literature.* Chapel Hill: University of North Carolina Press, 1997.

Schaffer, Simon. Afterword to Miller and Reill, *Visions of Empire,* 335–52.

Schama, Simon. *Landscape and Memory.* New York, NY: Knopf, 1995.

Schiebinger, Londa. *Plants and Empire: Colonial Bioprospecting in the Atlantic World.* Cambridge, MA: Harvard University Press, 2004.

Schiebinger, Londa, and Claudia Swan, eds. *Colonial Botany: Science, Commerce, and Politics in the Early Modern World.* Philadelphia: University of Pennsylvania Press, 2005.

Schlau, Stacey. *Spanish American Women's Use of the Word: Colonial through Contemporary Narratives.* Tucson: University of Arizona Press, 2001.

Schlereth, Thomas J. *The Cosmopolitan Ideal in Enlightenment Thought.* Notre Dame, IN: University of Notre Dame Press, 1977.

Schuller, Rodolfo R. Prologue. In Azara, *Geografía física y esférica,* ix–lxxii.

Scott, David. *Conscripts of Modernity: The Tragedy of Colonial Enlightenment.* Durham, NC: Duke University Press, 2004.

Scott, Nina. "'La gran turba de las que mercieron nombres': Sor Juana's Foremothers in 'La respuesta a Sor Filotea.'" In *Coded Encounters: Writing, Gender, and Ethnicity in Colonial Latin America,* edited by Francisco Javier Cevallos, Jeffrey A. Cole, Nina M. Scott, and Nicomedes Suárez-Aráuz, 206–23. Amherst: University of Massachusetts Press, 1994.

Seed, Patricia. *Ceremonies of Possession in Europe's Conquest of the New World, 1492–1640.* Cambridge, UK: Cambridge University Press, 1995.

Sellés, Manuel, José Luis Peset, and Antonio Lafuente, eds. *Carlos III y la ciencia de la Ilustración.* Madrid, Spain: Alianza, 1988.

Serrano, Diana. "Catalina de Jesús Herrera." Diss., University of Florida, 2004.

Seth, Vanita. *Europe's Indians: Producing Racial Difference, 1500–1900.* Durham, NC: Duke University Press, 2010.

Shell, Marc. *Money, Language, and Thought: Literary and Philosophical Economies from the Medieval to the Modern Era.* Berkeley: University of California Press, 1982.

Shtier, Ann. "'The Dream of the Botanical Monograph': Process Not Product." *Eighteenth-Century Studies* 40.1 (2006): 120–23.

Silva, Erika. *Los mitos de la ecuatorianidad: Ensayo sobre la identidad nacional.* Quito, Ecuador: Ediciones ABYA-YALA, 1992.

Silver, Sean R. "Locke's Pineapple and the History of Taste." *Eighteenth Century* 49 (2008): 43–65.

Simón, Pedro. *Noticias historiales de Venezuela.* 2 vols. Prologue by Guillermo Morón. Caracas, Venezuela: Ayacucho, 1992.

Slade, David. "Enlightened Archi-textures: Founding Colonial Archives in the Hispanic Eighteenth Century." Diss., Emory University, 2005.

Slade, David, and Karen Stolley. "On the *Brevísima relación*'s 'Black Legends': Eighteenth-Century Texts and Contexts." In *Approaches to Teaching the Writings of Bartolomé de*

Las Casas, edited by Santa Arias and Eyda M. Merediz, 92–105. New York, NY: Modern Language Association, 2008.

Smith, Adam. *The Wealth of Nations.* 1735. Amherst, NY: Prometheus Press, 1991.

Smith, Pamela H., and Paula Findlen, eds. *Merchants and Marvels: Commerce, Science, and Art in Early Modern Europe.* New York, NY: Routledge, 2002. Soto Arango, Diana, Miguel Angel Puig-Samper, and Luis Carlos Arboleda, eds. *La Ilustración en la América Colonial.* Madrid, Spain: Doce Calles, 1995.

Soto Arango, Diana, Miguel Angel Puig-Samper, Martina Bender, and María Dolores González-Ripoll, eds. *Recepción y difusión de textos ilustrados: Intercambio científico entre Europa y América en la Ilustración.* Madrid, Spain: Doce Calles, 2003.

Soto Arango, Diana, Miguel Angel Puig-Samper, and María Dolores González-Ripoll, eds. *Científicos Criollos e Ilustración.* Madrid, Spain: Doce Calles, 1999.

Spivak, Gayatri Chakravorty. "Can the Subaltern Speak?" In *Marxism and the Interpretation of Culture,* edited by Cary Nelson and Lawrence Grossberg, 271–31. Basingstoke, UK: Macmillan Education, 1988.

Stalnaker, Joanna. *The Unfinished Enlightenment: Description in the Age of the Encyclopedia.* Ithaca, NY: Cornell University Press, 2010.

Stein, Stanley J., and Barbara H. Stein. *Apogee of Empire: Spain and New Spain in the Age of Charles III, 1759–1789.* Baltimore, MD: Johns Hopkins University Press, 2003.

———. *Edge of Crisis: War and Trade in the Spanish Atlantic, 1789–1808.* Baltimore, MD: Johns Hopkins University Press, 2009.

———. *Silver, Trade, and War: Spain and America in the Making of Early Modern Europe.* Baltimore, MD: Johns Hopkins University Press, 2000.

Stepan, Nancy Leys. *Picturing Tropical Nature.* London, UK: Reaktion Books, 2001.

Stiles, Veronica. "Fact and Fiction: Nature's Endgame in Werner Herzog's *Aguirre, the Wrath of God.*" *Literature/Film Quarterly* 17.3 (1989): 161–67.

Still, Judith. *Enlightenment Hospitality: Cannibals, Harems and Adoption.* Oxford, UK: Voltaire Foundation/University of Oxford, 2011.

Stolley, Karen. "Amalgamación, negociación, y circulación: la economia discursiva del XVIII." *Dieciocho at 30 Treinta años de Dieciocho.* Anejos 4 (2009): 149–69.

———. "Death by Attrition: The Confessions of Christopher Columbus in Carpentier's *El arpa y la sombra.*" *Revista de Estudios Hispánicos* 31.3 (1997): 505–31.

———. "East from Eden: Domesticating Exile in Jesuit Accounts of the 1767 Expulsion from Spanish America." In Bernier, Donato, and Lüsebrink, *Jesuit Accounts.*

———. "The Eighteenth Century: Narrative Forms, Scholarship and Learning." In González Echevarría and Pupo-Walker, *Cambridge History of Latin American Literature,* 1:336–74.

———. *"El lazarillo de ciegos caminantes": Un itinerario crítico.* Hanover, NH: Ediciones del Norte, 1992.

———. "Llegando a la primera mujer: Catalina de Jesús Herrera y la invención de una genealogía femenina en el Quito del siglo XVIII." *Colonial Latin American Review* 9.2 (2000): 167–85.

———. "Oviedo y Baños en tierra de nadie: La conciencia criolla del historiador a principios del siglo XVIII." In *Crítica y descolonización: El sujeto colonial en la cultural latinoamericana,* edited by Beatriz González Stephan and Lúcia Helena Costigan, 569–84. Caracas, Venezuela: Academia Nacional de la Historia, 1992.

———. "Las pesadillas criollas en *Secretos entre el alma y Dios* (c. 1760) de Catalina de Jesús Herrera." *Guaraguao: Revista de Cultura Latinoamericana* 37 (2011): 15–33.

Subirats, Eduardo. *La ilustración insuficiente.* Madrid, Spain: Taurus, 1981.

———. *La modernidad truncada en América Latina.* Caracas, Venezuela: Centro de Investigaciones Posdoctorales, 2001.

Tandeter, Enrique. "Forced and Free Labour in Late Colonial Potosí." In Bakewell, *Mines of Silver* 10:131–69.

Tavard, George H. *Juana Inés de la Cruz and the Theology of Beauty: The First Mexican Theology.* Notre Dame, IN: University of Notre Dame Press, 1991.

Taylor, William B. "Between Nativitas and Mexico City: An Eighteenth-Century Pastor's Local Religion." In Nesvig, *Local Religion,* 91–117.

———. *Magistrates of the Sacred: Priests and Parishioners in Eighteenth-Century Mexico.* Stanford, CA: Stanford University Press, 1996.

Ten, Antonio E. "Ciencia y universidad en la América Hispana: La Universidad de Lima." In Lafuente and Sala Catalá, *Ciencia colonial en América,* 162–91.

TePaske, John Jay. "Economic Texts." In *Guide to Documentary Sources for Andean Studies, 1530–1900,* edited by Joanne Pillsbury, 120–28. Norman: University of Oklahoma Press, 2008.

———. "Integral to Empire: The Vital Peripheries of Colonial Spanish America." In Daniels and Kennedy, *Negotiated Empires,* 29–41.

Teresa de Jesús. *Libro de la vida.* Edited by Dámaso Chicharro. Madrid, Spain: Cátedra, 1997.

Thrower, Norman J. W. *Maps and Civilization: Cartography in Culture and Society.* 3rd ed. Chicago, IL: University of Chicago Press, 2008.

Tietz, Manfred, ed. *Los jesuitas españoles expulsos: Su imagen y su contribución al saber sobre el mundo hispánico en la Europa del siglo XVIII.* Madrid, Spain: Iberoamericana; Frankfurt, Germany: Vervuert, 2001.

Todorov, Tzvetan. *The Conquest of America: The Question of the Other.* Norman, OK: University of Oklahoma Press, 1999.

Torre Revello, José. *El momento histórico del virreinato del Río de la Plata.* Vol. 4 of *Historia de la nación argentina,* edited by Ricardo Levene. Buenos Aires, Argentina: Ateneo, 1940.

Trabulse, Elías. *Historia de la ciencia en México: Estudios y textos siglo XVIII.* Mexico City: Fondo de Cultura Económica, 1985.

Trouillot, Michel-Rolph. "Anthropology and the Savage Slot: The Poetics and Politics of Otherness." In *Recapturing Anthropology: Working in the Present,* edited by Richard G. Fox, 17–44. Santa Fe, NM: School of American Research Press, 1991.

Tudisco, Anthony. "America in Some Travelers, Historians, and Political Economists of the Spanish Eighteenth Century." *Americas* 15.1 (1958): 1–22.

Turnball, David. "Travelling Knowledge: Narratives, Assemblage and Encounters." In Bourguet, Licoppe, and Sibum, *Instruments, Travel and Science,* 273–94.

Turner, Victor, and Edith Turner. *Image and Pilgrimage in Christian Culture: Anthropological Perspectives.* New York, NY: Columbia University Press, 1978.

Twinam, Ann. *Public Lives, Private Secrets: Gender, Honor, Sexuality, and Illegitimacy in Colonial Spanish America.* Stanford, CA: Stanford University Press, 1999.

Ulloa, Antonio de. *Noticias americanas.* Granada, Spain: Universidad de Granada, 1992.

Urrutia y Montoya, Ignacio de. *Teatro histórico, jurídico y político-militar de la Isla Fernandina de Cuba y principalmente de su capital la Habana.* Havana: Comisión Nacional Cubana de la UNESCO, 1963.

Urton, Gary. *Signs of the Inka Khipu: Binary Coding in the Andean Knotted-String Records.* Austin: University of Texas Press, 2003.

Ustariz, Jerónimo de. *The Theory and Practice of Commerce.* 2 vols. London, UK: John and James Rivington, 1751.

Vaca de Osma, José Antonio. *Carlos III.* Madrid, Spain: RIALP, 1997.

Vargas, José María. *Historia de la iglesia en el Ecuador durante el patronato español.* Quito, Ecuador: Editorial Santo Domingo, 1962.

———. *Historia de la provincia dominicana de santa Catalina virgen y mártir de Quito.* Quito, Ecuador: Escuela Tipográfica y Encuadernación Salesianas, 1942.

———. *Sor Catalina de Jesús María Herrera: Religiosa dominicana.* Quito, Ecuador: Editorial Royal, 1979.

Varner, Jeanette Johnson. "Introduction." In Oviedo y Baños, *Conquest and Settlement,* xv–xxii.

Vega, Garcilaso de la. *Royal Commentaries of the Incas and General History of Peru.* Translated by Harold V. Livermore. Edited by Karen Spalding. Indianapolis, IN: Hackett, 2006.

Velasco, Juan de. *Historia del reino de Quito en la América meridional.* 1795. Quito: Casa de Cultura Ecuatoriana "Benjamín Carrión," 1994.

Velasco, Sherry M. *Demons, Nausea, and Resistance in the Autobiography of Isabel de Jesús, 1611–1682.* Albuquerque: University of New Mexico Press, 1996.

Verdesio, Gustavo. *Forgotten Conquests: Rereading New World History from the Margins.* Philadelphia, PA: Temple University Press, 2001.

———. *La invención del Uruguay: La entrada del territorio y sus habitantes a la cultura occidental.* Montevideo, Uruguay: Editorial Graffiti/Editorial Trazas, 1996.

———. "The Original Sin behind the Creation of a New Europe: Economic and Ecological Imperialism in the River Plate." In Arias and Meléndez, *Mapping,* 137–59.

Vila, Anne C. "Science, Identity, and Enlightenment in the Eighteenth Century: Four Biographical Perspectives." *Eighteenth-Century Studies* 39.1 (2005): 115–20.

Vilches, Elvira. *New World Gold: Cultural Anxiety and Monetary Disorder in Early Modern Spain.* Chicago, IL: University of Chicago Press, 2010.

Villalobos, Sergio R. "Guerra y paz en la Araucanía: Periodificación." In Villalobos, Casanova, Zapater, Carreño, and Pinto, *Araucanía,* 7–30.

———. *Vida fronteriza en la Araucanía.* Santiago, Chile: Andrés Bello, 1995.

Villalobos, Sergio R., Carlos Aldunate, Horacio Zapater, Luz María Méndez, and Carlos Bascuñán. *Relaciones fronterizas en la Araucanía.* Santiago: Ediciones Universidad Católica de Chile, 1982.

Villalobos, Sergio R., Holdenis Casanova, Horacio Zapater, Luis Carreño, and Jorge Pinto. *Araucanía: Temas de historia fronteriza.* Temuco, Chile: Ediciones Universidad de la Frontera, 1989.

Villarroel, Hipólito. *Enfermedades políticas que padece la capital de esta Nueva España.* 1787. Mexico City: Porrúa, 1999.

Viqueira Albán, Juan Pedro. *Propriety and Permissiveness in Bourbon Mexico.* Translated by Sonya Lipsett-Rivera and Sergio Rivera Ayala. 1987. Wilmington, DE: Scholarly Resources, 1999.

Vogeley, Nancy. "Enlightenment Ascriptions of Colonial Identity." Review of *Bárbaros: Spaniards and Their Savages in the Age of Enlightenment,* by David Weber, and *La escritura de la Independencia: El surgimiento de la opinión pública en México,* by Rafael Rojas. *Eighteenth-Century Studies* 39.4 (2006). 542–46.

Voigt, Lisa. *Writing Captivity in the Early Modern Atlantic: Circulations of Knowledge and Authority in the Iberian and English Imperial Worlds.* Williamsburg, VA: Omohundro Institute of Early American History and Culture; Chapel Hill: University of North Carolina Press, 2009.

Voltes, Pedro. *Carlos III y su tiempo.* 3rd ed. Barcelona, Spain: Editorial Juventud, 1964.

von Hagen, Victor Wolfgang, ed. *The Green World of the Naturalists: A Treasury of Five Centuries of Natural History in South America.* New York, NY: Greenberg, 1948.

Walckenaer, C. A. "Advertencia preliminar del Editor," "Nota adicional del Editor," "Noticia de la vida y escritos de D. Félix de Azara," "Piezas Justificativas," and "Introducción." In Azara, *Viajes,* 1:1–81.

Walker, Charles F., ed. *Entre la retórica y la insurgencia: Las ideas y los movimientos sociales en los Andes, siglo XVIII.* Cuzco, Peru: Centro de Estudios Regionales Andinos "Bartolomé de las Casas," 1996.

———. *Shaky Colonialism: The 1746 Earthquake-Tsunami in Lima, Peru, and Its Long Aftermath.* Durham, NC: Duke University Press, 2008.

Waller, Gregory A. "*Aguirre, the Wrath of God:* History, Theater, and the Camera." *South Atlantic Review* 46.2 (1981): 55–69.

Wallerstein, Immanuel. *The Modern World System: Capitalist Agriculture and the Origins of the European World-Economy in the Sixteenth Century.* New York, NY: Academic Presses, 1974.

Warf, Barney, and Santa Arias, eds. *The Spatial Turn: Interdisciplinary Perspectives.* London, UK: Routledge, 2009.

Weber, Alison. *Teresa of Avila and the Rhetoric of Femininity.* Princeton, NJ: Princeton University Press, 1990.

Weber, David J. *Bárbaros: Spaniards and Their Savages in the Age of Enlightenment.* New Haven, CT: Yale University Press, 2005.

———. *The Spanish Frontier in North America.* New Haven, CT: Yale University Press, 1992.

Webster, Susan Verdi. "Vantage Points: Andeans and Europeans in the Construction of Colonial Quito." *Colonial Latin American Review* 20.3 (2011): 303–30.

Wells, Byron R., and Philip Stewart, eds. *Interpreting Colonialism: Studies on Voltaire and the Eighteenth Century.* Oxford, UK: Voltaire Foundation, 2004.

Wernitznig, Dagmar. *Europe's Indians, Indians in Europe: European Perceptions and Appropriations of Native American Cultures from Pocahontas to the Present.* Lanham, MD: University Press of America, 2007.

Wertheimer, Eric. *Imagined Empires: Incas, Aztecs, and the New World of American Literature, 1771–1876.* Cambridge, UK: Cambridge University Press, 1999.

West, Robert C. "Aboriginal Metallurgy and Metalworking in Spanish America: A Brief Overview." In Bakewell, *Mines of Silver,* 10:41–56.

Whitaker, Arthur Preston. *The Huancavelica Mercury Mine: A Contribution to the History of the Bourbon Renaissance in the Spanish Empire.* 1941. Westport, CT: Greenwood Press, 1971.

———, ed. *Latin America and the Enlightenment.* 2nd ed. Ithaca, NY: Cornell University Press, 1961.

Williams, Jerry M. "Popularizing the Ethic of Conquest: Peralta Barnuevo's *Historia de España vindicada.*" In Bauer and Mazzotti, *Creole Subjects,* 412–41.

Williams, Roger L. *Botanophilia in Eighteenth-Century France: The Spirit of the Enlightenment.* Dordrecht, Netherlands: Kluwer, 2001.

Willingham, Eileen. "Creating the Kingdom of Quito: Patria, History, Language and Utopia in Juan de Velasco's *Historia del reino de Quito* (1789)." Diss., University of Wisconsin, 2001.

———. "Locating Utopia: Promise and Patria in Juan de Velasco's *Historia del reino de Quito.*" In Millones Figueroa and Ledezma, *El saber,* 251–77.

Withers, Charles W. J. *Placing the Enlightenment: Thinking Geographically about the Age of Reason.* Chicago, IL: University of Chicago Press, 2007.

———. "Where Was the Atlantic Enlightenment? Questions of Geography." In Manning and Cogliano, *Atlantic Enlightenment,* 37–60.

Wolff, Larry, and Marco Cipollini, eds. *The Anthropology of the Enlightenment.* Stanford, CA: Stanford University Press, 2007.

Woll, Allen. *A Functional Past: The Uses of History in Nineteenth-Century Chile.* Baton Rouge: Louisiana State University Press, 1982.

Worthen, Edward H. "A Mexican Historian Comes Home." *Journal of Church and State* 15.3 (1973): 455–63.

Yeo, Richard. *Encyclopaedic Visions: Scientific Dictionaries and Enlightenment Culture.* Cambridge, UK: Cambridge University Press, 2001.

Zamora, Margarita. "Epic Poetry." In González Echevarría and Pupo-Walker, *Cambridge History of Latin American Literature,* 1:231–59.

Zapata Silva, Claudia. "Identidad, nación y territorio en la escritura de los intelectuales mapuches." *Revista Mexicana de Sociología* 68.3 (2006): 467–509.

Index

frontiers, 108, 196–97n62, 200n111, 200n116, 201n128

Indian horse culture, 198n81

Indian-Spanish relations, 42, 50–51, 69, 76–77, 198n80, 201n125, 235n135

Spanish military, 201n120

Weiland, David, 236n148

Welsers, 16, 23–28, 33–34, 184n23, 185n35, 186n53, 187n58

Wertheimer, Eric, 81, 202n129

Whitaker, Arthur Preston, 228n36

Williams, Jerry, 7

Williams, Roger L., 208n61

Withers, Charles, 4, 56, 63, 180n14, 195n43, 197n64, 210n81

Woll, Allen, 202n129

women's spiritual autobiography. *See under* religion

Wunderkammer tradition, 97

Yeo, Richard, 206n34

zambos, 138

Zamora, Margarita, 61

Zapata Silva, Claudia, 202n138